DICTIONARY OF
LANGUAGE AND LINGUISTICS

DICTIONARY OF
LANGUAGE
AND
LINGUISTICS

R. R. K. HARTMANN, M.A., D.Comm., Transl. Dip.
Lecturer in Applied Linguistics, The Language Centre,
University of Nottingham

and

F. C. STORK, M.A., Ph.D.
Senior Lecturer in Applied Linguistics, Head of The Language Centre,
University of Sheffield

A HALSTED PRESS BOOK

JOHN WILEY & SONS
New York—Toronto

Published in the U.S.A. and Canada by
Halsted Press Division
John Wiley & Sons, Inc., New York

LIBRARY OF CONGRESS CATALOG CARD NUMBER 72–6251

ISBN 0 470–35667–7

© 1972 APPLIED SCIENCE PUBLISHERS LTD

Printed in Great Britain by Galliard Limited, Great Yarmouth, Norfolk, England.

CONTENTS

v

ACKNOWLEDGEMENTS

A work of this kind inevitably owes a great deal to the many authors of textbooks and articles dealing with the subject matter concerned. Without their work this dictionary could never have been conceived. The compilers would also like to thank their many colleagues and friends, too numerous to mention, in this country and abroad, who have given their advice or help or who have in any way contributed towards the compilation of this dictionary. Their help made the dictionary possible, but errors of commission or omission are the responsibility of the compilers.

INTRODUCTION

LANGUAGE AND LINGUISTICS

Language is one of the most fundamental aspects of human behaviour and the development of language into a refined instrument of expression and communication is probably man's greatest achievement. Linguistics is the study of language in all its forms, and is thus of direct relevance to all users of language. Every human being is born into a speech community and uses language throughout his whole life: in this sense everyone is a linguist.

Language studies have a long history, dating back at least as far as the Ancient Indian and Greek grammarians, yet modern linguistics is a young subject, applying rigorous scientific methods in a field which, at any rate since the Middle Ages, has been the domain of philosophical speculations and prescriptive value judgments. The application of linguistics to problems in related practical fields, e.g. language teaching, is even younger. There is still a certain mistrust of linguistics in some quarters, which is perhaps a reflection on the way the early scholars of modern linguistics put forward their ideas rather than on the ideas themselves. Be this as it may, it is now true that all linguistic studies, both theoretical and applied, are gaining recognition as academic disciplines in their own right and no one interested in languages, from the general reader to the teacher or communications engineer, can afford to ignore them.

The linguistic sciences are concerned with the way speech sounds are produced and transmitted, the way speech sounds operate in a system to produce meaningful utterances, and the way in which grammatical forms and vocabulary items are used in different varieties of language. Such studies may be confined to a particular speech community at one stage in its history, or they may transcend the boundaries of geography and time to include historical and comparative studies as well as investigations into the nature of language in general.

THE PURPOSE OF THIS DICTIONARY

The rapid development of all branches of language studies has led to a widespread and growing interest in the activities of the linguist. At the same time many new terms have been introduced which are often confusing to the beginner and specialist alike. Linguists have to use language to describe language, which is difficult enough, but the compiler of a dictionary of linguistics has to use language to describe the language used to describe language, which is an even more difficult task. Attempts have been made to present and explain these complexities of linguistic terminology, but such glossaries are often out of date, too specialised, or inaccessible to the English reader. (→ Appendix 2, Bibliography, Section 1.)

There is therefore a growing need for a dictionary which will explain the many new terms and at the same time relate the new approaches and concepts to the already familiar traditional grammatical terminology. It is hoped that this *Dictionary of Language and Linguistics* will be of help to students of linguistics and language teachers, including teachers of English as a foreign language, and to all those, whatever their fields, who are interested in the study of language.

Increasingly, linguists 'apply' themselves to practical problems such as translation, language teaching, communication technology and lexicography, whose practitioners in turn are interested in what linguistic knowledge has to offer them. Growing inter-disciplinary research, e.g. between linguists, psychologists, computer experts, sociologists, etc., calls for an elementary explanation of the most fundamental concepts under discussion.

NOTES ON COMPILATION

A few remarks seem appropriate to explain the basic methodological problems involved in writing this Dictionary, particularly the justification of its contents. What has been included and what had to be left out depended on a definition of the scope and coverage attempted. The first and most important criterion for selecting entries was a *general consensus of opinion among linguists*. This consideration called for a fairly detailed treatment of basic concepts, although it will be obvious that linguists are not even agreed on such fundamental ideas as LANGUAGE, GRAMMAR and WORD. Linguists, grammarians and phoneticians have always been prolific innovators of metaphorical expressions, an understandable and perhaps forgivable fact in a field so all-embracing as language. Some terms have been used to designate different concepts, e.g. ACCENT with the meaning of 'stress', 'diacritic mark', 'non-standard speech', while some concepts are known under different names, e.g. 'a feature of meaning' as SEMEME, SEMANTIC COMPONENT, PLEREME.

Although linguists agree on certain basic concepts, they are not usually willing to standardise terminology, a difficulty which also besets other disciplines. In a rapidly growing field this creates additional problems for the uninitiated. One should bear in mind that neither special terminologies nor language as a whole can be considered static. Any effort on the part of the compilers to lay down rules for the 'correct' use of terms is destined to fail, except where such codification has been achieved by the experts themselves, e.g. in certain branches of acoustic phonetics.

In selecting entries for inclusion in this Dictionary we have tried to bring together *representative samples of terminology* from the various branches of linguistic scholarship, e.g. PHONETICS, SEMANTICS, SYNTAX, as well as the approaches and methods used, e.g. SYN-CHRONIC, HISTORICAL, BRITISH LINGUISTICS. The major language types have been included under such headings as: AGGLU-TINATIVE, INFLECTED, ANALYTIC LANGUAGE, as well as the words used in describing them: traditional terms such as SUBJECT, PREDICATE, NOMINATIVE, and newer terms such as TRANS-FORMATION, DISTINCTIVE FEATURE, HEAD WORD. Definitions are also given of the major varieties of language, both spoken and written, e.g. DIALECT, STYLE, REGISTER. In addition, the more important notions from related and applied fields are repre-sented, e.g. from various branches of applied linguistics (LAN-GUAGE LABORATORY, MACHINE TRANSLATION, SPEECH THERAPY).

On the other hand, we have *excluded general non-technical terms* about which adequate information can be found in a good general dictionary. Foreign words have been excluded except in cases where they are in wide use, e.g. UMLAUT, SANDHI, LANGUE and PAROLE.

The varied potential readership of this Dictionary demanded that the notion of the 'common core' of widely accepted terminology be extended to *selected terms from specialised but important theories* and branches of linguistics. Thus we have provided entries on various 'schools' such as TRANSFORMATIONAL-GENERATIVE GRAM-MAR, SYSTEMIC GRAMMAR, TAGMEMICS together with the most basic concepts associated with them. Just as there is a danger of 'simplification' in presenting commonly used terms, it is impossible to avoid 'technicality' and (to a certain extent) 'circularity' in the rarer terms.

ix

Whilst most of the entries in this Dictionary are of an introductory nature, it is not intended to replace a textbook. Indeed it is hoped that with the help of the bibliographical references the more serious student will find himself guided towards the right textbook for more detailed studies.

Another major difficulty lies in the *arrangement of entries.* Some compromise had to be reached between the extremes of a smaller number of general entries (incorporating as much information as possible related to the topic in question) and a large number of individual entries (giving only a brief definition of that particular term and its reference). The general principle adopted was that whenever a set of terms is mutually defining, all related terms were brought together in a single article. Thus the entry STOP includes several types of speech sounds, SIMPLE STOP, COMPLEX STOP, etc. which are referred to the main heading STOP. When a term has an obviously technical sense by itself, e.g. UNIT NOUN, certain information is duplicated in both the individual entry and the joint entry NOUN. Terms with different senses are defined separately and/or cross-referenced to an appropriate head word, e.g. CENTRE, BASE, etc. Where necessary an entry assigns a term to the field to which it belongs, e.g. SPECTRAL ANALYSIS is part of phonetics. Within each entry the arrangement is from the older or traditional to the contemporary usage, and from the general to the specific sense. Where there is disagreement or controversy about a concept, this is indicated, e.g. PHONEME. Related terms are marked by means of cross-references, e.g. PHONEMICS, ALLOPHONE, etc. Entries giving details of individual languages have not been included in the main body of the work, but an appendix has been added listing the major languages of the world, grouped according to families. Biographical details of individual linguists are not given, but entries on major schools in linguistics have been included.

DIRECTIONS FOR THE USE OF THIS DICTIONARY

(1) Alphabetic order is based upon the first word of a compound, thus PHONETIC TRANSCRIPTION occurs before PHONETICS.

(2) Compound terms may be given in full form, e.g. COMPLEX WORD, but more often than not refer the reader to a more comprehensive entry, e.g. COMPLEX STOP → STOP. Alternative terms are listed at the end of the entry.

(3) Cross references are indicated by means of an arrow: →, which is the equivalent of 'see'. Other symbols and conventions used are explained in the list on pages xvii–xviii.

(4) Examples are given in *italics*; translations and glosses in single quotation marks. Double quotation marks are reserved for actual quotations. Phonetic transcriptions are in accordance with the International Phonetic Alphabet (→ chart pages 262–263).

(5) A number in brackets at the end of an entry, whether alone or with the name of an author, is a reference to the appropriate section of the Bibliography, pages 277–302. Thus (8.21 Barber) refers to *Linguistic Change in Present-day English* by C. L. Barber, listed in Section 8.21 of the Bibliography. A great deal of new and specialised material in linguistics appears in article form in journals; for this reason a separate list of journals has been included in the Bibliography.

(6) All languages mentioned in the entries are listed in their family groups in Appendix 1, pages 267–276.

(7) A typical entry will contain:

(a) a general definition, which is an interpretation of the concept in question. Thus the entry ARTICULATION begins: 'The production of speech sounds by the movement of the organs of speech';

(b) a further specification to classify or subdivide the general definition. Thus the entry ARTICULATION continues by making reference to the 'movable speech organs' and 'the parts of the vocal tract which cannot move';

(c) cross-references show the relationship of the term to other terms within the system. Thus in the entry ARTICULATION, cross-references are made to → ORGANS OF SPEECH, → POINTS OF ARTICULATION and → MANNER OF ARTICULATION;

(d) examples, wherever possible from English or other Indo-European languages, to illustrate the definition, e.g. the initial sound of the word *coal* to illustrate CO-ARTICULATION;

(e) bibliographical references, at the end of the more important entries, to indicate where further detailed information can be obtained. The name of an author in the bibliographical reference does not necessarily imply that this author coined the term in question, but simply that more information about this concept or related fields can be found in his work. Entries without bibliographical references explain general terms contained in most introductory textbooks.

LIST OF ABBREVIATIONS
USED IN LINGUISTICS

A	adjunct,
	affirmation (stress),
	affix (morpheme)
AP	adjective phrase
abl	ablative (case)
acc	accusative (case)
act	active (voice)
Adj	adjective
Adv	adverb(ial)
Af	affix (morpheme)
Art	article
Aux	auxiliary (verb)
B	base (morpheme)
C	common (noun),
	consonant,
	complement
cap	capital (letter)
CD	complementary distribution
cl	clause
coll	colloquial (style)
comp ⎫ compar(degree)	comparative (degree)
comp	complement
cond	conditional (tense)
conj	conjunction
cps	cycles per second/Hertz
{D}	past tense (morpheme)
d	deictic (modifier)
dat	dative (case)
db	decibel
decl	declension
def	definite (article)
del	deletion
Dem ⎫ Demonstr	demonstrative (pronoun)
Det	determiner
dial	dialect
dim	diminutive (affix)

diph	diphthong
dir	direct (object)
disj / disjunct	disjunctive (pronoun)
E	east (e.g. E–Germanic)
e	emphatic (adverb)
etym	etymology
f / fem	feminine (gender)
fam	familiar (style)
fig	figurative (expression)
fut	future (tense)
gen	genitive (case)
H	head (word)
hist	historical
I	initial
IA	Indo-Aryan
IC	immediate constituent
imp / imper	imperative (mood, sentence)
imperf	imperfect (tense)
impers	impersonal (verb)
indef	indefinite (article)
ind / indic	indicative (mood)
ind / indir	indirect (object)
infin	infinitive (mood)
insep	inseparable (prefix)
instr	instrumental (case)
Int	intensifier
Interj	interjection
inter / interrog	interrogative (pronoun, sentence)
i / intrans	intransitive (verb)
IPA	International Phonetic Alphabet
irreg	irregular (verb)
ITA	Initial Teaching Alphabet
K	consonantal (element of syllable)
L	language, lexical rule
l	linking (verb)
lit	literal (meaning)
l / loc	locative (case, adverb)
M	modal (verb), middle (e.g. M–English),

M	morphological rule
m, masc	masculine (gender)
Mn	modern (e.g. Mn–English)
Mod	modal (verb), modifier
MT	machine translation
MV	main verb
N	noun, new (e.g. N–English), numeral, north (e.g. N–Germanic), nucleus (of syllable)
n, nt	neuter (gender)
neg	negative (verb form)
nom	nominative (case)
N gp	nominal group
NM	noun modifier
NP	noun phrase
nondef	non-definite (article)
§No	number marker
O	old (e.g. O–English)
{0}, {Ø}	zero (morpheme)
obj	object
P	proto (e.g. P–Indo-European), predicator/predicate, phrase structure rule
p	pretonic (element of syllable)
p, pers	person
p, pl, plur	plural (number)
part, partic, ptc	participle
p part	past participle
phil	philology
perf	perfect (tense)
plup, pluperf	pluperfect (tense)
pos	positive (degree)
pos, poss	possessive (pronoun)
Pr, Pron	pronoun
pre	before (e.g. pre-Old English)

Prep	preposition(al)
pres	present (tense)
pret	preterite (tense)
princ	principal (clause)
prop	proper (noun)
Prt	particle
Q	qualifier
refl	reflexive (pronoun)
reg	regular (verb)
rel	relative (pronoun)
RP	received pronunciation
S	sentence, south (e.g. S–Germanic)
s, sg	singular (number)
s, subj	subject
sep	separable (prefix)
sl	slang
SL	source language
SM	sentence modifier
Spec	specifier
Sub	subordinator
subjunct	subjunctive (mood)
subord	subordinate (clause)
subst	substantive
suff	suffix
super	superlative (degree)
syl	syllable
syn	synonym
T	transformation rule
t	tonic (element of syllable), transitive (verb)
TL	target language
transl	translation
V	vowel
V, Vb	verb
voc	vocative (case), vocabulary
VP	verb phrase
W	west (e.g. W–Germanic)
wh	interrogative (pronoun)
{Z}	plural (morpheme)

LIST OF SYMBOLS
AND CONVENTIONS USED IN
LINGUISTIC STUDIES

[ ]	'square brackets' enclose phonetic items, allophones, e.g. [ʃiːp]
-	'hyphen' indicates position of phonetic item in word, e.g. [-n] in *man*
:	'colon' indicates opposition, e.g. [p]:[b], [t]:[d]
' ˊ ˋ ˬ ˜ ˮ ˉ ˆ →	'diacritic marks'
. . .	silence, pause
/ /	'slant lines', 'slant brackets', 'bars' enclose phonological items, phonemes, foot boundary, e.g. /ʃiːp/
// //	tone-group boundary
1, 2, 3, etc.	tone, pitch level
⟋ ↑	rising intonation
⟍ ↓	falling intonation
— —>	level intonation
+	'plus juncture' indicates open transition
‖	'double bar' juncture
#	'double cross' juncture
* *	'double asterisks' enclose morpho-phonemic items
~	phonological contrast
{ }	'wing brackets', 'braces' enclose grammatical forms, e.g. plural morpheme {-s} or syllable structure
+	'plus sign' indicates morpheme boundary, e.g. *man + ly*
		group boundary
‖	clause boundary
‖|	sentence boundary
(( ))	included clause

xvii

*	'asterisk' indicates ungrammatical or unacceptable form; reconstructed or hypothetical form
⟨ ⟩	'angle brackets' enclose graphic symbols, e.g. graphemes
italics	quotes of utterances in conventional spelling
>	developed to..., becomes..., is greater than
<	developed from..., from..., is less than
'gloss'	'glosses' enclose meaning of lexical item or translation
→	phrase structure arrow meaning 'rewrite as'...
⇒	transformation rule arrow meaning 'transform into'
=	equals, identical with
≠	is not equal, is not identical with
∅	zero
∈	is a member of
∉	is not a member of
⊂	is included in
⊃	includes
⊄	is not included in
⊅	does not include
≡	equivalence
∪	in union with
∩	intersects with

A

ABBREVIATION The shortening of certain forms of the language to reduce the time and effort spent on their use, both in speech and in writing. ACRONYMS are words formed from the initial letters of the words in a phrase, e.g. *NATO* from *North Atlantic Treaty Organisation*, CLIPPED WORDS are formed by retaining only part (usually the first syllable) of the original word, e.g. *lab* from *laboratory*, and CONTRACTIONS are formed by dropping part of the word or phrase, e.g. *you'd* from *you would*.

ABBREVIATION, LAW OF → Zipf's law.

ABERRANT A linguistic element which deviates from the grammatical pattern typical of its class, e.g. in English the nouns *oxen* and *children* have an irregular plural ending.

ABLATIVE A → case form in some inflected languages, e.g. Latin, often indicating such adverbial features as the manner or place of an action or the instrument with which it is carried out (→ instrumental), e.g. *"Dente lupus cornu taurus petit"* (Horace) 'The wolf attacks with his teeth, the bull with his horns'; *Aegypto advenio domum* 'I arrive home from Egypt'. Prepositions may also govern the ablative, e.g. Latin *magnā cum laude* 'with great renown'. In Latin the ablative is also used in the predicate after certain verbs such as *utor* 'to use', *fungor* 'to perform'. Finno-Ugric languages also have an ablative case usually denoting place.

ABLATIVE ABSOLUTE In Latin grammar the use of an → absolute construction consisting of a participle and a noun, both in the ablative case, e.g. *"Regibus exactis consules creati sunt"* (Livius) 'Kings having been abolished, consuls were elected'.

ABLAUT → Vowel gradation.

ABNORMAL VOWEL → Neutral vowel.

ABRIDGED CLAUSE A name given by some grammarians to a structure which functions as a → clause but which does not contain a finite verb, e.g. *Enthusiastic about the class, John...*

ABRUPT or INTERRUPTED versus CONTINUANT One of the basic oppositions in → distinctive feature phonology based on the analysis of a → spectrogram. 'Abrupt' indicates silence followed or preceded by a sudden spread of energy or rapid transition of vowel → formants as opposed to absence of rapid transition or sudden burst. In articulatory terms abrupt indicates rapid closure or opening of the vocal tract, e.g. to produce → stop consonants. Apart from stop consonants such sounds as a trilled or flapped /r/ have the feature abrupt, whereas sounds such as fricatives and /l/ have the feature 'continuant'.

ABSOLUTE CONSTRUCTION A structure isolated from the → main sentence by intonation or commas. An example of such a construction in English is the gerundial phrase in *Weather permitting, we shall go.*

1

Alternative terms: nominative absolute, dangling participle, absolute phrase. → sentence modifier, included position.

ABSOLUTE PHRASE → Absolute construction.

ABSORPTION → Assimilation resulting in the loss of a sound, e.g. *immobile* from *in* + *mobile*, or Latin *quindecim* < **quinque decem*.

ABSTRACT NOUN A noun referring to a non-material concept, e.g. *happiness* or *courage*. It rarely takes a determiner such as *a* or *the*, and if used in the plural the meaning may be changed, e.g. *kindness:kindnesses*. → concrete noun.

ABSTRACT SOUND A speech sound or → phoneme which is generalised from a → concrete sound by disregarding all dialectal or ideolectal variants, e.g. the English phoneme /r/ as an abstraction from the free variants [ɹ] fricative or [ɾ] flap.

ABSTRACTION The process or result of forming a theoretical concept which has no concrete identity but which is based upon observation and classification of concrete events. E.g. the concept of phoneme is an abstraction based upon observation of the form and behaviour of speech sounds. The phoneme has no physical identity but is represented in a given environment by a speech sound or → allophone. → categorisation.

ABUSIVE LANGUAGE The use of a word or phrase outside its normal → semantic range, e.g. the name of an animal applied to human beings, with insulting connotations. → vulgar.

ACCENT (*a*) The phonological feature of relatively high → stress, → pitch or → duration. (*b*) Alternative term for → diacritic mark. (*c*) A variety of a language differing from the → standard, particularly in pronunciation, e.g. in regional or social dialects or in the speech of foreigners.

ACCENTOLOGY The systematic study of → stress.

ACCENTUAL SYSTEM The → stress and/or pitch system of a language.

ACCENTUAL UNIT A stretch of speech containing one primary → stress, e.g. a single word such as *inventory* ['invəntrɪ] or a phrase such as *give it him* ['giv ɪt ɪm].

ACCENTUATION → Stress.

ACCEPTABILITY Information as to whether or not a native speaker regards an utterance as correct or appropriate is of particular interest in linguistics, particularly in a → generative grammar, the rules of which are intended to specify all well-formed sentences and no others of the language in question. Occasionally linguists design elicitation tests to determine whether or not a particular utterance is regarded as ACCEPTABLE to an informant. A distinction is often made between grammatical acceptability, i.e. whether an utterance conforms to the syntactic conventions, and semantic acceptability, i.e. whether an utterance has → meaning in a particular context. Forms quoted as unacceptable for one reason or another may be marked with an asterisk ⟨*⟩ and

2

called asterisk forms. → Grammaticality, correctness, nonsense form. (2.3 Quirk–Svartik).

ACCEPTABLE　→ Acceptability.

ACCESSORY VERB　→ Auxiliary verb.

ACCIDENCE The system and study of alterations in word form, often by the addition of affixes, to differentiate such grammatical categories as → case, → tense, → gender, → number, e.g. Latin *pater, patris, patrem* . . .; English *go, went, gone* or *make, made, making.* → inflexion.

ACCOMMODATION　Partial → assimilation of adjacent speech sounds in conformity with the phonemic pattern of the language, e.g. early Latin **ag-tos > actus,* where [g] is devoiced under the influence of the [t].

ACCOUNTABILITY A principle of → linguistic analysis which demands that all features of an actual or potential utterance must be made explicit in the description of the language. This is usually done by setting up units such as phonemes, morphemes, or sentences. Utterances are then said to be realisations of or reducible to these units at various levels of analysis. (4.2 Chomsky).

ACCULTURATION The process or result of cultural and linguistic contact between members of two speech communities, characterised by → borrowing of vocabulary or grammatical patterns, → bilingualism and loan-words, as between European settlers in North America and the indigenous population, or between different ethnic groups, e.g. the Pennsylvania Dutch of German

communities in the Eastern United States of America. (10.1 Hymes).

ACCUSATIVE A → case form in inflected languages denoting that the word in question is the → object of a transitive verb, e.g. Latin *agricola colit agros* 'the farmer cultivates the fields', or is governed by a certain preposition, e.g. Latin *post mortem* 'after death'. In English this relationship is often expressed by word order in the case of nouns, e.g. the difference between *The boy hits the ball* and *The ball hits the boy* or by a special form in the case of pronouns, e.g. the words *him* and *me* in *I see him* and *He sees me*. In some languages the accusative case may have special adverbial significance, e.g. the accusative of time: German *den nächsten Morgen* '(on the) next morning', or accusative of place: Latin *domum ire* 'to go home'. → objective pronoun.

ACOUSTIC FEATURES Characteristics of speech sounds as analysed in → acoustic phonetics in terms of pitch or amplitude, or in phonology in terms of oppositions such as → compact *versus* diffuse, → sharp *versus* plain, → continuant *versus* interrupted, etc.

ACOUSTIC FORMANT → Formant (*a*).

ACOUSTIC PHONETICS A branch of → phonetics which is concerned with the study of the physical properties of speech sounds, e.g. pitch, frequency and amplitude, during transmission from speaker to hearer. Recent developments of electronic and other instrumentation have improved techniques of observation, recording and measurement.

→ auditory phonetics. Alternative term: physical phonetics. (3.3 Jakobson–Fant–Halle, Joos).

ACOUSTICS A branch of physics which is concerned with the properties of sound. → acoustic phonetics.

ACQUISITION → Language acquisition.

ACROLOGY → Acrophony.

ACRONYM → Abbreviation.

ACROPHONY The use of a graphic sign which originally represented the initial sound or syllable of a word as a general alphabetic sign. Thus the second letter of the Greek alphabet, *beta*, is allegedly derived from the Semitic word *beth* meaning 'house'. Alternative term: Acrology. (7.2 Gelb).

ACTION NOUN A noun denoting an action, e.g. *a run*; *a walk*; *a fight*; *an arrival*.

ACTIVE The active → voice.

ACTIVE ARTICULATOR → Articulator.

ACTIVE CAVITY → Cavity.

ACTIVE VOICE → Voice (*b*).

ACTOR–ACTION–GOAL The normal word order in an English active sentence, where the → subject (the actor) precedes the → verb (the action), which precedes the → object (the goal), e.g. *The boy kicks the ball*. A different order is found in some other languages, e.g. Latin where case endings indicate these relationships.

ACTUALISATION → Realisation.

ACUTE → Grave *vs.* acute.

ACUTE ACCENT A → diacritic mark placed over a vowel in writing to indicate pitch, stress, or other qualities, e.g. close vowel in French *fiancé* or *cliché*. → grave accent.

ADAM'S APPLE Popular name for the front part of the → larynx which can be seen externally in adult males as a protruberance at the front of the throat.

ADAPTATION → Assimilation.

ADAPTATION THEORY The view that words with similar meanings influence each other's grammatical form, e.g. kinship words with suffix *-ther* such as *brother, mother, father*.

ADDITIVE CLAUSE A → clause which gives additional information to a main clause without modifying or affecting the original information, e.g. *and he sat down* in *The visitor came in and he sat down*.

ADDRESS Speech directed towards a specific person indicated by terms relating to a position in the social hierarchy, e.g. English *Mr.*, French *Madame*, etc., or by → familiar or → polite forms, e.g. French *tu* as opposed to *vous* 'you', or by special vocative case forms. Alternative term: allocution.

ADDRESSEE One of the participants in a conversation or other situation of language activity. In the spoken medium it is the hearer or auditor, in the written medium the reader, as opposed to the performer (speaker or writer). → Communication.

ADEQUACY A principle of linguistic analysis which demands that a theory must provide the means for making correct statements about the empirical facts. In → transformational-generative grammar a grammar is considered DESCRIPTIVELY ADEQUATE if it describes correctly the linguistic intuition of a native speaker of the language; EXPLANATORY ADEQUACY on the other hand means that it is also in keeping with an appropriate theory of language and language acquisition. (4.2 Chomsky).

ADHERENT ADJECTIVE → Attribute.

ADJECTIVAL A name given by some grammarians to a structure which functions as an → adjective or modifier, before or after a noun, but which cannot take the normal inflexions of an adjective, e.g. *the above statement,* or *A girl spoiled by her mother is not a good room-mate.*

ADJECTIVAL CLAUSE A → clause functioning as an → adjective or noun modifier, e.g. *I didn't like the show* (*that*) *we saw last night.* Alternative term: adjective clause.

ADJECTIVE A → part of speech used to describe or qualify a noun, either as a subordinate member of a noun phrase as in *the tall man* or predicatively as in *the man is tall.* In English most adjectives can have three forms: positive, comparative and superlative, usually formed by the addition of the inflexional endings -(*e*)*r* and -(*e*)*st* or by use of the words *more, most, less* or *least,* e.g. *tall, taller, tallest; beautiful, more*

beautiful, most beautiful; probable, less probable, least probable. Some grammarians restrict the term adjective to those which are regular in form, i.e. those which fit into the set - -, - - (*e*)*r,* - - (*e*)*st.* A word which forms the comparative and superlative degrees with *more, most,* etc. or in any other way is then called an → adjectival. (4.1, 4.2, 8.23).

ADJECTIVE CLAUSE → Adjectival clause.

ADJECTIVE GROUP An adjectival structure with at least one adjective and one or more → adjuncts, e.g. *not very interesting.*

ADJECTIVE PREDICATE → Predicative adjective.

ADJECTIVISATION The use of a word or phrase as an → adjective, e.g. *It's the up-and-coming thing.*

ADJUNCT A word or phrase which is used to extend the meaning of another word or phrase, but which is not one of the main structural elements of a sentence: e.g. *stone* in *He built a stone wall; always* in *I always work hard.* (4.1, 4.2, 8.23).

ADJUNCTIVAL A name given by some grammarians to a structure which functions as an → adjunct, e.g. prepositional or participial phrases such as *made-to-order.*

ADNOMINAL A part of speech or phrase which modifies a noun. → modifier.

ADOPTIVE FORM A form of a word created by → overcorrection.

ADSTRATUM The forms of a language which affect those of

5

another, more dominant, speech community, e.g. the speech of European immigrants influencing the English language in the USA, their adopted country. → substratum.

ADVERB A → part of speech which can be used to qualify a verb, adjective or other adverb. In English it usually fits into the → frame: *The man walked . . .* and often ends in *-ly*, e.g. *quickly*. Some grammarians would limit the term adverb to refer only to those words which are regular in form, i.e. which take *-ly*. A word having the same function but a different form, e.g. *He walked fast* or *He walked across the field* is then called an → adverbial. (4.1, 4.2, 8.23).

ADVERBIAL A name given by some grammarians to a structure which functions as an → adverb but which does not have the usual formal features, i.e. does not end in *-ly*. An adverbial may indicate place, as in *He stayed at home*; manner, as in *She worked hard*; time, as in *Bob is leaving next week*; frequency, as in *Such things seldom occur*; or degree, as in *The lecture was very good*.

ADVERBIAL CLAUSE A → clause which functions as an → adverb, modifying some other structure, e.g. in *Although he was very busy, he did it for me*. Such clauses are often classified by their influence on meaning into → adversative, → causal, → conditional, → confirmatory, → consequence clause, clause of degree, manner, etc.

ADVERBIAL CONJUNCTION → Conjunctive adverb.

ADVERBIALISATION The use of a word or phrase as an → adverb,

e.g. the prepositional phrase in *He stayed at home.*

ADVERSATIVE CLAUSE An adverbial clause introduced by an adversative conjunction expressing a contrast, e.g. *Though he was brave, he was prudent.*

ADVERSATIVE CONJUNC-TION A → conjunction joining two clauses which imply a contrast, e.g. *but* in *It's warm but it's raining.*

AFFECTIVE A type of style or meaning which is characterised by highly emotional connotations and spontaneous creations. → function (*a*). Alternative term: emotive.

AFFILIATION Genealogical relationship of descendant or daughter languages to their common ancestor or parent language, e.g. French and Spanish to Vulgar Latin or Proto-Romance. → family of languages. (6.1).

AFFINITY Close relationship between languages which show phonological or grammatical similarities due to typology or contact, but irrespective of genetic evolution. → classification (*a*). (6.1).

AFFIX A collective term for → prefix, → infix, → suffix, i.e. a morpheme added to the → base or root of a word to form a new → stem, e.g. *-y* and *un-* in *lucky, unlucky*, or to provide an inflexional element, e.g. *-er, -est*, as in *unluckier, unluckiest*. → word formation.

AFFIX CLIPPING → Met-analysis.

AFFIX INDEX → Index (*b*).

6

AFFIXATION The process or result of attaching or adding an → affix to a root, e.g. *Marx-ism, luck-y.*

AFFIXING INDEX → Index (*b*).

AFFIXING LANGUAGE A type of language in which grammatical relationships are expressed by adding modifying elements on to a base or root word. These elements may be either prefixes (prefixing languages such as Koptic or Bantu) or suffixes (suffixing languages such as Algonquian or Latin). → agglutinative language. (6.1, 8.1).

AFFRICATE A speech sound which is a combination of a → stop and a → fricative; the stop is released slowly with the result that a fricative is heard, e.g. [t͡ʃ] as in *chop* or [d͡ʒ] as in *judge.* Such a combination of sounds is usually called an affricate only if it functions as a single → phoneme. Thus /ts/ in English *coats* /kouts/ is not usually referred to as an affricate, but the same combination of sounds /ts/ in German *zu* /t͡suː/ is an affricate and is represented by the → ligature /t͡s/.

AFRICAN LINGUISTICS The linguistic description of the languages of Africa, a study in which much progress has been made in recent years, with teams of field workers from Europe and America making surveys of hitherto unrecorded languages and dialects and arriving at new classifications of language types and families. → Appendix 1, pp. 273–274. (8.8 Greenberg, Polomé).

AFRO-ASIATIC LINGUISTICS → Hamito-Semitic linguistics.

AGENT In a passive sentence the noun phrase preceded by the preposition *by*, e.g. *The letter was written by him.* In inflected languages the → instrumental case may be used to refer to the agent without a preposition.

AGGLOMERATING LANGUAGE → Agglutinative language.

AGGLOMERATION → Agglutination.

AGGLUTINATION (*a*) The adding of a suffix to a root to denote grammatical function. → agglutinative language. (*b*) The coalescence of speech sounds of closely linked words. → sandhi. Alternative term: agglomeration.

AGGLUTINATIVE INDEX → Index (*b*).

AGGLUTINATIVE LANGUAGE A type of language such as Finnish, Hungarian, Turkish, Swahili or Japanese where grammatical relationships and word structure are indicated by the free combination of elements, e.g. the Turkish *odalarimdan* 'from my rooms' where the elements *-lar -im -dan* are morphemes expressing one distinct category, i.e. plural, first person, ablative, respectively. In → inflected languages, however, one morpheme may stand for more than one category. Some linguists regard agglutinative languages as standing morphologically and historically between → isolating and inflecting types. English has agglutinating features in such compound words as *ungodliness* and *unavoidably.* Alternative terms: agglutinating, agglomerating, agglomerative language. (6.1, 8.1).

AGGREGATIVE COMPOUND
A compound word formed by multiple composition, often occurring in newspaper headlines, e.g. "*April Fool call-up joke...*" (*The Guardian*).

AGOGICS OF SPEECH The system and study of → rhythm in speech.

AGRAMMATISM Inability to comprehend or produce grammatical utterances due to psycho-physiological defects or other reasons. → aphasia. (9.5).

AGRAPHIA Inability to write due to malfunction in the central nervous system. (9.5).

AGREEMENT Correspondence in form or grammatical category of two or more items which indicates a specific syntactic relationship, e.g. in the English sentence *The boys are here*, the noun plural ending *-s* is in agreement with the plural verb *are* and vice versa; in the sentence *The boy is here*, the subject and predicate agree by their both being singular. In some languages adjectives agree with the nouns they qualify, e.g. French *la table est belle* (f), but *le cadeau est beau* (m). → number, gender, case, person. Alternative terms: concord, congruence, correspondence. (4.1, 4.2).

AIR CHAMBER → Cavity.

AIR STREAM Air, moving into or out of the vocal tract, which is used by the → speech organs to produce speech sounds. Alternative term: breath stream.

AIR-STREAM MECHANISM
Term first used by K. L. Pike to refer to parts of the vocal tract used to produce different types of sounds. An air stream is produced by an air-stream mechanism by means of an INITIATOR, a part of the vocal tract which moves in order to pull air in or push air out. There are three main types of air-stream mechanism and all three can be INGRESSIVE (i.e. the air moving inwards) or EGRESSIVE (i.e. the air moving outwards). The most important is the PULMONIC AIR-STREAM MECHANISM since air moving out of or in some cases into the lungs, with the lungs acting as the initiator, forms the basis of almost all human speech. The GLOTTALIC AIR-STREAM MECHANISM (or PHARYNGEAL AIR-STREAM MECHANISM) where the larynx acts as initiator pushing air out of or drawing air into the mouth and pharynx, is used to produce sounds heard in some African or Caucasian languages. Only a small volume of air is controlled by the glottalic mechanism so that only a small fraction of speech can be uttered with one movement of the initiator. The third type is the VELARIC (or as it is sometimes called ORAL) AIR-STREAM MECHANISM where the back part of the tongue moves backwards or forwards on the velum, acting as the initiator drawing air into or pushing air out of the mouth. The air in the rest of the vocal tract plays no part in this mechanism. The → clicks of some African languages are produced by velaric air stream. An ingressive velaric air stream is used to produce the expression of annoyance usually written *tut-tut*. Other common examples of the velaric air-stream mechanism in use are one type of 'raspberry' sound and the activity of

sucking through a straw. (3.1, 8.22).

AKUEME A minimum distinctive characteristic in the tone of voice of an individual speaker such as timbre, rhythm, tempo, loudness, etc. → voice quality.

ALALIA Inability to speak due to abnormality or malfunction of the external speech organs rather than of the central nervous system. (9.5).

ALEXIA Complete inability to learn to read. This complaint, like → dyslexia, has many associated learning difficulties. (9.5).

ALGEBRAIC LINGUISTICS The use of formal and context-free models, partly borrowed from logic and mathematics, in the theoretical analysis and description of languages. → glossematics, → transformational-generative grammar, → categorial grammar. (9.4, 10.4).

ALGORITHM A strategy for finding a solution to a problem which can be stated in a flow-chart form, e.g. as a computer programme.

ALIEN WORD → Alienism.

ALIENISM A loan word taken from another language, e.g. *mirage*, *blitz*; or a lapse on the part of a foreign learner, under the influence of his native tongue. Alternative terms: alien word, foreignism, peregrinism.

ALLEGRO FORM A contraction of word forms as pronounced in rapid speech; e.g. Latin *caldus* < *calidus*, or English *library* [laibri] as

opposed to the full or → lento form [laibrəri], or *I should have thought so* [aiʃdevθɔːtsou] as opposed to [ai ʃʊd hæv θɔːt sou].

ALLITERATION The technique of using the same initial sound in a number of successive words, e.g. *"When to the sessions of sweet silent thought..."* (Shakespeare). → rhyme. (7.3).

ALLO- A prefix used in connection with names of linguistic units to refer to non-distinctive → variants of a single distinctive unit, e.g. → allophones of a phoneme, → allomorphs of a morpheme, → allographs of a grapheme.

ALLOCHRONE A non-distinctive variation in the length of a speech sound, which does not affect the meaning of the word, e.g. the English *room* may be pronounced [rum] or [ruːm]. → chroneme.

ALLOCUTION → Address.

ALLOGRAPH One of a group of variants of a → grapheme or written sign. In Latin script, the writing system used by most West European languages, it usually refers to the different shapes of letters and punctuation marks, e.g. lower case, capital, cursive, printed, strokes, etc. → allophone, allomorph. (7.2).

ALLOKINE One of a number of non-distinctive variants of a → kineme or gestural unit.

ALLOLOG One of a number of non-distinctive variant forms of a word, e.g. the → allegro and → lento forms [mɑːm] and [mædəm] of *madam*, [kɑːnt] and [kænət] of *cannot*.

ALLOMORPH A non-distinctive variant of a → morpheme. In English the plural ending -*s* has the following variants: {s} as in *cats*, {z} as in *dogs*, and {zz} as in *houses*, or even {ø} as in *sheep*. By analogy with the phonological terms → phoneme/allophone, these are said to be different allomorphs of the English plural morpheme. Alternative term: morpheme alternant. (4.1).

ALLONYM One of a number of variant forms of a name, e.g. *Constantinople* and *Stambul* of *Istanbul*.

ALLOPHONE A speech sound which is one of a number of variants of a → phoneme. The occurrence of a particular allophone may be determined by its environment or it may be in free variation. An example of allophones determined by environment is the use of two different allophones of the same phoneme /l/, the so-called 'front' or 'clear' [l] as in *lamp* or *light* occurring before vowels, and the so-called 'back' or 'dark' [ɫ] as in *old* and *table* occurring before consonants and at the end of words. An example of allophones occurring in → free variation is the Southern British English /r/ between vowels, as in *very*, which can occur either as a flap [ɾ], or as a fricative [ɹ]. Alternative terms: phonetic variant, allophonic variant, subphonemic variant. (3.1, 3.4).

ALLOPHONIC CHANGE → Phonetic sound change.

ALLOPHONIC REALISATION A → phoneme is said to be represented or realised by one of its allophones in a given situation. Thus [pʰ] as in *pot* is the allophonic → realisation of /p/ in word-initial position, whereas [p] is the allophonic realisation of /p/ after initial [s] as in *spot*. (3.4).

ALLOPHONIC VARIANT → Allophone.

ALLOTAGMA In tagmemics a non-distinctive variant of a → tagmeme. Allotagma is to tagmeme as allomorph is to morpheme and as allophone is to phoneme.

ALPHABET A collection of graphic signs called → letters, to represent one or more single sounds of speech. Alphabetic writing is believed to have developed in stages from pictorial sketches to systems of LOGOGRAPHY (Chinese characters, Egyptian hieroglyphs) to SYLLABOGRAPHY (Mesopotamian cuneiform, Hindi devanagari, Japanese kana) and eventually to more segmental scripts. English and most other West European languages use a modification of the Latin alphabet which, like Cyrillic used for Russian, goes back to Greek. Some languages, such as Finnish, are consistent in their use of one symbol per → phoneme, whereas in other languages, such as English, the relationship between individual speech sounds and letters is often blurred by historical → spelling. → notation. See illustration p. 265. (7.2).

ALPHABETIC WRITING A system of writing based on an alphabet in which the letters represent speech sounds. (7.2).

ALPHABETOGRAPHY The study of → alphabetic writing.

10

ALPHABETOLOGY The study of → alphabetic writing.

ALTERATION A change in the meaning of a word or phrase due to technical innovation, cultural transfer or mutual contact between varieties of language, e.g. *jet* 'rush of liquid' > 'type of propulsion'. (5.1).

ALTERNANT → Variant.

ALTERNATION The existence of two or more variants, distinctive or non-distinctive, in a → paradigmatic relationship, e.g. the alternation of forms, as in the distinctive alternation of present and past tenses of strong verbs such as *bring, brought,* or the representation of one phoneme by more than one symbol, e.g. /i/ in English as *ee* as in *meet,* or *ea* in *meat,* or *ei* in *receive* or *ie* as in *retrieve.* → free variation.

ALTERNATIVE FORM → Variant.

ALVEOLAR A consonant pronounced with the tongue touching or in close proximity to the gum above the upper teeth, or alveolar ridge, e.g. [t], [s]. If the tip of the tongue is the articulator, the sound may be called → apico-alveolar, if the back part of the tongue is the articulator, the sound may be called → dorso-alveolar, if the point of articulation is towards the rear of the alveolar ridge approaching the palate, the sound may be called POST-ALVEOLAR. Alternative term: supra-dental. (3.1, 8.22).

ALVEOLAR RIDGE The ridge of bone above the gum behind the top teeth. See diagram p. 159. Alternative terms: alveolum, teeth ridge.

ALVEOLUM → Alveolar ridge.

AMALGAM (a) → blend. (b) → cumul.

AMALGAMATING LANGUAGE → Inflected language.

AMBIGUITY A construction is said to be AMBIGUOUS when more than one interpretation can be assigned to it. The English sentence *Patent medicines are sold by frightening people* is ambiguous since it is not clear whether *frightening* is describing *people* or expressing the act of 'putting fear into'. This particular ambiguity is resolved in speech by → intonation and stress.

AMBIGUOUS → Ambiguity.

AMBILINGUAL A person or speech community equally competent in both of two languages, e.g. Belgian nationals speaking both French and Flemish. → bilingualism.

AMBISYLLABIC CONSONANT A consonant which forms a transition between two → syllables, the syllable boundary occurring during the articulation of the consonant, e.g. [t] in *butter.*

AMBIVALENT WORD A word with two opposite meanings, e.g. French *hôte* 'guest' or 'host'.

AMELIORATION A type of → semantic change in which the meaning of a word assumes favourable connotations, e.g. *knight* 'lad', 'servant' > 'nobleman', *fond* 'insipid' > 'full of affection'. → deterioration. Alternative terms: melioration, elevation. (5.1).

AMELIORATIVE SUFFIX A → suffix which gives a word a more favourable meaning. Alternative term: meliorative suffix.

AMERICAN LINGUISTICS
Collective term for a number of
approaches to → linguistic analysis
by (North) American scholars.
American linguists of the early years
of the 20th century shared with
F. de Saussure (→ structural linguistics) the scepticism about looking at
language in comparative and historical terms. Supported by the field-
work techniques of → anthropological linguistics, men like F. Boas,
E. Sapir and B. L. Whorf established
a new tradition of descriptive linguistics based on the categories
appropriate to the indigenous languages of North and Central America
rather than those of Latin grammar.
L. Bloomfield (1887–1949) did much
to make linguistics into a respected
scientific discipline (BLOOMFIELDIAN-
ISM), which many have since helped
to modify and expand. The Bloomfieldians have been criticised for a
rigidly distributional and mechanistic
outlook, especially as regards their
association with stimulus-response
psychology (→ behaviourism).
Several alternative theories are being
developed (→ tagmemics, stratificational grammar), notably those based
on N. Chomsky's work (→ transformational-generative grammar).
American linguists have been actively
engaged in solving practical problems of language use (→ applied
linguistics), often in collaboration
with other fields (→ psycholinguistics,
computational linguistics). (2.1 Trager, Hall; 2.2 Hill, Joos; 2.3 Samarin; 2.4 Bloomfield, Sapir; 2.5 Cook;
4.2 Chomsky; 8.23 Gleason; 9.11
Lado; 9.12 Gunderson; 10.1 Hymes).

AMERINDIAN LINGUISTICS
The linguistic description of Ameri-
can Indian languages such as Hoka-
Siouan, Algonquian, Mayan and
Guaraní. → American linguistics. →
Appendix 1, p. 276. (8.8 Matteson).

AMPLIFICATIVE → Aug-
mentative.

AMPLITUDE Variation in air
pressure from a norm as a result of
a sound wave, measured as the dis-
tance from the peak of a wave to
its norm, e.g. A——B in the diagram
below. The greater the amplitude
of the sound wave at a given →
frequency, the greater the volume or
loudness of the sound. Amplitude
can be measured objectively, whereas
→ volume or loudness is a subjective
impression, depending on a combination of amplitude and frequency.
(3.1, 8.22).

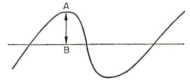

ANACHRONISM The use of a
word or expression which does not
correspond to the phonological,
grammatical or lexical norms of a
given period in the history of a
language, e.g. *erstwhile* or *unto* in
twentieth-century English.

ANACOLUTHON Beginning a
sentence in one way and continuing
or ending it in another, e.g. *I know
what you—but let us change the
subject.* Alternative term: anantapo-
doton, anapodoton.

ANAGRAM A word or group
of words made up of the same letters
as another word or group of words,
e.g. *petal* is an anagram of *plate.*
→ palindrome.

ANALOGICAL CHANGE →
Analogy.

12

ANALOGISM The view, first proposed by Zeno and other Greek Stoic philosophers, that the many grammatical and semantic irregularities in language are the product of natural usage and should not be tampered with by setting up normative standards. The controversy between the positions of analogism and → anomalism foreshadows a later distinction of descriptive and prescriptive grammar. (2.5 Robins).

ANALOGUE A word in one language which is the → equivalent of a word in another although its form and semantic range may not be identical, e.g. French *maison* and English *house*.

ANALOGY The process or result of grammatical and lexical forms changing under the influence of some other regular pattern in the language. Thus *hisn* for *his* may be used on the pattern of *my*:*mine*, *knowed* for *knew* by analogy with *mow*:*mowed*, *brang* for *brought* by analogy with *sing*:*sang*. Such modifications tend to bring about regularities in the forms of the language, often in contrast to → phonetic laws. Alternative term: analogical change. (6.1, 6.2).

ANALPHABETIC NOTATION A system of non-alphabetic graphic signs, → diacritic marks and other symbols used to represent the features of → articulation and → prosody in minute detail. Such notations have been devised by A. M. Bell ('Visible Speech'), H. Sweet ('Organic'), O. Jespersen, K. Pike and others. → transcription. (3.1 Abercrombie).

ANALYSIS → Linguistic analysis.

ANALYTIC LANGUAGE A type of language which shows syntactic relationships by → function words and → word order, as opposed to → inflected or → agglutinative languages, where such formal relationships are expressed by the close combination of elements (prefixes, infixes, suffixes) with the base or root word. Words tend to consist of simple free morphemes, and the composition of plurimorphemic words is irrelevant to their syntactic function. Examples of analytic languages are Vietnamese, Chinese, Samoan and, to some degree, English. → Synthetic language. (6.1, 8.1).

ANANTOPODOTON → Anacoluthon.

ANAPAEST → Foot.

ANAPHORA (*a*) The repetition of initial sounds, words or syntactic structures in successive verses or sentences to achieve a stylistic effect, e.g.

"Alone, alone, all, all alone,
Alone on a wide wide sea . . ."
(Coleridge)

or Latin *"Veni, vidi, vici,"* (Caesar) 'I came, I saw, I conquered'. (*b*) The reference back to an → antecedent by repetition or grammatical substitution, e.g. *You can't have this book, take that one!* Alternative term: back-reference, anaphoric reference.

ANAPHORIC REFERENCE → Anaphora.

ANAPHORIC SUBSTITUTE A word which refers back to another word already mentioned, either by repetition or by use of a → prop word, e.g. *You can't come, can you?* or *I don't want this; have you got* *another one?* Alternative term: anaphoric word.

ANAPHORIC WORD → Anaphoric substitute.

ANAPODOTON → Anacoluthon.

ANAPTYCTIC VOWEL A short vowel inserted into a word. → anaptyxis.

ANAPTYXIS The insertion of a short vowel into a word between two or more consonants to simplify the syllabic structure, e.g. when [ə] is inserted in English *athlete* ['æθəliːt], or when German *Landsknecht* 'mercenary' > French *lansquenet* or Italian *lanzichenecco*. → table p. 75.

ANARTHRIA Inability to articulate speech sounds due to brain lesion or damage to the nervous system. (9.5).

ANASTROPHE → Metathesis.

ANCESTOR LANGUAGE One of a family of related languages which is the common origin of all others. Thus, Vulgar Latin is regarded as the ancestor of all Romance languages such as French, Italian and Rumanian, which are called descendant or daughter languages. → glottochronology. Alternative term: parent language. (6.1).

ANIMAL CRY THEORY → Origin of Speech.

ANIMATE A class of → nouns referring to living persons or animals. The categories animate/inanimate operate like grammatical → genders in some languages. In Russian, for example, the form of the accusative of masculine nouns varies depending on whether reference is being made to an animate being or not.

ANNOMINATION → Pun.

ANOMALISM The view, first proposed by Aristotle and other Greek philosophers, that the proportional regularities in language are sufficient grounds for setting up normative standards of correctness which speakers of the language should follow. The controversy between the positions of anomalism and → analogism foreshadows a later distinction of prescriptive and descriptive grammar. (2.5 Robins).

ANOMALOUS An utterance is said to be anomalous when it does not comply with the grammatical and semantic conventions of the language. → grammaticality, nonsense form.

ANOMIA The inability to remember or to recognise names. (9.5).

ANTECEDENT A word or phrase referred back to by a subsequent word, usually a → pronoun. For example in *The man who was sitting in the car, man* is the antecedent of *who*, and in *Although John came, he did not speak, John* is the antecedent of *he*. There is usually formal correspondence between the two parts of the reference in → number and → gender, e.g. *Bob and his sister Mary went on their first holiday to Italy; Jean went to see her parents.* → back-reference.

ANTERIOR versus NON-ANTERIOR Cavity features in recent theories of → distinctive feature phonology. Anterior refers to sounds produced with an obstruction in front of the palato-alveolar region, e.g. labials, dentals, alveolars. Non-anterior refers to sounds produced with no obstruction in front of the palato-alveolar region, e.g. palatal, velar, pharyngeal consonants and, of course, all vowels.

ANTHROPO-LINGUISTICS → Anthropological linguistics.

ANTHROPOLOGICAL LIN-GUISTICS The use of special research techniques from the fields of anthropology and linguistics to study the languages of speech communities which have no writing system and literary tradition. Since there are no written texts, and often no previous scholarship to rely on, the pioneers in this field had to develop new procedures of eliciting linguistic information directly from native speakers (→ field-work). These general principles have also been applied to language families and types other than Amerindian, e.g. African and Malayo-Polynesian languages. Anthropological linguists since F. Boas and E. Sapir (→ American linguistics) have emphasised that language cannot be separated from its social setting, and that linguistics must therefore be regarded as a social science. → ethno-linguistics, culture and language. Alternative terms: anthropo-linguistics, linguistic anthropology. (10.1 Hymes).

ANTHROPONYMY The study of personal names. → Onomastics.

ANTHROPOPHONICS Old term used by Baudouin de Courtenay (1845–1929) to refer to the total sound productive potential of the human organs. Some modern phoneticians are reviving the term.

ANTICIPATION A sound change brought about by the speech organs anticipating and preparing the position necessary for the production of a following sound. → Umlaut is an example of vocalic anticipation, e.g. the *ō* of Old English *fōt* 'foot' changed before the *-i* ending of the plural *fōti* > fēt, hence Modern English *feet*. → prolepsis. (6.1).

ANTICIPATORY ASSIMILA-TION → Assimilation.

ANTICIPATORY DISSIMILA-TION → Dissimilation.

ANTIGRAMMATICAL CON-STRUCTION A structure which is not in keeping with the syntactic patterns of the standard language, e.g. the dialectal *I've never seen nothing like it*.

ANTI-MENTALISM → Mechanistic linguistics.

ANTONOMASIA The use of an adjective for a → proper noun, e.g. *The Almighty*, or the use of a proper noun as a generic term for a class, e.g. *Hoover* for *vacuum cleaner*. → appellative name.

ANTONYM One of two or more words with opposite meanings, e.g. *hot/cold* or *hope/despair*. True or pure antonyms are rare. → converse term, synonym. (5.1).

ANTONYMY The relationship between → antonyms.

15

AORIST In some inflected languages such as Greek, a form of the verb denoting a → tense or → aspect referring to the past but without limitations as to whether the action is completed or continued.

APERTURE The degree of opening at some point in the vocal tract for the pronunciation of a speech sound.

APEX (*a*) The tip of the tongue. → diagram p. 159. (*b*) A → diacritic mark indicating a long vowel, e.g. Latin *pōpulus* 'poplar' as opposed to *populus* 'people'.

APHAERESIS → Aphesis.

APHASIA Partial or complete loss of the ability to use spoken language as a result of maldevelopment, disease or injury to the brain. Alternative term: dysphasia. (9.5).

APHERESIS → Aphesis.

APHESIS The omission of one or more sounds or words from the beginning of an utterance, e.g. *Evening* for *Good evening!* or [baut] for *about*. → table p. 75. Alternative term: aph(a)eresis, prosiopesis.

APHRASIA The inability to produce or understand utterances phrased according to grammatical patterns. (9.5).

APICAL ARTICULATION The articulation of a speech sound using the apex or tip of the tongue, e.g. [t] in *tin*.

APICO-ALVEOLAR A consonant articulated by the tip, or apex, of the tongue touching or approaching the → alveolar ridge, e.g. [d] as in *dog*, [t] as in *tin* or [s] as in *sack*.

APICO-DENTAL A consonant articulated with the apex of the tongue touching or approaching the upper teeth, e.g. [t̪] and [d̪] in Spanish [t̪od̪os] 'every'.

APOCOPATION → Apocope.

APOCOPE The omission of one or more sounds or letters from the end of a word, e.g. Old English *helpe* > Middle English *help*, or *chapman* > *chap*. → table p. 75. Alternative term: apocopation.

APODOSIS → Consequence clause.

APOPHONY → Vowel gradation.

APOSIOPESIS The breaking off in the middle of a statement, e.g. *I wish you would . . .*

APOSTROPHE A diacritic mark used in writing to indicate omission of a sound or part of a word, e.g. *'aven't* or *'cello*, or (in English) the possessive case, e.g. *Mary's* or *the children's*.

APPELLATION In → semantics, the relationship between a term and the actual existent object for which it stands. (5.1).

APPELLATIVE FUNCTION The use of language for the purpose of asking for a response or action by the person addressed. → function (*a*).

APPELLATIVE NAME A personal name used as a → common

16

noun, e.g. *Wellingtons* 'rubber boots' or *Sam Brown* 'officers' leather belt'. → antonomasia.

APPLICATION In → semantics, particularly in the comparison of the semantic structures of different languages, the use of a particular expression in a particular situation. E.g. the German word *Land* may be said to have the same application on the whole as the English word *country*, although in certain cases related words (German *Staat, Gebiet*, etc. and English *province, state*, etc.) might be more appropriate as corresponding pairs. The concept of application is useful in discussing the problem of finding lexical equivalents in → translation. (2.1 Lyons).

APPLIED LINGUISTICS Collective term for the various applications of linguistic (and phonetic) scholarship to related practical fields. Linguistic knowledge can be used to solve practical language problems in → language teaching (acquisition of the native or a foreign language). Indeed some linguists use the term applied linguistics to refer solely to these pedagogical aspects. Other branches of applied linguistics are → lexicography (dictionary-making), → translation, → speech pathology and therapy. Applied linguistics in the widest sense borders on other disciplines, e.g. → sociolinguistics, psycholinguistics, biolinguistics, computational linguistics, stylistics, information theory. (9.1–9.6, 10.1–10.5).

APPOSITION A word or phrase modifying a preceding noun phrase or clause. It may be a close apposition, e.g. *Our friend Peter*, a loose apposition, e.g. *The man, my uncle*,

drives a red sportscar, or an appositive clause, e.g. *The question why he did it was never answered.*

APPOSITIVE CLAUSE A clause used in → apposition, either as a → non-restrictive sentence modifier with commas: *He walked to the garage, which was a mile away*, or as a → restrictive noun modifier with no commas: *This is the house that Jack built.*

APPROXIMANT Term used by some phoneticians to refer to → frictionless continuant.

ARABIC SCRIPT → Table p. 265. (7.2).

ARBITRARINESS The fact that the connexion between the meaning an utterance conveys and the phonic or graphic substance through which it is realised is not fixed. Languages differ, among other things, by the way they relate content with form, e.g. in their phonological, grammatical and semantic structures. → Convention. (2.1 Lyons).

ARCHAEOGRAPHY The study of ancient written documents. → palaeography, epigraphy. (7.2).

ARCHAISM A word or other linguistic item which is no longer used in speech or writing except to create a special effect or as a deliberate revival for practical purposes. Alternative terms: atavism, revival form.

ARCHEOGRAPHY The study of ancient written documents. → paleography, epigraphy. (7.2).

ARCHIPHONEME Term invented by N. Trubetzkoy (1890–

17

1939) for a unit of sound resulting from a neutralisation of certain features of → phonemes in a given environment, e.g. English distinguishes voiced and voiceless stops in most positions: *tip* ~ *dip*; *ketch* ~ *gets*; *pan* ~ *bann* but after [s] the feature of voice is irrelevant, e.g. *stop, sketch, span,* but not **sdop, *sgetch, *sban.* In this position in English the opposition voiced ~ voiceless is neutralized and in transcriptions the archiphoneme is sometimes written with a capital letter /P/, /T/, /K/. → neutralization.

AREA In → dialectology, a geographical region defined by similar typological features such as pronunciation, grammar or vocabulary. The FOCAL AREA is a region within a speech community from which certain features spread outwards to neighbouring regions, usually by imitation, and thus influence the linguistic habits of the majority of speakers. This may create a → standard language, e.g. the speech of London and Paris in the development of English and French. Certain features of the language at an earlier stage may be preserved in ISOLATED (or REMOTE or RELIC) AREAS and interchange with neighbouring speech communities through bilingualism may be strong in TRANSITION (or CONVERGENCE or GRADED) AREAS, where boundaries to adjacent dialect areas are not clear-cut. MARGINAL or LATERAL AREAS are those regions which are furthest removed from that where an innovation originates. (7.1, 8.1, 8.24).

AREA STUDIES The study of the geography, history and institutions of a particular geographical region in conjunction with the language of the speech community.

AREAL CLASSIFICATION → Geographical classification.

AREAL GROUP A number of languages with certain features in common as a result of geographical proximity rather than genealogical evolution. Alternative term: areal type. (6.2 Hoenigswald).

AREAL LINGUISTICS A branch of general linguistics studying the → classification of dialects and languages by relating the geographical location of a speech community to its historical development, and showing how typological similarities in pronunciation, grammar and vocabulary are related from one part of an area to another. (7.1 Kurath).

AREAL TYPE → Areal group.

ARGOT → Cant.

ARMENIAN ALPHABET → Table p. 265. (7.2).

ARRANGEMENT → Item-and-arrangement.

ARTICLE A word used as an adjunct to a noun to modify or limit its meaning. The English *the* or its equivalent in other languages is called the DEFINITE article, whereas *a* or *an* or their equivalents in other languages are called the NON-DEFINITE or INDEFINITE article. In some languages the article takes the form of a suffix to a noun, e.g. Danish *bordet* 'the table'; other languages have no articles at all, e.g. Latin and Russian. → determiner. (4.1, 4.2, 8.23).

ARTICULACY The active control of the spoken language, involving the linguistic skills of comprehension and speaking, as opposed to → literacy, the command of the written language. Alternative term: oracy. (9.11 Halliday *et al.*).

ARTICULATION The production of speech sounds by the movement of the → organs of speech. The movable speech organs are called active articulators (e.g. the tongue and lower lip) and the parts of the vocal tract which cannot move are called → points of articulation or passive articulators (e.g. upper teeth, alveolar ridge and palate). Consonants are described both in terms of articulator and point of articulation, e.g. as apico-alveolar, labio-dental, and according to their → manner of articulation, i.e. how the air stream is constricted or released, e.g. as stop, continuant or nasal. The neutral position of the speech organs at rest, which varies from one language to another, is called BASIS OF ARTICULATION. Two or more features of articulation occurring simultaneously or nearly simultaneously are referred to as CO-ARTICULATION, e.g. in the articulation of the initial sound of English *coal*, a voiceless dorso-velar stop with lip rounding, the most important factor is the contact between the dorsum region of the tongue and the velum (PRIMARY ARTICULATION). A second, in this instance less important, feature of the articulation of this sound is the lip rounding, occurring in anticipation of the rounded vowel which follows (SECONDARY ARTICULATION). → double articulation (*a*), speech production. (3.1, 8.22).

ARTICULATOR A part of the vocal tract involved in the production of speech sounds. A distinction is made between an ACTIVE ARTICULATOR or MOVABLE SPEECH ORGAN such as the tongue, lips, lower jaw, etc. which can be moved at will, and PASSIVE ARTICULATOR or IMMOVABLE SPEECH ORGAN such as upper teeth, palate, etc. which are not movable but with which other articulators may touch or approach. (3.1).

ARTICULATORY PARA-METER → Articulatory variable.

ARTICULATORY PHONETICS A branch of → phonetics concerned with the study of the function of the → organs of speech in the → articulation of speech sounds. Alternative terms: physiological phonetics, motor phonetics. (3.1, 3.3 Ecroyd *et al.*, 8.22).

ARTICULATORY SETTING Adjustments in the → vocal tract, adopting a posture of the articulatory organs which is maintained by a speaker throughout the whole time he is talking, but which is different from the relaxed position.

ARTICULATORY SYSTEM Term used to refer to the nose, the lips, the teeth, tongue, velum and other → articulators.

ARTICULATORY VARIABLE A feature of articulation which may be changed to produce a different distinct state of the speech organs, and hence a different speech sound. Voicing or lack of voicing, point of articulation, manner of articulation, for example, can all be varied to produce different speech sounds, e.g. [d] differs from [t] mainly in that the former is voiced and the latter voiceless and [b] differs from [d] mainly in that for the former the point of articulation is on the lips and for the latter on the alveolar ridge. Alternative term: articulatory parameter. (3.1).

ARTIFICIAL LANGUAGE
(*a*) A language invented with the specific aim of improving international communication. Artificial languages are usually composed of grammatical and lexical elements of groups of natural languages, e.g. Esperanto (created by L. Zamenhof in 1887), Volapük (J. M. Schleier, 1879), Interlingua (G. Peano, 1908 and later by the International Auxiliary Language Association), and Novial (O. Jespersen, 1928). None of these has had the impact the inventors hoped for. → standardisation. Alternative terms: auxiliary language, interlanguage, constructed language. (*b*) Code system of abstract symbols, signs and/or numbers such as are used in computer programming, e.g. ALGOL, COBOL, FORTRAN, ATLAS AUTOCODE. (9.4 Hays).

ARTIFICIAL SCRIPT A system of writing specifically designed for a particular purpose, e.g. shorthand, speedwriting, → Initial Teaching Alphabet, → analphabetic notation.

ARTIFICIAL SPEECH → Speech synthesis.

ASCENDING DIPHTHONG → Diphthong.

ASPECT A grammatical category of the verb marked by prefixes, suffixes or internal vowel changes, indicating not so much its location in time (→ tense) but the duration and type of action expressed. The term aspect (Russian вид) was first used to refer to the basic dichotomy perfective *vs.* imperfective in Russian

and other Slavonic languages. The IMPERFECTIVE or DURATIVE ASPECT describes an action which is regarded as having continuity or repetition in the past, present or future, e.g. the Russian verb *читать* 'to read' is imperfective and *я читал весь день* means 'I was reading all day, and *я буду читать весь день* means 'I shall read the whole day', thus emphasising the duration of the activity but not specifying that a particular book etc. was read to the end. The PERFECTIVE ASPECT on the other hand describes an action either completed in the past or to be completed in the future, e.g. the Russian verb *прочитать* is perfective and *я прочитал книгу* means 'I have (or had) read (and finished) the book', and *я прочитаю книгу* means 'I shall have read (and finished) the book' thus emphasising the completion of the action rather than its duration. Other languages beside Russian have aspectual systems which complement and overlap with the tense system; Ancient Greek, for example, had perfective, imperfective and → aorist. English has two aspects which combine with features of tense and mood: PERFECT ASPECT,

e.g. *I have read the newspaper*
I had read the newspaper
I will have read the newspaper etc.

and PROGRESSIVE or CONTINUOUS ASPECT:

e.g. *I am reading the newspaper*
I was reading the newspaper
I will be reading the newspaper etc.

In addition to the basic notions of imperfective and perfective aspect similar temporal distinctions are referred to in terms of aspects: INCHOATIVE or INCEPTIVE ASPECT expressing the beginning of an action; ITERATIVE or FREQUENTATIVE or HABITUAL ASPECT expressing repetition of an action; MOMENTARY or PUNCTUAL ASPECT expressing sudden interruption of the completion of an action; PERMANSIVE ASPECT expressing a permanent state as a result of a completed action etc. → tense, mood. (4.1, 4.2, 8.23).

ASPIRATE (*a*) A speech sound produced by cavity → friction, e.g. [h] as in *hand*. (*b*) → aspirated stop.

ASPIRATED STOP A → stop consonant released with a puff of breath. In most varieties of English, initial stop consonants are aspirated, e.g. [pʰ] as in *pin*, whereas they are not normally aspirated after [s], e.g. [p] as in *spin*. This difference does not constitute a → phonemic contrast in English.

ASPIRATION The articulation of a stop consonant with an audible puff of breath, e.g. [tʰ] in *too* or [pʰ] in *pin*. (3.1, 8.22).

ASSERTIVE → Exclamatory.

ASSIBILANT An → affricate articulated on the teeth, e.g. [t͡s] as in German [t͡suː] *zu* 'to'. Alternative term: assibilate.

ASSIBILATE → Assibilant.

ASSIBILATION The process by which a → stop consonant becomes a → sibilant consonant owing to → assimilation, e.g. Latin *vitium* > Italian *vezzo* 'habit'.

ASSIGN A linguistic symbol, the meaning of which is acquired not by direct → reference to a material object, but by association with other symbols, e.g. the word *zebra* by means of pictures and/or comparison with a 'horse'.

ASSIMILATION The process or result of two sounds becoming identical or similar, due to the influence of one upon the other. If the change affects adjacent sounds it is called CONTIGUOUS or JUXTA-POSITIONAL ASSIMILATION, e.g. [z] in *news* > [s] in *newspaper*. If the sounds involved are not adjacent it is called INCONTIGUOUS ASSIMILATION. (Alternative terms: DISTANT ASSIMILATION, DILATION, NON-CONTIGUOUS ASSIMILATION.) Umlaut or → vowel mutation is an example of incontiguous assimilation, e.g. Old English *fōt* has the plural of *fēt* (modern English feet) where the *ō* has changed to *ē* as a result of the influence of the *i* in the second syllable of an older form **fōti*. If a sound is changed under the influence of a following sound the term REGRESSIVE ASSIMILATION (alternative terms: RETROGRESSIVE ASSIMILATION, ANTICIPATORY ASSIMILATION) is used, e.g. the [v] in *five* > [f] in *fivepence*. If a sound influences a sound which follows, the term PROGRESSIVE ASSIMILATION (alternative term: LAG) is used, e.g. Latin *femina* > French *femme* 'woman', the *m* influencing and changing the *n* which follows. If two sounds influence each other mutually the term RECIPROCAL ASSIMILATION (alternative term: COALESCENT ASSIMILATION) is used, e.g. English *seven* pronounced as [se͡bm] where the labiodental [v] has become bilabial [b] which in turn influences the alveolar nasal [n] changing it to the bilabial nasal [m]. TOTAL ASSIMILATION occurs when the sounds involved become identical as in the case of *femina* > *femme* above. PARTIAL ASSIMILATION

21

occurs when the sounds involved become similar, not identical, e.g. in the case of [v] > [f] in *fivepence* above. The [v] adopts the voiceless character of the [p] but not its bilabial character. → dissimilation, absorption, accommodation. Alternative term: adaptation. (3.1, 6.1).

ASSOCIATION GROUP A group of words associated by meaning, e.g. *chair, table, couch, stool,* or by form, e.g. *walking, cleaning, sitting, reading.* → semantics. Alternative term: associative field. (5.2 Ullmann).

ASSOCIATIVE ETYMOLOGY → Folk etymology.

ASSOCIATIVE FIELD → Association group.

ASSOCIATIVE RELATIONS F. de Saussure's term for → paradigmatic relations along the axis of choice rather than that of chain (→ syntagmatic).

ASSONANCE The repetition of the same vowel sound, e.g. *"The rain in Spain stays mainly in the plain"*.

ASTERISK FORM (*a*) A word or sentence is marked with an asterisk to show that it is ungrammatically constructed or that it is a nonsense form, e.g. **the cat sats on the mat* or **colourless green ideas sleep furiously.* (4.1). (*b*) An item is marked with an asterisk to show that there is no written evidence of its existence and that its form has been theoretically reconstructed, e.g. */kmto/, the Indo-European reconstruction meaning 'hundred'. Alternative term: starred form. (6.1).

ASYLLABIC A sound which cannot form a → syllable nor be the nucleus of a syllable, e.g. a → stop consonant in English.

ASYMMETRIC CONSONANT → Lateral.

ASYNDETIC CONSTRUCTION → Asyndeton.

ASYNDETISM → Asyndeton.

ASYNDETON A construction in which clauses or sentences are joined without the use of conjunctions, e.g. *He came through the door: my long wait was over.* → syndeton, polysyndeton. Alternative terms: asyndetism, asyndetic construction.

ASYNTACTIC COMPOUND A compound word the parts of which would have a different relationship to each other if used as independent words, e.g. *worm-eaten,* the syntactic structure of which is different from *eaten by worms.*

ATAVISM → Archaism.

ATHEMATIC A kind of inflexion which consists of the root plus an affix without a stem morpheme, e.g. the Latin verb *rego* 'I rule' consisting of the root *reg-* plus the affix *-o* indicating first person singular present tense. → thematic inflexion.

ATLANTIC LINGUISTICS Term proposed by J. R. Firth (1890-1960) for what is common to (*a*) linguistic studies in America and Western Europe, (*b*) the study of the English language as spoken on either side of the Atlantic Ocean. → American linguistics, British linguistics.

ATLAS → Linguistic atlas.

ATONIC A sound or syllable pronounced with weak → stress. Alternative term: light.

ATTESTED FORM A word or phrase for which there is written historical evidence, as opposed to an → asterisk form which is hypothetical or ungrammatical.

ATTRACTION The influence of linguistic elements upon one another, e.g. phonetic → assimilation and dissimilation, grammatical → analogy. Thus in *Neither of these people were present*, *were* is plural because of the adjacent *people*, although *neither* is a singular concept.

ATTRIBUTE An → adjective modifying a noun within a noun phrase, e.g. *I like her new hat* as opposed to → predicative adjective, *Her hat is nice*. In English, adjectives usually precede the noun which they modify, in some languages they may follow, e.g. French *la phonétique*

acoustique 'acoustic phonetics'. Alternative terms: attributive adjective, adherent adjective.

ATTRIBUTIVE ADJECTIVE → Attribute.

ATTRIBUTIVE ENDOCENTRIC CONSTRUCTION → Endocentric construction.

AUDIBLE AREA The area on a graph of frequency plotted against amplitude within which fall those sounds which human beings are capable of hearing (Fig. 1). (3.3 Mol).

AUDIOGRAM A graph produced by an → audiometer showing hearing loss in decibels.

AUDIOLOGY The systematic study of the functions and disturbances of → hearing and the treatment of the patient. (9.5).

AUDIOMETER A device for testing → hearing and for measuring hearing loss.

AUDIBLE AREA

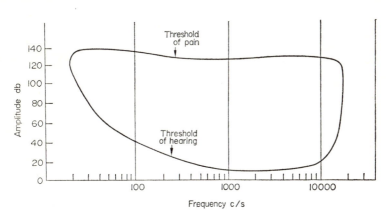

(Fig. 1)

23

AUDIOMETRY The measurement of → hearing.

AUDITORY AREA The region in the brain which controls hearing. Alternative term: auditory centre.

AUDITORY CENTRE → Auditory area.

AUDITORY DISCRIMINATION The ability to perceive and distinguish different speech sounds. Alternative term: aural discrimination.

AUDITORY FEEDBACK → Feedback (*a*).

AUDITORY LANGUAGE Human communication involving the organs of → hearing in the perception of speech sounds, as opposed to written, sign or gesture language. (3.1).

AUDITORY MASKING The situation which arises when the perception of one sound is impaired by the presence of other sounds.

AUDITORY PHONETICS A branch of → phonetics concerned with the study of → hearing and the → perception of speech. Alternative term: psychological phonetics. (3.3 Mol).

AUGMENTATIVE A form of a word made by the addition of a → suffix with the meaning 'great' or 'large', e.g. Italian *casone* 'big house' from *casa*. → diminutive. Alternative term: amplificative.

AURAL DISCRIMINATION → Auditory discrimination.

AUSTRONESIAN LINGUISTICS → Malayo-Polynesian linguistics.

AUTO-INSTRUCTION → Programmed instruction.

AUTOMATIC TRANSLATION → Machine translation.

AUTOMATIC VARIANT → Conditioned variant.

AUTONOMOUS SOUND CHANGE → Sound change.

AUTONOMOUS WORD → Content word.

AUXILIARY A word which has no independent function or meaning on its own but which can only be used in combination with other words, e.g. preposition, conjunction, → auxiliary verb, etc.

AUXILIARY LANGUAGE (*a*) → artificial language. (*b*) A language or dialect used as a means of communication between members of different speech communities and which is not the native language of its speakers, e.g. Swahili as spoken by non-Bantu people in East Africa, or Standard English as spoken by speakers of different regional or social dialects in Britain. (7.1).

AUXILIARY MARK → Diacritic mark.

AUXILIARY SIGN → Diacritic mark.

AUXILIARY VERB A word used in a verb phrase as an adjunct to another verb. It often serves in English to form → moods, tenses or → aspects of a full verb, e.g. *have* in *I have seen that film* or *am* in *I am reading this book*. Auxiliary verbs in English can be recognised by the

following features: they have a
special negative form, e.g. *haven't,
aren't, doesn't*; they can be used
with inversion after words like
seldom and *hardly*, e.g. *Seldom have
I seen such a sight*, or to form
questions, e.g. *Do you smoke?*; they
can be used to take the place of and
to refer back to a full verb, e.g. *am*
in *Are you going? I am*; they can be
stressed for special emphasis, e.g. *But
I do!*; or they often occur with a
weak stress and have special weak
forms, e.g. *'s* in *he's gone.* Apart from
the auxiliaries *be, have, do,* English
has a series of → modal auxiliaries
such as *can, shall, will.* Alternative
terms: helper verb, accessory verb.
(4.1, 4.2, 8.23).

AVAILABILITY The relative
ease of recall or frequent occurrence
of words in a particular context.
Thus, the words *table* or *chair* will
spring to mind immediately when
talking of 'furniture', and some
linguists suggest it is these lexical
items which should be emphasised
in practical language teaching rather
than isolated and unusual words.
(9.11 Halliday *et al.*).

AXIS The object of a preposition
in a prepositional phrase, e.g. *the
road* in *He is walking along the road.*
→ exocentric construction.

B

BABBLING → Language
acquisition.

BABY-TALK (*a*) A number of
basic items, usually 'conventionalised' words but differing from language to language, which are used for
communicating with small children
between the stages of babbling and
full language. Alternative term:
nursery language. (9.6). (*b*) A speech
defect characterised by the use of
speech sounds similar to those of a
child in the early stages of speech
development. Alternative term: infantile speech. (9.5).

BACK-FORMATION A type of
word formation by → derivation, e.g.
to sculpt is formed from the existing
word *sculptor* by analogy with an
established pattern, e.g. *act/actor.* In
this way the new word *sculpt* is considered to be the original word and
sculptor the derived word, whereas in
fact the opposite is true. Alternative
term: inverse derivation. (4.2, 8.23).

BACK-REFERENCE Reference
to an → antecedent by repetition or
grammatical substitution, e.g. *You
can't come, can you?* or *You can't
have this book, take that one!*
Alternative terms: anaphora, cross-
reference.

BACK VOWEL A → vowel
sound produced with the tongue
retracted towards the back of the
oral cavity, e.g. [ɑː] as in English
calm or [uː] as in English *soon.* →
front vowel. Alternative terms: dark
vowel, deep vowel, broad vowel.

BALANCE Symmetry in the phonemic, grammatical or semantic system of a language. The English phonemic system shows symmetry in the patterns of voiced stop consonants, as opposed to both voiceless stops and nasal continuants at three points of articulation:

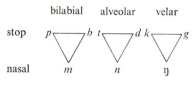

(2.1 Martinet).

BARBARISM A deviation in pronunciation, grammar or vocabulary from a recognised standard of → usage.

BASE (*a*) That part of a word which is left after all inflexional and derivational affixes have been removed. Thus *unluckiest* consists of the base *luck* plus the two derivational elements *un-* and *-i-* and the inflexion *-est*. → stem. Alternative terms: root, kernel. (4.2). (*b*) In historical and comparative linguistics, a reconstructed form from which words in cognate languages are said to have developed. → etymon. Alternative term: root. (6.1).

BASE COMPONENT A term used by some linguists to refer to the → phrase structure component of a transformational-generative grammar.

BASE COMPOUND → Primary compound.

BASE FORM That → variant of a → morpheme which is the most common and the least restricted and

is considered to be the most typical. Thus the past tense morpheme in English can be said to have the base form /-d/ which alternates with /-t/ as in *walked* /wɔːkt/, /ɪd/ as in *planted* /plɑːntɪd/, /ø/ (zero) as in *put* /pʊt/, etc. Alternative terms: canonic form, basic alternant.

BASIC ALTERNANT → Base form.

BASIC SENTENCE In language teaching, a syntactic structure such as the simple declarative sentence type *The dog bites the man*, which serves as the model for drilling similar and more complicated patterns, e.g. *After biting the man, the dog ran away.* → clause pattern. (4.1, 8.23, 9.11).

BASIC VOCABULARY → Vocabulary.

BASIS OF ARTICULATION The neutral position of the → organs of speech at rest, which varies from one language to another. → articulation.

BEHAVIOURISM The study of human behaviour in observable stimulus–response situations. Behaviourist studies have influenced the work of several linguists, particularly the Bloomfieldians (→ American linguistics), and contributed to the understanding of verbal skills and learning processes and to the development of → programmed instruction, but under the incisive criticism of N. Chomsky and his followers (→ transformational-generative grammar) has undergone considerable modification. → psycholinguistics. (10.2).

BIAS WORDS Expressions which deviate in meaning from a neutral term to imply a subjective evaluation or prejudice. The slant may be in a favourable or unfavourable direction, e.g. *established* as opposed to *old-fashioned* for 'traditional' and *progressive* as opposed to *new-fangled* for 'modern'. (5.1).

BILABIAL A speech sound in the articulation of which both lips are used to stop or modify the → air stream, e.g. [b] as in *bin*, [p] as in *pin*, [m] as in *man* or [w] as in *win*. Alternative terms: labio-labial, labial. (3.1, 8.22).

BILABIODENTAL A speech sound articulated by means of the upper lip and upper teeth touching the lower lip, e.g. the final consonant cluster in German *fünf* [fymf̑] 'five'.

BILATERAL CONSONANT → Lateral.

BILATERAL OPPOSITION Two phonemes are said to be in bilateral opposition when only one feature causes the contrast between them. If this feature is neutralised the phonemes will share the same → archiphoneme. Thus the English phonemes /p/ and /b/ are said to be in bilateral opposition, the feature distinguishing them is the voicing of the /b/.

BILINGUAL Involving two languages. This term may refer to individuals or communities speaking two languages, or to manuscripts, books, inscriptions and dictionaries using elements of two languages. → ambilingual.

BILINGUALISM The use of two languages by a speaker or speech community. There are many types of bilingualism, e.g. someone with parents of different native languages living in either speech community, or a person having learned to master a foreign language through intensive formal instruction. Bilingual speakers are not necessarily born translators and interpreters, as the skill of → switching between two languages must be acquired separately, and persons who are equally conversant in both languages and in all situations (→ ambilingual) are very rare. In areas of intensive language contact, e.g. in Switzerland, Holland or Wales, bilingualism is an important factor of linguistic → change. (9.2).

BINARISM The use of the concept of 'dichotomy' between pairs, introduced into liguistic analysis by R. Jakobson (b. 1896) and members of the → Prague School. In phonology, the basic unit → phoneme may be defined in terms of the presence or absence of certain → distinctive features. In grammar and semantics, an element may be 'marked' or 'unmarked' for a particular feature, e.g. *cats* (vs. *cat*) for 'plural', or *bitch* (vs. *dog*) for 'female sex'. A similar notion of binary distinctions is used in → information theory. Alternative term: binarity. (2.2 Garvin).

BINARITY The principle of a choice between two possibilities, e.g. singular/plural, voiced/voiceless, present/past, etc. → binarism.

BIO-LINGUISTICS The use of special research techniques from the fields of biology and linguistics to the study of language in relation to the growth and structure of living

27

organisms, particularly of man. There had been some early attempts to link up Darwinian evolutionary principles to 19th century historical-comparative studies (→ Indo-European linguistics), as well as several non-linguistic studies which related the statistical frequency of words and other linguistic units to underlying factors of human behaviour (→ Zipf's law), but not until very recently has there been interdisciplinary research by both linguists and biologists into such questions as whether language capacity in man is transmitted genetically and is independent of intelligence or brain weight. Further contributions from psychology, pathology and the study of speech defects (→ clinical linguistics) are likely to increase our knowledge of these processes. → zoo-semiotics. (10.2 Lenneberg).

BISEMY Double meaning of a word, e.g. Latin *sacer* 'sacred' or 'accursed'. → polysemy, synonymy.

BIUNIQUENESS In → phonology the principle of one-to-one correspondence between phonemic and phonetic representations: each sequence of phones being represented by a unique sequence of phonemes and each sequence of phonemes representing a unique sequence of phones. This principle is contested in → generative phonology. (2.3 Householder).

BLADE That part of the tongue which lies immediately behind the apex or tip. → diagram p. 159. (3.1, 8.22).

BLEND A type of → word formation in which two or more free morphemes are combined to form a new word which incorporates all the meanings of its constituents, e.g. *chuckle* and *snort* > *chortle*, *breakfast* and *lunch* > *brunch*, *smoke* and *fog* > *smog*. Alternative terms: telescoped word, portmanteau word, amalgam.

BLENDING The intimate fusion of words (→ blends like *brunch* from *breakfast* and *lunch*) or phrases (→ contamination as in *equally as good* from *equally good* and *as good*).

BLOCKED SYLLABLE A → syllable ending in a consonant. Alternative terms; closed syllable, checked syllable.

BLOCKED VOWEL A vowel in a → blocked syllable.

BLOOMFIELDIANISM → American linguistics.

BLUEBEARD COMPOUND → Compound noun.

BODY LANGUAGE → Kinesics.

BODY SEMANTICS → Kinesics.

BONE CONDUCTION → Feedback (*a*).

BOOK WORD → Learned word.

BORDER MARK → Boundary signal.

BORROWED ELEMENTS Sounds, grammatical forms or lexical items taken over from another language, e.g. English word *blitz* taken from German, or [ɛ] in the name *Chopin* when used in English [ʃopɛ̃].

28

BORROWING The introduction into a language or dialect of elements from another language or dialect by contact and/or imitation. The most common type of borrowing is that of vocabulary items, e.g. English LOAN WORDS *poet* from French, *blitz* from German, *sputnik* from Russian. Sometimes loan words such as the above mirror exactly the phonemes of the original language, but sometimes such words are adapted to fit the phonemic and morphemic patterns of the host language, e.g. *garage* from French when pronounced ['gærɪdʒ] on the pattern of *marriage*, or the French *redingote* 'riding coat' borrowed from English where the spelling is changed too. Another common type of borrowing is LOAN TRANSLATION, LOAN SHIFT or CALQUE where morphemes are translated in the host language. German has many examples of this type of borrowing, e.g. *Sauerstoff* (literally 'acid material') is a translation from the Greek word which we take into English without translation: 'oxygen'; the Russian word *sputnik* (literally 'fellow traveller') mentioned above is a loan translation from the Greek word which we take without translation: 'satellite'. Alternative term: loan. (5.1, 6.1, 9.2).

BOUND ACCENT → Stress.

BOUND FORM → Bound morpheme.

BOUND MORPHEME A → morpheme which cannot be used alone as a word with a distinct meaning, but only as an affix in conjunction with another morpheme, e.g. *-ly* in *quickly*, *-s* in *boys* or *-th* in *width*. Alternative term: bound form. (4.1, 4.2, 8.23).

BOUND SENTENCE A syntactic structure which cannot occur on its own without further specification, e.g. *Did you really?* → free sentence.

BOUNDARY MARKER In → transformational-generative grammar a symbol used in a string to indicate boundaries between the elements of the string, e.g. + in the string Det + Nom + V + Det + Nom.

BOUNDARY SIGNAL A feature such as fixed → stress, → intonation or → transition which may act as a device to separate linguistic units within longer stretches of speech. Thus in speech the different allophones [l] and [ɫ] may be used to help to distinguish *they lend it* from *they'll end it* by marking or 'signalling' the WORD BOUNDARY either before *lend* or after *they'll*. Alternative term: border mark. (3.4 Trubetzkoy).

BOUSTROPHEDON A method of → writing in which the lines run alternately in opposite directions.

BOW-WOW THEORY → Origin of speech.

BRACHYLOGY A shortened or condensed and grammatically incomplete expression, used in colloquial speech or specialised jargons to reduce time and effort, e.g. the greeting *Morning!* or the traffic sign *Road Up*.

BRACKETING One of several ways of indicating the hierarchical structure of a sentence. The relationship between the words in the sentence *The boy ate the apple* may be illustrated by brackets as follows:

((the boy) (ate (the apple))). → tree diagram.

BRANCH In the family tree model of genetically related languages, one language or group of languages which developed from a common ancestor is called a branch, e.g. Italic and Germanic are branches of Indo-European. → family of languages. (6.1).

BRANCHING The representation of elements of syntactic structure by means of tree diagrams, e.g. the sentence *The boy kicks the ball* could be diagrammed as follows:

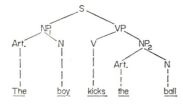

BRANCHING PROGRAMME A course of → programmed instruction which provides alternative routes along which the student can continue according to his achievements at each stage in the course, as opposed to a linear programme where there is a single sequence through the course.

BREATH GROUP A sequence of speech sounds produced between two intakes of air.

BREATH STATE → Glottis.

BREATH STREAM → Air stream.

BREATHED SEGMENT A stretch of sound produced with the → glottis open.

BREATHING An accent mark indicating → aspiration in Greek. → diacritic mark.

BREATHY PHONATION → Register (*a*).

BREATHY VOICE → Register (*a*).

BREVE A → diacritic mark used to indicate that a vowel is to be pronounced short or with weak stress, e.g. [ă].

BRIGHT VOWEL → Front vowel.

BRITISH LINGUISTICS Collective term for certain traditions and tendencies which have characterised linguistic studies in Britain. One such feature is the development of phonetics within the scope of 'the linguistic sciences' from H. Sweet (1845–1912) to D. Jones (1881–1967) and J. R. Firth (1890–1960). The latter also developed → prosodic phonology and a 'contextual' theory of meaning (FIRTHIAN LINGUISTICS) which owed much to the → ethnolinguistics of B. Malinowski (1887–1942). Out of this LONDON SCHOOL M. A. K. Halliday developed → systemic grammar. (1.1 Meetham; 2.2 Bazell, Minnis; 2.5 Langendoen; 9.11 Halliday *et al*.).

BROAD TRANSCRIPTION A type of → phonetic transcription using a restricted number of symbols to produce a readable transcript, based on a → phonemic analysis of the language being transcribed. → narrow transcription.

BROAD VOWEL → Back vowel.

BROCA'S AREA Area of the cerebral cortex in the brain which controls the function of speech production, as opposed to → Wernicke's area which controls comprehension of speech. Alternative term: centre of Broca.

BUCCAL A non-nasal sound produced in the oral cavity.

BUCCAL CAVITY → Cavity.

C

CACOGRAPHY (*a*) Handwriting which is difficult to read. → calligraphy. (*b*) Spelling which deviates from the accepted norm, e.g. *repetative* for *repetitive*. → orthography. (7.2).

CACOLOGY Speech which deviates from an accepted norm in pronunciation or grammar.

CACOPHONY A combination of sounds considered to be unpleasant. → euphony.

CACUMINAL → Retroflex.

CADENCE The rise and fall in pitch, volume or stress in speech, used particularly with reference to an → intonation pattern at the end of a sentence or before a pause.

CALLIGRAPHY The aesthetic qualities of → writing, particularly highly developed in Chinese, Arabic, and Indian languages. (7.2).

CALQUE → Loan translation.

CANONIC FORM (*a*) In phonology: the most usual and widespread → syllable structure in a given language, e.g. the structure consonant–vowel–consonant of English, or the avoidance of consonant clusters in Malay. → phonotactics. (*b*) In morphology: the form chosen to represent the basic form of a → morpheme, e.g. the past tense morpheme of English verbs has the canonic form [-d]. Alternants include [-t] after voiceless consonants, [-ɩd] after [-t] or [-d], or a change in the stem vowel in the case of strong verbs.

CANT A → jargon peculiar to a local, social or occupational group, particularly of the lower social strata. Alternative terms: argot, lingo.

CARDINAL NUMBER A simple numeral which answers the question *how many?* e.g. *one, two, three*, as opposed to → ordinal number.

CARDINAL VOWEL One of a series of → vowel sounds with defined features of articulation, invented by D. Jones and used by British phoneticians. In the diagram below the numbers 1–8 denote the PRIMARY cardinal vowels in relation to the position of the tongue in the mouth.

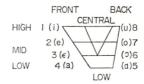

31

This system of cardinal vowels does not belong to any language, but is useful as a basis for comparison of vowel sounds within a language and between different languages. (3.1).

CARET A diacritic mark indicating insertion or → silent stress, e.g. *"To be or not to be ∧ that is the question"*.

CARTESIAN LINGUISTICS The view based on R. Descartes (1596–1650) and several rationalist French grammarians of the PORT ROYAL school that human language rests on a thought structure common to all mankind. The philosophical and linguistic works in this tradition are indebted to both Latin prescriptive grammar and the mathematical ideology of the Age of Enlightenment. Linguists interested in the problem of language → universals have recently re-examined some of these Cartesian premises. (2.5 Chomsky).

CASE A grammatical category of a → noun, or similarly inflected word such as a pronoun or adjective, indicating its relationship to other words in a sentence. In inflected languages, cases are usually distinguished by declensional endings (or lack of ending), e.g. in the German sentence *Der Hund beißt den Mann* 'The dog bites the man', *der Hund* is nominative and *den Mann* is accusative, or in Latin *Agricola colit agros* 'The farmer cultivates the fields', *agricola* is nominative and *agros* is accusative. The relationship between words in the above examples is independent of word order, and changing the order of words makes no difference to the meaning of the sentence, apart from emphasis. The

number of cases and the number of case inflexions in different classes of words varies from one language to another, e.g. German has four, Russian six, Finnish sixteen cases. In non-inflected languages such syntactical relationships are often indicated by means of → word order or → prepositions, e.g. in the English sentence *The dog bites the man* the meaning depends entirely on the word order, and if the word order is changed, the meaning is changed or destroyed. The term 'case' is often used to refer to such syntactic relationships in English, although in modern English only one case is inflexionally marked in nouns, the possessive, e.g. *men's*. Pronouns have more forms which could be described as subjective, objective, and two possessive forms, e.g. *I, me, my, mine; they, them, their, theirs,* etc. → ablative, accusative, common, dative, genitive, instrumental, locative, nominative, objective, oblique, possessive, prepositional, subjective, vocative. (4.1, 4.2 Anderson).

CASUAL SPEECH A → manner of discourse intermediate between politely informal and intimate.

CATACHRESIS The inappropriate use of a word or phrase for a meaning which is similar, but not the same, e.g. *luxuriant* 'profuse' for *luxurious* 'elegant'. → malapropism.

CATCH → Glottal stop.

CATEGORIAL COMPONENT In transformational-generative grammar a set of branching → rewrite rules which show explicitly the grammatical relations in the → deep structure of a sentence.

CATEGORIAL GRAMMAR
An approach to linguistic analysis
proposed by Y. Bar-Hillel and other
logicians which recognises only two
basic categories in grammar, the →
sentence and the → noun from which
all other items and relationships are
derived within a semi-algebraic
framework. (10.3 Bar-Hillel).

CATEGORISATION The
process and result of grouping
linguistic symbols and the sections of
human experience they represent
into classes. This process is very
complex and consists basically of
the abstraction of individual experi-
ences into general concepts. The
symbol *house*, for example, has
different denotative and connotative → meanings when used by a
housewife than when used by an
architect. Different languages have
different ways of classifying the
world around them into linguistic
categories. Alternative term: classification. (2.1 Hayakawa).

CATEGORY → Grammatical
categories.

CATEGORY SYMBOL A
symbol used to represent a whole
class of elements, e.g. in transformational-generative grammar the symbol NP is usually used to refer to
noun phrase.

CATENATION The linking
together of speech sounds, syllables,
and words by such devices as →
assimilation, → juncture and →
elision.

CATENATIVE VERB →
Copula.

CAUSAL CLAUSE An → adverbial clause which states the cause,
reason or purpose of what is mentioned elsewhere in the sentence,
usually introduced by a conjunction
such as *because* or *therefore*, e.g.
*The match was cancelled because it
rained.*

CAUSAL CONJUNCTION A
conjunction such as *in order that* or
therefore introducing a clause expressing a reason, purpose or effect,
e.g. *He said it, therefore it is true.*

CAUSATIVE FORM →
Causative verb.

CAUSATIVE VERB A verb
form which indicates that the →
subject caused an action to be
carried out, thus *to fell* is the causative form of *to fall*. Alternative
term: causative form.

CAVITY The vocal tract can be
divided into five cavities or AIR
CHAMBERS, the PULMONIC CAVITY
including the lungs and trachea; the
PHARYNGEAL CAVITY, the space between the root of the tongue and the
back wall of the throat; the NASAL
CAVITY including the nose and the
nasal pharynx; the ORAL or BUCCAL
CAVITY, the mouth; the (O)ESOPHA-
GEAL CAVITY including the stomach
and eosophagus, which although not
used in normal production of speech
sounds may be used by patients who
have undergone an operation for the
surgical removal of the larynx. The
pharyngeal, oral and nasal cavities
all being above the glottis are often
referred to as the SUPRA-GLOTTAL
CAVITIES. In the production of speech
sounds a distinction is made between
an ACTIVE CAVITY, directly involved
in some way with the production of a
particular sound, and a PASSIVE
CAVITY, not directly involved; e.g.

in the production of oral sounds the nasal cavity is passive, or in the case of a sound produced with a velaric → air-stream mechanism, all cavities except the oral cavity are passive. → diagram p. 159. (3.1 Pike).

CAVITY FEATURES → Distinctive feature.

CAVITY FRICTION → Friction.

CEDILLA A diacritic mark, usually placed under a letter to indicate a special feature of pronunciation, such as 'soft' *c* as in *garçon* or *façade*.

CELTIC LINGUISTICS Traditionally studied in → Indo-European comparative philology, the Celtic languages (Irish and Scottish Gaelic, Welsh, Breton, etc.) have recently experienced a revival both in their use as spoken and written languages and in their linguistic description. → Appendix 1, p. 269. (6.1 Lockwood).

CENEMATICS The system and study of → cenemes, the linguistic units of the sound system of a particular language.

CENEME Term used in → glossematics to describe the smallest unit of phonology. Since these primary units have no content, i.e. no semantic meaning in their own right, they are also called 'empty units'. → expression (*a*). (2.5 Hjelmslev).

CENETICS The system and study of the units of phonetics and phonology.

CENTRALISATION The process whereby a vowel tends to become a → neutral vowel, e.g. when *and* [ænd] > unstressed [ənd]. Alternative term: centring.

CENTRAL VOWEL → Neutral vowel.

CENTRE (*a*) The → head word in a phrase. → endocentric construction. (*b*) → Syllable nucleus. (*c*) The top region of the tongue.

CENTRE OF BROCA → Broca's area.

CENTRE OF WERNICKE → Wernicke's area.

CENTRING → Centralisation.

CENTRING DIPHTHONG → Diphthong.

CENTUM LANGUAGE One of the Indo-European languages in which the Proto-Indo-European velar stop *[k] was retained, e.g. in the initial sound of the Latin word *centum* 'hundred'. Centum languages include the sub-families Hellenic, Italic, Celtic, Germanic and the less documented Hittite and Tokharian. → satem languages. (6.1).

CEREBRAL → Retroflex.

CHAIN and CHOICE Two concepts borrowed from mathematics and information theory to denote the two axes along which linguistic units may be arranged: chain refers to the 'horizontal' or linear sequence of elements (→ syntagmatic), e.g. the successive words in a sentence, choice refers to the 'vertical' range of structural alternatives from which a selection can be made (→ paradigmatic), e.g. various synonymous expressions that may be used in a particular utterance. (10.4 Herdan).

CHANGE The modification and/ or replacement of features of a language from one stage in its historical development to the next. Such changes may affect the sound system or parts of it, the grammatical system, or the vocabulary. Changes may be caused by external influences on the language such as → borrowing, or by internal processes such as → analogy or pronunciation fashions. (6.1).

CHANNEL A medium through which information (electric impulses, sound waves, etc.) is carried from a sender (or source) to a receiver (or addressee). → communication.

CHARACTER A graphic sign used in logographic → writing systems such as Chinese to represent words or morphemes. The characters may be direct pictorial images of ideas, e.g. the character for 'tree' was stylised from a picture of a tree, but in the main they are combinations of two elements, the radical component indicating the meaning of the word and the phonetic component suggesting its pronunciation. → table p. 264. (7.2).

CHARACTERISTIC FEATURE → Acoustic features.

CHARACTEROLOGY OF SPEECH The particular characteristics or stylistics of the speech of an individual, including pronunciation, diction, choice of words, etc.

CHECKED SYLLABLE A → syllable ending in a consonant,

e.g. *hit, hat, hate.* Alternative terms: blocked syllable, closed syllable.

CHECKED versus UNCHECKED One of the basic oppositions in → distinctive feature phonology based on the analysis of a → spectrogram. 'Checked' indicates rapid discharge of energy within a short time, 'unchecked' a slower discharge of energy over a longer time. In articulatory terms checked indicates rapid stoppage of a pulmonic → air stream. Checked phonemes are of three types: → ejective consonants, implosive → stops or → clicks.

CHECKED VOWEL A vowel sound in a → checked syllable, e.g. in *hit, hat, hate.* Alternative terms: closed vowel, blocked vowel.

CHEST PULSE A muscular contraction involving the intercostal muscles and the diaphragm, which helps to expel air from the lungs. Several chest pulses make up one exhalation of air. In speech a chest pulse may be considered equivalent to a → syllable, but some phoneticians refute this. A chest pulse which occurs with an extra burst of energy is called a reinforced chest pulse or STRESSED PULSE. A stressed pulse produces a stressed syllable. (3.3 Ecroyd *et al.*).

CHILD LANGUAGE → Language acquisition.

CHINESE SCRIPT → Table p. 264. (7.2).

CHOICE → Chain and choice.

CHROMATIC ACCENT → Pitch accent.

CHRONE A unit of duration of speech sounds. → allochrone, chroneme.

CHRONEME A distinctive feature of length in a speech sound, usually a vowel. Languages which use vowel length as a → distinctive feature rarely have more than two chronemes: long and short; e.g. German *Rum* [ʀum] 'rum' *vs. Ruhm* [Ru:m] 'fame'. Some languages like Russian and Spanish do not use vowel length in this way. → allochrone. (3.1).

CIRCUMFLEX An accent mark indicating a degree of stress, pitch, length, vowel quality or similar feature of speech which is represented in the writing system of a particular language. → diacritic mark.

CITATION A quotation of an utterance in its traditional graphic form, e.g. in a dictionary.

CITATION SLIP In → lexicography, a verbatim quotation of a spoken or written utterance which is used for the arrangement and definition of individual entries in a dictionary.

CLASS CLEAVAGE The assigning of a word to different → word classes. Depending on the context in which it occurs, *home* is a noun in *A house is not a home*, but an adverb in *I am going home*. Alternative term: overlapping distribution.

CLASS DIALECT A social → dialect.

CLASS NOUN → Unit noun.

CLASSICAL LANGUAGE (*a*) The stage in the historical development of a language which is considered to be the peak of its cultural importance. (*b*) A term often used to describe Latin and ancient Greek and other ancient languages with an important literature. → modern language.

CLASSIFICATION (*a*) The process by which languages are grouped into different types according to their historical development or the relationships and correspondences between them. Two basic methods of classification may be distinguished: → GENEALOGICAL CLASSIFICATION attempts to find genetic relationships between different languages; → TYPOLOGICAL CLASSIFICATION uses strictly formal criteria, such as morphological indices, to differentiate types of languages. From the genealogical point of view, English is affiliated with other Indo-European languages such as Greek and Latin, and more closely to Germanic languages such as German and Dutch; from the typological point of view, however, certain aspects of its structure may be more easily compared with agglutinative and analytic languages such as Turkish and Chinese. → index (*b*). (6.1, 6.2). (*b*) The way in which words, morphemes and other grammatical units are assigned to different classes. → categorisation.

CLASSIFICATORY LANGUAGE A type of language, such as Swahili and other Bantu languages, which indicates grammatical categories and semantic classes by affixing → particles on to a → root. → agglutinative language. (6.1, 8.1).

CLASSIFIER (*a*) A word or form which indicates the class or category of an adjacent word or form, e.g. *-mente* signifies adverbs in Spanish and Italian. (*b*) An auxiliary sign used in some writing systems to indicate the semantic or morphological class of words, e.g. 'human beings', 'animals', 'gods', 'plural', etc. Alternative terms: determinative, determinant.

CLAUSE In traditional grammar a clause is a group of words containing a subject and a verb, as opposed to a → phrase which contains no finite verb. Under this definition clauses may be MAIN CLAUSES, i.e. able to stand alone and constitute a full sentence, or SUBORDINATE CLAUSES, linked to a main clause by a → subordinating conjunction. A simple sentence such as *The trees are green* is said to consist of one main clause; a complex sentence such as *It is cold although the sun is shining* is said to consist of a main clause (*it is cold*) and a subordinate clause (*although the sun is shining*); two main clauses can be joined by a → co-ordinating conjunction to form a compound sentence such as *He came in but he did not speak*. In this sentence the clauses *he came in* and *he did not speak* are said to be CO-ORDINATE CLAUSES. According to their function in the sentence subordinate clauses may be divided into categories such as ADVERBIAL CLAUSE, ADJECTIVAL CLAUSE, etc. In → systemic grammar a clause is one of the five grammatical units of English, second in rank to the sentence and consisting of one or more groups. (4.1, 4.2, 8.23).

CLAUSE EQUIVALENT A word or phrase which functions as a → clause, but which does not possess all the constituents of a clause, e.g. *now* in *When are you leaving? Now.* Alternative terms: sentence word, isolate.

CLAUSE MARKER A word or phrase or syntactic feature which indicates the function of a → clause, e.g. *Who* in *Who is that?* or inversion in *Is he going?*

CLAUSE PATTERN The basic 'blueprint' for a simple clause. Several types can be distinguished according to the number and types of constituent elements, e.g. subject, predicate, object(s), adverb(s), complement(s). (4.1, 4.2, 8.23).

CLAUSE TERMINAL → Juncture.

CLEAR 'L' The alveolar [l] used by most speakers of English before vowels, e.g. in *lamp*, as opposed to the → 'dark' or velarised [ɫ], used by most speakers of English before consonants and at the end of words, e.g. in *table*.

CLICHÉ A stereotyped word or phrase which has become almost meaningless through excessive use, particularly in such fields as political propaganda, e.g. *democracy*, advertising, e.g. *value for money*, and in certain jargons such as journalese, e.g. *inside information*.

CLICK A → stop produced by double contact of the tongue simultaneously released, creating suction of air by means of an ingressive velaric → air-stream mechanism. Certain African languages such as Bushman use clicks. One type of click can be similar to the sound often represented in English ortho-graphy by *tut-tut*. (3.1).

CLINE A continuous, graded scale with an infinite number of gradations. It is often easier to place a linguistic element on such a bipolar scale, e.g. between grammatical and semantic → meaning, than to assign it to a particular pigeon-hole cate-gory. Similarly, particular speech sounds are never exactly alike, but may be thought of as falling within a CONTINUUM of articulatory ranges.

CLINICAL LINGUISTICS
The use of special techniques from the fields of medicine and linguistics to study and treat speech defects and language disorders. Such defects may be due to physical disability from birth, to accident or illness, or to psychological disturbances. The linguistic sciences can help by pro-viding theoretical models, analytical techniques and descriptive data about language as a whole, the relationship between speech and writing, language varieties, articulation and classifica-tion of speech sounds, grammatical and semantic relationships, etc. → aphasia, speech therapy. (9.5).

CLIPPED A kind of pronuncia-tion characterised by → syncope, → fortis articulation and rapid tempo giving a staccato rather than a slurred impression, e.g. some dialects of British English in contrast to some varieties of U.S. American English. (8.24).

CLIPPED WORD → Abbrevia-tion.

CLIPPING The shortening of words resulting in new forms with the same meaning, e.g. *examination* > *exam, co-educational* > *co-ed*.

CLITICS In → tagmemics, bound forms which can hardly be considered as bound morphemes since they fill slots at the phrase or clause level, but which are not consistent with the criterion for the definition of a word as minimum free form since they cannot occur as free forms. In English the *'m* in *I'm* is a clitic: although it is phonologically attached to the *I* (and cannot occur without the *I*) it fills the predicate slot. The term PROCLITIC is used if the bound form is prefixed and ENCLITIC if the bound form is suffixed. (2.5 Cook).

CLOSE APPOSITION A word or phrase used in apposition and not separated by open transition in speech, nor by a comma in writing, e.g. *our friend Peter* in *I haven't seen our friend Peter for a long time.*

CLOSE APPROXIMANT Term used by some linguists to refer to a → fricative.

CLOSE JUNCTURE → Transi-tion.

CLOSE TRANSITION → Transition.

CLOSE VOWEL A → vowel sound pronounced with a narrow opening of the mouth and with the tongue raised either to the front [iː] or back [uː] of the mouth. Vowel sounds are usually classified accord-ing to the position of the tongue along a three point scale: high, mid, low, or a four point scale: close, half close, half open, → open vowel. → diagram p. 253. Alternative term: narrow vowel.

CLOSED-CLASS WORD → Function word.

CLOSED LIST → Closed system.

CLOSED SET → Closed system.

CLOSED STATE → Glottis.

CLOSED SYLLABLE A → syllable ending in a consonant. Alternative terms: blocked syllable, checked syllable.

CLOSED SYSTEM A paradigmatic series of a limited number of variants, e.g. English prepositions or inflexions, etc., the number of which is fixed and cannot be increased without the system being changed, as opposed to an → open set such as a list of lexical items, e.g. *chair*, *table*, *lamp*, etc. Alternative terms: closed list, closed set. (9.11 Halliday *et al.*).

CLOSED VOWEL A vowel sound in a → closed syllable, e.g. in *hit*, *hat*, *hate*. Alternative terms: blocked vowel, checked vowel.

CLOSING DIPHTHONG → Diphthong.

CLOSURE Blocking off the air stream momentarily at some point in the vocal tract. For the air-stream to be cut off completely there must also be a VELIC CLOSURE, i.e. the velum must seal off the nasal cavity so that no air escapes through the nose: stop consonants (except glottal and pharyngeal stops) are formed in this way. During such a blockage the air is imprisoned between an INNER CLOSURE, the one furthest removed from the lips, and an OUTER CLOSURE, the one furthest removed from the lungs. According to whether the inner closure occurs at the lungs, glottis or velum it is called a PULMONIC CLOSURE, GLOTTALIC CLOSURE or VELARIC CLOSURE respectively. The outer closure may occur at the lips, the teeth, the alveolar ridge, the palate, velum, pharynx or glottis or any intermediate point. → air-stream mechanism. (3.1, 8.22).

CLUSTER (*a*) A sequence of linguistic elements which may be sounds (→ consonant cluster, vowel cluster) or parts of speech (→ noun cluster, verb cluster). (*b*) In areal linguistics a group of dialects or languages which share common features as a result of their mutual geographical proximity.

CLUTTERING Rapid speech omitting sounds and syllables, usually due to nervous disorders. (9.5).

COALESCENCE → Fusion.

COALESCENT ASSIMILATION → Assimilation.

CO-ARTICULATION Simultaneous or nearly simultaneous occurrence of more than one feature of → articulation.

CODA The final part of the → syllable occurring between its peak and the onset of the next syllable, e.g. *n* in *manly*.

CODE A prearranged set of rules for converting messages from one sign system into another. Sign systems such as alphabetic writing are already derived arbitrary representations of items of a natural language and so codes based on alphabetic writing are 'twice removed' from natural languages. Examples of codes are the Morse code used in telegraphy and many binary systems of computer programming. In the so-called 'communication model' of → information theory, the message is said to be converted into signals by the sender or source (ENCODING) and reassembled into meaningful sequences by the 'receiver' or addressee (DECODING). → elaborated, restricted code. (10.5).

COGNATE LANGUAGE A language related genealogically to other languages. Thus in the Romance family of languages, French is a cognate of Italian, one of its sister languages, and of Latin, its parent language. (6.1).

COGNATE OBJECT The → object which is etymologically or semantically related to the verb by which it is governed, e.g. the nouns in *we sing a song* or *he runs a race*.

COGNATE WORD A word related in form and meaning to a similar word in another language, e.g. English *mother*, German *Mutter* and Latin *mater* (ETYMOLOGICAL COGNATES) or English *head* and German *Kopf* (cognates in usage) since they both refer to the same part of the body.

COGNITIVE FUNCTION The use of language for the purpose of intellectual activity such as reasoning. → function (*a*).

COGNITIVE MEANING Those aspects of the → meaning of a word or phrase which relate it to some feature(s) of the external world (denotative meaning) or of intellectual reasoning. Cognitive in this sense may be contrasted with →

expressive, → affective, → connotative, or → communicative. → denotation. (5.1).

COGNITIVE REALITY In → semantics, the validity of semantic components. The analysis of kinship terms has shown that at least parts of the vocabulary of a language can be viewed as consisting of certain universal categories, e.g. *brother* as 'male' + 'sibling'. → componential analysis. (5.1).

COHESION The degree to which two or more words or → morphemes seem to belong together in a syntactic structure. A → bound morpheme coheres more strongly with the element to which it is bound than to any other element, e.g. *-ly* in *He walks quickly*. In this same sentence *he* coheres more strongly with *walks* than with *quickly*. In the sentence *He used to sit here*, *to* coheres strongly with both *used* and *sit*. Some linguists have extended this term to cover those features in a text which link its component parts. (4.1, 4.2, 8.23).

COINAGE The process or result of deliberately creating a new word out of existing morphological elements by → derivation, → composition or → root-creation. → nonce-formation. (4.2, 5.1).

COINED WORD A new word deliberately created for a specific purpose.

COLLATION The collection and grouping of linguistic material gathered from native informants as a basis of the → linguistic analysis of their language. → field-work. (2.3 Samarin).

COLLECTIVE NOUN A → noun which refers to a group of persons, things or ideas. In English such nouns are usually inflected in the same way as other nouns, but usage often varies as to whether they are considered to be singular or plural, e.g. *It is a good team* as opposed to *They are a good team*, or *The parliament is in session; they will vote soon.*

COLLIGATION A group of words in sequence, considered not as individual lexical items, but as members of particular word classes. Thus the colligation *The boy kicks the ball* would be considered as noun phrase + verb + noun phrase. → collocation.

COLLOCATION Two or more words, considered as individual lexical items, used in habitual association with one another in a given language, e.g. in English *green* collocates with *grass, dark* with *night*, etc. Every individual word in a language has its range of collocations which limits its meaningful usage, and equivalent words in different languages rarely, if ever, have the same range of collocations. → colligation.

COLLOCATION ACCENT The → stress pattern within a group of words which distinguishes phrases such as '*two-hundred-year-old houses* or *two* ' *hundred-year-old houses* or *two hundred* ' *year-old houses.*

COLLOQUIAL SPEECH → Manner of discourse.

COLLOQUIALISM An expression which is used only in informal or colloquial speech and not, for example, in formal speech or writing.

COLOURING → Timbre.

COMBINATIVE SOUND CHANGE → Sound change.

COMBINATORIAL SEMANTICS → Semantics.

COMBINATORY SOUND CHANGE → Sound change.

COMBINATORY VARIANT → Conditioned variant.

COMMAND An utterance which demands or forbids an action to be carried out. A distinction must be made between the semantic term command and the formal or grammatical term → imperative since not all commands have the imperative form, e.g. *NCO's and other ranks will report at 6.00 a.m.* is a command but it is not an imperative. The same is true of a phrase such as *The tenant to pay the rates.* The relationship existing between command and imperative also exists between such terms as → question (semantic term) and interrogative (grammatical term), and between statement and indicative. (4.1, 4.2, 8.23).

COMMENT The statement that is made about the person or thing that is being discussed. The comment is often, but not necessarily, the predicate of the sentence, and may provide 'new' information about the topic, e.g. in *He plays well* the pronoun *he* is the topic and the verbal construction *plays well* is the comment which tells us more about the topic. → topic and comment, exocentric construction.

COMMON ASPECT The simple verb form in English, e.g. as in *I write to my parents regularly*, as opposed to the → progressive or continuous aspect, e.g. as in *I am writing a letter.*

COMMON CASE The uninflected form of the noun in English as opposed to the → possessive case with the *'s* inflexion.

COMMON CORE That part of the language which is used and understood by the majority of its speakers. → vocabulary.

COMMON GENDER A type of → gender. Also used sometimes with reference to → epicenes, i.e. nouns which can denote either male or female persons, e.g. *lecturer* or *driver.*

COMMON LANGUAGE Type of speech used by the majority of the population of a speech community in everyday situations, rather than specialised literary usage. Alternative terms: popular language, common speech, vernacular.

COMMON MOOD → Mood.

COMMON NOUN A → noun designating a general class of objects or concepts rather than an individual or personal name. Common nouns may be non-count or → mass nouns, e.g. *flour* and *courage*, or count or → unit nouns, e.g. *table* and *box.* → proper noun.

COMMON SPEECH → Common language.

COMMON VOICE Active → voice.

COMMUNICATION The passing of information from one point to another, one of the most basic uses of human language. Communication requires (1) a source or 'sender', (2) an addressee or 'receiver', (3) a 'channel' which acts as the medium and carrier of the message. Messages are usually in a recognisable form of text or utterance (4) made up from the inventory of a code (5), shared by both sender (encoder) and receiver (decoder). Communication is usually about a particular topic (6) within a physical and social context (7) common to the participants in the communicative situation. (9.11 Moulton, 10.5).

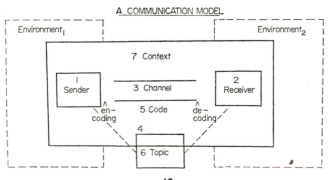

A COMMUNICATION MODEL

COMMUNICATION ENGIN-EERING The application of → information theory to → communication, i.e. the passing of messages from a source to a receiver via a channel. Alternative term: communication technology. (10.5).

COMMUNICATION TECHNO-LOGY → Communication engineering.

COMMUNICATIVE FUNC-TION The use of language for the purpose of conveying information between a speaker or writer and listener or reader. → function (*a*).

COMMUTATION Contrastive → substitution of phonemes.

COMPACT versus DIFFUSE One of the basic oppositions in → distinctive feature phonology based on the analysis of a → spectrogram. 'Compact' indicates a concentration of energy in a relatively narrow central region of the spectrum and 'diffuse' concentration in non-central regions. In articulatory terms this opposition indicates the relations of the shape and size of the resonance chamber behind and in front of the narrowest point (stricture). The English vowels /e/ in *pet*, /a/ in *pat* and /o/ in *pot* are compact while /ɪ/ in *pit*, /ʌ/ in *putt*, /u/ in *put* are diffuse. Consonants such as /k/ in *kill*, /ʃ/ in *shall* and /ŋ/ in *sing* are compact whereas /p/ in *pill*, /t/ in *till*, /m/ in *mill*, etc. are diffuse.

COMPARATIVE DEGREE → Degree.

COMPARATIVE GRAMMAR → Comparative linguistics.

COMPARATIVE LINGUISTICS An approach to language studies in which sets of phonological, grammatical and lexical correspondences between related languages or between different periods in the historical development of one language are listed and classified. Comparative → philology started with the discovery of the similarities between ancient Sanskrit and other languages of the Indo-European family such as Classical Greek and Latin, and 19th century linguists from J. Grimm to the → Neogrammarians did much to refine its techniques. One of the aims of these studies was to reconstruct the common ancestor of all → Indo-European languages. → Typological comparison, on the other hand, classifies languages into groups on the basis of shared structural features rather than genetic relationships. → Descriptive linguistics, historical linguistics. Alternative term: comparative philology, comparative grammar. (6.1, 6.2).

COMPARATIVE METHOD A method of establishing relationships between two or more related languages by comparing forms of → cognate words. The aim of this comparison is usually to reconstruct a common ancestor. → internal reconstruction. (6.1, 6.2).

COMPARATIVE PHILOLOGY → Comparative linguistics.

COMPARATIVE TRANSCRIP-TION → Phonetic transcription.

COMPARATIVISM Collective term for the work of the early pioneers in → comparative linguistics.

COMPARISON OF LAN-GUAGES The description and

analysis of similar and different items and patterns of two or more languages or of two or more periods in the development of one language to find genetic or typological relationships between them (→ comparative linguistics, historical linguistics, typology) or to find principles which may make language teaching and translation more effective (→ contrastive linguistics). (6.1, 9.13).

COMPATIBILITY The relationships that can be established between words with partly overlapping meanings. Thus the words *dark* and *night* are compatible in → collocations such as *It was a dark and rainy night.* (5.1).

COMPETENCE and PER-FORMANCE A distinction drawn originally by N. Chomsky: competence refers to the ability all native speakers have of being able to understand and produce sentences which they have never heard before; it refers in this sense to the code which underlies all utterances in a given language. Performance on the other hand refers to the realisation of this code in actual situations where language is used, and thus relates to the utterances themselves. In transformational-generative grammar features of competence are represented in the → deep structure exhibited by the syntactic component of the grammar, whereas features of performance are represented in the → surface structure produced by the phonological component of the grammar. (2.1 Chomsky).

COMPLEMENT That part of a verbal phrase which is required to make it a complete predicate in a sentence, e.g. the object noun that occurs with a transitive verb (*hit the ball*), the noun or adjective that occurs after a copulative verb (*became president* or *is beautiful*), or the adverb in the phrase *It happened yesterday.* Complements are obligatory constituents, as opposed to → adjuncts which are optional modifiers, e.g. the adverb in *He became president last night.* In traditional grammar the term complement is used to denote an element that 'completes' a sentence after a verb which does not usually take an 'object', e.g. the verb *to be.* In the sentence *He is a policeman, a policeman* is the complement. (4.1, 4.2, 8.23).

COMPLEMENTARITY In → semantics, the relationship between words with meanings that are mutually exclusive, e.g. *single : married* or *brother : sister.* As opposed to → antonyms such as *big* and *small*, complementary items are not usually 'gradable', i.e. *big, bigger, biggest*, but not *married, more married.* (5.1).

COMPLEMENTARY DISTRIBUTION Term used to describe a situation where two → variants are mutually exclusive in a particular environment. Thus in English, the two → allophones of the phoneme /p/, [pʰ] aspirate as in the word *pin* and [p] non-aspirate as in the word *spin*, are said to be in complementary distribution because only the non-aspirate form [p] occurs after /s-/ and only the aspirate form [pʰ] occurs at the beginning of a word.

COMPLETE VERB (*a*) → Intransitive verb. (*b*) A verb with forms corresponding to the forms of the majority of verbs in the same language, e.g. *make, makes, made, making; walk, walks, walked, walking,* as opposed to a → defective verb, e.g. *must* or *ought*.

COMPLETIVE FRAGMENT
→ Favourite sentence.

COMPLEX NUCLEUS
A → syllable nucleus consisting of a vowel cluster, e.g. the diphthong [ai] in *night*. Alternative term: complex peak.

COMPLEX PEAK
→ Complex nucleus.

COMPLEX SENTENCE
A → sentence which is made up of at least one independent or → main clause and one dependent or → subordinate clause, joined by a subordinating conjunction, e.g. *I don't know whether he called.* → compound sentence.

COMPLEX STOP
→ Stop.

COMPLEX WAVE FORM
→ Sound wave.

COMPLEX WORD
A word made up of one free → morpheme and one or more bound morphemes, e.g. *homeliness*, or two or more bound morphemes, e.g. *receive*.

COMPONENT
(*a*) → Semantic component. (*b*) In transformational-generative grammar, one of several parts of the theoretical model which accounts for or generates a sentence, e.g. phonology/graphology, syntax (phrase structures and transformations) and semantics (dictionary and projection rules). → level.

COMPONENTIAL ANALYSIS
A method of → linguistic analysis which shows how elements such as sounds or words are made up of component features. N. S. Trubetzkoy (1890–1938) and the → Prague School analysed phonemes into → distinctive features: thus /d/ can be regarded as being composed of 'oral' (*vs.* nasal) + 'voiced' (*vs.* voiceless) + 'dental' (*vs.* labial, velar, etc.). Some linguists have explained morphemes and other grammatical elements as being made up of distinctive 'categories'; thus *goes* may be said to be 'singular' (*vs.* plural), 'verb' (*vs.* noun), 'third person' (*vs.* first person), 'present' (*vs.* past). In semantics, componential analysis can show how sets of terms contain universal features or → semantic components, thus the proportional relations between words like *man/woman/child* and *bull/cow/calf* may be stated in terms of 'male'/'female', 'adult'/'non-adult', 'human'/'bovine', etc. (2.1, 3.1, 4.1, 5.1, 5.2 Bendix).

COMPOSITE TRANSFER
A semantic change of a word because it is related to another word in phonetic shape and/or meaning, e.g. when the Germanic *Bergfried* 'guard-peace' becomes English *belfry* with the meaning 'bell tower'. (5.2 Ullmann).

COMPOSITE VERB
A term used in transformational-generative grammar to refer to a verb consisting of two parts, sometimes called stem and complement, which are not adjacent in the structure but which are usually separated by the object of the verb, e.g. *rang ... up* as in *He rang her up.* → discontinuity.

COMPOSITION
The joining of two or more words to produce a → compound word in which the meanings of the component parts merge to

represent a phrase, e.g. *house-boat*, 'boat combined with and serving as a house'. → word-formation. (4.2, 5.1).

COMPOUND → Compound word.

COMPOUND GRAPHEME A combination of graphic signs representing one sound, e.g. *gh* in *laugh*. → digraph, ligature.

COMPOUND NOMINAL → Compound noun.

COMPOUND NOUN A → noun phrase which is made up of two or more words, e.g. *high school, blue-beard, machine-gun* with the stress pattern ′ ‵ which helps to differentiate the compound noun *bláckbird* from the structure modifier + noun *black bìrd*. Alternative terms: compound nominal, bluebeard compound.

COMPOUND PERSONAL PRONOUN The → pronouns formed by *my, your, our*, etc. combined with *self, selves*, e.g. *myself, ourselves*.

COMPOUND PHONEME A combination of vowel phonemes in one syllable, e.g. a diphthong functioning as a phonological unit. (2.4 Bloomfield).

COMPOUND PREDICATE A → predicate consisting of more than one verb phrase, e.g. *He came and looked* or *He was running and jumping*. → simple predicate.

COMPOUND SENTENCE A → sentence which is made up of at least two independent or → main clauses, connected by co-ordinating conjunctions such as *and* or *but* or by intonation, e.g. *We arrived in London and went to our hotel, (but) then her sister called.* → complex sentence. Alternative terms: multiple sentence, sentence compound.

COMPOUND SUBJECT A → noun phrase which consists of single nouns or pronouns joined by conjunctions or by intonation, e.g. *Either one man or two boys were needed.*

COMPOUND TENSE A → tense form made up of an auxiliary verb plus a full verb, e.g. in *We have been waiting for you for over an hour.*

COMPOUND WORD The combination of two or more words to form a new word. Most frequently two nouns are joined to form compounds, e.g. *typewriter, apple-tree,* but other parts of speech may also occur in compounds, e.g. *flyover, nevertheless, blue-eyed, overtake, forget-me-not,* etc. Compound words can often be distinguished from their two-word counterparts by means of different stress patterns, e.g. *White House* as opposed to *white house* or *moving van* as opposed to *moving van*. → word formation. (4.2, 5.1).

COMPREHENSION One of the basic linguistic skills, consisting of the ability to listen to and understand speech (aural comprehension) or to read and understand written language (visual comprehension). (3.3 Mol, 9.5, 9.11).

COMPROMISE LANGUAGE → Koine.

COMPUTATIONAL LINGUIS-TICS A branch of language studies which applies computer techniques to linguistic and literary research, particularly in word → frequency counts and other fields requiring statistical analysis, such as → concordance making, → machine translation, → speech recognition and → speech synthesis. → Mathematical linguistics. (9.4, 10.4).

CONCATENATION (*a*) The process of linking elements together by placing them in sequence to form strings. In transformational-generative grammar a language is considered as a set of strings which consist of elements linked together by the process of concatenation. (*b*) The → extension of the semantic meaning of a word in a linear development, e.g. German *Feder* 'feather' > 'quill' > 'pen'. → radiation.

CONCEPT The mental image of an object or process, e.g. the idea of 'heavenly body', which can be verbalised by definition, e.g. "luminous object in the sky, of certain consistency, temperature, etc." and given an agreed name or → term, e.g. *star*. (5.2 Zgusta).

CONCEPTUAL THEORY OF MEANING → Semantics.

CONCEPTUALISM → Semantics.

CONCESSIVE A conjunction or clause expressing a state or condition in spite of which the truth or validity of the main clause holds good, e.g. *We went out, although we knew that it would rain.*

CONCORD → Agreement.

CONCORDANCE A list of words with references to where and how often they occur in a particular text or set of texts, such as the Bible, or the works of a single author, arranged by alphabet, subject matter, or in chronological order. (7.3, 9.4).

CONCRETE NOUN A → noun referring to a material object, e.g. *table* or *animal*. It may take any → determiner and usually forms a plural. → abstract noun.

CONCRETE SOUND The actual pronunciation of a particular speech sound by a speaker, as opposed to an → abstract sound or → phoneme in which individual and dialectal variants are disregarded.

CONDITIONAL A verb form implying a condition or hypothesis. In some languages a special form of the verb exists for this purpose, e.g. French *vous iriez* 'you would go'. In English a compound form is used with the auxiliaries *should* or *would* plus the infinitive of the main verb. → conditional tense.

CONDITIONAL CLAUSE A clause expressing a condition, usually introduced by *if*, e.g. *If you walk too far, you will be tired.* → consequence clause. Alternative terms: hypothetical clause, protasis.

CONDITIONAL PERFECT TENSE Traditional term for the verb form occurring in English as *would have* + past participle, e.g. *He would have read.* This kind of time reference is now usually considered as a type of → aspect, since it refers to the type and state of the action, e.g. its completion, rather than location in time. Alternative term: future perfect in the past.

CONDITIONAL SOUND CHANGE → Sound change.

CONDITIONAL TENSE Traditional term for the verb form occurring in English as *would* + infinitive, e.g. *He would go.* This feature is now usually considered as a → mood rather than a → tense. Alternative term: future in the past. → aspect.

CONDITIONAL VARIANT → Conditioned variant.

CONDITIONED SOUND CHANGE → Sound change.

CONDITIONED VARIANT A particular variety of sound or grammatical form determined by its environment, e.g. the unaspirated [p] in *spin* where the lack of aspiration is conditioned by the preceding [s], or the variant *dep-* < *deep* which occurs before the suffix *-th* in *depth*. → complementary distribution. Alternative terms: automatic variant, combinatory variant, conditional variant, contextual variant, positional variant.

CONFIRMATIONAL INTER-ROGATIVE A shortened clause which implies the confirmation of the preceding statement, e.g. in *They said it would rain today, didn't they?* or *Nice day, isn't it?* Alternative terms: confirmatory clause, tag question.

CONFIRMATORY CLAUSE → Confirmational interrogative.

CONGENERIC GROUP → Synaesthesia.

CONGRUENCE → Agreement.

CONJUGATE To list the forms of a particular verb according to → tense, person and number. → conjugation.

CONJUGATION Classification of a verb according to its inflexional forms for → number, → person and → tense, etc. Latin verbs, for example, are classified into four conjugations: 1st conjugation: infinitive ending in *-are*, e.g. *amare* 'to love', 2nd conjugation: infinitive ending in *-ēre*, e.g. *monēre* 'to advise', 3rd conjugation: infinitive ending in *-ere*, e.g. *regere* 'to rule', 4th conjugation: infinitive ending in *-ire*, e.g. *audire* 'to hear'. The term conjugation is sometimes used to refer to other categories of verbs, e.g. → strong or irregular verbs such as English *drink/drank/drunk* and → weak or regular verbs such as *walk/walked*. → declension. (4.1, 4.2).

CONJUNCT FORM → Conjunctive pronoun.

CONJUNCTION An uninflected word used to link together words or sentence parts. Conjunctions are usually classified into two categories: CO-ORDINATING CONJUNCTION (alternative terms: CO-ORDINATOR, COUPLING CONJUNCTION), e.g. *and, but, or, nor, for*, which link together items of equal rank without syntactic or semantic implications; and SUB-ORDINATING CONJUNCTION (alternative term: SUBORDINATOR) which in turn may be classified into QUALIFYING CONJUNCTION, e.g. *when, if, because, although, while* which indicate semantic subordination of the clause introduced; PREPOSITIONAL CONJUNCTION, e.g. *as, than* used in comparisons to complete a syntactic structure; INCORPORATING CONJUNCTION, e.g.

that, whether, what, how which imply syntactic subordination. Alternative term: connective. (4.1, 4.2, 8.23).

CONJUNCTIVE ADVERB An → adverb which connects clauses, e.g. *consequently, nevertheless, indeed, hence, furthermore.* Unlike conjunctions, they need not be restricted to the beginning of the sentence which they introduce, e.g. *The chairman left; the meeting, however, continued.* Alternative terms: adverbial conjunction, introductory adverb.

CONJUNCTIVE PRONOUN A → pronoun used only in conjunction with a verb in Romance languages, e.g. French *je* 'I' or the object pronoun occurring before the verb as in *il me dit.* Alternative term: conjunct form. → disjunctive pronoun.

CONNECTING CONSONANT or VOWEL → Linking morpheme.

CONNECTIVE (*a*) → Conjunction. (*b*) → Sentence connector.

CONNECTIVE CONSTRUCTION → Exocentric construction.

CONNECTOR (*a*) A conjunctive adverb such as *therefore* which links two or more sentences. (*b*) A linking verb such as *be, seem* and *become* which relates the subject and complement in a sentence. → copula.

CONNOTATION That aspect of meaning of a particular word or group of words which is based on the feelings and ideas it arouses in the minds of speaker (or writer) and hearer (or reader). Thus the term *democracy* has different emotive associations in different political

contexts and it may be said that its original or literal sense has been extended to include different overtones. Connotation is opposed to → denotation or → cognitive meaning. Alternative terms: implication, overtone. (5.1).

CONNOTATIVE MEANING → Meaning.

CONSECUTIVE INTERPRETING → Interpreting.

CONSECUTIVE TRANSCRIPTION The rendering in → phonetic transcription of a consecutive text rather than of individual words.

CONSEQUENCE CLAUSE The → clause which states the expected result of the condition expressed in a conditional sentence, e.g. in *If the wind drops, it will rain, it will rain* is the consequence clause and *if the wind drops* is the → conditional clause. Alternative term: apodosis.

CONSONANCE Identical final consonant sounds of two or more words, e.g. in *dash* and *fish.*

CONSONANT (*a*) A → speech sound produced by obstructing or impeding the passage of air at some point in the vocal tract above the → glottis. It may or may not be accompanied by → voicing: [b, d, g, v, ð, ʒ, z] are voiced, [p, t, k, f, θ, ʃ, s] are voiceless. Consonants can also be classified according to (i) the point of → articulation: bilabial [p, b, m]; labiodental [f, v]; interdental [θ, ð]; dental or alveolar [t, d, n, l, r]; palatal [ʃ, ʒ, ɲ]; velar [x, ɣ, k, g, ŋ]; uvular [ʀ]; pharyngeal [ħ]; glottal or laryngeal [ʔ], (ii) the manner of articulation: stop [p, b, t, d, k, g, ʔ];

49

nasal [m, n, ɲ, ŋ]; lateral [l]; trill [r, ʀ]; fricative [f, v, θ, ð, ʃ, ʒ, x, ɣ]; affricate [t͡s, d͡z, t͡ʃ, d͡ʒ, p͡f], (iii) duration: long [lː] as in Italian *bella*; short [l] as in English *willow*. → Table p. 261. In phonology a consonant may also be defined as a speech sound which can occur at the margin of a → syllable and not as the nucleus. (*b*) A letter representing this type of speech sound. (3.1, 8.22).

CONSONANT CLUSTER A combination of two or more adjacent consonants occurring within the same → syllable. Languages differ in the consonant clusters they will allow and the position in which they will allow them; e.g. the combination [-ts] often occurs at the end of words such as *cats*, *hats*, etc., but except in the occasional rare borrowed word it does not occur at the beginning of words in English. In German and Russian, however, this cluster occurs in both positions.

CONSONANT MUTATION → Mutation.

CONSONANT SHIFT A series of regular changes in the articulation of consonant sounds at a particular stage in the history of a language. → first sound shift, second sound shift.

CONSONANTAL Term used to refer to the syllabic, non-semantic sign of some systems of writing such as ancient Egyptian, West Semitic and Arabic, where → vowels are not represented. (7.2).

CONSONANTAL versus NON-CONSONANTAL One of the basic oppositions in → distinctive feature phonology based on the analysis of a → spectrogram. 'Consonantal' indicates the lowering of the frequency of the first → formant with a reduction in overall intensity and 'non-consonantal' indicates the lack of these features. In articulatory terms consonantal indicates interference with the air stream above the glottis in the vocal tract. All consonants have the feature consonantal and all vowels have the feature non-consonantal.

CONSTITUENT A linguistic element which is a component part of a larger unit, e.g. a → morpheme within a word, a word within a construction, or subject and predicate in a → sentence. → immediate constituent analysis, discontinuity.

CONSTITUENT CLASS → Form class.

CONSTITUENT SENTENCE A term used in → transformational-generative grammar to refer to a sentence which is embedded into another sentence, the MATRIX SENTENCE. Constituent sentences often coincide with what are known in traditional grammar as dependent clauses: the sentence *The man who is driving the car is my uncle* can be considered as being derived from the two sentences *The man is my uncle*, *He is driving the car*, the second sentence, the constituent sentence, being embedded into the first, the matrix sentence, with the appropriate transformation of *the man* to *who* in the constituent sentence. In traditional grammar *who is driving the car* is a dependent clause, *The man is my uncle* being the main clause. → parenthetical clause. (4.1 Fowler).

50

CONSTITUENT STRUCTURE GRAMMAR An alternative term for → phrase structure grammar.

CONSTRATE In writing, the graphic marks that are applied to a surface. → substrate (*b*).

CONSTRICTED → Glottalised.

CONSTRUCTED LANGUAGE → Artificial language (*a*).

CONSTRUCTION The process or result of a grouping of morphemes within a word or of words within a sentence, e.g. the word *headmaster* may be regarded as a compound construction consisting of the morphemes *head* and *master*; or the sentence *The cat caught the mouse* can be described as a construction consisting of subject + verb + direct object, or noun + verb + noun.

CONSULTATIVE SPEECH A → manner of discourse intermediate between formal and casual.

CONTACT The influence of different languages upon each other due to frequent meetings between their speakers. Linguistic contact is characterised by → bilingualism, → borrowing, and → linguistic change, caused by direct learning, translation and deliberate language teaching. Sometimes mixing of different language forms may create creole or → pidgin languages. (9.2 Weinreich).

CONTACT VERNACULAR → Pidgin.

CONTAGION The process or result of confusing or blending two forms which are semantically linked, e.g. the association of *restive*, origin-ally 'inactive', 'persistent', with *restless*, gives the new meaning 'fidgety'. (5.2).

CONTAMINATION The process or result of confusing or joining two forms which are habitually or accidentally associated. Thus the combination of *equally good* with *as good* gives the expression *equally as good*.

CONTENT In → linguistic analysis, content refers to the level of lexical or semantic meaning of expressions. Many linguists have stressed that linguistic 'signs' have a content plane (what is meant) and an → expression plane (how it is said). (2.5 Hjelmslev).

CONTENT WORD A word which has a full lexical meaning of its own, e.g. *chair, table, book*, as opposed to a → function word which has no such independent lexical meaning but just contributes to the grammatical meaning of a construction, e.g. *the, of, but*. Alternative terms: full word, lexical word, notional word, open-class word, autonomous word. (4.1, 5.1).

CONTEXT (*a*) The sounds, words or phrases preceding and following a particular linguistic item in an utterance or text. Speech sounds are often influenced by the sounds adjacent to them and are thus said to be conditioned by their environment, e.g. [n] in English is usually articulated on the alveolar ridge, but in a word such as *tenth* [tʰen̪θ] it has a dental articulation in anticipation of the dental sound [θ] which follows. Alternative terms: linguistic context, co-text, environment. (3.1, 4.1).

(*b*) Those features of the external world in relation to which an utterance or text has meaning. The notions of context and situation are central in all branches of → semantics, since they account for the way that verbal and graphic symbols represent the world around the speaker. → systemic grammar. Alternative terms: environment, context of situation. (2.4 Firth, 5.1, 8.24).

CONTEXT OF SITUATION
→ Context (*b*).

CONTEXT-FREE GRAMMAR
A phrase structure grammar in which the rewrite rules such as X → Y (which means rewrite X as Y) apply irrespective of the context of X.

CONTEXT-RESTRICTED GRAMMAR A phrase structure grammar in which the rewrite rules indicate a restriction in the contexts in which they are to be applied, e.g. X → Y/a __ b/ means: X is to be rewritten as Y only in the context indicated between the slants where __ shows the place in the string which the replacement occupies. Alternative term: context-sensitive grammar.

CONTEXT-SENSITIVE GRAMMAR → Context-restricted grammar.

CONTEXTUAL ANALYSIS A type of → linguistic analysis which recognises that the meanings of linguistic units are determined by the → context in which they occur. Contextual constraints operate on the level of phonology and graphology, grammar and lexis (→ complementary distribution, selection restriction).

CONTEXTUAL MEANING →
Meaning.

CONTEXTUAL THEORY OF MEANING → Semantics.

CONTEXTUAL VARIANT →
Conditioned variant.

CONTIGUOUS ASSIMILATION → Assimilation.

CONTIGUOUS DISSIMILATION → Dissimilation.

CONTINUANT Any speech sound which is not a → stop, e.g. vowel, spirant, fricative. → interrupted, → abrupt *vs.* continuant.

CONTINUANT versus NON-CONTINUANT (STOP) Manner of articulation features in recent theories of → distinctive feature phonology. In continuant sounds the air stream is allowed to keep flowing past a constriction whereas in the case of non-continuant sounds the air stream is blocked.

CONTINUOUS ASPECT →
Aspect.

CONTINUOUS CONSTITUENT
A linguistic element within a larger unit which is preceded or followed by another element with which it is closely related without any break, e.g. *is* and *leaving* in *Mary is leaving now*, as opposed to discontinuous constituents, e.g. in *Is Mary leaving now?* → discontinuity.

CONTINUOUS SPECTRUM
→ Spectrum.

CONTINUUM → Cline.

CONTOID Name given by some linguists to an articulatory class of sounds more traditionally called → consonants, reserving the term consonant to refer to the consonant phonemes of a particular language and their written representation. Contoid is thus a phonetic term and consonant a phonological term. → vocoid. (3.1 Pike).

CONTOUR A sequence of → prosodic features such as pitch or stress over part or the whole of an utterance, e.g. the rising → intonation pattern in the question *Are you?* Such features are used in speech as → vocal qualifiers to convey information about the state of the speaker. (3.4, 8.22).

CONTRACTION The process or result of shortening a linguistic form, e.g. in the construction: pronoun plus auxiliary, *I've, you'd*, or auxiliary plus *not: won't, can't*, or in the French *au* for *à le*. → abbreviation.

CONTRAST (*a*) Between languages: → comparison. (*b*) In phonology, morphology, syntax, etc. the term contrast is used to refer to → opposition between → distinctive units. An opposition exists, for example, between voiced and voiceless stops at the beginning of words in English as in *pin ~ bin, tin ~ din* and between singular and plural of nouns such as *man ~ men*. Such opposition between linguistic elements is called contrastive or functional, and contrastive pairs involving only one opposition are referred to as → minimal pairs. Some British linguists, however, use the term opposition for the → paradigmatic

relationships outlined above and restrict the term contrast to a → syntagmatic relationship, e.g. in the word *pin* /p/ contrasts with /n/ as it differs from it; i.e. /p/ is a voiceless bilabial stop and /n/ is a voiced alveolar nasal continuant. In this usage the term contrast and opposition cannot be equated since it is not possible to talk about an opposition between /p/ and /n/ in the word *pin*. → binarism. (3.1, 4.1).

CONTRASTIVE → Distinctive.

CONTRASTIVE ANALYSIS A method of → linguistic analysis which shows the similarities and differences between two or more languages or dialects with the aim of finding principles which can be applied to practical problems in language teaching and translation, with special emphasis on transfer, interference, and equivalents. This approach is → synchronic in that it pays attention only to the contemporary forms of the languages in question, whereas → comparative-historical linguistics is usually → diachronic, concentrating on the forms of the languages at different periods of their development. Alternative terms: differential analysis, differential linguistics. (9.13).

CONTRASTIVE PAIR → Minimal pair.

CONTRASTIVE SUBSTITUTION → Substitution.

CONVENTION The fact that different speakers of a language follow very similar rules for using their language with reference to particular situations, e.g. in naming objects and ideas. Changes in usage are dependent on the need to agree on a common system of communication, or to improve the system. → arbitrariness. (2.1 Lyons).

CONVENTIONALISM → Nominalism.

CONVERGENCE (*a*) → Merger. (*b*) → De-dialectalisation.

CONVERGENCE AREA That region of a → speech community which touches on a neighbouring language, where frequent linguistic → contact produces mixed language forms, bilingualism and change. (7.1).

CONVERSATION → Spoken language used between at least two speakers. As opposed to written language and deliberate prose, conversation is often spontaneous speech (and sign language), and as such has not been subjected to large-scale and detailed analysis in linguistics.

CONVERSE TERMS A pair of lexical items which have opposite associative meanings, e.g. *buy* and *sell*, *husband* and *wife*. → antonymy. (2.1 Lyons).

CONVERSION (*a*) Alternative term for → transmutation, the change of function or class of a word, e.g. *condition* (n) becomes *to condition* (vb). Sometimes the change is limited to a change in suprasegmental features, e.g. *prèsent* becomes *to presént*. (*b*) The change from one code or recording medium to another, e.g. → translation, → transcription, → transliteration.

CO-OCCURRENCE A relationship permitted or required between two or more words of different types to form a sentence. Thus words of the class *man, boy*, etc. can be used or can co-occur with words of the class *sit, run, walk*, etc. to make sentences. Words of the former class, traditionally called nouns, may be preceded by *a, the*, etc., words of the latter class, traditionally called verbs, may be followed by *quickly, slowly*, etc. → colligation, collocation.

CO-ORDINATE CLAUSE A → clause which is joined to another by means of a conjunction but which is not grammatically dependent on it, e.g. *He went shopping but he did not buy a new hat* consists of two co-ordinate clauses joined by a → co-ordinator.

CO-ORDINATE CONSTRUCTION Syntactic units of equal rank or status, e.g. two words joined by *and* such as *bread and butter*, or sentences joined by → co-ordinating conjunctions such as *and, or*, e.g. *I walked into the room and he handed me the book*. Alternative terms: co-ordinative construction.

CO-ORDINATE ENDO-CENTRIC CONSTRUCTION → Endocentric construction.

CO-ORDINATING CONJUNCTION A → conjunction such as *and, but, or*, which connects words or clauses of equal status, e.g. *He handed me the book and I read it out to him.* → correlative. Alternative term: co-ordinator.

CO-ORDINATION The linking of words by means of → co-ordinating conjunctions. (4.1, 4.2, 8.23).

CO-ORDINATIVE CONSTRUCTION → Co-ordinate construction.

CO-ORDINATOR → Co-ordinating conjunction.

COPENHAGEN SCHOOL → Glossematics.

COPULA A → verb such as *be, seem, become, look,* etc. which relates the → subject to the → complement, e.g. in *He is a teacher, The policeman seemed not at all satisfied, It got worse and worse.* Alternative terms: copulative verb, linking verb, equational verb, catenative verb, connector. (4.1, 4.2, 8.23).

COPULATIVE COMPOUND A type of → compound word having two constituents of equal status as if joined by *and,* e.g. *bittersweet, Anglo-American.* Alternative term: dvandva compound.

COPULATIVE VERB → Copula.

CORONAL A sound produced by bringing the blade of the tongue into contact with the hard palate. → palatal.

CORONAL versus NON-CORONAL Cavity features in recent theories of → distinctive feature phonology. Coronal sounds involve the blade of the tongue being raised, thus dental, alveolar and palatal sounds are coronal. Sounds for which the blade of the tongue remains in the neutral position, e.g. labial consonants, uvular [R], glides, etc. are non-coronal.

CORPUS An unorganised mass of linguistic data collected in → field work or by compiling written → texts. The linguist analyses such data to make scientific statements about the phonological, graphemic, grammatical or lexical features of a language. (2.3 Samarin).

CORRECTNESS Traditionally, much attention was paid by grammarians to the question of 'right' and 'wrong' in speech and writing. Today most linguists try to avoid value judgments, basing their research on observable data of → usage. Recent investigations of social dialects have shown that each variety of a language has its own internal standard of → acceptability, but what is correct in one dialect may not be socially acceptable in another. → prescriptive linguistics, adequacy.

CORRELATION (*a*) The relationship existing between two series of sounds, e.g. [p t k f θ] which are voiceless sounds, and [b d g v ð] which are voiced. A correlation of voice is said to exist between them. → mark of correlation. (*b*) The attachment of semantic → meaning to linguistic units such as words.

CORRELATIVE A → conjunction consisting of a pair of words such as *either/or, both/and,* etc. connecting words or clauses of equal status, e.g. in *He was both shocked and entertained.*

CORRESPONDENCE → Agreement.

CORRESPONDENCE THEORY OF MEANING → Semantics.

CO-TEXT → Context (*a*).

COUNT NOUN → Unit noun.

COUNTABLE NOUN → Unit noun.

COUPLING CONJUNCTION
→ Conjunction.

**C O V E R E D versus U N -
COVERED** Cavity features in recent theories of → distinctive feature phonology. Covered sounds are produced with a tension and constriction in the pharynx, uncovered sounds are produced without such a constriction. The terms are used only with reference to vowels primarily in African languages exhibiting vowel harmony.

CRASIS A fusion of two vowels or diphthongs into one long vowel or diphthong as a result of their coming together at the end of one word and at the beginning of the next, e.g. Latin *co-ago* > *cogo* 'I drive'.

CREAK → Register (*a*).

CREAKY VOICE → Register (*a*).

CREATIVITY Term used by some linguists to refer to that quality of all human languages which enables speakers to understand and produce sentences never heard or produced before.

CREOLE A mixed natural language composed of elements of different languages in areas of intensive → contact, e.g. of European languages such as English, Portuguese, French and Dutch with native speech forms of Central America and Central Africa. → pidgin, lingua franca. Alternative term: creolised language. (8.8 Hall, 9.2 Hymes).

CREOLISED LANGUAGE → Creole.

CREST OF SONORITY → Peak of sonority.

CROSS-REFERENCE (*a*) → back-reference. (*b*) The practice in lexicography of referring the reader of a dictionary from one entry to another.

C R Y P T O G R A M A text written in a secret → code.

CRYPTOGRAPHY The study of secret codes, which may contribute to our understanding of extinct languages by the decipherment of ancient documents.

C U C K O O THEORY → Origin of speech.

CULTIVATED SPEECH → Manner of discourse.

CULTURAL OVERLAP The similarities in behaviour and attitudes, customs and institutions of two speech communities, reflected in corresponding linguistic features, e.g. translation-equivalents in the vocabularies. (2.1 Lyons).

CULTURAL SPEECH → Manner of discourse.

CULTURE and LANGUAGE Language is closely related to man's ecology, including his social environment and the literary, religious and other traditions of his society. Linguists, philosophers and anthropologists share an interest in the interrelationship of these fields, with a view to establishing the extent of their dependence upon one another (→ relativity). It is important to determine what is unique in a particular culture as well as to discover features which appear to be universal in all cultures. → anthropological linguistics. (10.1).

CUMUL A form which signals more than one grammatical category, e.g. the Latin ending -*a* in the noun *lingua* 'tongue, language' represents singular number, feminine gender, and nominative or ablative case. Alternative term: amalgam.

CUNEIFORM SCRIPT → Table, p. 264. (7.2).

CURSIVE WRITING Handwriting by linking up graphic signs such as letters to represent sequences of speech sounds and words, as opposed to print in which letters are not joined, shorthand in which they are joined so as to represent contracted forms, or → monumental writing. (7.2).

CYBERNETICS Collective name given to the study of communication and automatic control mechanisms in and between living organisms and machines, e.g. between man and computer. → Information theory. (1.1 Meetham, 9.4, 10.5).

CYCLE One complete repetition of a → sound wave, i.e. part of a wave between any point and the next point where the variations in air pressure start the same pattern of changes again.

CYRILLIC ALPHABET → Table p. 265. (7.2).

D

DACTYL → Foot.

DAMPING Reducing the amplitude of a wave. In the case of a sound wave, this causes the sound to die away. A sound with a high degree of damping has its energy spread over a wide range of frequencies which show up clearly on its → spectrum.

DANGLING MODIFIER A participial phrase used as a modifier when there is no appropriate word to which it can refer, thus producing a sentence which is nonsensical if taken literally from a grammatical point of view, e.g. *Being a nice day, we went to the beach*, or *Standing behind the closed door, his voice could not be heard.*

DANGLING PARTICIPLE An → absolute construction consisting of a participial phrase modifying a sentence, e.g. *Weather permitting, we shall go.*

DARK 'L' The → velarised [ɫ] heard in English before consonants and at the ends of words, e.g. *table*, as opposed to the alveolar or → 'clear' [l] which occurs in English before vowels, particularly front vowels, e.g. *light*.

DARK VOWEL → Back vowel.

DARMESTETER'S LAW A → sound shift first discovered by Darmesteter describing the fact that in the transition from Latin to French the syllable immediately preceding the stress syllable is lost unless it contains the vowel [a]. (6.1).

DATIVE → Case form in some inflected languages, primarily denoting that the word in question is the indirect → object of a verb, e.g. in Latin *Tibi librum damus* 'We give you the book', or is governed by certain prepositions, e.g. German *auf dem Lande* 'in the country'. In English this relationship is usually expressed by the prepositions *to* or *for*, but also by word order, hence the difference in meaning between *Show the boy a dog* and *Show the dog a boy*.

DAUGHTER LANGUAGE → Family of languages.

DEAD LANGUAGE A language no longer used as a medium of oral communication in a speech community, e.g. Latin, Gothic, as opposed to → living languages such as English, Japanese. Alternative term: extinct language.

DECISION PROCEDURE → Procedure.

DECLARATIVE MOOD → Mood.

DECLENSION The list of all possible inflected forms of a → noun, → pronoun, or → adjective, etc. An inflected language has several forms for both singular and plural of nouns, to show → number, → gender and → case. Latin has six cases but not all nouns have that number of different forms in the singular and plural: *civis* 'citizen', for example, has only four different forms in the singular and three in the plural:

	Singular	Plural
Nominative	*civis*	*cives*
Vocative	*civis*	*cives*
Accusative	*civem*	*cives*
Genitive	*civis*	*civium*
Dative	*civi*	*civibus*
Ablative	*civi*	*civibus*

The declension of an English noun has fewer forms, distinguishing only between common and possessive in both singular and plural: *man*, *man's*, *men*, *men's*. Pronouns in English show a greater diversity, distinguishing between common, objective and two possessive forms:

Common	Objective
I	*me*
you	*you*
he	*him*

1st Possessive	2nd Possessive
my	*mine*
your	*yours*
his	*his* etc.

→ conjugation. (4.1, 4.2).

DECLINE To list the various grammatical forms of a noun, pronoun, or adjective according to case and number etc. → declension.

DECODE To decipher a message from the signals of a → code.

DE-DIALECTALISATION The process whereby local and regional dialects become more like the → standard language, particularly by increased mobility, greater communication and better education. → dialectalisation. Alternative term: convergence. (7.1).

DEEP GRAMMAR → Deep structure.

DEEP STRUCTURE The grammatical relationships inherent in the elements of a phrase or sentence but not immediately apparent from their linear sequence. Consider the following English sentences:

(1) *John expected mother to bring a present.*

(2) *John persuaded mother to bring a present.*

The → surface structure of these two sentences is identical, as they both consist of

Nominal + verb + nominal + marked infinitive + determiner + nominal, but the deep structure of the two sentences is different as can be seen by the fact that (1) can be transformed as follows:

(3) *John expected that mother would bring a present.*

but not (2):

(4) **John persuaded that mother would bring a present.*

The difference between the two sentences can be shown diagrammatically as follows:

(1*a*)

John expected mother to bring a present.

(2*a*)

John persuaded mother to bring a present.

From the above diagrams it can be seen that the difference lies in the nature of the relationship of the verbs *expected* and *persuaded* with what follows them; in (1*a*) *expected* is directly related to all of what

follows; in (2*a*) *persuaded* is directly related only to *mother*. Alternative terms: deep grammar, underlying structure. (2.5 Lyons, 4.2 Chomsky).

DEEP VOWEL → Back vowel.

DE-ETYMOLOGISATION The fusing of two → morphemes in a compound in such a way that both form and meaning of the original morphemes are no longer recognised, e.g. *lady* < Old English *hlāf-dige* 'bread kneader'. (5.1, 6.1).

DEFECT → Speech defect.

DEFECTIVE VERB A verb which does not possess all the → conjugations typical of its class, e.g. auxiliary verbs such as *must* or *ought* in English have no past tense forms. → complete verb (*b*). Alternative term: incomplete verb.

DEFECTIVE WRITING A method of writing representing only the consonants as, for example, in Hebrew. Alternative term: plene writing. (7.2).

DEFERRED PREPOSITION → Preposition.

DEFINITE ARTICLE → Article.

DEFINITE DECLENSION → Weak declension.

DEFINITE DETERMINER A → determiner in a noun phrase specifying a → noun as a particular item, e.g. *the, this, those.* → indefinite determiner.

DEFINITION The process or result of stating the meaning of a word by characterising the component features of the 'concept' (REAL

DEFINITION), by explaining the derivation and use of the 'term' (NOMINAL DEFINITION), or by pointing to the 'thing' (OSTENSIVE DEFINITION). (5.2 Zgusta).

DEFLEXION, DEFLECTION In historical (diachronic) linguistics the loss of → inflexion, e.g. when several case endings merge into one. In synchronic linguistics, deflexion is said to occur when the function of inflexional morphemes is performed by other means such as the syntactic comparison of adjectives with *more* and *most* rather than with *-er* and *-est*. (4.1, 5.1, 6.1).

DEGENERATION → Deterioration.

DEGREE Adjectives and adverbs are usually classified into the following:

POSITIVE DEGREE: the statement of a quality or attribute but implying no comparison; the basic form of the adjective or adverb as listed in a dictionary, e.g. *sad, beautiful, quickly*.

COMPARATIVE DEGREE: expressing a higher or lower degree of a particular quality or attribute in relation to a reference point, e.g. *a hotter day than yesterday*. In English the comparative degree is formed with the inflexion *-er*, e.g. *hotter, faster*, or by the use of the words *more* or *less* as in *more beautiful, less quickly*, or by a special irregular form, e.g. *better, worse*.

SUPERLATIVE DEGREE: expressing the highest or lowest degree of a quality or attribute. In English it is formed by adding the inflexion *-est*, e.g. *quickest, fastest*, etc. or by the use of the words *most* or *least*, e.g. *most beautiful, least able*, or by the use of a special irregular form, e.g. *best, worst*. (4.1, 4.2, 8.23).

DEICTIC FUNCTION → Deixis.

DEICTIC WORD A word, the function of which is to point out or specify an individual person, thing or idea. DEIXIS, the act of pointing out or indicating, is a feature of such words as personal pronouns, *I, he, you*, etc., demonstrative pronouns such as *this, that*, relatives such as *who, which*, etc. and particularly the definite article *the*. (4.1, 4.2, 8.23).

DEIXIS The role played by a → deictic word. Alternative term: deictic function.

DELABIALISATION The absence or removal of → labialisation. Alternative term: unrounding.

DELAYED SPEECH In → language acquisition of children, the late transition from the prelinguistic to the 'linguistic' stage, due to slow maturation or psycho-physiological disturbances. (9.6).

DELETION (*a*) The process or result of leaving out part of a construction. Thus in some grammars the relative pronoun can be said to have been deleted from the sentence *Have you read the book (that) I told you about?* → zero.

(*b*) In transformational-generative grammar the removal of an item from a string by means of a DELETION TRANSFORMATION such as X + Y + Z ⇒ X + Z which means that X + Y + Z is transformed into X + Z, thus deleting Y.

DELETION TRANSFORMATION → Deletion (*b*).

DELIBERATE SPEECH A formal style of speech. → manner of discourse.

DELICACY The depth of detail in the analysis of linguistic phenomena. Thus an analysis of a sentence which isolates → parts of speech is more delicate than one which simply divides it into → subject and → predicate. → Systemic grammar.

DELIMITATION A graphemic, phonological or grammatical device for signalling the boundary between words or clauses, e.g. by stress or juncture as in *I scream* [ai + 'skriːm] as opposed to *ice cream* ['ais + kriːm]. A feature used for this purpose may be said to have a DEMARCATIVE FUNCTION. Stress has a demarcative function in languages such as Hungarian or Czech where it is fixed in relation to the word boundary. Alternative terms: boundary marking, demarcation.

DEMARCATION → Delimitation.

DEMARCATIVE FUNCTION → Delimitation.

DEMOGRAPHY → Linguistic demography.

DEMONSTRATIVE Words such as *this, that, these, those, some, such,* used to point out or indicate persons or things specifically. If used as → determiners they may be called DEMONSTRATIVE ADJECTIVES, e.g. *That book is mine,* but if used as nominals they may be called DEMONSTRATIVE PRONOUNS, e.g. in *That is right* or *These are they.* (4.1, 4.2, 8.23).

DEMONSTRATIVE ADJECTIVE → Demonstrative.

DEMONSTRATIVE PRONOUN → Demonstrative.

DEMOTIC SCRIPT → Table p. 264. (7.2).

DENASALISATION The process or result of removing or losing → nasalisation.

DENOTATION That aspect of meaning of a particular word or group of words which is based on a clear → reference to a given section of the observable 'external world' and on some kind of conventionalisation, e.g. dictionary definition. Thus the word *girl* denotes something that is 'real' and can be easily related to other concepts such as 'living being', 'female sex', 'age', 'behaviour', etc., although in a particular context there may, of course, be emotive overtones or → connotations beyond the 'original' or 'literal' sense. Alternative terms: designation, cognitive meaning. (5.1).

DENOTATIVE MEANING → Meaning.

DENSITY OF COMMUNICATION The relative frequency of linguistic → contact between individual speakers or speech communities. This notion is useful in determining the boundaries between different → dialects and languages, since different varieties in speech tend to become eliminated with increased density of communication. (7.1, 8.1).

DENTAL A consonant which involves the teeth, normally the upper teeth, as the passive articulators in its → articulation. The tip or apex of the tongue usually acts as the active articulator, in which case the sound may be called → apico-dental, e.g.

61

[ʈ] and [ɖ] as in Spanish *netto* and *de*. If the point of articulation is to the rear of the top teeth almost or partially on the alveolar ridge, the term POST-DENTAL is used. (3.1, 8.22).

DEPALATALISATION The process or result of eliminating → palatalisation.

DEPENDENCE → Dependency.

DEPENDENCY The link between grammatical items of different → rank. Of two constituent items in a construction the one which cannot substitute for the whole construction is said to depend on the other: in the noun phrase *those beautiful houses* the last item is independent as it can stand on its own, the other two are dependent on the noun. Similarly the two morphemes *house* and *-s* may be said to be independent ('free form') and dependent ('bound form') respectively. The dependencies within the above noun phrase may be called unilateral, while those between the noun phrase and verb phrase in the sentence *I love those beautiful houses* may be termed mutual. Together with → cohesion, dependency is a useful criterion in segmenting sentences, clauses and words. → immediate constituent analysis. Alternative term: dependence. (4.1, 4.2, 8.23).

DEPENDENCY GRAMMAR Collective term for a number of semi-algebraic models of syntactic analysis which explain relationships between the elements of a sentence in terms of their mutual → dependency or subordination. In one such theory, proposed by the French linguist L. Tesnière (1893–1954) such syntactic relations are claimed to hold uni-versally and said to rest on the central role of the verb and the way it governs other elements, its 'satellites' (VALENCY). Some of these principles have been applied in → computational linguistics. (8.4 Helbig–Schenkel, 9.4 Hays).

DEPENDENT CLAUSE → Subordinate clause.

DEPENDENT SOUND CHANGE → Sound change.

DEPONENT VERB A term from Latin grammar which refers to verbs which have forms of the passive voice but the meaning of the active voice, e.g. Latin *loquor* 'I speak'.

DERIVATION (*a*) In descriptive linguistics the process or result of forming a word by adding an → affix to a → root. A derivational affix may or may not change the class of a word, e.g. *king—kingdom*, *man—manhood* (all nouns) as opposed to *modern* (adjective)—*modernise* (verb), *slow* (adjective)—*slowly* (adverb), *prison* (noun)—*imprison* (verb), *read* (verb)—*reader* (noun). → word formation. (*b*) In historical linguistics the origin or → etymology of words, e.g. English *foot* is derived from Latin *pedes*. (*c*) In → transformational generative grammar a list of all strings, from initial string to terminal string, showing the application of successive phrase structure or transformation rules. Such a list is said to be the derivation of a sentence. → inflexion. (4.2, 5.1, 6.1).

DERIVATIONAL AFFIX An affix which is used to form a → derivation, e.g. *re-* in *rewrite*, *-ness* in *happiness*, or *-ly* in *quickly*. → word formation.

DERIVATIVE A word consisting of one stem plus an affix. → word formation.

DERIVED FORM A word consisting of one stem plus an affix. → word formation.

DERIVED PHRASE MARKER → Phrase marker.

DERIVED PRIMARY WORD A word consisting of two bound morphemes. → word formation.

DERIVED SECONDARY WORD A word consisting of one stem plus a derivational affix. → word formation.

DERIVED SENTENCE → Transformed sentence.

DESCENDANT LANGUAGE → Family of languages.

DESCENDING DIPHTHONG → Diphthong.

DESCRIPTIVE ADEQUACY → Adequacy.

DESCRIPTIVE GRAMMAR The → grammar of a language based on observed → usage rather than on prescriptive or normative rules. → prescriptive linguistics (*a*).

DESCRIPTIVE LINGUISTICS In the widest sense, any study which observes and analyses the sound features, grammar and vocabulary of a language at a particular point in time. In the narrowest sense, the term 'descriptive linguistics' has been used to refer to the approach of American linguists such as L. Bloomfield (1887–1949) who studied pre-viously unrecorded American Indian languages using techniques of → field-work and a terminology specially suited to the language system under observation. Descriptive linguistics is often opposed to → historical linguistics which looks at the way groups of related languages develop, and to → prescriptive linguistics which attempts to lay down rules for how a language ought to be used. → Structural linguistics. (2.1 Gleason, 2.2 Joos, 2.5 Dixon).

DESIDERATIVE VERB A verb expressing desire to carry out an action. For example, Latin *esurire* 'to be hungry' is a desiderative verb derived from *esse* 'to eat'.

DESIGNATION → Denotation.

DETERIORATION A type of → semantic change in which the meaning of a word assumes unfavourable connotations, e.g. *villain* 'farm-servant' > 'slave' > 'criminal'. → amelioration. Alternative terms: degeneration, pejoration. (5.1).

DETERIORATIVE SUFFIX A suffix which gives a word a deprecative connotation, e.g. *-ish* in *childish*. Alternative term: pejorative suffix.

DETERMINANT (*a*) In → compound words, the element which qualifies the meaning of the base word or → determinatum, e.g. *door* in *doorknob*. (*b*) → Classifier (*b*).

DETERMINATIVE (*a*) A prenominal element such as article or pronoun. → determiner. (*b*) That part of a logographic character which indicates the semantic meaning of the word represented. → radical (*b*).

DETERMINATIVE COM-POUND A compound word one part of which determines or qualifies the other, e.g. *armchair* or *horseshoe*. → determinant (*a*), determinatum.

DETERMINATIVE PRONOUN Alternative name for the traditional demonstrative pronoun or possessive pronoun, i.e. → demonstratives such as *this, that, these, those, other, yours*, etc. which can function as nominals, e.g. *Those are better than ours*. Alternative term: pronominal adjective.

DETERMINATUM In → compound words, the base word which is qualified by the → determinant, e.g. *knob* in *doorknob*.

DETERMINER A word class, members of which function as → adjunct words in a → noun phrase. It may be any of the following types of word: (1) pre-article or noun phrase initiator such as *all, both, half*; (2) article or possessive such as *the, a, an, my, our, your, his, her, their*; (3) demonstrative such as *this, that, these, those*; (4) words such as *more, most, much, neither, some, enough, either, any, each*, which operate in → complementary distribution with articles; (5) numerals such as *one, two, first, second*, etc. Some linguists extend this term to cover modifiers in verbal, adjectival and adverbial phrases, e.g. → modal auxiliaries and → intensifiers. Alternative term: determinative. (4.1, 4.2, 8.23).

DETERMINISM → Relativity.

DEVANAGARI → Table p. 265. (7.2).

DEVELOPMENTAL LINGUISTICS Collective term for the study of → language acquisition in children. A number of different disciplines (psychology, biology, medicine as well as linguistics) contribute to our knowledge of these processes, e.g. the stages of language acquisition (babbling, nursery language, etc.), the order in which items and constructions are acquired, how much in this is instinctive, universal or due to deliberate teaching, what social and intellectual factors promote or hinder development, etc. (9.6).

DEVIANCE Collective term for any utterance which is not in keeping with the accepted grammatical and semantic norms of the standard language.

DEVIANT → Nonsense form.

DEVOICING The loss of → voice in a normally voiced consonant because of certain conditions. In English, for example, the [v] in the word *of* [ɔv], [əv] is devoiced before a voiceless consonant in rapid speech, e.g. *piece of toast* ('piːsəf'toust]. → assimilation.

DIACHRONIC LINGUISTICS An approach to linguistic studies which concentrates on the changes that languages undergo over longer periods of history. There is a long tradition of historical studies, particularly since it was discovered that many European and Asian languages are genetically related (→ Indo-European linguistics). The → synchronic study of language as carried out in the first half of the 20th century was a reaction against the 19th century comparative philology, but today the value of both synchronic and diachronic linguistics is generally recognised. The best developed branch in these studies is DIACHRONIC PHONOLOGY which investigates → sound changes. Alternative term: diachronist(ic) linguistics. (6.1, 6.2).

DIACHRONIC PHONOLOGY
→ Diachronic linguistics.

DIACHRONIST(IC) LIN-GUISTICS → Diachronic linguistics.

DIACRITIC MARK An auxiliary mark or symbol added above, below, or after conventional graphic → signs to give more information about the pronunciation of the sound represented in writing. Such diacritic marks include:

acute accent	′
apostrophe	’
caret	ᴧ
cedilla	˒
diaeresis or umlaut	··
grave accent	ˋ
macron	−
tilde	~
circumflex	ᴧ

→ punctuation. Alternative terms: accent, auxiliary sign, auxiliary mark.

DIAERESIS, DIERESIS A → diacritic mark indicating → umlaut, e.g. *Schönberg*, or separate pronunciation of vowels, e.g. *naïve*. → syneresis. Alternative term: trema.

DIAGRAMMATIC SIGN An abstract picture acting as a → sign of writing, e.g. a mathematical symbol.

DIALECT A regional, temporal or social → variety of a language, differing in pronunciation, grammar and vocabulary from the → standard language, which is in itself a socially favoured dialect. If the variant differs only in pronunciation it is often called ACCENT. Sometimes it is difficult to decide whether a variant constitutes a dialectal subdivision or a different language, since it may be blurred by political boundaries, e.g. between Dutch and some Low German dialects. REGIONAL DIALECTS (or LOCAL or GEOGRAPHICAL or TERRITORIAL DIALECTS) are spoken by the people of a particular geographical area within a speech community, e.g. Cockney in London, but due to the increase in education and mobility they are receding. SOCIAL DIALECTS (or CLASS DIALECTS or SOCIOLECT), on the other hand, are spoken by the members of a particular group or stratum of a speech community. A variety of language used at a particular stage in its historical development, e.g. mid-19th century British English, may be called TEMPORAL DIALECT or ÉTAT DE LANGUE or STATE OF LANGUAGE. → dialectology. (7.1, 8.24).

DIALECT AREA The geographical region covered by a dialectal variant of a language, bounded by → isoglosses on a linguistic atlas delineating differences of → pronunciation, → grammar and → vocabulary.

DIALECT ATLAS → Linguistic atlas.

DIALECT BORROWING The INTERNAL LOAN of an element from one dialect to another.

DIALECT BOUNDARY A number of differences in →

pronunciation, → grammar and → vocabulary in adjacent regions, usually shown on linguistic atlases by bundles of → isoglosses. It is often difficult to distinguish between a dialect boundary and a language boundary, e.g. along national frontiers where dialects of two different languages converge on each other and where there is a low → density of communication. (7.1, 8.1).

DIALECT GEOGRAPHY → Dialectology.

DIALECTALISATION The process whereby a → national language disintegrates into a number of local and regional → dialects, particularly through the lack of standardised educational facilities and mobility. → de-dialectalisation. Alternative term: divergence. (7.1).

DIALECTOLOGY A branch of general → linguistics concerned with the analysis and description of regional, social or temporal varieties of a language, showing how they differ in → pronunciation, → grammar and → vocabulary and how they are geographically distributed. A shift of emphasis has taken place since the first compilation of → linguistic atlases around 1900, from the study of DIALECT GEOGRAPHY to social stratification in language. Earlier work with questionnaires has been supplemented by interview and sample techniques, and dialects are no longer considered as deviant from a national or literary standard, but as language systems in their own right. (7.1, 8.24).

DIALINGUISTICS The study of the relationship between different languages used within one community with a view to determining → bilingualism among its speakers.

DIALOGUE → Monologue.

DIAPHONE Phonemes from different dialects which are phonetically different but phonologically equivalent, e.g. /o/ in British [kɔt] and American [kɑt], *cot*.

DIA-SYSTEM The phenomenon of two systems operating side by side, which may influence the development of the two systems, e.g. the two → phonemic systems of neighbouring dialects.

DICTION In carefully prepared public speaking, the choice of words and clarity of the sounds produced, to achieve a particular effect. → elocution.

DICTIONARY A list of lexical items, e.g. → words, → phrases or → terms, usually in alphabetical order and in book form, giving information about any or all of the following: → pronunciation, → spelling, → etymology, → meaning, → usage, → equivalents in one or more other languages, → part of speech or other grammatical data. Dictionaries may be classified by size and coverage into unabridged, shorter, collegiate, desk, concise and pocket. → lexicography. (5.1, 5.2 Zgusta, 8.25).

DIERESIS → Diaeresis.

DIFFERENTIAL ANALYSIS → Contrastive analysis.

DIFFERENTIAL LINGUISTICS → Contrastive analysis.

DIFFUSE → Compact versus diffuse.

DIFFUSION → Expansion (*b*).

DIGLOSSIA The presence in a language of two standards, a 'high' language used for formal occasions and in written texts, and a 'low' language used in colloquial conversation, e.g. in Swiss German, Greek, Arabic, etc. In certain situations, a MIDDLE LANGUAGE between the high and low standard may be appropriate. → bilingualism, status, intimacy. (Ferguson in 10.1 Fishman, Giglioli, Hymes).

DIGRAPH The combination of two letters representing a single speech sound, e.g. [dʒ] as in *judge*. Also used for a ligature such as [æ] representing the vowel in *man*.

DILATION → Assimilation.

DIMINUTIVE A form of a word, usually made by the addition of a SUFFIX with the meaning 'little' or 'small', e.g. *cigarette* < *cigar*, *rivulet* < *river*, *kitchenette* < *kitchen*. This reference to size is often transferred to a → term of endearment, e.g. English *pussikins* or German *Schätzchen* 'sweetheart'. → augmentative.

DIMINUTIVE SUFFIX → Diminutive.

DING-DONG THEORY → Origin of speech.

DIPHTHONG A vowel sound within a syllable with a perceptible change in its quality during its production. The tongue moves constantly and hence the quality changes constantly in the production of this type of sound, which makes any division into diphthong, suggesting only two sounds, and TRIPHTHONG, suggesting three sounds, an arbitrary distinction, since in theory there is

an infinite number of stages between the beginning and the end of the vowel. Phonetic symbols used to represent diphthongs suggest the beginning and the end of the vowel: e.g. [ei] for the sound in *day* or [ou] for the sound in *go*. The terms RISING or ASCENDING DIPHTHONG and FALLING or DESCENDING DIPHTHONG refer to the position of the most sonorous part of the sound, its 'peak of sonority' or the length of a particular element: in the case of a rising diphthong the most sonorous part occurs after an initial 'glide', e.g. [ŭo] in Italian *scuola* 'school', and in the case of a falling diphthong the most sonorous part occurs first and is followed by a 'glide', e.g. [ei] and [ou] in the English examples above. The terms CENTRING and CLOSING DIPHTHONG are used to refer to a diphthong which ends with a central or neutral vowel, e.g. [iə] in *here* or [ɛə] in *there*. Diphthongs may also be classified into narrow and wide. In a NARROW DIPHTHONG the displacement of the tongue is relatively small, e.g. [ou] in *go*, whereas in a WIDE DIPHTHONG the displacement of the tongue is greater, e.g. [ai] in *my*. → monophthong. (3.1, 8.22).

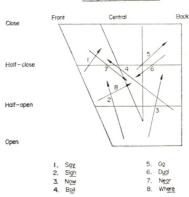

THE ENGLISH DIPHTHONGS

1. Say	5. Go
2. Sigh	6. Dual
3. Now	7. Near
4. Boil	8. Where

67

DIPHTHONGISATION The process whereby a → monophthong becomes a → diphthong.

DIPS A formula used in → glottochronology to determine the degree of lexical relationship between two or more languages:

$$d = \frac{\log c}{2 \log r} \times 0.014,$$

where *d* is dips, *c* the percentage of → cognate words in the languages, and *r* the percentage of cognates retained after 1,000 years of separation. (6.1 Lehmann).

DIRECT CASE Term sometimes used to refer to the → nominative, or to the nominative and → vocative cases, as opposed to → oblique case.

DIRECT DISCOURSE → Direct speech.

DIRECT METHOD A method of foreign language teaching where the aim is the direct association between language and experience in situation without the mediation of the native language. Several types of direct method exist, using conversation and reading rather than traditional → grammar-translation methods. (9.14).

DIRECT OBJECT → Object.

DIRECT QUESTION A question asked in → direct speech, e.g. *Do you really believe that?* → indirect question.

DIRECT SPEECH A quotation of actual speech as opposed to → indirect speech which reports what has been said using different words, word order or verb forms. Direct

speech is usually set off by intonation or punctuation, e.g. *"It was," she said, "as I had expected."* → indirect speech. Alternative term: direct discourse. (4.1, 4.2, 8.23).

DIRECTIVE CONSTRUCTION → Exocentric construction.

DIRECTIVE PARTICLE The initial element in a directive → exocentric construction, e.g. the preposition in the phrase *along the river* or the subordinating conjunction in the phrase *while we have the time.*

DIRECTOR The initial element in an → exocentric construction such as *in the corner, if he comes, saw a ship.*

DISAMBIGUATION The process or result of resolving → ambiguity by intonation, by syntactic analysis, or by meaning in a specific context. (4.1, 5.1, 8.23).

DISCONTINUITY The separation of otherwise continuous elements by the insertion of other elements, e.g. *You are not to tell anyone* becomes *You are not under any circumstances to tell anyone* with the insertion of the phrase *under any circumstances.* Sometimes an insertion can be made for humorous effect, e.g. *abso-bloody-lutely.* When a single morpheme is interrupted in this way the term DISCONTINUOUS CONSTITUENT or DISCONTINUOUS MORPHEME is used, e.g. in German the prefix *ge-* and the suffix *-en* together can form a unit indicating past participle, but they are separated by the stem of the verb in *gesehen*, etc.; the French *ne … pas* is also a unit indicating negation and it too is separated by the verb in *Je ne sais pas* 'I do not know', etc. The term discontinuous morpheme is also used by some linguists, particularly in → immediate constituent analysis, to refer to number, gender and case agreement in inflected languages, e.g. in Latin *puella pulchra* 'a beautiful girl'. (4.1, 5.1, 8.23).

DISCONTINUOUS CONSTITUENTS → Discontinuity.

DISCONTINUOUS MORPHEME → Discontinuity.

DISCOURSE A → text which forms a fairly complete unit. It is usually restricted to the successive utterances of a single speaker conveying a message. → discourse analysis, speech event.

DISCOURSE ANALYSIS The → linguistic analysis of stretches of language longer than a sentence with the aim of finding sequences of utterances with similar environments (equivalence classes) and of establishing regularities in their distribution. (2.3 Harris, 2.5 Cook, 4.1 Elson–Pickett).

DISCOVERY PROCEDURE → Procedure.

DISCRETE UNIT A → segment or → prosodic feature which is relevant in distinguishing meaning.

DISJUNCTION The relationship between structures separated by conjunctions such as *or* and *but* implying a contrast or disassociation, e.g. *They weren't exactly happy, but at least they never quarrelled.* The term disjunctive is used to refer to either the conjunction or the whole clause. → disjunctive pronoun.

DISJUNCTIVE → Epenthetic.

DISJUNCTIVE PRONOUN A personal → pronoun used alone or after a preposition or for particular stress, e.g. French *moi* 'me', *lui* 'him'.

DISPLACED SPEECH The use of words to refer to something which is not physically present, e.g. in the question *When does the train arrive?* → immediate speech.

DISSIMILATION The process or result of two sounds becoming dissimilar owing to the influence of one upon the other. If the change affects adjacent sounds it is called CONTIGUOUS DISSIMILATION (alternative term: JUXTAPOSITIONAL DISSIMILATION), e.g. Latin *anima* > *anma* > Spanish *alma*. If the sounds involved are not adjacent it is called INCONTIGUOUS DISSIMILATION (alternative term: DISTANT DISSIMILATION), e.g. French *marbre* > Middle English *marbel* 'marble' by dissimilation of the second *r* into *l*. If a sound is changed under the influence of a following sound, the term REGRESSIVE DISSIMILATION is used (alternative terms: ANTICIPATORY DISSIMILATION, RETROGRESSIVE DISSIMILATION), e.g. Latin *peregrinus* > French *pélerin* 'pilgrim' when the first *r* is dissimilated to *l*. If a sound influences a sound which follows the term PROGRESSIVE DISSIMILATION is used, e.g. Old High German *himil* 'heaven' (Modern German *Himmel*) comes from an older form *himin*, the second nasal *n* having changed from a nasal to a lateral *l*. → assimilation. (3.1, 6.1).

DISSONANCE A combination of sounds considered unpleasant.

DISTANT ASSIMILATION → Assimilation.

DISTINCTIVE Those features of a linguistic unit are said to be distinctive which help to distinguish it from other units. Thus, voicing has a distinctive function in differentiating the initial sounds of the two words *bin* and *pin* in English, and the difference between the first consonants of the two words is phonemic. → non-distinctive. Alternative terms: functional, contrastive, relevant, significant. (3.1, 8.22).

DISTINCTIVE FEATURE

Any feature which distinguishes one linguistic unit from another. The term is very common in → phonology where phonemes may be defined in terms of distinctive features. Thus [d] and [t] in English are both alveolar stops but are distinguished by the feature of voice which is present in [d] but lacking in [t]. In → Prague School phonology, developed to a large extent by N. Trubetzkoy, phonemes are defined as bundles of distinctive features, e.g. /d/ is *alveolar* + *stop* + *voice*. In the phonological theories of the 1950s, particularly in the work of R. Jakobson and M. Halle, distinctive features are based on acoustic criteria which can be read from a → spectrogram. There are three classes of this type of distinctive feature: (*i*) SONORITY FEATURES including such contrasts as → vocalic *versus* non-vocalic, → consonantal *versus* non-consonantal, → nasal *versus* oral, → compact *versus* diffuse, → abrupt *versus* continuant, → strident *versus* mellow, → checked *versus* unchecked, → voice *versus* voiceless; (*ii*) PROTENSITY FEATURES with the contrast → tense *versus* lax; (*iii*) TONALITY FEATURES with the contrasts → grave *versus* acute, → flat *versus* plain (non-flat), → sharp *versus* non-sharp. In more recent work on generative phonology, particularly by N. Chomsky and M. Halle, these features have been extensively modified and placed into categories such as (1) MAJOR CLASS FEATURES relating to such features as sonorant *versus* non-sonorant, vocalic; (2) CAVITY FEATURES relating to the shape of the oral cavity and the point of articulation with such features as → coronal *versus* non-coronal, anterior *versus* non-anterior, etc.; (3) MANNER OF ARTICULATION FEATURES such as → continuant *versus* non-continuant, → tense *versus* lax; (4) SOURCE FEATURES such as → voice *versus* voiceless, → strident *versus* mellow, and (5) PROSODIC FEATURES such as stress, pitch, etc. (3.3 Jakobson *et al.*, 8.22 Chomsky-Halle).

DISTINGUISHER

In → semantics, a device for separating different meanings of a word by subcategorisation. E.g. the word *bachelor* may be said to have the → semantic components or markers 'animal', 'human', 'male', 'young', etc., but it can be further specified by the distinguishers 'seal when without a mate during the breeding time' or 'having a first academic degree'. (10.3 Fodor–Katz).

DISTRIBUTED versus NON-DISTRIBUTED

Cavity features in recent theories of → distinctive feature phonology. Distributed refers to consonant sounds produced by means of a constriction which extends some length along the vocal tract in the direction of the air flow. Non-distributed refers to consonants produced by means of a constriction extending only a short way along the direction of the air flow. Palatalised dental consonants e.g. are distributed, non-palatised dental consonants are non-distributed.

DISTRIBUTION The number of possible environments or → contexts in which a particular linguistic item such as a speech sound or word can occur in a given language, dialect, or portion of text. → complementary distribution, free variation.

DISTRIBUTIONAL ANALYSIS A method of → linguistic analysis which shows the → distribution of phonological, grammatical or lexical elements within larger sequences, e.g. phonemes in words or words in sentences. The frequency of occurrence of individual items in restricted environments is considered here as important as their functional interrelationships. → functional analysis. Alternative term: distributionalism. (2.3 Harris).

DISTRIBUTIONALISM → Distributional analysis.

DISTRIBUTIONAL NUMERAL A → numeral referring to groups consisting of a certain number of members, e.g. *in twos, by the score, in thousands*.

DISYLLABIC Consisting of two → syllables.

DIVERGENCE → Dialectalisation.

DOMAIN (*a*) → Semantic field. (*b*) In the representation of a sentence by a tree diagram, that part of the diagram over which a particular node is said to dominate. → domination.

DOMINATION In syntactic analysis relationships between elements can be explained by means of tree diagrams. A certain constituent such as a noun may be dependent on or dominated by the node above it,

e.g. a noun phrase, which in turn may be part of, or dominated by, the node above it, e.g. as object in a verbal complex, as represented in the following diagram.

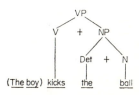

DORSAL A speech sound produced with the dorsum or back of the tongue as the active articulator, e.g. the → dorso-velar stop [k] as in *cool*. (3.1, 8.22).

DORSO-ALVEOLAR A speech sound articulated by the → dorsum region of the tongue touching or approaching the → alveolar ridge, e.g. [s] as in some speakers' pronunciation of *sit*.

DORSO-PALATAL A speech sound articulated by the → dorsum region of the tongue touching or approaching the palate, e.g. [ç] in German *ich* 'I'.

DORSO-UVULAR A speech sound articulated by contact or close approximation between the → uvula and the → dorsum region of the tongue, e.g. [ʀ] in French *rue* 'street'.

DORSO-VELAR A speech sound articulated by the → dorsum region of the tongue touching or approaching the → velum, e.g. [g] as in *gun*.

DORSUM Term used by many phoneticians to mean the part of the tongue behind the blade, i.e. to include front and back. Others use it to refer more specifically to the part of the tongue which lies directly

71

beneath the velum when the speech organs are at rest. → diagram p. 159. (3.1, 8.22).

DOUBLE ARTICULATION

(*a*) The production of a speech sound with two simultaneous strictures of equal importance, e.g. labial-velar stops such as [g͡b], [k͡p] found in some African languages. Double articulation must be distinguished from secondary articulation where one feature of articulation is subordinate to another, e.g. → retroflexion in the case of a retroflexed vowel, i.e. a vowel sound produced with the tip of the tongue curled back towards the palate. (3.1, 8.22).

(*b*) Term used by the French linguist A. Martinet to refer to the double segmentation of the continuum of speech, first into a series of units of grammar or meaning, i.e. → morphemes, or in Martinet's terminology monèmes, which are themselves then capable of division into a series of units of sound, i.e. → phonemes. Double articulation accounts for the special feature of human language that only a very small number of phonemes, usually fewer than 50, are required to form an infinite number of meaningful utterances. → first articulation, second articulation.

DOUBLE-BAR JUNCTURE
→ Juncture.

DOUBLE COMPARISON
The formation of the → comparative and → superlative degrees of adjectives or adverbs by both morphemic and syntactic devices; this is considered ungrammatical in Standard English, e.g. *She couldn't be more unhappier*, or *The most handsomest man. . . .*

DOUBLE CONSONANT →
Duration.

DOUBLE-CROSS JUNCTURE
→ Juncture.

DOUBLE NEGATIVE The
use of two → negatives in the same phrase or sentence. Except when used for a special positive effect, e.g. *it is not unlikely. . .*, it is considered substandard in modern English, e.g. *I haven't seen nothing*, but it is often heard in dialect form. In some languages the syntactic structure requires a double negative where it would not occur in other languages, e.g. Russian *Я никогда не видел его* 'I have never seen him', where both *никогда* 'never' and *не* 'not' are negatives.

DOUBLE VOWEL → Duration.

DOUBLET
A pair of items in a language which are similar in origin, form or meaning. ETYMOLOGICAL DOUBLETS are derived ultimately from the same word, e.g. *wine/vine* or *warden/guard*. Choice between MORPHOLOGICAL or SYNTACTIC DOUBLETS is determined by environment or function in the sentence, e.g. *a/an* or *shall/will*. (4.1, 5.1, 6.1).

DOUBLING → Geminate.

DOWNGRADING The
embedding of a grammatical unit (such as the phrase) within a unit at a lower level or rank of structure (such as the word), e.g. *over-the-counter sale* where the phrase *over the counter* is downgraded to the word level since it has a function which is usually fulfilled by a single word, e.g. *autumn sale* or *bargain sale*, etc.

DOWNWARD COMPARISON
→ Inferior comparison.

DRAMATIC DIALECT The imitation of a regional or social → dialect on the stage, usually by selecting a few typical features of pronunciation, grammar and vocabulary. → eye dialect.

DRIFT Successive changes in the historical development of a particular language with → sound shifts, → borrowing and other modifications, e.g. the loss of final syllables in Germanic languages. → dialectalisation.

DRILL A series of exercises devised for giving practice in, teaching, or testing a → linguistic skill. Drills may be classified by their contents into phonetic drills, grammatical drills and vocabulary drills, or by their arrangement into two-phase drill (single repetition or modification of a stimulus by the student), three-phase drill (stimulus —response by student—correct or 'master' response supplied by model), four-phase drill (stimulus—student response—master response—repetition of correct response by student). Comprehension drills give practice in 'passive' skills such as listening and reading, drills of production or expression give practice in 'active' skills such as speaking and writing. → pattern drill. (9.13, 9.14).

DUAL A grammatical category of → number referring to two items as opposed to → singular (one item) or → plural (more than two items). Ancient Greek, Sanskrit and Old Slavonic all had three number forms, singular, dual and plural. In many modern languages the dual form

tends to be merged with the plural, a change which had already started in Ancient Greek. In most modern European languages, duality is therefore a lexical, not a grammatical feature, i.e. duality is referred to by the use of the lexical item *two* or its equivalent, but it does not involve any special form other than the plural. (4.1, 4.2).

DUALIST THEORY OF MEANING In semantics, an approach to linguistic → meaning which assumes a two-way relationship between a symbol (the spoken or written word) and the object or concept to which it refers, as opposed to a triadic theory of meaning which postulates a three-way link between 'thing', 'symbol' and 'sense' (→ semantic triangle). Alternative term: dyadic theory of meaning. (5.1, 5.2).

DUMMY ELEMENT A grammatical element which is postulated by the linguist in the deep structure to explain the surface structure of a particular utterance, e.g. the 'understood' subject *you* in the imperative sentence *Come and see me tomorrow* or the 'zero' morpheme {ø} in the plural forms *sheep* and *fish*.

DURATION The length of time given to the articulation of a speech sound. Some sounds such as → flaps are essentially momentary, but other types of sounds can vary in their duration, e.g. stops can be held as long as breath can be held, a trill can be prolonged as long as the air stream can be kept moving. Duration is a phonetic concept, but it is exploited phonologically in many languages where it is usually referred to as LENGTH, e.g. German uses the distinction between long and short vowels to distinguish *Rum* 'rum' from *Ruhm* 'glory'. In phonology a distinction must be made between LONG CONSONANTS (or LONG VOWELS) and DOUBLE CONSONANTS (or DOUBLE VOWELS). The duration of a long segment (consonant of vowel) is restricted to a single syllable, e.g. *l* in Italian *bello* 'beautiful' or [i:] in English *bead*, whereas the duration of a double segment (consonant or vowel) extends over two syllables, e.g. *l* in English *wholly*, or [ıı] in one possible pronunciation of English *pitying*. → quantity. (3.1, 8.22).

DURATIVE ASPECT → Aspect.

DVANDVA COMPOUND → Copulative compound.

DYADIC THEORY OF MEANING → Dualist theory of meaning.

DYNAMIC ACCENT → Expiratory accent.

DYSARTHRIA Defective articulation due to abnormality or malfunction in the central nervous system. (9.5).

DYSLALIA Defective speech due to abnormality or malfunction of the external speech organs rather than of the central nervous system. (9.5).

DYSLEXIA Partial inability to read. This complaint, like → alexia, has many associated learning difficulties. (9.5).

DYSPHASIA → Aphasia.

DYSPHONIA A general term for any defect in the phonation of speech sounds. (9.5).

E

ECHO QUESTION A question asking for confirmation of a previous statement, e.g. B in the following: A: *I am going to the library*. B: *To the library?* A: *Yes*.

ECHO WORD → Onomatopoeic word.

ECOLOGY OF LANGUAGE The study, in such fields as → ethnolinguistics, → anthropological linguistics and → sociolinguistics, of the interactions that exist between a language and its environment, i.e. the speech community using it as one of its means of communication. (7.1, 8.1, 8.24, 9.2, 10.1).

ECONOMY (*a*) The reduction of → redundancy in language with the effect of making only those distinctions which are necessary for efficient communication. If certain distinctions are not used to set off linguistic items from one another, they tend to disappear. In → phonology it may be claimed that there are always more → oppositions than → distinctive features. (2.1 Martinet). (*b*) A principle of → linguistic analysis which demands that the regularities in a language be stated in the smallest possible number of rules, e.g. by stating irregular forms first and then summarising all other forms by one general statement. (2.2 Garvin).

EDITING Deliberate rephrasing or re-structuring of material to produce a polished or final version. Even in the spoken language unconscious lapses or blunders are often 'corrected' immediately. Hockett suggests that this latter phenomenon together with others such as → blending and → analogy is an important factor in linguistic change. (2.5 Hockett).

EGRESSIVE A speech sound produced with the air stream moving out of the vocal tract, as is the case in the production of all English speech sounds under normal conditions. → ingressive.

EGRESSIVE AIR-STREAM MECHANISM → Air-stream mechanism.

EGRESSIVE STOP → Stop.

EJECTIVE A speech sound, usually a → stop characterised by closure in the glottis and another stricture above the glottis. Pressure is created by the larynx moving upwards so that on release a glottalic egressive air stream is set in motion. This type of air-stream mechanism is used widely in Caucasian and American Indian languages. Some phoneticians use the term GLOTTALISED STOP for such speech sounds, others restrict glottalised stops to such sounds where the → glottal stop is a secondary feature of articulation, e.g. in French where consonants are often

articulated with a glottal stop such as [pʔ] in *pain* 'bread'.

ELABORATED CODE → Restricted code.

ELECTROMYOGRAPHY The observation and measurement of muscle movement during speech by means of inserting electrodes or applying surface pads to various parts of the → vocal tract. (3.1, 8.22, 9.5).

ELEMENT A constituent part of a whole which can be recognised as a feature in analysis, e.g. the phonemes /d/, /ɔ/ and /g/ are elements of the word *dog*, and the words *he*, *is* and *here* are elements of the sentence *He is here.*

ELEVATION → Amelioration.

ELICITATION A procedure for testing the → acceptability of an utterance by asking native speakers to use or comment on it in an appropriate context. (2.3 Quirk–Svartvik, Samarin).

ELISION The omission of speech sounds between syllables or words in connected speech, usually for ease of pronunciation, as in the phrase *there's*. (See table below.)

	at beginning of word	in middle of word	at end of word
ELISION (omission)	APHESIS PROSIOPESIS	SYNCOPE	APOCOPE
→ INTRUSION (addition)	PROTHESIS	ANAPTYXIS EPENTHESIS	PARAGOGUE

ELLIPSIS The process or result of omitting some part of a word or sentence. The words or parts of words missing are often said to be 'understood' or necessary to make the construction grammatically complete, e.g. in *Is he coming? Yes*, *yes* may be considered as an ellipsis of *Yes, he is coming.*

ELOCUTION A type of speech training which attempts to teach a socially correct → accent for public speaking or regional pronunciation, or a → dramatic dialect for professional acting. Alternative terms: speech improvement, speech education, speech.

EMBEDDED CLAUSE A term used in → transformational-generative grammar to refer to a clause which is built in, i.e. embedded, into the structure of another clause as a result of the application of a transformation rule, e.g. *The girl is sitting by the window* can be embedded into *The girl is my sister* to give *The girl (who is) sitting by the window is my sister*. → parenthetical clause.

EMBEDDING In transformational-generative grammar the process of inserting a → constituent structure into a → matrix structure. (4.1, 4.2, 8.23).

EMIC A term abstracted from such words as *phonemic, morphemic, graphemic*, etc. to mean → distinctive. → etic.

EMOTIVE → Affective.

EMPHASIS High → pitch or heavier → stress or both, given to a word or part of a word to indicate that it has special importance in an utterance.

EMPHATIC PRONOUN A form of the → personal pronoun used for emphasis, e.g. French *moi* in *Moi, je suis français.* → disjunctive pronoun.

EMPHATIC WORD A form expressing emphasis, e.g. the specially stressed auxiliary verb in *He does work hard.*

EMPIRICISM An approach to language which recognises only observable reality, either in terms of restricting → linguistic analysis to the real data in a corpus (→ field-work), or of relating words to the things for which they stand (positivism in philosophical → semantics). (2.2 Garvin).

EMPIRICISTS → Renaissance linguistics.

EMPTY WORD → Function word.

ENCLISIS The joining of one word to another, either in speech or writing, e.g. [ɔlrait] *all right*, sometimes written *alright*.

ENCLITIC A word in an unstressed form attached to another word which carries the stress, e.g. *stop her* [stɔ́pĕ], *piece of* [píːsĕv], or *drinka pinta milka day*. → clitics.

ENCODE To convert a message into → code, e.g. ideas into speech, sound into electric impulses, letters into binary digits.

ENDING → Suffix.

ENDOCENTRIC CONSTRUCTION A construction which functions syntactically in the same way as one of its constituents. Thus, *the three wise men* is an endocentric construction since the whole construction can have the same function as the noun. (→ exocentric construction). There are two major types of endocentric constructions in English: (*i*) CO-ORDINATE endocentric construction, often constructed with *and*, *or*, e.g. in *boys and girls*, *man or woman*, or by apposition, e.g. in *Mister Smith*, *Peter the Great*; (*ii*) ATTRIBUTIVE or SUBORDINATE construction where one constituent, the HEAD or CENTRE, is modified by one or more other constituents, e.g. *green cheese* which consists of the head *cheese* and the attributive modifier *green*, or *incredibly beautiful* which consists of an adjective *beautiful* as the head and the adverb *incredibly* as the modifier. (4.1, 4.2, 8.23).

ENDOPHASIA Subvocal inaudible language, e.g. silent reading. → exophasia. Alternative term: internal speech.

ENGRAM A memory trace of a sound, word or syntactic rule, imprinted and stored in the human brain. The notion of such localised neural correlates of linguistic symbols has been disputed. (5.1 Ogden–Richards, 10.2 Lenneberg).

ENVELOPE → Spectrum.

ENVIRONMENT → Context.

ENVIRONMENTAL CONDITIONING The influence of adjacent sounds on a particular speech sound, e.g. the devoicing of [v] in *fivepence* [faifpəns] is conditioned by the voicelessness of the [p]. → assimilation, dissimilation.

EOSOPHAGEAL CAVITY → Cavity.

EPANALEPSIS The repetition of a word for emphasis, e.g. the obligatory use of a personal pronoun in a question such as French *Votre sœur, comment va-t-elle?* 'How is your sister?', literally 'Your sister, how is she?'.

EPENTHESIS The insertion of one or more sounds or letters into a word, particularly in loan words, to make it conform to the phonological pattern of the borrowing language, e.g. Latin *schola* 'school' > Spanish *escuela* and French *école*; German *Landsknecht* 'mercenary' > French *lansquenet* or Italian *lanzichenecco*; English *sack* > German *Sekt*. → table p. 75.

EPENTHETIC A vowel or consonant inserted into a word to make pronunciation easier. → excrescent. Alternative terms: intrusive, parasitic, disjunctive vowel/consonant.

EPHEMERAL WORD → Nonce-formation.

EPICENE A noun which may refer to a male or female person, e.g. *teacher, driver*. → gender noun.

EPIGLOTTIS A protrusion or tongue situated above the larynx, serving to protect the larynx during swallowing. It does not normally play a part in the formation of any speech sounds. → diagram p. 159. (3.1).

EPIGRAPHY The study of ancient inscriptions on hard surfaces such as stone. → palaeography. (7.2).

EPIPHORA The repetition of final sounds, words or syntactic structures in successive verses or sentences, to achieve a particular stylistic effect, e.g. → rhyme at the ends of lines of verse. (7.3).

EPISTEMOLOGY The study of the origin and organisation of scientific knowledge. In linguistics epistomological questions are linked to the basic problem of having to describe language in terms of language (→ metalanguage). → philosophical semantics, logic in language. (10.3).

EPITHET Alternative term for an → adjective used to qualify a noun in a → noun phrase.

EPONYM The name of a geographical location or institution based on the name of a person, e.g. *Leningrad* or *Washington*.

EQUATIONAL SENTENCE A sentence in which an adjectival or nominal phrase in the predicate is identified with the subject, e.g. *Mr Smith is a policeman*, or *The weather is fine*. The verb used in such a sentence is called an equational verb or → copula. Some languages have special verb forms for the copula, other languages have equational sentences with no copula, e.g. Russian *Эта книга очень интересна* 'This book (is) very interesting'.

EQUATIONAL VERB → Copula.

EQUIVALENT A word or phrase which corresponds to a similar word or phrase in another language, e.g. cognate words *мать* in Russian and *mother* in English, or words with no etymological connection but similar meaning such as German *Autostoppen* and English *hitch-hiking*. → application. Alternative term: analogue. (5.1, 9.3).

EQUIVOCATION The phenomenon of two words being exactly alike in written and spoken form, but having different meanings, e.g. *meal* 'repast' and *meal* 'powdered grain'.

ERGATIVE Name of the grammatical case used to mark the subject of a transitive verb. (4.1, 4.2).

ERROR ANALYSIS In language teaching and testing, a technique of measuring progress by recording and classifying the mistakes made by individual or groups of students. Programmed instruction aims at avoiding the production of errors, although many linguists and psychologists claim that errors are necessary in the gradual acquisition of a language. In foreign language teaching, error analysis can be supplemented by → contrastive analysis to measure the degree of interference between source and target languages. (9.13, 9.14).

ESOPHAGEAL CAVITY → Cavity.

ÉTAT DE LANGUE A temporal → dialect.

ETHNOGRAPHIC LINGUISTICS The study of the physical and cultural environment of a speech community, as pursued by anthropologists like B. Malinowski (1887–1942) and A. L. Kroeber (1876–1960), using the techniques of → field-work to describe the situational contexts of speech acts. (10.1 Hymes).

ETHNO-LINGUISTICS A branch of → anthropological linguistics which studies the relationships between a person's language and his attitudes towards it, especially in terms of the speech levels he uses (degrees of 'intimacy') and the prestige he accords to different levels ('status'). Some ethno-linguists like W. von Humboldt and B. L. Whorf have advocated a principle of linguistic → relativity which claims that each language has its own way of structuring reality for its speakers. (10.1 Hymes).

ETIC A term abstracted from such words as *phonetic, graphetic*, etc. to mean → non-distinctive. → emic.

ETYMOLOGICAL COGNATE → Cognate word.

ETYMOLOGICAL DOUBLET Two or more words in a given language which are derived from the same basic word but are used with different meanings, e.g. *wine/vine*, < Latin *vinum*; *frail/fragile* < Latin *fragilis*. → doublet.

ETYMOLOGY The study of the source and history of words, the changes in their forms and meanings, including → borrowings from other languages. This branch of linguistics had close ties with → lexicology and → semantics, that is the analysis of the vocabulary items of a language and their meanings in different contexts of situation. (5.1, 6.1).

ETYMON A linguistic form from which another is derived, e.g. English *three*, German *drei*, Latin *tres*, Greek *trêis* all come from the Proto-Indo-European **treys* 'three'. → reflex. (5.1, 6.1).

EUPHEMISM The substitution of a non-committal, more pleasant or vague expression for one with unpleasant connotations or less prestige, e.g. *pass away* for *die, sanitary engineer* for *dustman*. → taboo. (5.1).

EUPHONY A combination of sounds which is considered to be pleasant. → cacophony.

EVALUATION PROCEDURE → Procedure.

EVOCATORY The power of a word or phrase to cause an emotional reaction in the hearer or reader by its ameliorative or pejorative → connotations, e.g. *democracy* or *red tape*.

EXCEPTIONS Forms which are not in keeping with the phonological or grammatical norms of a particular language or language family owing to such features as dialectal variation, → analogy or other features not accounted for by → phonetic laws. (6.1).

EXCLAMATION An utterance conveying intensity of emotion, often by means of particular → emphasis, → stress, → pitch, or → intonation, e.g. *Good heavens!*

EXCLAMATION MARK → Punctuation.

EXCLAMATION THEORY → Origin of speech.

EXCLAMATIVE A word or phrase used to introduce an exclamation, e.g. the pronoun *what* and the adverb *how* in the sentences *What a shame! How nice!*

EXCLAMATORY A clause or sentence containing a strongly emphasised opinion, different from the declarative form either in intonation, e.g. *It was a beautiful day!,* or in structure, *What a beautiful day it was!* → exclamative. Alternative term: assertive.

EXCLAMATORY FRAG-MENT → Favourite sentence.

EXCLAMATORY PITCH Exaggerated change of → pitch for special emphasis, e.g. when *are* is stressed with an extra high pitch in *What are you doing?*

EXCLUSIVE PERSONAL PRONOUN → Person.

EXCRESCENT A vowel or consonant added to a word to make pronunciation easier, e.g. German *Sekt* 'champagne' from English *sack.* → epenthetic.

EXHALATION The process or result of breathing out. One exhalation of air is made up of several → chest pulses. Alternative term: expiration. (3.1, 8.22).

EXISTENTIAL SENTENCE A name given by some grammarians to a sentence which expresses or denies the existence of something, e.g. *There is a chair in this room* or *There is no justice in the world.*

EXOCENTRIC CONSTRUC-TION A construction which does not function as a whole in the same way as any of its constituents, e.g. a prepositional phrase such as *on the table* which can function as an adverb, although none of the individual words is an adverb. There are three major types of exocentric construction:

(*i*) DIRECTIVE CONSTRUCTIONS of which the constituents are 'director' and 'axis', e.g. *in the corner, from the window,* etc. where the preposition acts as director and the noun as the axis, or the complement phrases *read a book, saw a ship,* where the verb is the director and the object the axis, or *if he comes, while we have time* where the conjunctions *if* and *while* act as directors and the rest of each clause as axis;

(*ii*) CONNECTIVE CONSTRUCTIONS which consist of a 'connector' or copula and a 'predicative attribute', e.g. *he is tall, he is clever, it grew darker;*

(*iii*) PREDICATIVE CONSTRUCTIONS which consist of a 'topic' and a 'comment', e.g. *he plays well* where *he* is the topic and *plays well* the comment, or *I saw the match* where *I* is the topic and *saw the match* the comment. (4.1, 4.2, 8.23).

EXOLINGUISTICS → Metalinguistics (*b*).

EXOPHASIA Audible vocalisation of language as opposed to subvocal language or → endophasia.

EXPANDED VERB FORM Any verb form which requires the use of an → auxiliary with a main verb, e.g. the emphatic mood in English *He did come after all*; the auxiliary *do* used in a question: *Do you smoke?*; or any → compound tense form *I shall go, he was reading,* etc.

EXPANSION (*a*) The addition of further elements in a sentence without

80

changing its basic structure, e.g. *John has a sister* can be expanded by *little* and/or *beautiful* occurring before *sister*: *John has a beautiful little sister*, or by adding *big* to *John*: *Big John has a sister*, or by adding a negative particle to the verb: *John hasn't a sister*. → modifier (*a*).

(*b*) The linguistic effects of migration and transmission of cultural institutions across language boundaries, in particular → innovation and → borrowing. Alternative term: diffusion (6.1).

(*c*) Widening of meaning. → extension (*a*).

EXPANSION RULE In transformational-generative grammar a rewrite rule which indicates the structure of the element to the left of the arrow, e.g. S → NP + VP which means 'rewrite sentence as nominal phrase plus verbal phrase', i.e. a sentence has the structure nominal phrase plus verbal phrase. → phrase structure rule.

EXPERIMENTAL PHONETICS A general term for phonetic studies which involve the use of mechanical or electronic apparatus such as → tape recorder, → spectrograph or → oscilloscope, for recording, analysing and measuring the properties of speech sounds. → phonetics. Alternative terms: laboratory phonetics, instrumental phonetics. (3.1 Ladefoged, 3.3).

EXPIRATION → Exhalation.

EXPIRATORY ACCENT → Stress conditioned by the relative degree of energy during the production of egressive speech sounds. The variations in energy are heard as variations in loudness. Alternative terms: dynamic accent, intensity accent, stress accent.

EXPLANATORY ADEQUACY → Adequacy.

EXPLETIVE (*a*) A word used as a filler, e.g. *there* or *it* in sentences where the logical subject follows the → copula, as in *There's no food in the larder* or *It is almost certain that the meeting will be called off*. Such expletives usually carry weak stress, except when they are used as adverbials, e.g. *There goes that song again*. Alternative term: floating element. (4.1, 4.2, 8.23). (*b*) Exclamation or oath.

EXPLOSION → Plosion.

EXPLOSIVE → Stop.

EXPONENCE → Systemic grammar, → realisation.

EXPRESSION (*a*) In → linguistic analysis, expression refers to the level of phonological or graphological form in which meaning is represented. Many linguists have stressed the distinction between 'what is meant' (→ content) and 'how it is said' (expression). → glossematics, sign (*b*). (*b*) An utterance which conveys a distinct meaning in a special context, e.g. the word *court* or the phrase *plead guilty* in legal terminology.

EXPRESSIVE FUNCTION The use of language for the purpose of verbalising a person's feelings. → function (*a*).

EXTENDED MEANING → Meaning.

EXTENSION (*a*) The process
or result of widening the meaning of
a word or phrase by an expansion of
the contexts in which it can occur, e.g.
place 'broad way' > 'any location',
dog 'hound of ancient breed' >
'any canine animal'. Alternative
terms: expansion, widening of meaning. (*b*) The term extension is sometimes contrasted with → intension;
the former designates the things to
which a word refers, the latter
designates the features which are
necessary to describe or define the
thing. Extension and intension are
in inverse proportion to one another:
the greater number of things covered
by an expression, the fewer defining
characteristics are necessary. (5.1).

EXTENSIONAL MEANING
→ Meaning.

EXTERNAL MEANING →
Meaning.

EXTINCT LANGUAGE →
Dead language.

EXTRALINGUAL FEATURES
→ Feature.

**EXTRALINGUISTIC FEAT-
URES** → Feature.

EYE DIALECT A written
form suggesting a regional or social
variant of a language, e.g. . . . *an' he
wuz sayin'* . . . Such literary imitations
do not portray speech forms accurately, but select a few features to
convey the register of folk speech. →
dramatic dialect.

F

FACTITIVE VERB A type of
→ transitive verb such as *make,
choose, elect, judge, name,* which may
take two → complements, e.g. *They
elected Mr Miller chairman of the
meeting* where *Mr Miller* is the direct
object or noun complement and
chairman of the meeting is the second
complement.

FACT MOOD Indicative →
mood.

FACULTATIVE VARIANT →
Free variant.

FADING The lowering of →
pitch and the gradual transition into
silence at the end of an utterance.

FADING JUNCTURE →
Juncture.

FALLING DIPHTHONG →
Diphthong.

FALLING JUNCTURE →
Juncture.

FALLING–RISING An →
intonation pattern where the voice
first falls and then rises, e.g. the
word *so* might have such an intonation in the following sequence:

A: *I wanted to tell you that my car
is broken down.*
B: *So?* (in other words: *so what?* or
why are you telling me this?)
A: *Well, I won't be coming to work
tomorrow.*

FAMILIAR FORM A
grammatical form which denotes a

degree of → intimacy between speakers or, occasionally, lack of respect towards the person addressed. French and German, for example, have special familiar forms of second person pronouns *tu* and *du*, as opposed to the → polite forms *vous* and *Sie*. Some languages (e.g. Japanese) have a more fully developed system of indicating relationships between speakers which is manifested more on a grammatical level with different vocabulary and grammatical forms for varying levels of politeness. → honorific form. (4.1, 10.1).

FAMILY OF LANGUAGES A model used by many linguists, although refuted by others, likening relationships between languages to a GENETIC RELATIONSHIP similar to family relationships. In this way a 'linguistic group', i.e. a group of related languages, is called a family of languages, e.g. the → Indo-European family. Based on this model Indo-European may be called the PARENT LANGUAGE of languages such as Latin and Greek, which in turn are called SISTER LANGUAGES. French and Italian are said to be DESCENDANT or DAUGHTER LANGUAGES of Latin. A further development of this model was the → FAMILY TREE developed by a German linguist, A. Schleicher, comparing relations between languages of a linguistic group to the branches of a tree. Alternative terms: language family, linguistic group. (6.1).

FAMILY TERMS → Kinship terms.

FAMILY TREE A model used in → historical linguistics to explain the relationships between the ancestor or parent languages and the descendant or daughter languages within a → family of languages.

FAUCALISATION A secondary feature of articulation producing a 'harsh' quality of sound by restricting the size of the opening in the pharynx.

FAVOURITE SENTENCE A sentence which has all the elements typical of the most frequently used sentence types of a given language, e.g. in English the FULL SENTENCE which contains a subject and a predicate, in that order: *John caught the fish yesterday*. A sentence which does not have all the features of a favourite sentence is a NON-FAVOURITE SENTENCE or MINOR SENTENCE; in English, minor sentences include commands, e.g. *Go away!* vocatives, e.g. *Waiter!* COMPLETIVE FRAGMENTS, e.g. *Tonight* in *When is he coming? Tonight.*, EXCLAMATORY FRAGMENTS, e.g. *Heavens above?* (4.1, 4.2, 8.22).

FEATURE In → linguistic analysis, any 'quality' or 'component part' of an element which may serve as the basis for describing regular patterns. Those aspects of an utterance which are regarded as coming within the central concern of linguistics are called INTRALINGUISTIC FEATURES, e.g. the 'distinctive features' of phonological units or the 'semantic components' of lexical items. Those aspects which are not strictly speaking relevant to language as an act of communication or to linguistics as its study are called EXTRALINGUISTIC or EXTRALINGUAL FEATURES, e.g. certain gestures (→ kinesics), the tone of voice (→ paralinguistics), or even the culturally determined context of the speech situation (→ metalinguistics). Intralinguistic features may be called FORMAL when they help in establishing explicit and internally consistent basic units (→ formal features), and DISTINCTIVE when they help to differentiate them from one another (→ distinctive features). Depending on the level and emphasis of analysis, features may be classed into ACOUSTIC, PHONOLOGICAL (segmental, suprasegmental, prosodic), GRAMMATICAL, SEMANTIC, SECONDARY, etc.

FEEDBACK (*a*) In → phonetics, the processes by which a speaker is consciously aware of his own → speech production, e.g. through the movements of his articulatory organs (KINAESTHETIC FEEDBACK) or through hearing his own voice (AUDITORY FEEDBACK) or through sound vibrations to the inner ear (VIBRATORY FEEDBACK, BONE CONDUCTION). A speaker hears his own voice through a mixture of bone and air conduction, which accounts for the fact that he does not always recognise it when he hears it by air conduction alone, e.g. from a tape recording. (*b*) In communication systems (→ information theory, → language teaching), those signals which are reported back indirectly to the 'input' or source from the 'output' or addressee, thus giving information on the 'efficiency' of the transmission. (3.1, 10.5).

FEMININE   → Gender.

FIELD (*a*) The FIELD OF DISCOURSE or subject-matter of a speech act. → register (*b*). (*b*) The → semantic field formed by lexical items of related meaning.

FIELD OF DISCOURSE → Field (*a*).

FIELD STUDY   → Field-work.

FIELD THEORY The view that sections of the vocabulary are structured into → semantic fields.

FIELD-WORK A method of collecting linguistic data from native → informants. The phonetic, grammatical and lexical features resulting from such surveys may be recorded by using → tape recorders, questionnaires, and/or → phonetic transcription. Alternative term: field study. (2.3 Samarin).

FIGURATIVE LANGUAGE The use of → figures of speech to heighten the effect of a statement or description.

FIGURE OF RHETORIC → Figure of speech.

FIGURE OF SPEECH A device for extending the semantic meaning of a word or a group of words to achieve a particular effect. This is usually done by associating or comparing two things, the so-called 'tenor' or primary term and the 'vehicle' or secondary term, e.g. *She is a devastating dancer* where the dancing and its effect is likened to 'destruction'. About 20 different types of rhetorical figures have been distinguished in → rhetoric and literary studies, the most important being the SIMILE in which something is described by comparison with a concrete image, e.g. *He is as blind as a bat*, and the METAPHOR in which similarity is suggested by transplanting a word into a different context, e.g. *a sea of faces*. Alternative terms: figure of rhetoric, rhetorical figure. (5.1, 7.3).

FILLER CLASS In → tagmemics the list of forms which can occupy a particular slot.

FINAL GLIDE   → Off-glide.

FINITE-STATE GRAMMAR A grammar which can produce a

limited number of sentences. Such a simple grammar is not adequate for dealing with natural languages, since all natural languages can produce an infinite number of sentences. (10.4 Marcus).

FINITE VERB A form of the verb which is limited in time by a → tense and also, in many languages, shows → agreement with person and number, e.g. *went* and *is* in *Yesterday he went fishing, but today he is staying at home.*

FINNO-UGRIAN LINGUISTICS → Ural-Altaic linguistics.

FIRST ARTICULATION The division of reality into discrete units represented by a sequence of sounds, e.g. *chair* 'a seat usually having four legs and a back rest'. → second articulation, double articulation (*b*). (2.1 Martinet).

FIRST INFINITIVE The → infinitive used without the particle *to*, e.g. *he must go.* → second infinitive.

FIRST LANGUAGE → Native language.

FIRST-ORDER LANGUAGE → Object language.

FIRST PERFECT → Perfect tense.

FIRST PERSON → Person.

FIRST POSSESSIVE The possessive forms of the → personal pronouns *my, your, his, her, its, our* and *their*, which are used primarily as determiners, in contrast to the → second possessive forms *mine, yours, his, hers, its, ours, theirs.*

FIRST SOUND SHIFT A series of regular consonant changes which took place in Primitive Germanic within the Indo-European family and which distinguish the Germanic languages from other varieties of Indo-European. The changes which took place are complex and can only be fully exemplified by a detailed comparison of older Germanic and other Indo-European languages, but perhaps the most striking changes were those affecting stop consonants and some of the results of these changes can be seen by comparing English (a Germanic language) and Latin (a non-Germanic but Indo-European language):

[p] > [f]		*pater*	*f*ather
[t] > [θ]		*tenuis*	*th*in
[k] > [x] > [h]	*cord-*	*h*eart

Alternative term: Germanic sound shift. (6.1).

FIRTHIAN LINGUISTICS → British linguistics.

FIXATION An archaic form surviving in the modern language in a stereotyped phrase, e.g. *an* in *If ifs and ans were pots and pans . . .* or *wend* in ". . . *wends his weary way*". Alternative term: fossilised form.

FIXED ACCENT → Stress.

FIXED STRESS → Stress.

FIXED WORD ORDER → Word order which is used to indicate grammatical relationships and which cannot be changed without altering or destroying the meaning of the sentence, e.g. the structure Subject + Verb + Object in the English sentence *The dog bites the man* as opposed to *The man bites the dog.* In non-inflected languages such as English, word order often takes the place of → inflexions in showing grammatical relationships within a sentence. → free word order.

FLAP A speech sound produced when an active articulator such as the tongue or lower lip is in rapid momentary loose contact with a passive articulator, e.g. the dental alveolar /r/ in Japanese or certain 'retroflex' alveolar sounds in a number of Indian languages. Flaps may be said to be intermediate in length of contact between a → stop and a → trill. (3.1).

FLAT versus NON-FLAT or PLAIN One of the oppositions in → distinctive feature phonology based on the analysis of a → spectrogram. 'Flat' indicates a weakening of the high frequency components of the spectrum, 'non-flat' or 'plain' the absence of this feature. In articulatory terms this indicates a narrow mouth orifice with velarisation. Sounds produced with rounded lips have the feature flat, whereas sounds with spread lips have the feature non-flat.

FLECTION → Inflexion.

FLEXION → Inflexion.

FLEXIONAL ENDING → Inflexional suffix.

FLEXIONAL LANGUAGE → Inflected language.

FLOATING ELEMENT → Expletive (a).

FLUENCY A person is said to be a fluent speaker of a language when he can use its structures accu-

rately whilst concentrating on → content rather than → form, using the units and patterns automatically at normal conversational speed when they are needed. (9.11). → articulacy.

FOCAL AREA → Area.

FOLK ETYMOLOGY The replacement of an unknown word by a more familiar one, e.g. *asparagus* by *sparrow-grass*, *Enfant de Castile* by *Elephant and Castle*, *sur-loin* by *sirloin*, etc. Such formations are the result of → analogy and assimilation and often obscure the etymological derivation of words. Alternative terms: popular etymology, associative etymology. (5.1, 6.1).

FOOT (*a*) A unit of → stress pattern used for measuring → verse structure. According to the arrangement of stressed and unstressed or long and short syllables the following basic types of 'metrical' feet can be distinguished:

IAMB	˘ /	e.g.	*To be or not to be* or *Cologne*
TROCHE	/ ˘	e.g.	*Goosy, goosy, gander* or *London*
SPONDE	/ /	e.g.	*Baa, baa, black sheep* or *Hong Kong*
DACTYL	/ ˘ ˘	e.g.	*Wit with his wantonness lasteth death'n bitterness* or *Washington*
ANAPAEST	˘ ˘ /	e.g.	*With a hey and a ho and a hey nonny no* or *Santa Fé.*

(*b*) A phonological unit consisting of a group of stressed and/or unstressed syllables. In a stress-timed language an utterance can be divided into feet each of which, though they may contain a different number of syllables, takes approximately the same amount of time to pronounce, e.g. *he saw/a black/bird* (i.e. the bird was black) or *he saw a/blackbird* (i.e. the species was blackbird). (3.1, 7.3, 8.22).

FOREIGN LANGUAGE Any language other than the → native language or mother tongue. A foreign language is usually learned not by interaction with others in childhood, but by formal → language teaching. Alternative terms: second language, secondary language. (9.11, 9.13).

FOREIGNISM → Alienism.

FORLORN ELEMENT → Suppletive.

FORM The shape or appearance of a linguistic unit. The form of a word often indicates its morphological and/or its syntactical relationship with other words, e.g. in the form *tables* the *s* denotes plural. Lexical and grammatical forms are said to be represented by → phonemes or → graphemes. → substance, systemic grammar, formal. Alternative term: linguistic form.

FORM CLASS A group of linguistic forms which are considered to be members of a single category, either because they have phonetic or morphological similarities, e.g. *-ing* forms such as *walking*, *sitting*, *living*, etc., or because they can occur in the same linguistic environment, which is sometimes termed sharing the same 'privilege of occurrence', e.g. the three items *John*, *He*, *The boy in the blue suit* can all occur in the slot or frame...*can swim*, and therefore can be said to belong to the same class. Alternative term: constituent class.

FORM WORD → Function word.

FORMAL Those criteria or features of language which can be used in → linguistic analysis as a basis for setting up certain categories and units such as word shapes (→ morpheme), sound patterns and word order. Linguists contrast formal features either with semantic features (in which case form is in opposition to 'meaning') or with the phonetic or graphic medium by which they are expressed (in which case form is in opposition to 'substance'). In either case the aim is greater explicitness or → formalisation. (2.1 Lyons).

FORMAL GRAMMAR A set of rules describing a language, based on observable features of linguistic behaviour and formulated in such a way that each → rule automatically defines its place in the whole system. → grammar. (4.2 Gross–Lentin).

FORMAL ITEM → Item.

FORMAL SPEECH A deliberate style of speech. → manner of discourse.

FORMAL UNIVERSAL → Universal.

FORMALISATION A type of → linguistic analysis which aims at making formal relationships in language as explicit as possible by describing them in terms of general → rules. An example of this approach is → generative grammar.

FORMANT (*a*) Term used in acoustic phonetics to indicate a frequency band which is shown on a → spectrogram to be reinforced. The areas of reinforcement which differ from one sound to another are due to resonance in the vocal tract. All vowel sounds have a fundamental tone and at least two frequency bands where the sound is intensified, i.e. they have two formants. Earlier it was considered that one area of intensity was due to resonance in the throat and another to resonance in the mouth, and the terms 'mouth formant' and 'throat formant' are still used by some phoneticians although the idea of the resonance being attributed to individual cavities has been rejected. On a spectrogram the formants show up as dark bands in a horizontal direction on a line → spectrum they are seen as peaks of amplitude at a given frequency (see diagram p. 214). Alternative term: acoustic formant. (3.1–3.3, 8.22). (*b*) → formative (*a*).

FORMATIVE (*a*) Collective term for → bound morphemes which are used either to form stems, e.g. *fif-* in *fifth*, or as inflexional or derivational affixes, e.g. *un-* and *-y* in *unlucky*. Alternative term: formant. (*b*) In → transformational-generative grammar the elements in a → terminal string which are the minimal units functioning in the syntax of the string. (4.1, 4.2, 8.23).

FORMLESS LANGUAGE (*a*) A type of speech or dialect considered to be lacking in grammatical precision. Linguists, however, would regard this idea as a contradiction in terms since all languages, → standard as well as dialect, possess a well-ordered morphological and syntactic structure. (*b*) → isolating language.

FORMULAE Sets of symbols used to express certain relationships between languages or linguistic units, e.g. PIE p t k k^w > P Gmc f θ x x^w is an abbreviated statement about the transition of Proto-Indo-European → stops to Proto-Germanic → fricatives.

FORMULAIC LANGUAGE → Special language.

FORTIS A consonant produced with strong muscular tension, as opposed to → lenis which is a consonant produced with weak muscular tension in the articulatory organs. In English voiceless consonants are usually aspirated and fortis, whereas voiced consonants are usually unaspirated and lenis. (3.1, 8.22).

FOSSILISED FORM → Fixation.

FOURIER ANALYSIS A mathematical formula for analysing a complex wave form into its constituent simple wave forms. → sound wave.

FRAME (*a*) → Substitution frame. (*b*) In → programmed instruction, one of a sequence of items in the teaching programme, which may be a statement or question with alternative answers, a picture, an audio stimulus, etc.

FREE ALTERNANT → Free variant.

FREE FORM → Free morpheme.

FREE MORPHEME A morpheme which can be used on its own as a word with a distinct meaning, e.g. *table*, *quick*, *pen*, as opposed to a → bound morpheme such as *-ly* in *quickly* or *s* in *tables*. Alternative term: free form. (4.1, 8.23).

FREE SENTENCE A syntactic structure which does not need additional context to be meaningful, e.g. *Mount Everest is the highest mountain in the world.* → bound sentence.

FREE STRESS → Stress.

FREE SYLLABLE A → syllable ending in a vowel. Alternative term: open syllable.

FREE TRANSLATION → Translation.

FREE VARIANT One of a number of forms which can function in → free variation, e.g. the alternative pronunciation of *room* as [rʊm] or [ruːm]. Alternative terms: free alternant, facultative variant, optional variant, non-functional variant, non-contrastive variant, individual variant.

FREE VARIATION Two or more linguistic elements are said to be in free variation when they occur non-distinctively in the same environment. For example, the word *either* may be pronounced as [aiðə] or [iːðə] without affecting its meaning. → free variant. Alternative term: non-functional variation.

FREE VOWEL A vowel sound in an → open syllable.

FREE WORD ORDER → Word order which, although not completely free in the literal sense, is not used to signal grammatical relationships and which can be varied without necessarily destroying

or changing the meaning, particularly in inflected languages where structures are sufficiently marked by endings, e.g. in Latin. → fixed word order.

FREQUENCY (*a*) The number of times a linguistic item such as word, syllable or phoneme occurs in a portion of text or recording. Statistical counts of WORD FREQUENCY (→ computational linguistics) may help to assess characteristics of authorship and style or the vocabulary of a → special language, or to select a minimum vocabulary for language teaching. → Zipf's Law. (*b*) A term used in acoustic phonetics for the number of vibrations per second of sound waves (measured in cycles per second). → Pitch rises as frequency increases. (3.1, 3.2, 8.22).

FREQUENCY ANALYSIS The analysis of the frequency of occurrence of linguistic elements in a corpus, e.g. by a → frequency count of the words in a text.

FREQUENCY COUNT A numerical procedure employed by researchers in linguistic and literary studies to determine the number of occurrences of single structural elements of language material, e.g. sounds, words or sentences in recordings or texts. The total → corpus must contain a fairly large number of items covering all possible contexts to yield statistically reliable results. (9.4, 10.4).

FREQUENTATIVE ASPECT → Aspect.

FREQUENTATIVE VERB A → verb form denoting an habitual or repeated action, e.g. the Russian

89

verbs of motion of the type *ходить*, 'to go', *ездить* 'to drive', *носить* 'to carry', as opposed to verbs such as *идти*, *ехать*, *нести* which can only refer to a single movement in a definite direction. (4.1, 8.5).

FRICATIVE A speech sound which is produced as a continuous sound by forcing the air through a partially obstructed vocal tract in such a way that the friction is audible with or without voice. Fricatives include all the non-nasal, non-lateral open consonants and are more numerous in type than any other consonant. They may be classified in various ways, including the location of the point of articulation as follows: bilabial [β] as in Spanish *lobo* 'wolf'; labiodental [f] as in *fan* or [v] as in *van*; dental or interdental [θ] as in *thin* or [ð] as in *this*; alveolar [s] as in English *some* or [ɹ] as used by some speakers of English in *drive*; palatal [ç] as in German *ich* 'I'; velar [x] as in German *Buch* 'book' or [ɣ] as in Dutch *groot* 'big'; pharyngeal [ħ] as in Arabic *Ahmed*; laryngeal [ɦ] as in Dutch *hoek* 'corner' pronounced with rather more audible friction than [h] in English *hook*. Alternative terms: spirant, close approximant. (3.1, 8.22).

FRICTION Sound production as a result of air stream passing through a stricture in the → vocal tract. Audible friction is produced in the glottis during whispering, whilst friction which occurs above the glottis is referred to as SUPRAGLOTTAL FRICTION. A distinction is also made between CAVITY FRICTION when there is voiceless resonance of a whole cavity as the air passes through it, e.g. in the pronunciation of the English [h] in *hand*, and LOCAL FRICTION

produced by the action of an articulator at a specific point in the vocal tract, e.g. the fricative [f] in *fan* with the lower teeth on the upper lip or [s] in *sit* with the tongue approaching the alveolar ridge. (3.1, 8.22).

FRICTIONLESS CONTINUANT A → continuant produced with minimal audible friction, i.e. with unobstructed passage for the air along a central channel. All vowels fall into this category (including so-called semi-vowels such as [r] and [w]) and some consonants such as [h] in *hook*. Some linguists prefer the term OPEN APPROXIMANT to refer to these sounds, referring to the fact that they are produced with open approximation of the articulators.

FRONT MUTATION → Vowel mutation.

FRONT VOWEL A vowel sound produced with the highest part of the tongue towards the front of the mouth, e.g. [æ] in *bad*. → back vowel. Alternative terms: slender vowel, bright vowel.

FRONTAL A speech sound, articulated by the front of the tongue touching or approaching a passive articulator, e.g. [ts] in German *zu* 'to'.

FRONTING (*a*) A → sound change which results in a vowel sound being articulated in the front of the mouth, e.g. [u]>[y]. (*b*) Environmentally conditioned allophones may be fronted, i.e. produced further forward in the mouth. The [k] in *keen* is articulated further to the front of the velum than that in *calm*. (3.1, 6.1, 8.22).

FROZEN SPEECH An extremely formal → manner of discourse.

FULL SENTENCE → Favourite sentence.

FULL STOP → Punctuation.

FULL VERB A → verb form expressing the main 'action' of the sentence, as opposed to an → auxiliary verb. In English, full verbs combine with auxiliaries to form verb phrases like *have been going*, *will have gone*, *was about to go*, etc., in which the full verbs carry the lexical meaning and the auxiliaries perform syntactic functions. Alternative terms: main verb, principal verb.

FULL WORD → Content word.

FUNCTION (*a*) The use of language for a particular purpose, e.g. to portray a situation (REPRESENTATIONAL FUNCTION), to convey information between speaker and hearer (COMMUNICATIVE FUNCTION), to make the hearer respond (APPELLATIVE FUNCTION), to verbalise feelings (EXPRESSIVE FUNCTION) or intellectual reasoning (COGNITIVE FUNCTION). (*b*) The role played by an element within an utterance and its structural relationship to other elements. Thus the phonological elements /p/, /i/, and /n/ may be said to make up the function *pin*, and each has a part in making it a complete unit. In grammar the term function refers to the role that a particular word plays in a larger syntactic unit, e.g. a noun 'acting' as subject or object in a sentence. Certain categories of such word classes, e.g. tense and

number of verbs, may also be referred to as function.

FUNCTION WORD A word which does not carry a full lexical meaning, but rather a grammatical or functional significance, e.g. words like *the, for, since, to*, etc. which are used to indicate relationship or function of other words as opposed to → content words which have lexical meaning, e.g. *paper, stool, telephone*, etc. Function words are usually uninflected in form. Alternative terms: grammatical word, closed-class word, form word, empty word, structural word. (4.1, 4.2, 8.23).

FUNCTIONAL → Distinctive.

FUNCTIONAL ANALYSIS A type of → linguistic analysis which is based on → function rather than → form. Most contemporary linguistics since the → Prague School is 'functional' in that it looks at the structural relations of units of speech within larger stretches of which they are a part. The linguist establishes basic elements and shows how they combine into environments of a higher rank, e.g. phonemes into syllables, syllables into morphemes, morphemes into words, words into phrases, phrases into sentences, etc. Functional analysis attempts to indicate the role which a constituent plays in an utterance, e.g. a noun phrase 'functioning' as 'subject' or 'actor' in a sentence. (2.1 Martinet, 2.2 Hamp, 2.5 Vachek).

FUNCTIONAL CHANGE (*a*) → Phonemic sound change. (*b*) The use of the same form in different syntactic functions, e.g. *in* in *in the house, the 'in' fashion, the in's and out's of the problem*. Alternative terms: transmutation, conversion.

FUNCTIONAL LINGUISTICS
A type of → linguistic analysis which stresses functional relationships (→ function), e.g. the work of several scholars on the Continent associated with the → Prague School and → glossematics. (2.1 Martinet, 2.5 Hjelmslev, Vachek).

FUNCTIONAL LOAD
The extent to which a linguistic contrast is exploited. → functional yield.

FUNCTIONAL MEANING
→ Meaning.

FUNCTIONAL YIELD
A measure of the use a particular language makes of phonemic → oppositions. In English, for example, the opposition /t/ : /d/ has a high functional yield, i.e. there are many pairs of words in which this distinction plays a part, e.g. *tin/din, bad/bat, at/add, latter/ladder*; on the other hand, the opposition /θ/ : /ð/ has a low functional yield, i.e. there are only a few words in which this distinction plays a part, e.g. *ether/ either*. (2.1 Martinet).

FUNCTOR
Collective term for → bound morpheme and → function word.

FUNDAMENTAL FREQUENCY
The greatest common divisor of the component → frequencies of a sound wave, in other words the frequency of repetition of a complex wave.

FUSED COMPOUND
→ Primary compound.

FUSING LANGUAGE
→ Inflected language.

FUSION
The close merging of linguistic elements, e.g. of speech sounds (→ crasis); of morphemes (*strong + th > strength*); or of words (*player-manager*, 'member of a football team and at the same time its manager'). → blend. Alternative term: coalescence. (3.1, 4.1, 5.1, 6.1).

FUSIONAL LANGUAGE
→ Inflected language.

FUTHORK
A name given to the runic alphabet which was devised from Latin and Greek letters adapted for easy carving on wood or stone. → table, p. 265.

FUTURE IN THE PAST
→ Conditional tense.

FUTURE PERFECT IN THE PAST
→ Conditional perfect tense.

FUTURE PERFECT TENSE
Traditional term for the verb form occurring as *will have + past participle* in English, e.g. *I will have read*. This kind of time reference is now usually considered as a type of → aspect rather than → tense, since it refers more to the type and state of the action, e.g. that it will be completed, than to its location in time. Alternative term: second future.

FUTURE TENSE
A → tense form of a verb referring to an action which will take place at some future point in time. In some languages the future tense may be expressed by a special verb form, e.g. French *je donnerai* 'I shall give'. In English the future is a compound tense formed with the help of auxiliaries, e.g. in *He will go* or *They will be leaving tomorrow* and has more in common with the category → mood than tense and in any case does not always imply futurity, cf. *This*

material will wash or *He will be home by now.* Note, also, that futurity is not always expressed by the 'future tense', e.g. English *I am going home tomorrow.* Alternative term: present future.

G

GEMINATE A geminate can be defined phonetically as a sequence of identical articulations. On the phonological level, i.e. with reference to specific languages, it usually refers to the lengthening of consonants, e.g. Italian *donna* 'woman' which has a long [nː]. If the geminate is a stop consonant, e.g. [t] Italian *brutto* 'ugly', the period of complete closure before the release is lengthened. The term DOUBLING is sometimes used to refer to this phenomenon, but note that in some orthographies doubling a consonant in writing may have nothing to do with the pronunciation of the consonant in speech: compare, e.g. English *hope* and *hopping*. (3.1).

GENDER A grammatical category based on the forms of nouns, pronouns, adjectives and articles. The traditional names for GRAMMATICAL GENDERS: MASCULINE, FEMININE and NEUTER are misleading since in many languages they are grammatical categories which do not often coincide with NATURAL GENDER, a biological rather than a linguistic classification. Languages vary in the number of gender distinctions made and the importance attached to these distinctions. French has two genders:

masculine, e.g. *le livre* 'the book', and feminine, e.g. *la table* 'the table'; German has three: masculine, e.g. *der Tisch* 'the table', feminine, e.g. *die Hand* 'the hand' and neuter, e.g. *das Mädchen* 'the girl'. As can be seen from the examples above the gender is shown in French and German by means of the form of the article, whereas the form of the noun itself gives no certain indication of its gender. In other languages, e.g. Russian and Latin, gender distinctions are based on the forms of the nouns themselves. Apart from the three mentioned above other gender classifications include: COMMON GENDER, replacing masculine and feminine in its opposition to neuter in Danish and Dutch, and a binary system of ANIMATE as opposed to INANIMATE found in some American Indian languages. Grammatical gender does not play an important role in English grammar although pronominal distinctions are made, usually on the basis of natural gender, between *he, she* and *it.* Note, however, that even in English the use of these pronouns does not always coincide with natural gender, e.g. *a car, ship* or *aeroplane* may be referred to as *she, a baby* or *an animal* may be referred to as *it.* Natural gender occasionally plays a role in the form of nouns, cf. *actor : actress* → epicine nouns but many can apply to both sexes. (4.1, 4.2).

GENDER NOUN A noun which follows natural → gender, e.g. *waitress* (as opposed to *waiter*).

GENEALOGICAL CLASSIFICATION The → classification of languages according to their genetic relationships into families. Alternative term: genetic classification.

GENERAL GRAMMAR → Universal grammar.

GENERAL LINGUISTICS A collective name given to those branches of linguistic study which provide the basic concepts, theories, models and methods. General linguistics usually comprises the principles of analysis and description in → phonology, → grammar and → vocabulary studies as well as graphemic, historical and comparative studies, and dialectology. → applied linguistics. Alternative term: theoretical linguistics. (2.1–7.3).

GENERAL SEMANTICS A philosophical doctrine of → meaning in language communication, rejecting the Aristotelian view that words have only one lexical meaning. (2.1 Hayakawa).

GENERALISED TRANS-FORMATION In transformational generative grammar a → transformation rule which operates on two strings at once, joining them, embedding them, etc. Thus a generalised transformation rule would enable *The book on the table is mine* to be derived from *The book is mine* and *The book is on the table.*

GENERATION The specification of new utterances, e.g. sentences, from a limited inventory of linguistic items, by applying a series of grammatical → rules. The linguist tries to account for the 'intuitive' behaviour of the native speaker by devising analytic models of these processes. → generative grammar.

GENERATIVE GRAMMAR A series of explicit → rules assigning structural descriptions to stretches of language or speech and identifying such stretches as properly formed or grammatical sentences of a given language. An ideal generative grammar will generate all and only the grammatical sentences of a given language. → transformational-generative grammar. (2.1 Chomsky, 4.2 Lakoff, 8.23 Langendoen).

GENERATIVE PHONOLOGY → Phonology.

GENERATIVE SEMANTICS → Semantics.

GENERIC TERM A word which denotes a whole range of members of a given subclass, e.g. *furniture* is a generic term for *chair, table, settee, couch,* etc.

GENEROUS PLURAL The addition of a second plural marker to a word which is already plural, e.g. the Southern American English *you-all.*

GENETIC CLASSIFICATION → Genealogical classification.

GENETIC RELATIONSHIP → Family of languages.

GENEVA SCHOOL → Saussurean linguistics.

GENITIVE A → case form in some inflected languages indicating such relationships as possession or source, e.g. Latin *regis copiae* 'the king's troops'; German *Das Buch der Lieder* 'the book of songs'. Prepositions may also govern the genitive, e.g. Russian *от начала до конца* 'from beginning to end'. Some languages use the genitive for certain adverbial constructions, e.g. Russian *первого мая* 'on the first of May'. In English the 'genitive' relationship is usually expressed by

94

means of the preposition *of*, e.g. *the blue of the sky* or by the possessive *'s*, e.g. *Shakespeare's works.* Note, however, that the preposition *of* in English is followed by a pronoun which at any rate historically speaking is genitive, e.g. *He is a friend of mine.* The 'genitive' notion is still there if *'s* is used with a noun after *of*: *He is a friend of John's.*

GEOGRAPHICAL CLASSIFICATION The → classification of languages according to their geographical location, e.g. the languages of the Balkans. → areal linguistics. Alternative term: areal classification. (6.1, 7.1, 8.1).

GEOGRAPHICAL DIALECT A regional → dialect.

GEOGRAPHICAL LINGUISTICS The study of the regional distribution of dialects (→ dialectology) and/or of languages (→ areal linguistics). (6.1, 7.1, 8.1).

GERMANIC LINGUISTICS Collective term for the linguistic description of Germanic languages such as German, English, Dutch, Swedish, etc. → Appendix 1 p. 268. (6.1, 8.2, 8.4, 8.7 Haugen–Markey).

GERMANIC SOUND SHIFT → First sound shift.

GERUND (*a*) A → verbal noun in Latin formed with the suffix *-andum* or *-endum*, often used after prepositions or in the genitive or dative to modify another noun, e.g. *Ad bene vivendum breve tempus satis est longum*, 'For living well a short time is long enough' (Cicero) or *ars vivendi* 'the art of living'. (*b*) A linguistic form in a language other than

Latin which is felt to be analogous with the Latin gerund, e.g. the *-ing* form of the verb in English, such as *living* in the translations in (*a*) above. → present participle. (4.1, 4.2, 8.23).

GERUNDIAL CLAUSE An absolute → participial phrase, e.g. *Weather permitting, we shall have a picnic.* → absolute phrase.

GERUNDIVE A word having characteristics of both verb and adjective. This word class is not usually distinguished in English, but is traditionally described in Latin grammars as a verbal adjective, e.g. *amandus, –a, –um*, 'worthy or fitting to be loved', i.e. 'lovable'.

GESTURE A form of communication by movement of parts of the body, e.g. a nod of the head or a wave of the hand. Gestures are usually connected with, but not essentially part of, language. → kinesics. (2.3 Birdwhistell).

GHOST FORM A word originally coined in error by a scribe or lexicographer or by misinterpretation of a word heard in a foreign language. Alternative terms: ghost word, phantom word, vox nihili. (5.1, 6.1).

GHOST WORD → Ghost form.

GINGIVAL → Alveolar.

GLAGOLITIC ALPHABET → Table p. 265.

GLIDE (*a*) Alternative term for → semi-vowel. (*b*) The adventitious production of an intermediate sound when the speech organs pass from the position of one speech sound to the position of another, e.g. [j] in one possible pronunciation of *the ice* [ǒi'jɑis]. Alternative term: transitional sound.

GLOSS A word used to circumscribe another word, e.g. the English 'four' is used to refer to, translate, explain or identify the German word *vier*. (5.1, 6.1).

GLOSSARY A → dictionary with definitions of the terms used in a special field, e.g. the vocabulary of swimming or of nuclear physics.

GLOSSEMATICS A type of linguistic analysis based on the work of the Danish linguist L. Hjelmslev (1899–1965). Like many other scholars following F. de Saussure he insisted that language must be considered as a self-contained system at a particular time rather than an amalgam of philological facts (→ historical linguistics). Thus linguistics was an 'immanent' discipline independent of other sciences, with its own methodological and terminological apparatus. Starting with complete texts, the linguist must analyse utterances in terms of the → paradigmatic and syntagmatic relationships between constituent elements and within a framework of form (internal grammatical relations), substance (external categories of material objects), expression (verbal or graphic medium) and content (significance or meaning). This analytic and semi-algebraic procedure is intended to yield the basic invariant unit GLOSSEME. → function (*b*). Alternative terms: Copenhagen School, Neo-Saussurean linguistics. (2.5 Hjelmslev).

GLOSSEME The basic unit established in the → linguistic analysis of several different schools. →

morpheme, taxeme. (2.4 Bloomfield; 2.5 Hjelmslev).

GLOSSOGRAM → Palatogram.

GLOSSOLALIA Collective term for a number of different kinds of 'speaking in tongues', used by certain members of some tribal societies and religious sects for magical or spiritual effects. The utterances which are often produced in conditions of trance are within the conventions of the sound system of the language(s) known by the speaker, but usually unintelligible to the audience. (10.1 Burling).

GLOSSOLOGY Obsolete term for → linguistics, or → semantics.

GLOTTAL → Laryngeal.

GLOTTAL CATCH → Glottal stop.

GLOTTAL STOP A closure of the → glottis followed by its sudden release. It occurs in English when a speaker pronounces the words *there are* in such a way as to separate them distinctly as in RP with no linking [r], or in such dialect forms as Cockney ['wɔːʔə] for *water*. A glottal stop may also occur in English as a reinforcement of another stop, particularly in final position, e.g. [kʌpʔ] *cup*. In some languages such as Danish, the glottal stop is phonemically distinctive, e.g. *anden* ['anʔən] 'the duck' in contrast to *anden* ['anən] 'other'. Alternative term: glottal catch. (3.1, 8.22).

GLOTTALIC AIR-STREAM MECHANISM → Air-stream mechanism.

96

GLOTTALIC CLOSURE → Closure.

GLOTTALISATION The articulation of a → glottal stop as a secondary feature of a speech sound, e.g. as reinforcement of other stops, particularly at the end of a word in some English pronunciations, e.g. [wɔʔt] *what*, [gɒʔt] *got*.

GLOTTALISED Pronounced with a → glottal stop. Alternative term: constricted.

GLOTTIS The gap between the vocal cords in the → larynx. The glottis may be in one of four 'states', (1) open, i.e. BREATH STATE as for normal breathing, (2) vibrating, i.e. VOICE STATE as during the production of voiced sounds, (3) narrowed, i.e. WHISPER STATE as during whispering, (4) CLOSED STATE sealing off the top of the trachea and preventing the escape of air from the lungs. → diagram p. 159.

GLOTTOCHRONOLOGY Lexicostatistical techniques to establish mutual family relationships between languages; several mathematical formulae have been worked out based on → cognate basic vocabulary items, e.g. for the degree of lexical relationship (→ dips) and for the number of years two related languages have been separated (→ time depth). (6.1 Lehmann, 10.1 Hymes).

GLOTTOGONIC LINGUISTICS Those branches of linguistic studies which are concerned with the question of when, where and how human speech developed. Various theories have been proposed by philosophers, linguists and others, e.g. on whether language originated in one or in several places (→ monogenesis, polygenesis theory), or what form of social, anatomical, etc. processes were responsible for the → origin of speech. (2.3 Haas).

GLOTTOLOGY Obsolete term for → linguistics.

GLOTTOPOLITICS The study of how a national → standard language is promoted by various decision-making bodies in a culturally and linguistically diverse country. → institutional linguistics. Alternative term: institutional linguistics. (2.1 Hall; 10.1 Fishman).

GNOMIC PRESENT TENSE A present tense denoting a continuous or habitually repeated action, not emphasising the temporal concept, e.g. *Birds fly.*

GOAL A term used to describe the direct object in an active sentence. In *The boy caught the ball, the ball* is the direct object and the 'goal' of the action of the verb. In a passive sentence the goal is the subject, e.g. *The ball was caught by the boy* where *the ball* is the subject and *the boy* the → agent. → voice, actor–action–goal.

GOTHIC ALPHABET → Table p. 265.

GOVERNMENT The determination of the morphological form of one word by another word. Prepositions are said to govern nouns, e.g. *to the town, under the bridge*, and in inflected languages they determine the case and hence the inflexion of different nouns, e.g. Latin *ad astra* 'to the stars', *cum laude* 'with distinction', etc. Other forms of government include the subject determining the person and number of the verb, or a transitive verb governing a direct object. → agreement. Alternative term: rection. (4.1, 4.2, 8.23).

GRADATION → Vowel gradation.

GRADED AREA → Area.

GRADING Arranging a limited inventory of language items into a convenient order for the purpose of teaching them. This usually involves some STAGING, i.e. the division of the course into periods of time (lessons), SEQUENCING, i.e. the ordering of the teaching items into successive sections, and LIMITATION of teaching items (vocabulary) to a useful minimum. (9.11 Mackey).

GRAMMAR In its widest sense, the term grammar refers to generalised statements of the regularities and irregularities found in language. For the Greeks, grammar was a branch of philosophy concerned with the 'art of writing'. By the Middle Ages grammar had come to be regarded as a set of rules, usually in the form of a textbook, dictating 'correct' usage. TRADITIONAL GRAMMAR was PRESCRIPTIVE, i.e. it attempted to provide universally valid rules to show how a language ought to be spoken or written. Today most linguists agree that grammar should be DESCRIPTIVE, i.e. it should record actual usage and formulate the rules whereby sentences are generated and understood; in this way grammar becomes a valuable instrument in improving a learner's performance in either his native language or a foreign language. Grammars designed specifically for teaching purposes are often referred to as PEDAGOGICAL GRAMMARS, while

grammars investigating language in general or a specific language may be called SCIENTIFIC GRAMMARS. Grammars may be SYNCHRONIC, i.e. describing the language of a particular period, or DIACHRONIC, i.e. describing the development of a language, or COMPARATIVE, i.e. comparing and contrasting two or more different languages. A grammatical description which is based entirely on the observable forms of a language may be called FORMAL GRAMMAR, whereas a description based on meanings rather than forms is called a NOTIONAL or PHILOSOPHICAL GRAMMAR. Thus, a formal definition of noun in English might be: 'a word which distinguishes between singular and plural and possibly has a possessive form', whereas a notional definition might be: a 'naming word'. Traditional grammar has always been a mixture of notional and formal elements, which has often led to inconsistencies and discrepancies. Until recently grammar was seen as a branch or 'level' of linguistic study intermediate between → phonology and → semantics, and comprising morphology (i.e. the study of word forms) and syntax (i.e. the study of the way words are linked together in larger structures). Some contemporary linguists regard grammar as an all-encompassing theory of → linguistic analysis, e.g. → transformational-generative grammar, → systemic grammar, → tagmemics, → stratificational grammar. UNIVERSAL (or GENERAL) GRAMMAR sets out to establish what is common to all languages. Traditional grammarians accepted the categories of Greek and Latin in this role. Contemporary grammatical theories, however, are more concerned to find a logically consistent framework which will permit the adequate description of specific languages. (4.1, 4.2, 8.23).

GRAMMAR-TRANSLATION METHOD A method in → language teaching in which passages are translated from or into the foreign language. In addition, the teacher may supply comments in the pupils' native language on the grammatical constructions and vocabulary of the original or the translation. → direct method. (9.14).

GRAMMARIAN A person concerned with the study of → grammar.

GRAMMATICAL → Grammaticality.

GRAMMATICAL ANALYSIS The analysis of linguistic material to establish grammatical categories such as → parts of speech, → inflexions, etc. → grammar.

GRAMMATICAL CATEGORY Classes of grammatical items distinguished by form, function, or meaning. → parts of speech, number, gender, case, tense.

GRAMMATICAL CHANGE (*a*) An alternative term for the sound changes associated with → Verner's Law. (*b*) Any change in the morphology (MORPHOLOGICAL CHANGE) or syntax (SYNTACTIC CHANGE) of a language as a result of such developments as → analogy, → folk etymology, → borrowing from other languages, etc. (5.1, 6.1).

GRAMMATICAL EQUIVALENTS Words which are interchangeable in a given grammatical environment without substantially

affecting the meaning, e.g. *will/shall* in the first person singular and plural future 'tense' in modern British English.

GRAMMATICAL FEATURE A → feature of grammatical arrangement, e.g. word order or inflexion. → taxeme.

GRAMMATICAL GENDER → Gender.

GRAMMATICAL ITEM An element of form or syntax which can be isolated and shown to have a distinctive function, e.g. *s* in *chairs*, *ing* in *meeting*.

GRAMMATICAL MEANING → Meaning.

GRAMMATICAL SUBJECT → Subject.

GRAMMATICAL UNIT A unit of linguistic structure. In → systemic grammar five grammatical units are often recognised, e.g. in English → sentence, → clause, → group, → word, → morpheme. The hierarchical relationship existing between these categories, called → rank scale, is such that a sentence consists of one or more clauses, a clause of one or more groups, a group of one or more words and a word of one or more morphemes. (8.23 Halliday).

GRAMMATICAL WORD → Function word.

GRAMMATICALITY An utterance is said to be GRAMMATICAL if it is in agreement with the conventions of the → standard language. Traditionally this implied a value judgment on what should be considered appropriate (→ correctness), but more recently tests have been devised to elicit the regular and varying patterns of actual usage. Some linguists have restricted the notion of grammaticalness to those conventions of the language which have been 'generated', i.e. specified, by the → rules of the grammar. Thus the sentence *Colourless green ideas sleep furiously* might be regarded grammatically well-formed, although from the point of view of semantic context it is hardly meaningful. → acceptability. Alternative term: grammaticalness.

GRAMMATICALISATION The change of a free morpheme with → semantic meaning into a bound morpheme with a largely → grammatical meaning, e.g. *wise* in *moneywise*.

GRAMMATICALNESS → Grammaticality.

GRAMMATOLOGY → Graphetics.

GRAMMEME Older term for → tagmeme.

GRAMMETRICS The study of the linguistic patterns used by a writer and how they deviate in their arrangement from the grammatical norm. → poetic licence, verse. (7.3).

GRAPH In the analysis of continuous text, any written sign which recurs as a unit. By analogy with → phone/phoneme and morph/morpheme, a distinction has been made between graph as any graphic sign and → grapheme as the minimal unit of a particular writing system.

GRAPHEME A minimum distinctive unit of the → writing system of a particular language. Like the concept of → phoneme and → morpheme, the grapheme has no physical identity, but is an abstraction based on the different shapes of written signs and their distribution within a given system. These different variants, e.g. the cursive and printed shapes of letters in an alphabetic writing system *m*, *м*, *M*, M, m, etc., are all → allographs of the grapheme ⟨m⟩. (7.2, 8.21 Francis).

GRAPHEMICS The study of the graphic signs used in a particular language, as opposed to → graphetics which is concerned with shapes and substances used in writing generally. Alternative term: graphology. (7.2).

GRAPHETICS The study of the graphic substance and the shapes of written signs without regard to a particular language or writing system, as opposed to → graphemics which is concerned with those graphic signs which are distinctive in a particular language. Alternative terms: graphonomy, graphics, grammatology. (7.2).

GRAPHIC SIGN → Sign (*a*).

GRAPHIC SUBSTANCE As opposed to the phonetic and gestural features of language, graphic substance refers to the visual marks and signs used in different languages to represent speech in → writing. The relative shapes and combinations of graphic elements of a particular writing system are the subject of → graphemics, while orthography refers to the spelling conventions in a language. For the purpose of → phonetic transcription of speech special notations have been devised, often based on existing scripts, e.g.

the International Phonetic Alphabet. → Table p. 262.

GRAPHICS → Graphetics.

GRAPHOLOGY → Graphemics.

GRAPHONOMY → Graphetics.

GRASSMANN'S LAW A → sound shift first discovered by H. G. Grassmann (1809–1877) describing differences between Greek and Sanskrit and the other Indo-European languages. When two aspirate sounds occurred in neighbouring syllables → dissimilation took place, and the first of the two aspirates became a voiceless stop in Greek and a voiced stop in Sanskrit. (6.1).

GRAVE versus ACUTE One of the oppositions in → distinctive feature phonology based on the analysis of a → spectrogram. 'Grave' indicates predominance of lower frequencies in the spectrum and 'acute' the predominance of high frequencies. In articulatory terms grave versus acute indicates the opposition 'peripheral' versus 'medial', i.e. sounds produced on the velum or lips (peripheral) are grave and sounds produced on the palate and teeth (medial) are acute. For example the English consonants /f/, /p/, /b/, /m/ and the front vowels /i/, /e/, /a/ etc. have the feature grave, and /s/, /t/, /d/, /n/ and the back vowels /o/, /u/ etc. have the feature acute. In recent theories, particularly those of N. Chomsky and M. Halle, the features grave and acute have been modified or linked with cavity features such as coronal, back, etc. → distinctive feature.

GRAVE ACCENT A → diacritic mark placed over a vowel in writing to indicate stress, tone or other qualities, e.g. open vowel in French *père* 'father'. → acute accent.

GREAT ENGLISH VOWEL SHIFT A series of changes in certain Middle English vowels resulting in an upward shift of long vowels and a diphthongisation of the two highest vowels which could not be shifted upwards. Diagrammatically it could be represented as:

Thus ME *grēne* > *green* /griːn/; *spōn* > *spoon* /spuːn/; *hūs* > *house* /haus/, etc. (6.1, 8.21).

GREEK ALPHABET → Table p. 265.

GRIMM'S LAW The consonant changes in the → first sound shift and → second sound shift, which were responsible for separating the Germanic languages from other Indo-European languages and High German from Low German, named after the famous German grammarian Jacob Grimm (1785–1863). (6.1).

GROOVE FRICATIVE → Sibilant.

GROOVE SPIRANT → Sibilant.

GROUP One of the five grammatical units of → rank scale. A → word or phrase which functions as a constituent of a → clause, e.g. in *The tall lady is my aunt*, *the tall lady* is a group acting as subject of the verb. → sentence, morpheme. (8.23 Halliday).

GROUP GENITIVE A whole phrase or group of words which seems to take a possessive inflexion, e.g. *The Lord Mayor of London's residence,* or *The man who is digging our garden's hat.*

GROUP-INFLECTED LANGUAGE → Inflected language.

GUTTURAL General lay term for → velar and → pharyngeal.

H

HABITUAL ASPECT → Aspect.

HALF CLOSE VOWEL A → vowel sound produced with the tongue in a medium high position. → diagram p. 253.

HALF OPEN VOWEL A → vowel sound produced with the tongue in a medium low position. → diagram p. 253.

HAMITO-SEMITIC LINGUISTICS Collective term for the linguistic description of Hamitic and Semitic languages such as Hausa, Arabic, Hebrew, etc. → Appendix 1, p. 273. Alternative term: Afro-Asiatic linguistics. (8.8 Beeston).

HAPLOGRAPHY The omission in writing of one or more similar letters in succession, e.g. *acommodation* or *accomodation* for *accommodation.*

HAPLOLOGY The omission in speech of one or more similar sounds in succession, e.g. when *temporary* is pronounced [tempri].

HARD Alternative term for non-palatalised. → palatalisation.

HARD PALATE → Palate.

HARD SIGN The symbol ⟨ъ⟩ used in the Cyrillic alphabet in Russian and Bulgarian to indicate that the preceding consonant is hard or non-palatalised. In modern Russian script it is often represented by an apostrophe.

HARMONIC Vibrations at a frequency which is a multiple of the fundamental → frequency. Resonant vibrations at twice the fundamental frequency are called 'second harmonic', at three times the fundamental frequency 'third harmonic', etc. The type and degree of harmonic resonance present is responsible for the → quality of a sound. Alternative term: overtone. (3.3 Joos).

HEAD A word which is syntactically dominant in a group and could have the same syntactic function as the whole group if it stood alone. Thus in *Green cheese tastes nice, green cheese* is a group which consists of a noun head word *cheese* and a subordinate adjective modifier *green.* When an adverb and adjective occur together in a group, e.g. *incredibly beautiful,* the adjective is the head word and the adverb the modifier, since the group has the same syntactic function as a simple adjective. →endocentric construction. Alternative term: centre. (4.1, 4.2, 8.23).

HEAD WORD → Head.

HEARING The process by which the brain is able to perceive and interpret sounds. → listening. (3.3 Mol, 9.5, 9.11).

HEAVY STRESS → Stress.

HELPER VERB → Auxiliary verb.

HESITATION FORM A sequence of neutral sounds articulated in speech pauses, e.g. *er . . . er* or *well, mhm.*

HETEROCLITE (*a*) A noun which has more than one stem form in its → declension, e.g. Latin nominative *iter*, genitive *itineris* 'journey'. (*b*) A → suppletive, e.g. Latin *tuli* and *latum* in the verb *ferō, ferre, tuli, latum* 'to carry'.

HETEROGRAPH One of two or more words which are identical in meaning and perhaps in sound, but different in spelling, e.g. *inquiry, enquiry.*

HETEROGRAPHY A writing system or spelling in which words of the same meaning and/or pronunciation are represented by different graphic signs, e.g. *fare, fair*; *inquiry, enquiry.* → homography.

HETERONYM One of two or more words which are identical in spelling, but different in sound and meaning, e.g. *bow* 'for shooting arrows', *bow* 'of a ship'. → homograph.

HETERONYMY The relationship between → heteronyms.

HETEROPHEMY The unconscious misuse of a word in speech or writing, e.g. *revelant* for *relevant.*

HEY-NONNY-NONNY THEORY → Origin of speech.

HIATUS Break between two adjacent monophthongs forming two successive syllables, as opposed to a diphthong which involves a change of vowel quality within a syllable, e.g. in *Noël* as opposed to the diphthong in *Knowles* (personal name). → diaeresis.

HIERARCHY In → linguistic analysis, the ordered arrangement which may be established between elements of language on several interrelated levels, strata, or planes. Thus language as a whole can be said to be divided into the sub-systems of phonology, grammar, and lexis. Within each of these, units may be ranked in hierarchical order, e.g. distinctive feature, phoneme, syllable, etc. in phonology, or morpheme, word, phrase, etc. in grammar. There have been attempts to classify the vocabulary of a language according to grammatical or semantic features of individual items (→ thesaurus). → stratification, rank, level. (3.1, 4.1, 5.1).

HIERATIC SCRIPT → Table p. 264.

HIEROGLYPHIC SCRIPT → Table p. 264.

HIGH-FALLING An → intonation pattern on a word which falls in pitch after starting on a high level, e.g. on *well* in *Well, I don't know!* (as an expression of surprise).

HIGH GERMAN SOUND SHIFT → Second sound shift.

HIGH, LOW, BACK Cavity features in recent theories of → distinctive feature phonology referring to the position of the tongue.

HIGH VOWEL A → vowel sound produced with the tongue in a relatively high position in the mouth. → diagram p. 253.

HIRAGANA A syllabic writing system used in Japanese. → Table p. 264.

HISTORICAL GRAMMAR → Historical linguistics.

HISTORICAL LINGUISTICS An approach or method used in any branch of linguistics to study short-term shifts and long-term changes in the sound system, grammar and vocabulary of one or more languages. Thus, HISTORICAL PHONOLOGY is concerned with → sound change; HISTORICAL GRAMMAR with changes in → morphology and → syntax; and HISTORICAL SEMANTICS with the change in → meaning of lexical items. Historical linguistics is traditionally linked with → comparative philology which studies structural affinities between languages with the aim of finding their common ancestor language. Historical (or → diachronic) linguistics studies the development of a language from one stage in its history to the next, while → synchronic studies are concerned with the structure of a language at one (usually the contemporary) stage only. (6.1, 6.2).

HISTORICAL PHONOLOGY → Historical linguistics.

HISTORIC(AL) PRESENT The use of the present → tense forms of verbs to narrate events which occurred in the past, often to give a sense of immediacy or urgency.

HISTORICAL SEMANTICS → Historical linguistics.

HOLD The period of time during the → articulation of a speech sound in which the organs of speech retain the position for its production, e.g.

the duration of the closure in the production of a → stop.

HOLE IN THE PATTERN The phonological systems of most languages have a symmetrical arrangement of → oppositions. If there are three voiceless stops /p/, /t/, /k/, there are usually also three voiced stops /b/, /d/, /g/. A hole in the pattern occurs if a phonological system is asymmetrical in some way, e.g. Dutch has three voiceless stops /p/, /t/, /k/, but only two voiced stops /b/, /d/, with [g] occurring only as an → allophone of /k/. (2.1 Martinet).

HOLOPHRASE A word which expresses on its own the meaning of an entire sentence. This may be at a particular stage of language development, e.g. when a child speaks in single-word utterances, or a characteristic of a particular language, e.g. Russian *холодно* 'it is cold'.

HOLOPHRASTIC LANGUAGE Term used to refer to the stage in language acquisition when a child uses single word utterances.

HOMOGRAM One of two or more words which are → homographs with different etymologies, e.g. *fair* 'collection of exhibitions and/or amusements' or *fair* 'beautiful, just'.

HOMOGRAPH One of two or more words which are identical in spelling, but different in meaning, e.g. *lead* 'to guide' and *lead* 'metal'. If they are also identical in sound they may be called → homonyms, e.g. *rest* 'remainder' and *rest* 'to relax'. If they differ in both sound and meaning they may be called → heteronyms, e.g. *bow* 'for shooting arrows', *bow* 'of a ship'.

HOMOGRAPHY (*a*) The relationship between → homographs. (*b*) A type of writing system or spelling in which one particular graphic sign always represents the same speech sound, e.g. a phonetic alphabet. → heterography.

HOMOIONYM → Near-synonym.

HOMONYM One of two or more words which are identical in sound, but different in meaning, e.g. *flour* and *flower*. If they are also identical in spelling they may also be called → homographs, e.g. *rest* 'remainder' and *rest* 'to relax'. Homonyms may be derived from the same word by a split in semantic meaning, e.g. *game* 'organised play' and 'object of hunt'.

HOMONYMIC CLASH Ambiguity arising from the use of → homographs or → homophones, e.g. *red* 'colour' or *read* 'perused' in the schoolboy riddle:

Q. *What is black and white and* [red] *all over?*
A. *A newspaper.*

Alternative terms: homophonic clash, homonymic conflict.

HOMONYMIC CONFLICT → Homonymic clash.

HOMONYMY The relationship between → homonyms.

HOMOPHONE One of two or more words which are identical in sound but different in meaning and/or spelling, e.g. English *heir* and *air*.

HOMOPHONIC CLASH → Homonymic clash.

HOMOPHONY The relationship between → homophones.

HOMORGANIC SOUNDS Different speech sounds which are articulated at the same → point of articulation, e.g. [b] and [m] which are both bilabials.

HONORIFIC FORM A grammatical form indicating humbleness or inferiority of the speaker. The term honorific is usually used in respect of languages which differentiate several different degrees of → polite form on a grammatical level.

HUMANISM An approach to language which stresses the spiritual quality of man's communicative abilities, either in contrast to 'vulgar' deviations from the classical literary norm (→ Renaissance linguistics) or in reaction against attempts to formalise linguistic descriptions into a system of logical rules (idealism in Neo-linguistics). Scholars like the Dane L. Hjelmslev maintained that it should be possible to combine a humanistic regard for man's linguistic creativity with scientific statements about the formal regularities underlying it. (2.5 Hjelmslev).

HUMANISTS → Renaissance linguistics.

HUMBOLDTISM → Relativity.

HYBRID WORD A → compound word made up of components which originate from different languages, e.g. *television* where *tele-* is from Greek *tēle* 'far' and *-vision* is from Latin *visio* 'sight'. Alternative term: mongrel word. (5.1, 6.1).

HYDRONYMY → Onomastics.

HYPER-CORRECTION → Overcorrection.

HYPER-FORM The result of → overcorrection.

HYPER-URBANISM → Overcorrection.

HYPHEN → Punctuation.

HYPONYM A word the → meaning of which may be said to be included in that of another word. In the two examples below, the more specific words (in the bottom line) are co-hyponyms of the more general words (in the top line) which are said to be SUPERORDINATE to their hyponyms. (2.1 Lyons).

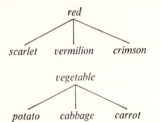

HYPONYMY The relationship between → hyponyms. Alternative term: inclusion.

HYPOTACTIC CLAUSE → Subordinate clause.

HYPOTAXIS The joining together of sentences and clauses by means of → conjunctions, e.g. *He walked in because the door was open*, as opposed to → parataxis, e.g. *The door was open: he walked in.*

HYPOTHETICAL CLAUSE → Conditional clause.

I

IAMB → Foot (*a*).

ICONIC SIGN → Sign (*a*).

ICONOGRAPHY The drawing of pictures or images on concrete objects as a primitive method of → writing. (7.2).

ICTUS The stressed part of a → foot.

IDEOGRAM A graphic sign used in a writing system to represent a stretch of speech. This term may be used for a character sign which stands for units larger than individual speech sounds, e.g. words (LOGOGRAM), or for a visual image representing a message, e.g. a traffic sign (PICTOGRAM). Alternative term: ideograph. (7.2).

IDEOGRAPH → Ideogram.

IDEOGRAPHY → Logography.

IDIOLECT A → variety of language used by one individual speaker, including peculiarities of → pronunciation, → grammar and → vocabulary. A → dialect is made up of the idiolects of a group of speakers in a social or regional subdivision of a speech community. Linguists often analyse their own idiolect to make general statements about language. (7.1, 8.24).

IDIOM (*a*) A group of words which has a special connotation not usually equal to the sum of the meanings of the individual words, and which usually cannot be translated literally into another language without the special meaning being lost, e.g. *that's not my cup of tea* or *hold the line please*. Alternative term: idiomatic expression. (*b*) A term used in a more technical sense by some linguists to refer to a linguistic or non-linguistic convention which takes on a certain symbolic significance in its context, e.g. a certain word or utterance used as a 'password' or understood only by a restricted audience, or a certain look, gait or secret sign, etc. (2.1 Hockett).

IDIOMATIC EXPRESSION → Idiom (*a*).

IDIOMATIC TRANSLATION → Translation.

IDIOMATOLOGY The system and study of characteristic tendencies in a given language, e.g. the use of inflexions, frequency of homonyms, vocabulary structure, word order, etc. (5.2 Ullmann).

IDIOPHONE A speech sound which is characteristic of, or peculiar to, one → idiolect.

ILLITERACY The inability to read and/or write. About half the world's population is illiterate and efforts are now under way to teach them the skills of reading and writing. → literacy. (7.2 I.B.E.).

ILLITERATE (*a*) Unable to read and/or write. (*b*) A → manner of discourse which is noticeably different from the accepted → standard language.

IMITATION → Language acquisition.

IMITATIVE WORD → Onomatopoeic word.

IMMANENCE A principle of describing language as a self-contained → system, without any reference to external factors such as philosophy, sociology, etc. (2.5 Dixon, Hjelmslev).

IMMEDIATE CONSTITUENT → Immediate constituent analysis.

IMMEDIATE CONSTITUENT ANALYSIS (IC ANALYSIS) A method of analysing sentences or words by dividing them into their component parts. Thus the sentence *The book is good* may be divided into two parts as follows: *The book| |is good*. The components resulting from this first division of a unit are termed IMMEDIATE CONSTITUENTS. The immediate constituents themselves may be further divided and when no further divisions can be made on the same linguistic level the resultant divisions are termed ULTIMATE CONSTITUENTS. In the case of the sentence quoted the ultimate constituents are the individual words *The| |book| |is| |good*; in the case of an IC analysis of a word such as *happiness*, the ultimate constituents are the individual morphemes *un| |happi| |ness*. (8.23 Nida).

IMMEDIATE SPEECH Speech referring to a tangible or observable situation present at the time of speaking, as opposed to → displaced speech.

IMMIGRANT LANGUAGE (*a*) The native language of a minority immigrant population in a speech community, e.g. Urdu as spoken by Pakistanis in Great Britain. (*b*) A variety of the host language spoken by immigrants living in the speech community, e.g. the type of English spoken by some Pakistani immigrants to Great Britain. → indigenous language. (7.1, 8.1).

IMMOVABLE SPEECH ORGAN → Articulator.

IMPERATIVE A sentence or verb form which commands, requires or forbids an action to be carried out, e.g. *Stand up!, Do sit down, Don't talk!, Everybody start now.* A distinction must be made between the grammatical term imperative and the semantic term → command since not all commands are imperatives. → mood. (4.1, 4.2, 8.23).

IMPERFECT A → tense form traditionally associated with a continuous or habitual action in the past, e.g. *She was reading all day yesterday,* or *He read for an hour every day,* as opposed to the → perfect tense which is usually associated with a single completed action, e.g. *I have read that book.* → past tense.

IMPERFECTIVE ASPECT → Aspect.

IMPERSONAL VERB A verb used only in the third person singular with no reference to a particular subject, e.g. *It is raining,* or French *Il faut ....* 'it is necessary ...'. → personal verb. Alternative term: monopersonal verb.

IMPLICATION → Connotation.

IMPLOSION The movement of air inwards upon release of a → stop.

IMPLOSIVE STOP → Stop.

IMPRESSIONISTIC TRANSCRIPTION → Phonetic transcription made with no knowledge or reference to the system of a particular language. A phonetician making an impressionistic transcription tries to represent everything he hears, being prepared to use any symbols required. Transcription of an unknown language has to be of this type in the first instance, later a SYSTEMATIC TRANSCRIPTION can be used where the segments are known and a limited number of symbols are used to represent them. (3.1 Abercrombie).

IMPROPER COMPOUND A → compound word of which all parts are inflected, e.g. French *monsieur, messieurs,* or Russian numerals such as *пятьдесят* 'fifty', genitive: *пятидесяти.* → proper compound.

IMPROPER SPEECH The substandard forms of a language, used by certain groups in certain situations, e.g. → slang, and regarded by others as socially unacceptable.

INACTIVE VOICE The passive → voice (*b*).

INANIMATE → Gender.

INCAPSULATING LANGUAGE → Incorporating language.

INCAPSULATION → Incorporation.

INCEPTIVE ASPECT → Aspect.

INCHOATIVE ASPECT → Aspect.

INCLUDED POSITION When a linguistic form appears as part of a larger construction, it is said to be in

108

an included position, e.g. *The man in the car* in the sentence *The man in the car is my uncle*. If, however, in reply to the question *Who is your uncle?* the answer is *The man in the car*, it constitutes a free sentence. → absolute construction.

INCLUSION → Hyponymy.

INCLUSIVE PERSONAL PRONOUN → Person.

INCOMPATIBILITY The relationship that can be established between words with similar but contradictory meanings. Thus the word *chair* in the sentence *This chair is comfortable* is incompatible with other lexical items in the → semantic field of 'furniture' such as *stool* or *settee*. (2.1 Lyons).

INCOMPLETE VERB (*a*) A → transitive verb which requires an object to complete its sense. (*b*) → Defective verb.

INCONGRUITY The difference in range of meaning denoted by seemingly equivalent words in different languages, e.g. German *Land* '(open) country', 'state', but English *land* 'ground', 'territory'. (5.1).

INCONTIGUOUS ASSIMILATION → Assimilation.

INCORPORATING CONJUNCTION → Conjunction.

INCORPORATING LANGUAGE A type of language such as Eskimo, where grammatical relationships and word structure are indicated by the successive juxtaposing of affixed → bound morphemes into single words. This language type is morphologically

more complex than → agglutinative or → inflected languages. English has a few incorporating features in such contractions as *won't* which incorporates *will* and *not*. Alternative terms: polysynthetic, incapsulating language. (6.1, 8.1).

INCORPORATION The intimate fusing of words or word parts into a single word. Alternative term: incapsulation. → fusion.

INDECLINABLE Having only one form, incapable of taking → inflexions to show number, gender or case, etc. → invariable word. Alternative term: inflexible.

INDEFINITE ARTICLE → Article.

INDEFINITE DECLENSION → Strong declension.

INDEFINITE DETERMINER A → determiner in a noun phrase expressing generality, e.g. *a, any, some, every*. → definite determiner.

INDEFINITE PRONOUN (*a*) A → pronoun which does not refer to a definite person or thing, e.g. *anybody, anything, something, nobody*, etc. (*b*) → Predeterminers such as *both, all, several*.

INDEPENDENT CLAUSE → Main clause.

INDEPENDENT ELEMENT A word or phrase, usually an → interjection or → exclamation, which has no grammatical connexion with the rest of the sentence in which it functions, e.g. *well* in *Well, what about it?*

INDEPENDENT SOUND CHANGE → Sound change.

109

INDEX (*a*) A non-linguistic feature of handwriting, pronunciation, voice quality, gesture, etc. which gives information about the social or regional origin, physical state or attitude of speaker or writer, or indicates idiosyncratic features. (3.1 Abercrombie). (*b*) A ratio between particular elements in a language which may serve as a measure for a certain feature. Thus the numerical relationship between words and smaller grammatical units, e.g. the number of morphemes or affixes per word, may be used to compare and classify languages into different types. Thus linguists like J. H. Greenberg have proposed the so-called AFFIXING) INDEX, AGGLUTINATIVE INDEX, SYNTHETIC INDEX, NEXUS INDEX, etc. to characterise respectively → affixing, → agglutinative, → synthetic, → inflected, etc. languages. (2.3 Greenberg).

INDIC LINGUISTICS Collective term for the linguistic description of Indian languages such as ancient Sanskrit, Hindi, Bengali, Urdu, etc. → Appendix 1, p. 270. (8.7 Miltner, Ray).

INDICATIVE MOOD → Mood.

INDIGENOUS LANGUAGE A language spoken by the native population of a given area and one which has developed among that population, e.g. American Indian languages before European colonisation or French in France, as opposed to an imported or → immigrant language. (7.1, 8.1).

INDIRECT DISCOURSE → Indirect speech.

INDIRECT OBJECT → Object.

INDIRECT QUESTION A question quoted in → indirect speech, e.g. *She asked me if I was satisfied, She asked me why I had come.* → direct question. Alternative terms: reported question, oblique question.

INDIRECT QUOTATION → indirect quotation. (4.1, 4.2, 8.23).

INDIRECT SPEECH The paraphrasing of an utterance without quoting verbatim the actual words used by the original speaker. Special grammatical and syntactic features such as tense forms or subordinate clauses distinguish indirect from → direct speech, e.g. *He has come* may become (*He said that*) *he had come* in indirect speech. Alternative terms: reported speech, indirect discourse, indirect quotation. (4.1, 4.2, 8.23).

INDIVIDUAL VARIANT → Free variant.

INDO-EUROPEAN LINGUISTICS In the widest sense, the linguistic description of the languages of the Indo-European family, i.e. Germanic linguistics, Romance linguistics, Latin linguistics, Russian linguistics, Celtic linguistics, etc. More specifically, 'Indo-European' linguistics refers to those → comparative and historical studies which are concerned with the similarities that exist between these languages in phonology, grammar and vocabulary and their genealogical relatedness. Since scholars such as Sir William Jones (1746–1794), R. Rask (1787–1832) and J. Grimm (1785–1863) established sets of correspondences between ancient Sanskrit, Greek, Latin and other European languages, such diachronic studies have made considerable progress, and chairs in

Indo-European and general 'philology' have been established in many major European universities. Efforts to reconstruct the common ancestor of this family of languages ('Stammbaum' or 'pedigree' theory) have been modified since the end of the 19th century by considerations of geographical and social impacts on language (→ dialectology, Prague School, Neo-linguistics) and partly replaced by descriptive and → synchronic work on contemporary languages. Recent contributions to this field have come through the decipherment of ancient inscriptions, e.g. Mycenaean 'linear B', and the discovery and re-grouping of earlier language forms in central Europe and the Mediterranean (Illyrian, Hittite, Anatolian, etc.). → centum, satem languages, philology, etymology, sound shift. Appendix 1, pp. 268–270. Alternative terms: Indo-Germanic Linguistics, Indo-European Philology. (6.1, 8.2–8.7).

INDO-GERMANIC LINGUISTICS → Indo-European linguistics.

INFANTILE SPEECH → Baby-talk (*b*).

INFERIOR COMPARISON A comparative form of an adjective or adverb expressing lesser quantity or intensity of the content of the adjective or adverb. In English the words *less . . . than* or *not . . . so* are used for this purpose, e.g. *She is not so beautiful as her sister.* → superior comparison. Alternative term: downward comparison.

INFINITE VERB FORM → Non-finite verb form.

INFINITIVE A form of the verb which is not limited by → person, → number or → tense; the form usually listed in dictionaries. In English it may stand alone (→ first infinitive), e.g. *I must go*, or it may be preceded by the particle *to* (→ second infinitive), e.g. *I want to go.* Apart from this verbal usage the infinitive may also be used as a noun, e.g. *To see is to believe*, as an adverbial, e.g. *He studied hard to pass*, as a form of command, e.g. *The tenant to pay the rates.* (4.1, 4.2, 8.23).

INFINITIVE PHRASE A phrase consisting of an → infinitive with or without a complement, e.g. *He came to see the film* or *It is better to have played and lost than not to have played at all.*

INFIX An → affix which is inserted within a word. Infixes are used extensively in Cambodian, Sudanese and in some American Indian languages. An example from English might be the colloquial *abso-bloomin'-lutely.*

INFLECTED LANGUAGE A type of language in which grammatical relationships are shown by → inflexion rather than word order. Affixes are merged closely with a base or root word so that they become part of the word, e.g. the endings of the 'conjugated' Latin verb *amare* 'love', *amo* 'I love', *amas* 'you love', *amat* 'he loves', etc. Inflexions often indicate more than one category, e.g. *-a* in Latin *lingua* 'tongue' marks singular number, nominative case, and feminine gender. In ROOT-INFLECTED (or FUSIONAL or FUSING) languages such as Arabic the vowel distribution in the root of a word changes, e.g. [jalasa] 'to sit', [jəːlis] 'I am sitting', [jəluːs] 'they are sitting',

111

similar to 'vowel gradation' in English *sing/sang/sung*. In STEM-INFLECTED languages such as Sanskrit or Latin, suffixes expressing different functions are added to an unchanged base (see Latin examples above). In GROUP-INFLECTED (or AMALGAMATING) languages such as Georgian affixes are intimately joined with the base. Alternative terms: inflecting, inflexional, flexional language (6.1, 8.1).

INFLECTION → Inflexion.

INFLEXIBLE → Indeclinable.

INFLEXION, INFLECTION The process or result of adding → affixes to the base or root of a word to determine and limit its grammatical significance. Examples are case endings on nouns in such languages as Greek, Latin and Russian or, in English, the plural morpheme -*s*, e.g. *hat/hats, dog/dogs*; the possessive -'*s*, e.g. *boy's/boys'*; tense morphemes, e.g. *go/went/gone*, or *walk/walked*. Alternative terms: flexion, flection. → word formation. (4.1, 5.1, 6.1).

INFLEXIONAL SUFFIX An inflexional ending added to a base or stem, e.g. the plural ending -*s* on *boys*. → derivational affix. Alternative terms: flexional ending, inflexional ending.

INFORMANT A native speaker who acts as the model for someone who is studying his language. In linguistic → field-work, particularly in dialectology and in anthropological linguistics, informants should be well chosen to represent a sample of a speech community. Often linguists use themselves as informants to study features of pronunciation, grammar and vocabulary. In language teaching, too, native speakers are needed as models for the student of that language. (2.3 Samarin).

INFORMATION The content of a message communicated from a → source to a → receiver. In communication engineering it refers to the minimum amount of binary digits necessary to encode a message to be sent through a communication channel, and may thus be a measure of → information content. (1.1 Meetham, 10.5).

INFORMATION CONTENT In a communication system or in a particular linguistic environment, the ratio of actual to probable occurrence of an item. Thus, in the English sentence *We are going away* the fourth item *away* has a higher information content than the second, because it is one of several possible words which could occur in that position and therefore gives the most important piece of information about the context. The second item *are* is highly likely to occur between *we* and *going*, and therefore conveys only little information. In general, information content is inversely proportional to distribution, i.e. probability of occurrence. (10.5).

INFORMATION THEORY The study of → communication or the transmission of information. Early work by N. Wiener (→ cybernetics), C. Shannon and W. Weaver concentrated on the technological and mathematical aspects of sending messages from a 'sender' or 'source' to an 'addressee' or 'receiver' by encoding and decoding it (→ code). These principles were later applied by electrical engineers to the study of the efficiency of communication channels in relation to → noise and other factors in the process of transmitting

information (COMMUNICATION ENGIN-
EERING or COMMUNICATION TECHNO-
LOGY). Linguists, too, are interested in
the amount of information of a particular item in a particular context
(INFORMATION CONTENT). Information content, measured in 'bits' or
binary digits, is inversely proportional
to redundancy and probability of
occurrence: the more likely (and thus
more redundant) a word is in a given
context, the smaller is the amount of
information conveyed by it. Thus the
word *are* in the sentence *We are going
away* is highly predictable in that
position and therefore has less information content than, say, the word
away. Alternatively we might say
that *away* gives more SEMANTIC
INFORMATION than the three other
words in that sentence. Some of these
ideas have brought new approaches
in → semantics, → computational
linguistics and → distinctive feature
analysis. → noise, → redundancy, →
Zipf's Law. (10.5).

INGRESSIVE A speech sound
produced with the air stream moving
into the vocal tract, as often heard in
Swedish *ja* 'yes'. → Clicks are
examples of velaric ingressive sounds.

**INGRESSIVE AIR-STREAM
MECHANISM** → Air-stream
mechanism.

INGRESSIVE STOP → Stop.

INHALATION The act of
breathing in. Alternative term: inspiration. (3.1, 8.22).

INITIAL GLIDE → On-glide.

INITIAL MUTATION →
Mutation.

INITIAL STRESS → Stress on
the first → syllable of a word.

**INITIAL TEACHING ALPHA-
BET (ITA)** A near-phonemic →
alphabet used sometimes in teaching
English-speaking children to read:

a littl girl næmd jɛɛn cæm tɷ
liv nɛɛr jonny and jæn. ʃhɛɛ had
a pɷdl caulld twiŋkl. and ʃhæ
wer bɷʈh raʈher 'sueperior'.
'ʃhɛɛ duʌ not wont tɷ nɷ us and
our dog biŋglʌ,' sed jonny.

(7.2, 9.12 Gunderson, 9.13 Lee).

INITIATION The physical process whereby the breath stream is set
in motion by the action of an →
initiator in the vocal tract. → air-
stream mechanism, speech production.

INITIATOR Any moving part of
a cavity or chamber which changes
the size of the cavity, thus causing
movement of air. The lungs are the
most frequently used initiators in
speech, others are larynx, velum, lips.
→ air-stream mechanism, speech
production.

INNER CLOSURE → Closure.

INNER FORM In the continuing
discussion of what languages have in
common and what distinguishes
them from one another, many linguists and philosophers since W. von
Humboldt (1767–1835) have com-
mented on the fact that the grammatical and semantic structure of a
particular language is unique to that
language (INNER FORM), however
susceptible its sound system (OUTER
FORM) may be to influences from
other languages. The distinction is
sometimes reinterpreted from different vantage points in terms of →
content and expression or → deep
structure and surface structure. (2.4).

INNOVATION A → change in sound, form or meaning, resulting in the creation of a new word. Such innovation may be due to accident, e.g. lapses, or a deliberate act, e.g. → neologisms. In dialectology such changes are usually held to begin at a certain geographical point and spread outwards to other areas of the speech community. (5.1, 6.1, 7.1).

INORDINATED ADJECTIVE If more than one adjective modifies the same noun, the most important adjective or the one most closely connected with the noun is called the inordinated adjective. Thus in *the cool dark night*, *dark* is the inordinated adjective.

INORGANIC FEATURE An element in a word or group of words which does not historically belong to that particular word or group, e.g. *r* in *-groom* in the compound *bridegroom*.

INSEPARABLE An → affix which cannot be separated from its stem, particularly certain verbal prefixes in German which remain attached to the verb for all conjugational forms, e.g. *Er übergeht den Fehler* 'he ignores the mistake', as opposed to the → separable verb form *Er geht zum Feind über* 'he defects to the enemy'. → discontinuity.

INSERTED CLAUSE → Parenthetical clause.

INSPIRATION → Inhalation.

INSTANTANEOUS RELEASE versus DELAYED RELEASE Manner of articulation features in recent theories of → distinctive feature phonology. Plosives have instantaneous release whereas affricates have delayed release.

INSTITUTIONAL LINGUISTICS The application of linguistic knowledge to the problem of creating or promoting a national → standard language in a politically, culturally and socially diverse country. → Language planning of this kind involves decisions as to which native dialect or foreign language is to serve as the general vehicle of communication in education, commerce and technology (→ standardisation) or which → alphabet is to be adopted for developing writing and literature. Alternative term: glottopolitics. (2.1 Hall; 10.1 Fishman, Tauli).

INSTRUMENTAL A → case form in some inflected languages denoting the agent or the origin of an action, e.g. Russian *Он пишит карандашом* 'he writes with a pencil'. Prepositions may also govern the instrumental, e.g. Russian *хлеб с маслом* 'bread and (with) butter'. Some verbs in Russian require the predicate to be in the instrumental case, e.g. the past tense of the verb *to be* in *Он был солдатом* 'he was a soldier'. The 'instrumental' relationship is usually expressed in English by means of the prepositions *by*, *with*, *by means of* or *through*. → ablative.

INSTRUMENTAL PHONETICS → Experimental phonetics.

INSTRUMENTATIVE VERB A verb which shows the instrument of the action in its meaning, e.g. *to horse-whip*.

INTENSIFIER An → adverbial of degree which intensifies the meaning of a word, e.g. *bone* in *bone idle*

114

or *extremely* in *extremely lucky*. Alternative term: intensive. (4.1, 8.23).

INTENSION The connotative and denotative → meaning which a speaker or writer gives a word or phrase by implication or definition. The term intension is sometimes contrasted with → extension (*b*). (5.1).

INTENSIONAL MEANING → Meaning.

INTENSITY ACCENT → Expiratory accent.

INTENSIVE → Intensifier.

INTENSIVE PRONOUN → Reflexive pronoun.

INTERCONSONANTAL Occurring between → consonants.

INTERDENTAL A speech sound which is articulated between the teeth, e.g. [θ] as in *thin* or [ð] as in *this*.

INTERFERENCE The errors made by carrying over the speech habits of the native language or dialect into a second language or dialect. Features of → pronunciation, → grammar and → vocabulary may cause interference when a person is learning to master the patterns of a second language. (9.11, 9.13, 9.2, 9.3).

INTERJECTED CLAUSE A → clause which is interpolated into a sentence, but which is not part of the structure of the sentence into which it is placed, e.g. *she said* in "*It was*," *she said*, "*as I had expected*."

INTERJECTION An indeclinable form which has no syntactic relationship with other forms, and which is used in an exclamation to express emotion. Some interjections correspond to forms which can be used in other functions, e.g. *Hell!* or *Bother!* whereas others are unrelated to other forms in the language and may often have combinations of sounds which do not otherwise occur in the language, e.g. *Ugh! Phew! Psst!* Some theories on the → origin of speech suggest that language may have started with interjections. (4.1, 8.23).

INTERJECTIONAL THEORY → Origin of speech.

INTERLANGUAGE → Artificial language.

INTERLINGUISTICS The comparative study of different languages to establish common elements between them, often with a view to devising an international → artificial language, or to finding equivalent and/or contrasting patterns, e.g. in translation and language teaching. (9.1, 9.3, 10.1).

INTERLUDE A consonant cluster occurring between vowels, e.g. [-kn-] in *picnic*. (2.1 Hockett).

INTERMEDIATE VOWEL (*a*) → Neutral vowel. (*b*) A vowel sound with a quality intermediate between two → cardinal vowels.

INTERNAL CHANGE → Vowel gradation.

INTERNAL HIATUS → Transition.

INTERNAL INFLEXION → Vowel gradation.

INTERNAL LOAN → Dialect borrowing.

115

INTERNAL MEANING → Meaning.

INTERNAL MODIFICATION → Vowel gradation.

INTERNAL OPEN JUNCTURE → Transition.

INTERNAL RECONSTRUC-TION A method of reconstructing older forms of a language by observation of modern structural patterns within that language. An example in English could be the comparison of patterns such as *luck/lucky/luckless*; *hair/hairy/hairless* with ----/*happy*/ *hapless* and the reconstruction on the basis of this of the form **hap* in order to complete the pattern. This method is particularly useful for languages with no older written records and with no written records of related languages of the same family, when the → comparative method which was developed to a high degree in the 19th century cannot be used. (6.2 Hoenigswald).

INTERNAL SPEECH Subvocal talking to oneself or verbalising, as in silent reading. Alternative term: endophasia.

INTERNATIONAL PHONETIC ALPHABET (IPA) System of → phonetic transcription devised by the International Phonetic Association to provide an internationally standardised method of recording the sounds of speech on paper. It was originally devised by P. Passy in 1886, based on the work of H. Sweet, and subsequently revised. → chart pp. 262–263. (3.1, 8.22).

INTERNATIONAL WORDS Words which are known internationally in all the major languages. They are usually borrowed from the language of origin with minor phonological changes, e.g. *sport* in French borrowed from English, or *sputnik* in English and *spoutnik* in French, borrowed from Russian. (5.1, 6.1).

INTERPRETER A person engaged in → interpreting.

INTERPRETING Oral → translation by a person who is proficient in the two languages and conversant in the terminology of the subject under discussion. In CONSECUTIVE INTERPRETING, usually done at small private or business meetings, or on guided tours, the interpreter renders his version of the original talk in short stretches, while the speaker of the original pauses periodically. In SIMULTANEOUS INTERPRETING, usually done at large conferences either from the inside of a booth via headset and microphone or by whispered speech, the interpreter listens to the original and at the same time renders his translation without the speaker of the original making any pauses. (9.3 Longley).

INTERROGATION MARK → Punctuation.

INTERROGATION POINT → Punctuation.

INTERROGATIVE A verb form or sentence type which is one way of expressing a question. Not all questions are formed by the interrogative, however, and a distinction must be made between the formal or grammatical term interrogative and the semantic term → question. In English an interrogative sentence is often characterised by inverted word order, e.g. *Are you going?*, the use of a special auxiliary verb, e.g. *Do you*

116

like it? or the use of a special interrogative word in conjunction with one of the above, e.g. *Where are you going? Why do you like it?* → mood. (4.1, 4.2, 8.23).

INTERROGATIVE ADJECTIVE
→ Interrogative word.

INTERROGATIVE ADVERB
→ Interrogative word.

INTERROGATIVE PRONOUN
→ Interrogative word.

INTERROGATIVE SENTENCE
A structure containing a question as opposed to one expressed in declarative → mood. In English an interrogative sentence is characterised by a rising final intonation with normal word order, e.g. *You're going?*, or inverted word order predicate–subject often with a special verb form with rising or falling intonation. e.g. *Do you like it?* or by the use of a special → interrogative word with rising or falling final intonation, e.g. *Why did he say that?*

INTERROGATIVE WORD A word used at the beginning of a clause or sentence to mark it as an → interrogative sentence. In English, these words usually begin with *wh-* and include the following: INTERROGATIVE ADJECTIVES such as *which* or *what* when part of a noun phrase, e.g. *Which model did you prefer?*; INTERROGATIVE PRONOUNS such as *who, which* or *what*, when used on their own, e.g. *What did you say?* or *Who did it?*; INTERROGATIVE ADVERBS such as *where, why, how*, e.g. *Why didn't you go there?* or *I don't know when he is coming.* Alternative term: question word. (4.2, 8.23).

INTERRUPTED A → consonant sound during the articulation of which the air stream is stopped, e.g. [t] in *tap*, as opposed to a → continuant, e.g. [l] in *lap*.

INTERVIEW A technique in linguistic → field-work for collecting data on the phonology, grammar and vocabulary of a language from native → informants by means of conversations. (2.3 Birdwhistell, Pittenger *et al.*, Samarin).

INTERVOCALIC A consonant occurring between two → vowels.

INTIMACY The extent to which social informality and solidarity is expressed in language, e.g. by the use of special forms of → address or by silence fillers like *you know* and *sort of*. Intimacy correlates inversely with → status. (10.1 Fishman).

INTIMATE SPEECH A very informal → manner of discourse used in communication with one's relatives and social equals.

INTONATION Melodic pattern produced by the variation in → pitch of the voice during speech. In English and many other languages (intonation languages) these melodic patterns convey information about the speaker, whether he is angry, surprised, polite, etc., and often indicate whether a sentence is a question, a statement or a command. Sometimes intonation carries other information: thus in response to the statement *John has a new girl friend*, the question *Who?* with a rising intonation requires the answer *John*, but *Who?* with a falling intonation is asking for further information about the new girl friend. The situation is different in a tone language where words, meanings and/or grammatical categories may be distinguished by pitch features which are as much a part of the structure of words as the segmental speech sounds. (3.1–3.4, 8.22).

INTONATION CONTOUR → Intonation pattern.

INTONATION FORMANT → Intonation morpheme.

INTONATION LANGUAGE A language in which melodic pitch patterns form part of the structure of sentences rather than words. → intonation.

INTONATION MORPHEME An → intonation pattern which in itself serves to distinguish different types of utterance, e.g. the rising intonation in English at the end of questions formed without → interrogative words, e.g. *You're coming?* Alternative term: intonation formant.

INTONATION PATTERN A chronologically significant melodic pattern of → pitch differences occurring during speech. English → declarative sentences are usually spoken with a falling intonation pattern, as also are questions introduced by → interrogative words. Alternative term: intonation contour. (3.1, 8.22).

INTRALINGUISTIC FEATURES → Feature.

INTRANSITIVE VERB A → verb which makes complete sense on its own without an → object. In English there is usually no formal distinction between → transitive and intransitive verbs, e.g. *He drinks*

when he is thirsty (intransitive) and *He drinks a pint of milk* (transitive); some verbs can by their nature not take a direct object and can therefore only be used intransitively, e.g. *Time elapsed.* (4.1, 4.2, 8.23).

INTRODUCTORY ADVERB → Conjunctive adverb.

INTROFLEXION → Vowel gradation.

INTRUSION The addition of a speech sound between syllables or words in connected speech, usually for ease of pronunciation, e.g. the INTRUSIVE [r] in *law and order* pronounced [lɔːrən'ɔːdə]. → table p. 75, elision.

INTRUSIVE R → Intrusion.

INVARIABLE WORD A word which never changes its form in whatever construction it occurs in a given language. Most languages have two large classes of words: variables and invariables. Examples of invariable words in English are → prepositions and → interjections. → indeclinable. Alternative term: invariant.

INVARIANT → Invariable word.

INVERSE DERIVATION → Back-formation.

INVERSE SPELLING A written form of → overcorrection, e.g. *maintainance* for *maintenance*.

INVERSION → Inverted word order.

INVERTED (*a*) → Retroflex. (*b*) → Inverted word order.

INVERTED COMMAS → Punctuation.

INVERTED WORD ORDER An arrangement of words within a sentence that is different from the normal declarative pattern, e.g. the subject occurring after an auxiliary verb to produce an → interrogative sentence in English: *I do* > *Do I?* Alternative term: inversion. (4.2, 8.23).

IRRADIATION → Radiation.

IRREGULAR VERB A → verb which exhibits certain forms which do not coincide with a particular paradigm considered as the norm for that type of verb, e.g. French *aller* 'to go' has the irregular future form *ir-* as in *j'irai* 'I shall go'. The term is also used to refer to English and German verbs which change the vowel of the root to form the past tense, e.g. *sing/sang/sung* as opposed to → weak verbs which add inflexions, e.g. *walk/walked*.

IRREGULARITY The phenomenon of a linguistic form deviating from the grammatical rule, e.g. the English noun *oxen* is irregular because it does not conform to the pattern of the majority of nouns forming the plural by adding *-s*. → regularity.

IRRELEVANT A linguistic feature which is present in an utterance, but has no influence on the meaning, e.g. the aspiration of /p/ as in *pin* [pʰɪn] and the lack of aspiration of /p/ after /s/ as in *spin* [spɪn], or the alternative pronunciation of *direction*

as [dɪrekʃən] or [daɪrekʃən]. → distinctive. Alternative terms: non-distinctive, non-functional, non-significant. (3.1, 8.22).

ISOCHRONISM → Tempo.

ISOERG → Isopleth.

ISOGLOSS In a linguistic atlas or map, a line drawn around an area in which a particular feature of pronunciation, grammar or vocabulary is found. Bundles of such isoglosses may be used to establish → dialect boundaries. Alternative terms: isoglottic line, isograph. (6.1, 7.1, 8.1).

ISOGLOTTIC LINE → Isogloss.

ISOGRADE → Isopleth.

ISOGRAPH → Isogloss.

ISOLATE (*a*) A single word functioning as a clause. → clause equivalent. (*b*) A term used occasionally as an alternative to → segment.

ISOLATED AREA → Area.

ISOLATING LANGUAGE A type of language which uses invariable root words and distinctive word order rather than → inflexion to show grammatical relationships. Examples are the ROOT-ISOLATING Chinese and the STEM-ISOLATING Samoan. → analytic language. Alternative term: formless language. (6.1, 8.1).

ISOLATIVE SOUND CHANGE → Sound change.

ISOLEX An → isogloss on a linguistic map drawn around an area of one particular feature of vocabulary. Alternative term: isolexic line. (6.1, 7.1, 8.1).

ISOLEXIC LINE → Isolex.

ISOMORPH An → isogloss on a linguistic map drawn around an area of a particular feature of → morphology. Alternative term: isomorphic line. (6.1, 7.1, 8.1).

ISOMORPHIC LINE → Isomorph.

ISOMORPHISM Similarities between two or more languages in their phonological, grammatical or semantic structure. Even in genealogically related language families, complete isomorphism is non-existent, as every language has its own organisation of → meaning into → form, e.g. the vocabulary relating to colour and kinship concepts. Even from one stage in the historical development of a single language to the next the various structures are not isomorphous. (2.1 Lyons).

ISOPHONE An → isogloss on a linguistic map drawn around an area of a particular feature of → pronunciation. Alternative term: isophonic line. (6.1, 7.1, 8.1).

ISOPHONIC LINE → Isophone.

ISOPLETH A line drawn on a linguistic map around an area not only of common linguistic features, but also of features of folklore, geography and cultural institutions which have a unifying influence on regional dialects. Alternative terms: isoerg, isograde. (6.1, 7.1, 8.1).

ISOSYLLABISM → Tempo.

ISOSYNTAGMIC LINE An → isogloss on a linguistic map delineating an area with similar features of → syntax. (6.1, 7.1, 8.1).

ISOTONIC LINE An → isogloss on a linguistic map which delineates an area with similar features of → tone. (6.1, 7.1, 8.1).

ITEM A linguistic form which can be isolated and quoted as part of a list. The following kinds of linguistic item may be distinguished: LEXICAL ITEM or vocabulary item, e.g. *chair*, *seat*, *table*, etc.; → GRAMMATICAL ITEM, e.g. -*s* in *chairs*; PHONOLOGICAL ITEM, e.g. /s/, /iː/, /t/ in *seat*. Lexical and grammatical items are usually classed together as FORMAL ITEMS and listed in → dictionaries as terms, lexemes or morphemes. For the purpose of language teaching, formal items and items of sound feature must be selected, graded, and presented in a particular order. (9.11 Halliday *et al.*).

ITEM-AND-ARRANGEMENT (IA) An approach to linguistic analysis which excludes all consideration of time and describes language in terms of lists of items and the arrangements in which these items occur. Passive and active sentences, for example, are considered to exist regarding one as being derived from the other as opposed to an → item-and-process approach. → word-and-paradigm. (2.2 Lyons).

ITEM-AND-PROCESS (IP) An approach to linguistic analysis which describes language as a dynamic system, i.e. with one item being derived from another by a series of changes, e.g. passive sentences being transforms of active sentences, in contrast to the → item-and-arrangement approach. The item and process approach is the basis of transformational grammar. → word-and-paradigm. (2.2 Lyons).

ITEM ANALYSIS In language → testing the careful evaluation of each of the elements in a test battery to ensure its reliability from the statistical, linguistic and paedagogical points of view. (9.14 Davies).

ITERATIVE ASPECT → Aspect.

ITERATIVE COMPOUND A → compound word made up of two identical halves, e.g. *bye-bye*.

ITERATIVE NUMERAL → Multiplicative numeral.

J

JARGON (*a*) A set of terms and expressions used by a social or occupational group, but not used and often not understood by the speech community as a whole. Outsiders often regard jargons such as 'officialese', 'journalese', 'medicalese', etc. as 'bad style'. → terminology. (*b*) → Language acquisition.

JUNCTURE A significant → intonation pattern marking the joining of one phrase or clause with another or with silence. Three types of terminal juncture are distinguished by most linguists:

(*i*) SUSTAINED JUNCTURE, represented in transcription by an arrow ⟨ → ⟩ or a single line ⟨/⟩ and often called a SINGLE-BAR JUNCTURE, which occurs when the pitch of the voice is sustained or rises very slightly, e.g. when words are in apposition as in *Mr Smith, | the gardener, | is out.*

(*ii*) RISING JUNCTURE, represented in transcription by a rising arrow ⟨↗⟩ or a double line ⟨//⟩ and often called a DOUBLE-BAR JUNCTURE, which occurs when the pitch of the voice rises before a pause, e.g. in counting or listing items or at the end of questions such as *Are you going?||.*

(*iii*) FALLING JUNCTURE, represented in transcription by a falling arrow ⟨↘⟩ or a double cross ⟨#⟩ and often called DOUBLE-CROSS JUNCTURE or FADING JUNCTURE, which occurs when there is a drop in pitch as the voice fades into silence, e.g. at the end of an utterance. → transition. Alternative terms: terminal juncture, clause terminal. (3.1, 8.22).

JUNGGRAMMATIKER → Neogrammarians.

JUXTAPOSED COMPOUND A compound made up of two elements which are placed next to each other, but written as separate words, e.g. *university student*.

JUXTAPOSING LANGUAGE A type of language such as Coptic and some Bantu languages, where grammatical relationships are shown by the adding of short formal elements or 'classifiers' to the base of words. (6.1, 8.1).

JUXTAPOSITIONAL ASSIMI-LATION → Assimilation.

JUXTAPOSITIONAL DISSIMI-LATION → Dissimilation.

121

K

KANA Collective term for *hiragana* and *katakana*, the Japanese syllabic writing systems. → Table p. 264.

KATAKANA A syllabic writing system used in Japanese, largely for transcription of foreign words. → Table p. 264.

KERNEL (SENTENCE) (*a*) In transformational-generative grammar originally a sentence which is generated by the phrase structure rules and obligatory transformations, but without optional transformations. Kernel sentences are usually simple, declarative indicative statements which can be transformed into more complex, e.g. passive, sentences, by means of optional transformation rules. The term is sometimes used as an alternative to the basic → clause pattern. (*b*) → base (*a*).

KEY One of a series of styles of speech (→ manner of discourse). One well-known classification proposes five such keys. The same message can be expressed in all keys according to context, e.g. a request for people to remain seated:

(1) FROZEN or ORATORICAL:
   Participants should remain seated throughout the ceremony.
(2) FORMAL or DELIBERATE:
   Those taking part should sit during the proceedings.
(3) CONSULTATIVE:
   Would you please stay in your seats.
(4) CASUAL:
   Don't get up.
(5) INTIMATE:
   Sit tight.

(8.24 Joos).

KEY-WORDS Those terms which represent the concepts and ideals typical of a period or social group, e.g. *automation, free enterprise, technocrat.* (5.2 Ullmann).

KINAESTHETIC FEEDBACK The process by means of which a speaker is aware of the movements of his articulatory organs. → feedback (*a*).

KINE The representation of a → kineme or minimum unit of gesture abstracted from the continuum of speech or non-verbal communication. → kinesics.

KINEME A term coined by analogy with → phoneme to refer to a minimum unit of → gesture such as the raising of eyebrows or shrugging of shoulders in speech or non-vocal communication. → kinesics. (2.3 Birdwhistell).

KINEMICS → Kinesics.

KINESICS The system and study of → gesture in speech or non-verbal communication, including facial expressions and body motion. By analogy with other branches of linguistic analysis (phonemics, morphemics) scholars have tried to isolate basic units (→ kine, kineme, allokine) and the pattern of arrangement between them has been termed KINEMICS. Alternative terms: body semantics, body language. (2.3 Birdwhistell; 10.1 Hymes).

KINETIC CONSONANT A consonant such as a → stop which cannot be prolonged without changing its quality.

KINSHIP TERMS Those terms which represent the members of a biologically related group, e.g. *father, uncle, cousin*, etc. Alternative term: family terms. (10.1 Burling).

KOINE A spoken dialect which becomes the common standard language for a politically unified region, e.g. Hellenistic Greek in the Mediterranean before Roman rule, or Hindi in large parts of India. Alternative term: compromise language. (7.1, 8.1, 8.8 Hall, 9.2 Hymes).

KYMOGRAPH An early mechanical device for the graphic representation of certain → acoustic features of speech.

L

LABIAL A speech sound which involves the use of the lips. If both lips are used to stop or modify the air stream the sound is called → bilabial or labio-labial. If the lower lip is brought into contact with the upper teeth, the sound is called → labio-dental. (3.1, 8.22).

LABIALISATION The articulation of a speech sound accompanied by lip movement, extending the oral cavity and producing a round aperture between rounded lips, e.g. [u:] in *room*. Alternative terms: lip rounding, rounding. (3.1, 8.22).

LABIO-DENTAL A speech sound articulated by bringing the lower lip near or into contact with the upper teeth, e.g. [f] as in *fat* or [v] as in *vat*.

LABIO-LABIAL → Bilabial.

LABIOVELAR A → velar speech sound produced with rounded lips, e.g. [kʼ] in *quill*.

LABORATORY PHONETICS → Experimental phonetics.

LAG → Assimilation.

LALLATION The second stage in → language acquisition when the infant begins at about six months of age to utter distinct vowel sounds, as opposed to → babbling. (9.6).

LAMBDACISM The replacing of a speech sound (usually [r]) by the sound [l], e.g. [tli:] instead of [tri:] *tree*. Alternative term: lamdaism.

LAMDAISM → Lambdacism.

LAMINAL Term used to indicate that the blade of the tongue is used as the active → articulator, as opposed to the apex. A distinction can thus be made between apico-alveolar, etc. and lamino-alveolar, etc. Some linguists use the term dorsal to refer to this articulation, but others use → dorsal to refer to articulation with the back part of the tongue. (3.1 Abercrombie).

LANGUAGE The most fundamental means of human communication. Language is the primary object of the study of → linguistics, and linguists approach the notion of 'language' from differing points of view. Some of these are contained in the well-known definition given by the American anthropological linguist E. Sapir (1884–1939): "Language is a purely human and non-instinctive method of communicating ideas, emotions and desires by means of a system of voluntarily produced symbols." This definition emphasises a number of important aspects of language. Language is a purely human activity, although some animals have communication systems which have certain analogies to human language. All human beings use language to interact with other members of the same speech community. Language is not only used as an instrument of communication, however, but also as a means of individual expression. Language is not instinctive; it has to be learnt as a system of arbitrary conventional symbols. Such symbols are primarily vocal, produced by the so-called → organs of speech, but secondary systems such as → writing and other → codes may complement the vocal system. Some linguists, such as F. de Saussure (1857–1913), have stressed the view of language as general patterns in the speech of a community and as the speaking activity of an individual in a particular situation (→ langue and parole); others, with N. Chomsky, regard language as the innate capability of native speakers to understand and form grammatical sentences and as the actual utterances produced at a given time (→ competence and performance). Linguists attempt to develop adequate theories of language phenomena in general as well as special techniques to describe particular languages in detail (→ grammar). Other disciplines have a contribution to make in addition to that of the linguist. Anthropologists regard language as a form of cultural behaviour, sociologists as an interaction between members of a social group, students of literature as an artistic medium, philosophers as a means of interpreting human experience, language teachers as a set of skills. → dialect. (2.1, 2.2).

LANGUAGE ACQUISITION

Several stages can be distinguished in the chronological development of the native language in children, although the processes leading from the 'prelinguistic' to the 'linguistic' stages are continuous, and there may be considerable individual variation:

3–6 months BABBLING or vocal play: understanding of facial expressions and tones of voice; exercising of organs of speech to produce a wide variety of sounds, but no coherent utterances;

6–9 months LALLATION: reaction to gestures and simple commands; continuation of self-stimulated combination of sounds;

12 months IMITATION: active response to outside influences; first 'words' (one-word sentences) and repetitive verbal play;

15 months JARGON: incorporating elements of the talk of environment into flow of uncontrolled speech; vocabulary rises to over 20 words; communication through two-word phrases;

2 years TALKING: full understanding of instructions; beginnings of verbalisation of wants in phrases;

4 years LOQUACITY: full understanding of adult speech directed at him and almost complete mastery of patterns.

In the acquisition of the mother tongue, various factors such as trial-and-error learning, imitation and analogy are at work; the acquisition of a second language may be made more difficult by age, lack of contact with the foreign speech community, interference between the two languages, insufficient motivation, etc. (9.1, 9.6, 10.2).

LANGUAGE ACQUISITION DEVICE Linguists and psychologists study the process of language learning by comparing input with output, i.e. by comparing the language an infant is exposed to with the language an infant produces. Exactly how the brain acquires language competence is not known, but the term language acquisition device, often abbreviated L.A.D., is applied to the unknown quantity in the model roughly as below:

input → ⟨ L.A.D. ⟩ → output

(2.1 Chomsky, 9.1, 9.6, 10.2).

LANGUAGE BARRIER The difficulties of communication between speakers of different languages. Among the solutions to this problem are increased and improved → language teaching, and more and better → translation and interpreting services. (8.1, 9.1, 9.3).

LANGUAGE BOUNDARY The line drawn between different speech communities. It is difficult in some cases to determine where one language ends and another one begins, particularly where dialects of different but related languages converge. → dialect boundary. (7.1, 8.1, 9.2).

LANGUAGE CHANGE → Change.

LANGUAGE CONTACT → Contact.

LANGUAGE FAMILY → Family of languages.

LANGUAGE LABORATORY An arrangement of electronic equipment and furniture to help in → language teaching by giving the opportunity for practice in the listening and speaking skills. It usually consists of acoustically treated booths, where each student has his own → tape recorder and headset. From a control desk or console the teacher can monitor (listen in) and/or interrupt the students individually or in groups and exercise remote control over the equipment in the students' booths. The students work independently and intensively with specially prepared tapes, which ideally should form part of a course of → programmed instruction. A distinction may be made between the BROADCAST SYSTEM in which students work together on material transmitted from the teacher's console, and the LIBRARY SYSTEM in which students work individually with pre-recorded tapes taken from a library or archive. A LISTENING INSTALLATION is a simple form of language laboratory for listening only, a LISTEN-AND-SPEAK LABORATORY (or LISTEN-RESPOND LABORATORY) has no recording facilities and students listen to a broadcast lesson. A LISTEN-SPEAK-RECORD LABORATORY is fully equipped with recording facilities at the individual booths. Film projection facilities may also be included. (9.14 Hayes, Stack).

LANGUAGE LEARNING The process by which human beings acquire either their native speech or a foreign language. Learning as a

125

psychological and social activity is not fully understood, and several theories and models have been put forward. It is generally accepted, however, that trial-and-error learning can be speeded up by systematic → language teaching in which all phonological, grammatical and lexical items are selected, graded and presented in an organised fashion. → Programmed instruction. (9.11, 9.6, 10.2).

LANGUAGE PLANNING

Collective term for a complex of efforts to improve interdialect and international communication *either* by studying the relationships between pairs of languages (dialects) *or* by creating a new language system. Whereas attempts to devise → artificial auxiliary languages have not had any marked success, the comparison of languages has proved very helpful in many ways, e.g. in → translation, by research into and standardisation of specialised terminologies, by the design of → union languages and → writing systems, etc. → institutional linguistics. Alternative terms: planned language change; prescriptive linguistics. (10.1 Tauli).

LANGUAGE SKILL →

Linguistic skill.

LANGUAGE STANDARDISA-
TION → Standardisation.

LANGUAGE TEACHING A

collective term used to denote all educational theory and practice concerned with instruction in both the native language and a foreign language. Recently there has been a trend towards increased and more efficient modern language teaching. Traditionally, languages were taught by the → grammar-translation method and by reading literature. Contemporary methods concentrate more on the practice of actual skills, such as comprehension, speaking, reading, etc. → Language laboratory, grading, drill. (9.1).

LANGUAGE UNIVERSAL →
Universal.

LANGUAGE VARIETY →
Variety in language.

LANGUE and PAROLE

Language may be said to have two facets: *Langue* refers to the → system of language which is passed on from one generation to another, e.g. the grammar, syntax and vocabulary, whereas *parole* refers to all that which a speaker might say or understand. Langue is the social, conventional side of language; parole is individual speech. Another way of expressing the difference is to say that langue is the → code and parole the → message. (2.4 Saussure).

LAPSE
The spontaneous creation of meaningless or unintended forms during speech, usually under special circumstances or in special contexts; e.g. a slip of the tongue in rapid speech.

LARYNGEAL
A speech sound which is produced in the larynx, e.g. the → glottal stop. Alternative term: glottal. (3.1, 8.22).

LARYNGEALISED VOICING
→ Register (*a*).

LARYNGECTOMY
Surgical removal of the → larynx. (9.5).

126

LARYNGOSCOPE An instrument for looking down the throat to examine the → larynx.

LARYNX A frame of cartilage or muscle, situated at the top of the trachea or windpipe, containing the → vocal cords. → diagram p. 159.

LATERAL A consonant produced whilst allowing air to escape around one or both sides of a closure formed by the tongue with the roof of the oral cavity. A typical example is the sound [l]. If the air escapes around only one side of the tongue the terms UNILATERAL CONSONANT, MONOLATERAL CONSONANT or ASYMMETRIC CONSONANT are used. If the air escapes around both sides of the tongue, the term BILATERAL CONSONANT is used. (3.1, 8.22).

LATERAL versus NON-LATERAL Cavity features in recent theories of → distinctive feature phonology. These features apply only to coronal consonants. Lateral sounds are produced with the air escaping along one or both sides of the tongue; in non-lateral sounds air does not escape in this way.

LATERAL AREA → Area.

LATERAL PLOSION The → release of a stop consonant in such a way as to allow the air to escape around the sides of the tongue: e.g. [t] in *brittle* [brɪtl]. → nasal plosion.

LATERAL RELEASE → Release.

LATIN ALPHABET → Table p. 265.

LATINATE GRAMMAR The tradition of prescriptive grammar based on the categories used in the description of ancient Latin. (2.5).

LAW IN LINGUISTICS A generalisation based on empirical → observation of regular processes and expressed in the form of an abbreviated statement. Various such laws or principles have been discovered about regular patterns in language. They are usually named after the author who first formulated them. One type of law deals with sound changes in the development of one or more languages (phonetic laws, e.g. → Darmesteter's law, → Grassman's law, → Grimm's law, → Verner's law, etc.); another is concerned with establishing the relationships between length and frequency of vocabulary items, e.g. → Zipf's law. (2.1, 6.1).

LAW OF ABBREVIATION → Zipf's law.

LAX A → vowel sound produced with relatively little muscular tension, e.g. [ɪ] in *bit*, as opposed to the → tense vowel [i:] in *beat*. This difference in tension can be felt by placing the thumb and forefinger under the lower jaw whilst pronouncing the words one after the other. → tense versus lax. (3.1, 8.22).

LAYERED → Layering.

LAYERING A term used in → tagmemics to refer to what in other forms of linguistic analysis might be called embedding, i.e. the inclusion of a string of tagmemes constituting a unit of a particular level into a string of tagmemes constituting a unit of the same level, e.g. in *the very good film*, *very good* is a phrase LAYERED within the phrase *the film*. → parenthetical clause.

LEARNED WORD A word used in literary style, e.g. *epistle*, as opposed to a popular word such as *letter*. Alternative term: book word.

LEIPZIG SCHOOL → Neogrammarians.

LENGTH → Duration.

LENIS A → consonant produced with weak muscular tension as opposed to → fortis, a consonant produced with strong muscular tension. In English, voiced consonants are usually unaspirated and lenis, whereas voiceless consonants are usually aspirated and fortis. (3.1, 8.22).

LENITION A relaxation in muscular tension during articulation, thus changing a → fortis consonant into a → lenis.

LENTO FORM The full form of a word or phrase in carefully articulated speech, e.g. *library* as [laibrəri], as opposed to the shortened or → allegro form [laibri].

LETTER A sign used in → writing to represent sounds of human speech. It usually refers to the single graphic unit of alphabetic scripts and its written or printed shape rather than to the characters and symbols of logographic or syllabographic writing systems. In many languages the correspondence between letters and sounds is often arbitrary, as the rules of → spelling tend to be conventional and do not keep up with phonological changes in the language. → alphabet. (7.2).

LEVEL (*a*) In → linguistic analysis, one of several planes which may be set up to divide language into manageable subsystems, e.g. sound or → phonology, form or → grammar, meaning or → semantics. Within these subsystems further divisions may be made as hierarchical arrangements of units on related strata, ranks, or levels, e.g. in → tagmemics the basic syntactic units are on the level of morpheme, word, phrase, clause, sentence, paragraph, and discourse. (*b*) In the study of language varieties, level refers to a stylistic, social or situational plane of speech. → manner of discourse. (*c*) The → volume or loudness of sound.

LEVEL-SKIPPING In → tagmemics when a particular level in the grammatical hierarchy is omitted in a grammatical construction, e.g. the whole phrase *the man who digs my garden* within the genitive construction *the man who digs my garden's spade*.

LEVEL STRESS The phenomenon of two adjacent syllables having a certain degree of prominence such as English *home-made* or *oatcake*. In fact the stress is not level in the sense of 'equal', since it consists of a combination of primary and secondary → stress.

LEVELLING The regularisation of differences in a paradigmatic set by → analogy, e.g. in the principal parts of English strong verbs the plural merged with the singular, as in Old English *sang, sungon* > Modern English *sang*.

LEXEME Name given by some linguists to a basic unit of the → vocabulary of a language, as opposed to a grammatical unit such as the → morpheme and a semantic unit such as the → sememe. (5.2 Zgusta).

LEXICAL FIELD → Semantic field.

LEXICAL ITEM A unit of the → vocabulary of a language such as a word, phrase or term as listed in a → dictionary. It usually has a pronounceable or graphic form, fulfils a grammatical role in a sentence, and carries semantic meaning. → lexeme.

LEXICAL MEANING → Meaning.

LEXICAL SELECTION The compatibility of words within larger syntactical units or as members of a grammatical sub-class, e.g. in sentences of the type *He eats fish* and *He drives a car*, verbs concerned with 'eating' can collocate with *fish* but not *car*; verbs concerned with 'driving' can collocate with *car* but not *fish*; *fish, meat, bread*, etc. belong to a different sub-class from *car*; and *car, van, locomotive*, etc. belong to a different sub-class from *fish*. (4.1, 5.1).

LEXICAL STRESS The stressing of an item when it is isolated from its usual context, e.g. the pronunciation of the indefinite article *a* as [ei] rather than [ə].

LEXICAL SYSTEM The relations that may be established between groups of vocabulary items in a → semantic field.

LEXICAL TONE → Tone.

LEXICAL WORD → Content word.

LEXICALISATION The expression of a grammatical or semantic category by a → lexical item, e.g. English 'make' + 'dead' together are lexicalised as *kill*, in German 'tot' +

'machen' > *töten*, or the close linking of lexical items in an idiomatic phrase, e.g. *bring pressure to bear on*...

LEXICOGRAPHER A person engaged in → lexicography or dictionary-making.

LEXICOGRAPHY A branch of applied → lexicology, concerned with the principles and practice of dictionary-making, i.e. compiling, comparing, defining and grouping → lexical items in book form. (5.2 Householder–Saporta, Zgusta).

LEXICOLOGY A branch of linguistics concerned with the study and analysis of the vocabulary items of a language as well as their meanings and evolution.

LEXICON A collection of the vocabulary or lexical items in a language or language variety, e.g. the words listed in a general → dictionary, or the terms listed in a specialised → glossary.

LEXICOSTATISTICS The statistical study of the basic → vocabulary of two or more languages to determine their mutual intelligibility, to find relationships between them, and to classify them into types and groups. (6.1, 8.1, 10.1).

LEXIS A name given by some linguists to that level of linguistic analysis which is neither phonological nor grammatical in nature. This usually comprises the vocabulary items of a language as well as their lexical or semantic meaning in specific contexts. (5.1, 5.2).

LEXOTACTICS The system and study of the characteristic arrangement of → lexemes in sequence.

LIAISON The joining of one word to the next with close → transition, e.g. French *il est aimable* [ilɛtɛmablə] 'he is likeable'.

LICENCE → Poetic licence.

LIGATURE The linking of written signs in writing or in print, e.g. <f+i> in <field>, or in phonetic transcription, e.g. [æ].

LIGHT → Atonic.

LIMITATION → Grading.

LINE SPECTRUM → Spectrum.

LINEARITY In phonology the principle of a → sequence of phonemes representing a sequence of phones in consecutive order: thus phoneme /A/ occurring to the left of phoneme /B/ means that the phone represented by /A/ occurs before the phone represented by /B/.

LINEAR PROGRAMME A course of → programmed instruction where the student is obliged to follow a set sequence of exercises or frames, as opposed to a branching programme where there are alternative routes according to the student's previous achievements.

LINEAR PHONEME → Phoneme.

LINEAR SCRIPT A form of writing using abstract signs or characters, e.g. an → alphabet, as opposed to earlier forms of pictorial writing which used recognisable pictures or sketches. (7.2).

LINGO → Cant.

LINGUA FRANCA In areas of intensive language → contact, a language adopted by speakers of different speech communities as their common medium of communication, e.g. Latin in medieval Europe, Arabic in the Near East, Swahili in Central Africa, and Malay in South East Asia. → creole, pidgin. (8.8 Hall, 9.2 Hymes).

LINGUAGRAM A picture of the → tongue.

LINGUIST (*a*) A person whose scholarly interest is language (linguistician), e.g. grammarian, phonetician, lexicologist, etymologist. (*b*) A person who is skilled in more than one language (polyglot), using this ability in a profession, e.g. translator, interpreter, language teacher.

LINGUISTIC ANALYSIS Collective term for various operations that the linguist performs on data he has obtained from → field-work or by collecting → texts. Linguists attempt to find the regular patterns in this material by breaking it down into minimal elements (→ segmental analysis), by establishing how these elements are made up (→ componential analysis), by examining the relationships between them (→ distributional analysis, discourse analysis), and by determining their arrangement within longer sequences (→ immediate constituent analysis, functional analysis). Such procedures are used on the levels of sound (→ phonemic analysis), grammar (→ morphological analysis, grammatical analysis), and vocabulary (→ semantic analysis). Special techniques are used for specific purposes, e.g. →

contrastive analysis and → error analysis in language teaching. → procedure.

LINGUISTIC ANTHROPO-LOGY →Anthropological linguistics.

LINGUISTIC AREA → Area.

LINGUISTIC ATLAS A collection of maps and charts illustrating the geographical distribution of features of pronunciation, grammar and vocabulary of a language or → dialect or both. The data are collected by trained field workers from carefully selected native → informants by means of informal conversations, questionnaires and tape recordings, plotted on maps and published in book form. Famous examples are the *Atlas linguistique de la France*, the *Linguistic Atlas of the United States and Canada* and various dialect surveys in Germany, the Soviet Union, Italy, Switzerland, England, Scotland, and other countries. Alternative term: dialect atlas. (7.1, 8.24).

LINGUISTIC BORROWING → Borrowing.

LINGUISTIC CHANGE → Change.

LINGUISTIC CIRCLE A group of linguists and scholars from related disciplines, usually based on a particular university, who meet periodically to discuss questions of common interest, often publishing transactions. Especially famous are the Linguistic Circles of Prague in the 1930s, Copenhagen in the 1940s, Paris, New York, and Ann Arbor, Michigan. (2.2 Sebeok).

LINGUISTIC CONTEXT → Context (*a*).

LINGUISTIC DEMOGRAPHY The study, largely by means of statistical surveys, of the different groups of users of the languages and language varieties within a speech community, classified by factors of social class, religion, age and regional distribution. (10.1 Fishman).

LINGUISTIC FORM → Form.

LINGUISTIC GEOGRAPHY The study of the regional distribution of dialect or language areas. → dialectology, areal linguistics. (7.1, 8.1).

LINGUISTIC GROUP → Family of languages.

LINGUISTIC MINORITY → Minority language.

LINGUISTIC NORM → Norm.

LINGUISTIC PHILOSOPHY → Philosophy of language.

LINGUISTIC PSYCHOLOGY → Psychological linguistics.

LINGUISTIC RELATIVITY → Relativity.

LINGUISTIC SCIENCES → Linguistics.

LINGUISTIC SEMANTICS → Semantics.

LINGUISTIC SIGN → Sign (*b*).

LINGUISTIC SKILL The ability of an individual speaker to use his language well. Most linguistic analysis has to do with 'idealised'

language knowledge or → competence, although linguists are aware
of the considerable variations in
actual performance from speaker to
speaker. During language acquisition or in → language learning an
extremely complicated set of skills
are learned and perfected to achieve
full fluency. These have been divided
into 'formal' skills (such as identification and recognition, control of
articulatory and graphic processes)
and 'thematic' or 'institutional' skills
such as correct response to a verbal or
written stimulus, use of appropriate grammatical patterns and vocabulary, translating from one language
or language variety into another, etc.
→ listening, speaking, reading, writing.
Certain virtuoso skills such as oratory
and literary creativity are held in great
esteem. Alternative terms: language
skill, verbal skill. (2.3 Samarin, 9.11).

LINGUISTIC TABOO →
Taboo.

LINGUISTIC TYPOLOGY
→ Typology.

LINGUISTICIAN A word coined
by analogy with mathematician,
politician, etc. to denote a specialist
in → linguistics. The term probably
came into being because of the confusion between the two meanings of
linguist, 'specialist in linguistics' and
'polyglot'. Linguistician is also used
occasionally to denote a specialist in
the application of linguistics to →
language teaching.

LINGUISTICS The field of study
the subject of which is → language.
Linguists study language as man's
ability to communicate, as individual
expression, as the common heritage
of a speech community, as spoken
sound, as written text, etc. Such

different approaches to language have
in fact led to the development of
linguistic schools and theoretical →
models, each with its own techniques
and methods of observing, classifying
and explaining the facts of human
speech. The major branches of linguistic knowledge include → phonology, → grammar (morphology and
syntax) and → lexicology. GENERAL
LINGUISTICS or THEORETICAL LIN-
GUISTICS provides the theoretical
concepts and apparatus and a
common framework for → descriptive, → historical, → comparative, empirical and other types of linguistic
studies, including → dialectology.
The term LINGUISTIC SCIENCES is used
to incorporate the above as well as →
phonetics and → semantics. The
history of linguistic scholarship goes
back over many centuries, when
ancient Indian and Greek linguists
first observed certain regularities in
language, e.g. between 'sounds' and
'meanings' or between 'speech' and
'writing'. Since then, linguistics has
moved away from philosophical and
literary studies to become an autonomous discipline between the 'arts'
and 'sciences'. Recent trends point
to more intensive contacts with the
social sciences (→ anthropological
linguistics, psycholinguistics, sociolinguistics), greater use of experimental and mathematical techniques,
and increasing applications to practical fields (→ applied linguistics,
→ feature, philology). Alternative
terms: linguistic science, glottology
(obsolete), glossology (obsolete). (2.1–
2.5).

LINGUOSTYLISTICS →
Stylistics.

LINKING MORPHEME An
element placed between two parts of

a compound to join them together, e.g. *-o-* in *psycholinguistic* or *socio-political*, or *-t-* in French *A-t-il un livre?* 'Has he got a book?'. Alternative term: connecting vowel, connecting consonant.

LINKING R The sound [r] used intervocalically between syllables or words. In English it may be etymologically justified as in [mɔːrən + mɔː] *more and more* or → intrusive as in [drɔːriŋ + pin] *drawing pin.*

LINKING VERB → Copula.

LIP ROUNDING → Labialisation.

LIP SPREADING Alternative term for → delabialisation or unrounding, referring to the posture of the lips during the production of a speech sound.

LIQUID A term used to refer collectively to apico-alveolar continuant sounds such as [r] and [l].

LISPING The pronunciation of [θ] and [ð] instead of [s] and [z] or vice versa, either deliberately or because of a confusion between dental and alveolar fricatives.

LISTENING One of the basic linguistic skills; the ability to identify and comprehend speech. → hearing.

LITERACY In languages with a system of writing, the ability to read or write as opposed to → articulacy, the active command of the spoken language. Only about half the world's population is literate in this sense. → illiteracy, preliteracy. (7.2 I.B.E.).

LITERAL TRANSLATION → Translation.

LITERARY LANGUAGE A → variety of language which is considered 'best' in certain social or teaching situations. It is usually equivalent to the → standard dialect of the language as used in → written language and in works of → literature, and opposed to the colloquial or vernacular styles. (7.1–7.3).

LITERARY TRANSLATION → Translation.

LITERATURE In the widest sense the term literature applies to any collection of → texts of a writer, period, subject field, or language variety. More specifically, it denotes those writings which are considered worth preserving and subjected to aesthetic evaluation ('literary criticism'). Apart from the classification by subjects, literary works are usually categorised by form into the 'genres' drama, poetry, prose, etc. The term ORAL LITERATURE is used for the stories, poems and songs which are passed on by word of mouth from one generation to another, e.g. in children's stories or by illiterate speech communities. (7.3, 10.1).

LIVING LANGUAGE A language which is the current native language of a speech community, e.g. English, German, Japanese, etc. → artificial language, → dead language.

LOAN The process or result of → borrowing elements from one language or dialect by another. This may occur on the phonological, grammatical and/or lexical levels, although the borrowing of vocabulary items is by far the most frequent.

LOAN BLEND The formation of a → compound word or phrase by combining native forms with → borrowed elements from another language, e.g. *co-worker*.

LOAN SHIFT The → borrowing of a word or phrase from another language with a simultaneous modification of its phonological shape, so that it is taken for a native one, e.g. *bungalow* from Hindi.

LOAN TRANSLATION The → borrowing of a compound word or phrase in which the total grammatical pattern and semantic meaning are imported, but the individual constituents are replaced from the stock of native sounds and morphemes, e.g. *Neogrammarian* < German *Junggrammatiker*, German *Ausdruck* 'expression' < Latin *expressio*. Alternative term: calque.

LOAN WORD A word introduced into a language directly from a foreign language or by translation or imitation of a concept taken over from another language, e.g. English *husband, skill, wrong, get*, etc. from Old Norse, *council, navy*, etc. from Old French and later borrowings, e.g. *Blitz* from German, *sputnik* from Russian. → borrowing.

LOCAL DIALECT → Dialect.

LOCAL FRICTION → Friction.

LOCATIVE A → case form in some inflected languages indicating the location at which an action takes place. In classical Latin this function is carried out largely by the ablative, but a few distinct locative forms remain, e.g. *Romae* 'at Rome', *domi* 'at home'.

LOGIC IN LANGUAGE The problem of whether human language can be treated as a logical system has occupied linguists and philosophers for centuries. Many traditional grammarians held the 'rational' view that language use must conform to universal rules of → philosophical grammar. Some groups of philosophers have maintained that since ordinary language is not logical enough for scientific and philosophical discourse, it must be extended or replaced for this purpose by artificial systems. Some of these ideas have been applied to linguistic theory and methodology, thus improving the efficiency of formal descriptions (→ glossematics, transformational-generative grammar, computational linguistics). Most linguists agree that the techniques of formal logic should be used to explain rather than regulate the patterns of language usage. (10.3 Dixon).

LOGICAL SUBJECT → Subject.

LOGOGRAM A graphic sign used in logographic systems of → writing to represent a word, e.g. ancient Egyptian hieroglyphs and Chinese characters. Logographic writing is believed to have originated from pictorial sketches used for recording messages, and later developed into more sound-based scripts such as syllabary and → alphabet. Logograms in alphabetic writing systems include symbols like % 'per cent', & 'and', + 'plus', etc. and abbreviations like Mr and Co. Alternative terms: logograph, word sign. → ideogram. (7.2).

LOGOGRAPH → Logogram.

LOGOGRAPHY A writing system using → logograms. Alternative term: ideography. (7.2).

LOGOP(A)EDICS → Speech therapy.

LOGO-SYLLABIC WRITING A system of writing using → logograms and → syllabograms.

LOGOTACTICS The study of the characteristics of words in sequence. → tactics.

LONDON SCHOOL → British linguistics.

LONG CONSONANT → Duration.

LONG VOWEL → Duration.

LOOK-AND-SAY A method of teaching → reading, sometimes also used in teaching a foreign language, by associating word shapes with the ideas and actions they stand for. (7.2, 9.14).

LOOSE APPOSITION A word or phrase used in → apposition and often separated by sustained → juncture in speech or by commas in writing, e.g. *My uncle, the manager, drives a red sports car.*

LOQUACITY → Language acquisition.

LOSS The discarding of phonological, grammatical or lexical items at a particular stage in the history of a language, either because they are replaced by others, or because the things they refer to have become obsolete. The relative loss and retention of items in the basic → vocabulary are studied in → glottochronology. (6.1).

LOUDNESS → Volume.

LOW VOWEL A → vowel sound pronounced with the tongue low in the mouth. → diagram p. 253.

M

MACHINE TRANSLATION The automatic production of a → translation by computer or similar machine. The machine programme must contain rules to analyse the original text in the → source language to find grammatical and lexical equivalents contained in its dictionary store, and to synthesise a new version of the original text in the → target language. Fully automated high-quality translation has proved a very difficult and expensive operation, but research in this field has contributed to progress in → linguistic analysis. Alternative terms: automatic translation, mechanical translation. (9.4 Hays).

MACROLINGUISTICS Those aspects of language study which are concerned with all types of human → communication. From this point of view macrolinguistics may be said to include not only → microlinguistics (phonology, grammar, semantics), but also 'pre-linguistic' phenomena such as miming and gestures as well as → paralinguistic features and problems of cultural behaviour. Some linguists regard macrolinguistics as the study, by statistical means, of large-scale linguistic phenomena, e.g. the distribution of phoneme or word frequencies. → Metalinguistics (*b*), → linguistics.

MACRON A → diacritic mark indicating syllable length and other features, e.g. Latin *pōpulus* 'poplar'.

MAIN CLAUSE A clause which has full meaning when standing alone and which is not dependent on any other clause, although it may be modified or expanded by a dependent clause or clauses, e.g. in the sentence *The sun shone although it was raining*, *the sun shone* is the main clause and *although it was raining* is a → subordinate clause. Alternative term: independent clause. (4.1, 4.2, 8.23).

MAIN VERB → Full verb.

MAJOR CLASS FEATURES → Distinctive feature.

MALAPROPISM The inappropriate use of a word because it is similar in sound to the appropriate word. → catachresis.

MALAYO-POLYNESIAN LINGUISTICS Collective term for the linguistic description of Malayo-Polynesian languages such as Malay, Javanese, Tagalog, etc. → Appendix 1, p. 275. → Oceanic linguistics. Alternative term: Austronesian linguistics. (8.8 Longacre, Milner–Henderson).

MALFORMATION Improper formation of a word by false analogy, e.g. *catched* for *caught*, by analogy with *cooked*, *watched*, *laughed*, etc.

MANIFESTATION → Realisation.

MANNER OF ARTICULATION The way in which the air stream is constricted or released in the vocal tract, used as a way of classifying speech sounds. The main classifications are → stop, → nasal, → fricative, → affricate, → lateral, → trill, → flap, → semi-vowel, → vowel. → chart p. 262. Alternative term: mode of articulation. (3.1, 8.22).

MANNER OF ARTICULATION FEATURES → Distinctive feature.

MANNER OF DISCOURSE A → variety of language used in a particular situation. Features of pronunciation, grammar and/or vocabulary may indicate a speaker's attitude to the subject under discussion or his social relationship to the intended listener. Several scales of LEVELS OF SPEECH have been set up, notably by M. Joos into 5 → keys: (1) frozen or oratorical, e.g. *Participants should remain seated throughout the ceremony*, (2) formal or deliberate, e.g. *Those taking part should sit during the proceedings*, (3) consultative, e.g. *Would you please sit during the proceedings*, (4) casual, e.g. *Don't get up*, (5) intimate, e.g. *Sit tight*. Other terms used to classify manner of discourse include CULTIVATED or CULTURAL, a type of speech used by educated speakers of the standard language, COLLOQUIAL, a type of speech used in everyday informal talk, SUB-STANDARD (or NON-STANDARD or ILLITERATE or VULGAR), a type of speech noticeably different from the 'accepted standard'. In dictionaries which contain information on stylistic variants, these may be designated by 'usage labels'. (7.1).

MARGIN The initial or final parts of a → syllable, e.g. [s] and [t] in *sit*. → onset (*b*), coda.

MARGIN OF SECURITY The range of possible allophonic variations of a → phoneme without the danger of its becoming confused with another phoneme.

MARGINAL AREA → Area.

MARGINAL ELEMENTS → Syllable.

MARK OF CORRELATION A phonological feature which distinguishes one set of phonemes from another, e.g. voicing in the series /b/,/d/,/g/:/p/,/t/,/k/ in English. (3.4 Trubetzkoy).

MARKED INFINITIVE → Second infinitive.

MARKED (MEMBER) That member of a binary pair which carries a distinctive feature to distinguish it from the other member of the pair. Marked *vs.* unmarked binary pairs operate at all levels of linguistic analysis: they may be phonemes such as /p/:/b/ where /b/ is marked for voicing, grammatical items such as *boy:boys* where *boys* is marked for plurality, and semantic contrasts such as *deep:shallow* and *high:low* where the first item is the primary or UNMARKED MEMBER, which can be used with neutral meaning (*cf. How deep is it?* but not *How shallow is it?* unless it has already been established that the thing referred to is 'shallow').

MARKER (*a*) A special feature of a linguistic unit which indicates its class or function. Markers may indicate the category of a linguistic unit at any level of analysis. At the phonological level, a certain intonation pattern may indicate the presence of a question. At the morphological level the morph /s/ in English

may indicate plurality. At the syntactic level the article *the* indicates the presence of a noun phrase. A SEMANTIC MARKER indicates a particular feature of the meaning of a word or phrase, e.g. one meaning of *bachelor* can be described in terms of the semantic components 'male' + 'unmarried'. (*b*) → phrase-marker.

MASCULINE → Gender.

MASS NOUN A term used by some grammarians to denote nouns which do not usually form a plural, e.g. *sugar, flour, sand, happiness*, etc. or, if a plural does exist, the meaning of the plural is different from that of the singular, e.g. *sugars, sands*, as opposed to → unit nouns which can be counted. A few mass nouns such as *oats* have only the plural form. Alternative terms: non-count noun, quantifiable noun, unbounded noun, uncountable noun. (4.1, 4.2, 8.23).

MATHEMATICAL LINGUISTICS Collective term for a number of applications of mathematical models and procedures to linguistic studies. Mathematical linguistics may be said to begin with the counting of linguistic units such as phonemes, graphemes, or vocabulary items (STATISTICAL LINGUISTICS). Towards the end of the 19th century, literary scholars and shorthand experts became interested in the → frequency of such items in specific contexts, but it was not until the Russian A. Markov had laid the mathematical foundation for the study of probability and the American G. K. Zipf had related the frequency distribution of words to underlying biological 'principles of least effort' (→ Zipf's law) that the linguists became interested in the use of quantitative counts

(QUANTITATIVE LINGUISTICS), using several different models for handling the data. Statistical criteria for determining style and authorship have also been worked out by a number of scholars (STYLOSTATISTICS), and mathematical formulae were adopted in → comparative linguistics to measure the degree of relatedness of languages (→ lexicostatistics) and to improve methods of dating different periods in their historical development (→ glottochronology). Another impetus came from → information theory which enabled communication engineers and linguists to measure content in terms of the redundancy of transmitted signals. The term ALGEBRAIC LINGUISTICS is sometimes used for the introduction of mathematical models into the theoretical analysis and description of the formal features of language (→ glossematics, transformational-generative grammar). Syntactic models have been set up in many projects in → machine translation and other computer-assisted linguistic operations (COMPUTATIONAL LINGUISTICS). (7.3, 9.4, 10.4, 10.5).

MATRIX SENTENCE In transformational-generative grammar a sentence into which a → constituent sentence is embedded. Matrix sentences often coincide with what is known in traditional grammar as main clauses. (4.1 Fowler).

MATRONYMIC A name given to a person based on the mother's name, e.g. *Nelson < son of Nel.* → patronymic, teknonymic. Alternative term: metronymic.

MEANING The sense that a word or group of words conveys. The term 'meaning' has caused much controversy both within and outside the field of linguistics, and numerous approaches to a consistent theory of meaning have been tried (→ semantics). Linguists usually distinguish between 'grammatical' meaning as the relationships that may be said to exist between linguistic elements such as the words within a sentence, and 'lexical' meaning as the sense a speaker attaches to linguistic elements as → symbols of actual objects and events. Thus, in a list of words such as *ball, boy, hits,* all the words have LEXICAL (or SEMANTIC or EXTERNAL) MEANING which may be found in dictionaries, but they do not have GRAMMATICAL (or FUNCTIONAL or STRUCTURAL or INTERNAL) MEANING until they are put together in a special way which indicates the formal relationship between them, e.g. *The boy hits the ball.* When there is a definite → reference relation between a word and the object or idea which it signifies, the word is said to have REFERENTIAL MEANING, while the relation between an utterance and the situation in which it is used is called CONTEXTUAL or SITUATIONAL MEANING. A distinction is often made between EXTENDED or WIDENED MEANING, e.g. when the word *boy* is used to refer to 'any immature man' rather than to 'non-adult male', and SPECIALISED or NARROWED MEANING, e.g. when the word *ball* is used to refer to 'round object used in particular game' rather than to 'any circular shape'. Other distinctions sometimes made are between INTENSIONAL and EXTENSIONAL MEANING (depending on whether the emphasis is on what the speaker 'implies' or on how many things to which the word may be applied), or between CONNOTATIVE and DENOTATIVE MEANING (depending on whether the word carries emotional 'overtones' or is conventionalised

MEANINGFUL Term used to refer to those words or utterances which give information to a hearer or reader even when used without a context. Some socially prescribed phrases such as *How do you do ?* have meaning only in the situation in which they occur. → nonsense form.

MEANINGLESS → Nonsense form.

MECHANICAL TRANSLATION → Machine translation.

MECHANISTIC LINGUIS-TICS Collective term for a number of approaches to language which have insisted on observing actual utterances as the result of a speaker's behaviour in a particular situation rather than the intuitive interpretation of man's ability to use language well (→ mentalistic linguistics). The emphasis is on 'real' data and referential context, e.g. in Bloomfieldian → distributional analysis or in → Neogrammarian sound laws. Alternative term: anti-mentalism. (2.5).

MEDIAE Older term for voiced → stops, e.g. [b], [d], [g]. → tenues.

MEDIAEVAL LINGUISTICS Collective term for a number of grammatical treatises written during the Middle Ages. Linguistic studies were closely linked with Latin, the common language of the church and the educated in Europe, and modelled first on → Latinate grammar. Latinate grammars were used both for prescriptive teaching of the language and as a basis of a few descriptions of vernacular languages such as Old English and Irish. → Phonetics and phonology were limited to the design of writing systems, and → etymology made no progress. Grammatical theory, regarded as one of the seven 'arts', came under the influence of SCHOLASTIC philosophy which sought a common causal basis to all scholarship. The scholastic authors of grammars during the 13th and 14th centuries were called MODISTAE, since it was the 'modus significandi' which for them represented reality through classes of words (which 'stand for' things). New in these → universal SPECULATIVE GRAMMARS was not the conceptual theory of semantic relations (based on Aristotelian views) or the distinction between *dictio* (or formal meaning) and *vox* (or sound substance), but the refinements in syntactic analysis, e.g. the function of prepositions, the formal criteria of grammatical acceptability, and the concepts of dependency, government and transitivity. The crusades and missionary contacts with non-Latin cultures and languages such as Arabic prepared the ground for→Renaissance linguistics. (2.5 Robins).

MEDIOPALATAL → Palatal.

MEDIO-VELAR → Velar.

MEDIUM VOWEL → Neutral vowel.

MELIORATION → Amelioration.

MELIORATIVE SUFFIX → Ameliorative suffix.

MELLOW → Strident versus mellow.

MELODICS The system and study of → intonation patterns.

MELODY The pattern of → pitch changes in an utterance.

MENTALISM → Mentalistic linguistics.

MENTALISTIC LINGUISTICS Collective term for a number of approaches to language which have stressed the speaker's inborn knowledge of language rather than the result of his behaviour in an actual speech act (→ mechanistic linguistics). The linguist's intuition is regarded as a better guide to the understanding of how language operates than the 'mere' data in a corpus of utterances. → mediaeval linguistics, → neo-linguistics, conceptual → semantics, → transformational-generative grammar. Alternative term: mentalism. (2.5 Chomsky, Hall).

MERGER A sound change which results in the contrast between two phonemes being neutralised, e.g. Middle English [æː] and [eː] merged into Modern English [iː]

Middle English	Modern English
see, eest [æː]	
	sea, east, green,
grene, deep [eː]	deep [iː]

→ sound change. Alternative term: convergence.

MESSAGE Information in the form of ordered signs or signals conveyed in a → communication system from a source through a channel to a receiver.

METALANGUAGE (*a*) The language or set of symbols which is used to analyse and describe another language (the observed or → object language), e.g. the words which paraphrase another word or the native language in foreign language teaching. Alternative term: second-order language. (*b*) A language which shares features of two or more languages to improve communication between them. → artificial language. (10.3).

METALINGUISTICS (*a*) The study of → metalanguage. In linguistic analysis it is important to distinguish between the language observed by the linguist (object language) and the language he uses to observe it (metalanguage). (9.3, 10.3). (*b*) The study of language in relation to such aspects of human behaviour as 'culture' or the 'speech act'. → anthropological linguistics, → features. Alternative term: exolinguistics. (10.1).

METANALYSIS Faulty → boundary signalling resulting in the formation of a new lexical item, e.g. *an adder* < *a nadder*, or *a newt* < *an ewt*, or *cherries* (plural) < French *cerise* (singular). → folk etymology. Alternative term: affix clipping.

METAPHONE A → free variant of a phoneme, e.g. [ai] or [iː] in *neither*.

METAPHONY → Vowel mutation.

METAPHOR A → figure of speech in which a name or descriptive term is applied to a person or object to which it is not literally applicable thus implying a comparison, e.g. '*There is a tide in the affairs of men which taken at the flood, leads on to fortune*' (Shakespeare, *Julius Caesar*, Act IV, Sc. 3). The term MIXED META-PHOR is used to refer to a combination of two or more, often incompatible different metaphors, e.g. *He burnt his boats when he bit off more than he could chew.* → simile.

140

METAPHRASE The process or result of converting an utterance from one language into another, e.g. by means of a → translation, without altering the meaning. → paraphrase.

METATHESIS A change of order, either of words in a sentence or speech sounds in a word, which deviates from normal usage and may in some cases lead to permanent changes in the language, e.g. *aksed* for *asked*. This feature was quite common in some Old English dialects, e.g. West Saxon *axian* 'ask', *dox* 'dusk'. Some linguists restrict the term to interchange of vowel and consonant such as Old English *ðridda* > *ðirda* 'third' or *hros* > *hors* 'horse'. Alternative term: anastrophe. (6.1).

METHOD A way of approaching, observing, analysing and explaining a particular phenomenon. In linguistics, this term refers to: (1) the different attitudes of groups of scholars to → language and → linguistics, e.g. atomistic, comparative, contrastive, descriptive, diachronic, mentalistic, prescriptive, structural, etc.; (2) the different techniques of establishing and measuring linguistic features, e.g. statistical counts, field study, work with literary texts, laboratory experiments, logical reasoning, segmental procedures, etc.; (3) the different principles and practices of language teaching, e.g. direct method, grammar-translation method, programmed instruction, etc. → linguistic analysis, → procedure. (2.5, 9.14).

METONYMY A type of → semantic change in which the meaning of a word or group of words is changed by using it for another word with which it is connected, e.g. *the bar* to refer to 'lawyer's profession' or *kettle* to refer to 'water' (in *the kettle is boiling*).

METRE The arrangement of stressed and unstressed → syllables to form a rhythmical pattern in → verse structure. The → foot is a subdivision of a metrical line and may be used to identify different types of metrical structure, e.g. an iambic pentameter consists of five iambic feet, "*If music be the food of love play on*". (7.3).

METRICS The system and study of the structure of metrical → verse.

METRONYMIC → Matronymic.

MICROLINGUISTICS Those aspects of linguistic studies which are concerned with the direct analysis of linguistic material, e.g. → phonology, → grammar, → lexicology. These studies form the basis for more peripheral studies, sometimes described as pre-linguistics, → macrolinguistics and → metalinguistics. (10.1 Whorf).

MIDIMENSIONAL PHONOLOGY → Prosodic analysis.

MID VOWEL → Neutral vowel.

MIDDLE LANGUAGE → Diglossia.

MIDDLE VOICE → Voice (*b*).

MIDDLE VOWEL → Neutral vowel.

MIMETIC WORD (*a*) → Onomatopoeic word. (*b*) A word coined to imitate the sound of another

141

word, e.g. *op art* 'optical art' on the pattern of *pop art*, or *wise buys* 'bargains' on the pattern of *wise guys*.

MIMICRY Imitation of the voice-quality features of another person.

MINIMAL CONTRAST The smallest possible → contrast the phonemic structure of a language will allow, e.g. *thin:sin:fin*. → minimal pair.

MINIMAL PAIR Two items which → contrast only in a single unit, e.g. words which contrast only in a single phone, e.g. *pin:bin*; *cob:cop*; *ample:amble*, or sentences by intonation pattern: e.g. *He's here*: *He's here?* etc. Alternative term: contrastive pair.

MINIMAL STRESS → Stress.

MINOR SENTENCE A sentence which does not possess all the features of a → favourite sentence. Alternative terms: non-favourite sentence, sentence fragment, verbless sentence.

MINORITY LANGUAGE A speech community which uses a different language from the majority of people living in the same political or national environment. Such speech communities are often groups of immigrants or colonisers. → immigrant language, → substratum. Alternative term: linguistic minority.

MIXED A noun or verb is said to be of mixed → declension or → conjugation if its inflexions have characteristics of more than one regular paradigm of the appropriate word class of the language concerned.

MIXED LANGUAGE The result of intensive interchange between two or more languages, usually in areas of → contact, e.g. → pidgin or → creole.

MIXED METAPHOR → Metaphor.

MIXING OF LANGUAGES The intermingling of phonological, grammatical and/or lexical elements from different languages in areas of intensive → contact, e.g. → pidgin, → creole. (8.8 Hall, 9.2 Hymes).

MOBILE STRESS → Stress.

MOCK FORM A neologism deliberately created for humorous effect, e.g. *supercalifragilisticexpialidocious*.

MODAL AUXILIARY VERB An auxiliary verb used to express a → mood such as optative, obligative, etc. Like all → auxiliary verbs in English the modal auxiliaries have special negative forms, can form the interrogative by inversion and have special → weak forms in speech in unstressed position, but in addition to these features modal auxiliaries can be recognised by the fact that they have no third person singular inflexion (present), e.g. *can, dare, may, must, need, ought, shall, used, will*. (4.1, 4.2, 8.23).

MODALITY The way in which a speaker can express his attitude towards a situation in interpersonal communication, usually realised in English by modal auxiliaries (→ mood) and/or adverbials such as *possibly* or constructions like *it is certain that...*

MODE (*a*) → Mood. (*b*) In → tagmemics, one of the three interlocking levels of phonology, grammar and lexicon.

MODE OF ARTICULATION → Manner of articulation.

MODE OF DISCOURSE → Register (*b*).

MODEL (*a*) → Informant in field-work and in language teaching. (*b*) Concrete picture or abstract formula used to describe or explain relation-ships. Examples of models in linguist-ics are: the tripartite division of language into speech sounds, gram-matical forms, and vocabulary items; the idea that communication consists of source, channel and receiver; the view of genetically related languages as a family tree showing affiliations by branches; the concept of language varieties as levels of dialects and styles; the mathematical formula $F \times R = C$ where F = frequency, R = rank and C = constant (→ Zipf's law).

MODERN LANGUAGE (*a*) In the historical development of lan-guages, the contemporary rather than classical period. (*b*) In language teaching a contemporary language (i.e. not Sanskrit, Latin, Greek, etc.) other than the → native language.

MODIFICATION (*a*) The altera-tion of a linguistic form through → borrowing, phonetic → assimilation, or → morpho-phonemic variation. (*b*) The relationship between a → head word and a → modifier.

MODIFIER (*a*) In syntax, an adjunct which limits or qualifies a → head word in a noun or verb phrase. Some linguists limit this term to pre-

nominal constructions, e.g. *the four tall boys*, while calling post-nominal constructions QUALIFIERS, e.g. *boys of a certain age*. → sentence modifier. (*b*) In phonetics, anything which affects the air stream in the vocal tract, e.g. vibration of the vocal cords.

MODISTAE → Mediaeval linguistics.

MODULATION (*a*) Collective term used by some linguists for → prosodic features such as stress, intonation, etc. (*b*) Collective term for those grammatical or lexical features which systematically express 'volition', 'ability', 'permission', 'ne-cessity', etc., e.g. by the use of → modal auxiliary verbs.

MOMENTARY ASPECT → Aspect.

MONEME Term used by some linguists for → morpheme. (2.1 Martinet).

MONGREL WORD → Hybrid word.

MONOGENESIS THEORY The theory that all the languages of the world developed from one original parent language. → polygenesis. (2.1 Hockett).

MONOGLOT → Unilingual.

MONOLATERAL CONSONANT → Lateral.

MONOLINGUAL → Unilingual.

MONOLOGUE The linguistic activity of a single speaker, e.g. in the form of a speech or lecture, or as internal speech. If no other person is present, the term SOLILOQUY is used; DIALOGUE refers to communication between two speakers, while a MULTILOGUE or POLYLOGUE includes more than two contributing speakers, e.g. in a discussion. → conversation.

MONOMORPHEMIC Consisting of a single → morpheme, e.g. the English word *home* as opposed to *homeliness.*

MONOPERSONAL VERB → Impersonal verb.

MONOPHONEMIC Consisting of one → phoneme. Sometimes it is difficult to decide whether a certain sound is made up of one phoneme or several, e.g. the English sounds [t͡ʃ] and [d͡ʒ] as in *chop* and *dodge* are regarded as one phoneme in some analyses, but as two phonemes in others. If they are considered to represent single phonemes they can be transcribed with a ligature as above; if they are considered to represent two phonemes they are written with two separate symbols: [tʃ], [dʒ]. (3.1, 8.22).

MONOPHTHONG A single → vowel sound with no change in quality from beginning to end of its production, as opposed to → diphthong. Alternative term: pure vowel, simple vowel. (3.1, 8.22).

MONOPHTHONGISATION In diachronic phonology, the process of change from a → diphthong to a → monophthong.

MONOSEMY When a word or phrase has only one semantic meaning, e.g. *ball-point pen*, as opposed to → polysemy or multiple meaning, e.g. *star* 'luminous heavenly body', 'asterisk', 'famous actor', etc. (5.1).

MONOSYLLABIC (*a*) Consisting of one → syllable. (*b*) A type of language in which most of the words consist of one syllable. → isolating language. (6.1, 8.1).

MONOSYLLABISM The predominance of words with only one syllable in the phonological and morphological structure of a language, e.g. in Chinese.

MONOSYLLABLE A word of one → syllable.

MONOSYSTEMIC versus POLYSYSTEMIC Traditional → phonology is monosystemic in the sense that it sets up one system of → phonemes for a particular language and this system is held to be valid for all environments and distributions. → Prosodic analysis is polysystemic in the sense that it sets up differing systems for different environments, e.g. word initial, word final, etc. (3.4 Palmer).

MONUMENTAL WRITING Ornate handwriting or printing used for special decorative purposes. → cursive writing. (7.2).

MOOD Grammatical distinctions in verb forms which express a speaker's attitude to what he is saying. Moods may be distinguished by means of inflexions, e.g. special subjunctive forms in French, German, etc., or by the use of auxiliaries, e.g. the → modal auxiliaries in English. Simple declarative statements which are grammatically 'unmarked' with respect to mood are said to be in the INDICATIVE, DECLARATIVE, COMMON or FACT mood, e.g. *He returned at dawn.* The IMPERATIVE mood is used for expressing commands or prohibitions, e.g. *Report back to me at once!* Note, however, that not all commands are expressed in the imperative mood, e.g. *All men will report at dawn.* Some linguists consider interrogative sentences to be modal and hence use the term INTERROGATIVE mood, but note again that not all questions are interrogatives. *You can come?* is a question but it is not an interrogative construction. The SUBJUNCTIVE mood expresses doubt or uncertainty, particularly in subordinate clauses. In some languages subjunctive forms occur regularly after certain conjunctions, e.g. French *Je parle lentement pour que vous me compreniez* 'I am speaking slowly so that you can understand me', or under certain syntactic conditions, e.g. reported speech in German: *Seine Mutter sagte, er wäre krank* 'His mother said he was ill'. The subjunctive mood may also be used for what is often described in traditional grammar as a THIRD PERSON IMPERATIVE, e.g. *Dieu vous bénisse* 'May God bless you' or English *God save the Queen.* Other moods such as OPTATIVE, expressing a wish, OBLIGATIVE, expressing compulsion, etc. are expressed in English by the modal auxiliaries *will, must, ought, may, can,* etc. Alternative terms: mode, modality. (4.1, 4.2, 8.23).

MORA The smallest unit for measuring quantity or length in a prosodic system. The mora is usually shorter than a syllable. (3.1, 8.22).

MORPH Phonological or orthographical representation of a → morpheme. A particular morpheme, which is an abstract element of form, may be represented in different environments by several different morphs: the plural morpheme in English, for example, may occur as

/s/, /z/, /iz/, etc. Morphs which are alternative representations of the same morpheme are called → allomorphs, by analogy with → allophone.

MORPHEME A minimum distinctive unit of grammar, i.e. a → grammatical unit of the lowest rank: a → word is composed of one or more morphemes. Like phoneme and grapheme, a morpheme is a formal element, and a particular morpheme may be represented by different variants or → allomorphs in different environments, e.g. the English plural morpheme often symbolised as {-s₂} may occur as /-s/ in *cats,* /-z/ in *dogs* or /-iz/ in *horses,* etc. The realisation of a single morpheme is the smallest potentially meaningful unit in a language; thus the word *home* cannot be divided into parts such as *h, ho, ome, me,* etc. without the original meaning being lost or changed. Thus *home* represents a single morpheme. A morpheme is said to be a → free morpheme if it can stand alone, e.g. *home, chair, table,* or a → bound morpheme if it can only occur in conjunction with another form, e.g. the English plural morpheme {-s₂} or the case endings of an inflected language such as Latin. Other basic units with grammatical and/or lexical meaning that have been proposed by different schools of linguistic analysis include → moneme and → glosseme. (4.1, 4.2, 8.23).

MORPHEME ALTERNANT → Allomorph, morpho-phoneme.

MORPHEME WORD A word consisting of one morpheme. → word formation.

MORPHEMIC ANALYSIS → Morphological analysis.

MORPHEMIC SCRIPT A writing system which uses one symbol per → morpheme, e.g. logography.

MORPHEMICALLY CON-DITIONED ALTERNATION → Morpho-phonemic variation.

MORPHEMICS A technique for analysing a language into → morphemes, including a description of their form and their arrangement. Morphemics usually refers to a → synchronic study, the historical aspect of word-formation being included in → morphology. (4.1, 4.2, 8.23).

MORPHOLOGICAL ANALYSIS The observation and description of the grammatical elements in a language by studying their form and function, their phonological variants, and their distribution and mutual relationships within larger stretches of speech. A morphological analysis may also be diachronic and take account of historical factors. → morphemics. (4.1, 4.2, 8.23).

MORPHOLOGICAL ASSI-MILATION A change in number, gender, or case ending of a word, brought about by the influence of a word or words nearby in the sentence, e.g. *these* in *these kind of things.*

MORPHOLOGICAL CHANGE → Grammatical change (*b*).

MORPHOLOGICAL DOUBLET → Doublet.

MORPHOLOGICAL EXTEN-SION Word-formation by adding affixes, e.g. *muchness* in *much of a muchness* on the pattern of *happiness, kindness,* etc.

MORPHOLOGY A branch of → grammar concerned with the study and analysis of the structure, forms and classes of words, e.g. declensional endings such as *walks, walked, walking,* derivational endings such as *-ness* in *happiness,* etc. Morphology includes not only synchronic studies (→ morphemics), but also the history and development of word-forms (historical morphology). (4.1, 4.2, 8.23).

MORPHONEME → Morpho-phoneme.

MORPHO-PHONEME A phonological unit consisting of a set of phonemes occurring in the variants (allomorphs) of a particular → morpheme: e.g. the English plural morpheme {-s} may occur as /-s/, /-z/, /-iz/, /-en/ or /ø/ as in *cats, dogs, horses, oxen, sheep.* Alternative terms: morpheme alternant, morphoneme.

MORPHO-PHONEMIC STRESS The difference in stress pattern which distinguishes such forms as *bláckbìrd* 'a species of bird' from *blàck bírd* 'a bird coloured black'.

MORPHO-PHONEMIC VARIA-TION Change in the phonemic form of a → morpheme, e.g. the English plural morpheme {-s} may occur as /-s/, /-z/, /-iz/, /-en/ or /-ø/ as in *cats, dogs, horses, oxen, sheep.* → morpho-phoneme. Alternative term: morphemically conditioned alternation.

MORPHO-PHONEMICS → Morpho-phonology.

MORPHO-PHONOLOGY The study of phonological variations

146

in → allomorphs which accompany their grouping into words, e.g. the changes in the English plural morpheme {-s₂} occurring as /s/, /z/, /iz/, /ø/, /en/, or the changes from /sliːp/ to /slep-/ before adding the past tense morpheme {t} in *slept*. Alternative terms: morpho-phonemics, phono-morphology.

MORPHO-SEMANTIC FIELD A lexical field or → association group, in which words are linked by similarities in meaning and/or sound.

MORPHOTACTICS The system and study of the characteristic arrangement of → morphemes in sequence.

MOTHER TONGUE → Native language.

MOTOR PHONETICS → Articulatory phonetics.

MOVABLE SPEECH ORGAN → Articulator.

MOVABLE STRESS → Stress.

MOVEMENT OF EXPRESSION Collective term for gestural movements of parts of the body which supplement speech. → kinesics.

MULTIDIMENSIONAL PHONOLOGY → Prosodic analysis.

MULTILINGUAL Involving more than one language. This term may refer to individuals or communities, or to manuscripts, books, inscriptions and dictionaries using several languages. Alternative terms: polylingual, polyglot.

MULTILINGUALISM The use of two or more languages by a speaker or speech community. Persons with equal competence in a number of languages are extremely rare, and usually their proficiency is exaggerated by laymen. → bilingualism. Alternative term: plurilingualism. (9.2).

MULTILOGUE → Monologue.

MULTIPLE MEANING In → semantics, the truism that words can have more than one meaning. → polysemy.

MULTIPLE SENTENCE → Compound sentence.

MULTIPLICATIVE NUMERAL A → numeral indicating the number of times an action takes place, e.g. *once, twice, thrice*. Alternative term: iterative numeral.

MULTI-SEGMENTAL FEATURE → Suprasegmental feature.

MULTISYLLABLE → Polysyllable.

MURMUR VOWEL → Neutral vowel.

MUTATION Collective term for the modification of sounds in a word under the influence of sounds in neighbouring words. Such changes can affect the whole sound system of a language from one stage in its historical development to the next, e.g. umlaut or → vowel mutation. Consonants may also be affected, as in INITIAL MUTATION, e.g. Welsh *tad* 'father', but *fy nhad* 'my father', *ei dad* 'his father'. → vowel gradation.

MUTE (*a*) A written symbol which does not represent a speech sound in a particular word, e.g. *h* in *hour*, *b* in *debt* or *e* in *house*. (*b*) An obsolete term for → stop.

MUTUAL INTELLIGIBILITY The ability to understand the speech of other speakers and to be understood by other speakers. In determining dialect and → language boundaries, tests of mutual intelligibility may show whether or not the members of a particular speech community comprehend vocabulary items used in a neighbouring speech community. → lexicostatistics.

MUTUALLY EXCLUSIVE Two varieties of a speech sound are said to be mutually exclusive if they are in → complementary distribution, i.e. if they do not occur in the same environment. Thus in English the prevelar [k̟] in *kill* and the mediovelar [k] in *call* are mutually exclusive: [k̟] only occurs before front vowels and [k] only occurs before back vowels. (3.1, 8.22).

N

NAMING Finding a suitable linguistic symbol (sound sequence or word) to refer to a new material object or abstract concept, usually by drawing on words with similar meanings, by extension or metaphor, e.g. *sky-scraper*. Alternative term: onomathesia. (5.1).

NARROW DIPHTHONG → Diphthong.

NARROW TRANSCRIPTION A type of → phonetic transcription to represent the continuum of speech as accurately as possible on paper. → broad transcription.

NARROW VOWEL → Close vowel.

NARROWED MEANING → Meaning.

NARROWING OF MEANING → Reduction (*b*).

NASAL A speech sound produced with the velum lowered so that air can escape through the nasal cavity which acts as a resonator. In the case of NASAL CONSONANTS, e.g. bilabial [m], alveolar [n], velar [ŋ], etc., the air escapes only through the nose, but in the case of a NASAL VOWEL, e.g. French bon [bõ] 'good', vin [vẽ] 'wine', the air escapes through both nose and mouth. French has both oral and nasal vowels in its phonological system whereas English only has oral vowels. Sometimes, however, nasalisation occurs in English as a secondary feature, e.g. in some pronunciations of *can't* [kõnt]. Phoneticians usually use the term NASALISED VOWEL to refer to this secondary feature and reserve the term nasal vowel for the phonological item as in French. (3.1, 8.22).

NASAL versus ORAL One of the basic oppositions in → distinctive feature phonology based on the analysis of a → spectrogram. 'Nasal' indicates presence of nasal → formant and damping of oral formant, 'oral' the absence of this feature. In articulatory terms nasal indicates that the nasal cavity supplements the mouth as a resonance chamber.

French, for example, has both oral and nasal vowels /bo/ *beau* 'beautiful' (oral) /bõ/ *bon* 'good' (nasal). In English the consonants /b/, /d/, /g/, etc. are oral whereas /m/, /n/, /ŋ/ are nasal.

NASAL CAVITY → Cavity.

NASAL CONSONANT → Nasal.

NASAL PHARYNX That part of the → pharynx which forms part of the nasal cavity: the space between the rear part of the → velum and the back wall of the throat. → diagram p. 159.

NASAL PLOSION The → release of a stop consonant in such a way as to allow the air to escape through the nose: e.g. in the pronunciation of [p] in *cup and saucer* [kʌpm̂sɔːsə] or [t] in *button* [bʌtn̩]. → lateral plosion.

NASAL RELEASE → Release.

NASAL TWANG Regional pronunciation involving nasalisation of vowels which are oral in the standard pronunciation. (8.24 Reed).

NASAL VOWEL → Nasal.

NASALISATION Timbre or quality given to a speech sound by allowing air to escape into the nasal cavity by lowering the velum. Nasalisation is a secondary feature of articulation and nasalisation of a vowel is a phonetic variant rather than a phonological feature, e.g. [ɑ̃ː] (nasalised [ɑ]) can be heard in some pronunciations of English *can't*. → nasal. (3.1, 8.22).

NASALISED → Nasal.

NASALISED VOWEL → Nasal.

NATIONAL LANGUAGE A regional → dialect or 'second' language which has become the → standard language or lingua franca in a particular country through historical development or government proclamation, e.g. Riksmål in Norway, Mandarin Chinese in China. In some multilingual communities there may be several OFFICIAL LANGUAGES, e.g. English and Hindi in India. → institutional linguistics. (10.1).

NATIVE LANGUAGE The first language which is normally acquired by a human being in early childhood through interaction with other members of his speech community. → foreign language. Alternative terms: first language, primary language, mother tongue. (9.6).

NATIVE WORD A word which has developed from the original sources of a particular language and not one which can be identified as a → loan word from another language.

NATIVISTIC THEORY → Origin of speech.

NATURAL GENDER → Gender.

NATURAL LANGUAGE A language which is the native tongue of a human speech community such as English or Japanese, as opposed to → artificial languages such as Esperanto or ALGOL.

NATURALISM In → philosophical semantics the view held since the Greeks that there is a fundamental connexion between the meaning of a word and the thing it signifies. Words are but the natural names we give to objects of the real or outside world. By contrast → nominalism claims that the shape of words is agreed upon by human custom and convention. Alternative term: realism. (2.5 Robins, 5.1).

NEAR-SYNONYM One of two or more words which are similar in meaning but not → synonyms, e.g. *help/aid/assistance*, or *female/woman/lady*. Alternative term: homoionym, pseudo-synonym. (5.1).

NEGATION The process or result of making a → negative statement. Sometimes this is achieved by a grammatical particle such as *not*, as in *He is not coming*, or by lexical means such as *failed* in *He failed to come*. → double negative.

NEGATIVE A grammatical form usually implying negation, e.g. *He did not eat the cake* as opposed to *He ate the cake*. Sometimes, however, a grammatical negative does not mean that an action did not take place, for example, *He did not eat the cake because he was hungry, but because he liked it* contains a grammatical negative, but the action of eating was carried out. Conversely, negation can be implied without the presence of a grammatical → negation. (4.1, 4.2, 8.23).

NEGATIVE CONJUNCTION A conjunction such as *nor* which implies a → negative.

NEGATIVE PARTICLE A grammatical form used to turn a declarative into a negative sentence, e.g. *not* in *I have not the time* or French *ne . . . . pas* in *Je ne sais pas* 'I don't know'.

NEO-FIRTHIAN LINGUISTICS → Systemic grammar.

NEOGRAMMARIANS A linguistic school centred on the University of Leipzig in the 1870s, led by S. A. Leskien and K. Brugmann. They stated categorically that → phonetic laws admit no exceptions. This statement was really nothing more than what scholars had taken for granted for a long time, but the abrupt overconfident way in which the Leipzig group put forward their ideas made them unpopular and earned them the name of JUNG-GRAMMATIKER 'young grammarians'. Alternative term: Leipzig School. (2.5 Robins, 6.1 Lockwood).

NEO-LINGUISTICS A school of grammarians, predominantly German and Italian, who rejected the ideas of the → Neogrammarians who had claimed that → phonetic laws have no exception; instead they stressed the role of the individual speaker, his social and geographical links, as well as his capability of linguistic → innovation. (2.5 Hall).

NEOLOGISM A newly coined word or phrase which has not yet received general acceptance, e.g. *boatel* from *boat* and *hotel* by analogy with *motel* (< *motor* and *hotel*).

NEO-SAUSSUREAN LINGUISTICS → Glossematics.

NESTING The embedding of a phrase or clause within an → endocentric phrase to modify its head word, e.g. the recursive structure: *The dog that chased the cat that ate the bird...*

NEUTER → Gender.

NEUTRAL VOWEL A → vowel sound, usually unstressed, pronounced with the tongue in a neutral position, i.e. mid central, not high, not low, not front, not back. One such sound is represented in phonetic transcription as [ə] as in *about* [ə'baut]. → vowel quadrilateral p. 253. Alternative terms: murmur vowel, medium vowel, central vowel, middle vowel, schwa, intermediate vowel, abnormal vowel, mid vowel.

NEUTRALISATION The cancelling of a phonemic → opposition in certain positions. In German, for example, voiced consonants do not occur at the ends of words and so the opposition which exists between pairs of voiced and voiceless consonants is neutralised in the final position. Thus [p] and [b] both occur at the beginning of words *Paar* [pɑːʀ] 'pair', *Bar* [bɑːʀ] 'bar', but only [p] occurs at the end of words, e.g. *gelb* [gelp] 'yellow'. → archiphoneme. (3.4 Trubetzkoy).

NEXUS INDEX → Index (*a*).

NIGORI MARK A diacritic mark ⟨″⟩ used in Japanese *kana* syllabic writing systems to indicate that the syllable begins with a voiced consonant sound.

NOA WORD A euphemistic word replacing a → taboo word, e.g. *crikey* for *Christ*.

NODE In a tree-diagram representing the constituent structure of a sentence, the point where 'branches' divide, e.g. the point

labelled 'verb phrase' (VP) in the phrase marker below.

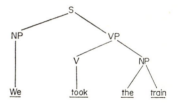

NOEME The meaning of a → glosseme.

NOISE Any undesirable interference in the transmission of information which is caused by the communication channel, not by the source of the messages, e.g. distortions in recordings or misprints in texts. A language makes allowances for such disturbances by means of → redundancy. (10.5).

NOMENCLATURE The standardised → terminology in a special field, e.g. the terms used in chemistry or articulatory phonetics.

NOMINAL A name given by some grammarians to a word which functions as a → noun, but does not have all the formal characteristics of a noun (i.e. in English the distinction between singular and plural and between common and possessive cases). In this type of description *The dead* in *The dead are honoured* would be considered a nominal: it functions as a noun, but it has no plural **deads* nor a possessive **dead's*. Alternative terms: substantive, noun-equivalent. (4.1, 4.2, 8.23).

NOMINAL CLAUSE A clause which is rank-shifted to function as a nominal group, i.e. one which could be replaced by a noun or noun phrase: e.g. *what I saw* in *From what I saw, I thought he was wrong.* Alternative term: noun clause.

NOMINAL DEFINITION → Definition.

NOMINAL GROUP → Noun phrase.

NOMINAL PHRASE → Noun phrase.

NOMINAL SEQUENCE → Noun phrase.

NOMINALISATION (*a*) The process or result of forming a → noun from some other part of speech by the use of an appropriate derivational affix, e.g. *green + ness, odd + ity.* (*b*) The process or result of using a noun phrase instead of a verbal construction or subordinate clause, e.g. *The acceptance of this proposal is a first requirement* instead of *It is first of all required that you accept what we propose here.* (4.1, 4.2, 8.23).

NOMINALISM In → philosophical semantics the view held since the Greeks that the forms of words we use to signify things are not inherently connected with the objects to which they refer (→ naturalism), but rather that they are arbitrarily chosen by custom and convention. Alternative term: conventionalism. (2.5 Robins, 5.1).

NOMINATIVE A → case form in some inflected languages, usually indicating that the noun in question is functioning as the subject of a sentence. It is usually considered the first case and is the form which appears in dictionaries. → oblique case.

NOMINATIVE ABSOLUTE → Absolute construction.

NON-ANTERIOR → Anterior *versus* non-anterior.

NON-CONSONANTAL → Consonantal *versus* non-consonantal.

NON-CONTIGUOUS ASSIMILATION → Assimilation.

NON-CONTINUANT → Continuant *versus* non-continuant.

NON-CONTRASTIVE VARIANT → Free variant.

NON-CORONAL → Coronal *versus* non-coronal.

NON-COUNT NOUN → Mass noun.

NON-DEFINITE ARTICLE → Article.

NON-DISTINCTIVE FEATURE A phonetic feature of an utterance which is not significant phonemically, i.e. is not used to distinguish one → phoneme from another. The first sound in the English word *pin*, for example, is an aspirated voiceless bilabial stop, but the aspiration, i.e. the audible puff of breath that occurs with the /p/, is a non-distinctive feature since [pʰ] with aspiration and [p] without it are not realisations of separate phonemes, but → allophones of the same phoneme. On the other hand, the feature of voice, or in this case the lack of it, is significant here because it helps to distinguish /p/ from /b/ and hence the word *pin* from the word *bin*. → distinctive feature. (3.1, 8.22).

NON-FAVOURITE SENTENCE A sentence which does not possess all the features of a → favourite sentence. Alternative term: minor sentence.

NON-FINITE VERB FORM A form of the verb which is not limited by person, number or time, e.g. → participle, → gerund, → infinitive. Alternative term: infinite verb form.

NON-FLAT → Flat *vs.* non-flat.

NON-FUNCTIONAL VARIATION → Free variation.

NON-PAST TENSE A → tense form of a verb which relates to an action other than one which took place prior to the time of the utterance. The distinction non-past : past is the basic distinction of the English tense system. → aspect, mood.

NON-RESTRICTIVE A structure within a sentence which gives additional information about some element in the sentence but which is not essential to the general meaning of the sentence: e.g. the relative clause in *Mr Smith, who used to be my teacher, is coming tomorrow*, gives us additional information about *Mr Smith* but it is not essential to convey the meaning that Mr Smith is coming tomorrow. Non-restrictive elements are usually set off from the rest of the sentence or utterance by means of commas or intonation. → restrictive.

NON-SHARP → Sharp *versus* non-sharp.

NON-SIGNIFICANT Not playing a role in any contrast of form or meaning, e.g. the feature of vowel length is non-significant in the pronunciation of the English word

room since both [rum] and [ruːm] occur. (3.1, 8.22).

NON-STANDARD A → manner of discourse which deviates in pronunciation, grammar or vocabulary from a recognised standard. A less neutral term with pejorative connotations is → sub-standard.

NON-SYLLABIC A speech sound which does not carry the → peak of sonority of a syllable, e.g. the second component of a falling → diphthong, as [i] in [dei] *day*, or a consonant accompanying a vowel in the same syllable, as [h] and [t] in [hɔt] *hot*.

NON-VOCALIC → Vocalic *versus* non-vocalic.

NONCE-FORMATION A linguistic form deliberately or accidentally made up for one particular purpose, e.g. abbreviations in newspaper headlines. Alternative terms: nonce-word, ephemeral word. (4.2, 5.1).

NONCE-WORD → Nonce-formation.

NONSENSE FORM An utterance may be considered NONSENSICAL if it is in keeping with the phonological and grammatical conventions of the language, but semantically meaningless, e.g. *Colourless green ideas sleep furiously*. Alternative terms: anomalous, deviant, meaningless.

NONSENSICAL → Nonsense form.

NORM That which is taken as the recognised standard of spoken or written language. Depending on the type of communicative situation (individual speaker or groups in the speech community) and on the theoretical approach (psycholinguistics or sociolinguistics), different strata or standards of usage may be established as an aid to determining various and sometimes conflicting norms:

NOTIONAL WORD → Content word.

NOUN A → part of speech traditionally defined as a word denoting or naming a person, thing or concept. This type of definition leads to difficulties, since e.g. the word *red* is still the 'name' of a

	individual	bi-personal	collective
potential	competence	code	functional system
realised	performance	discourse	institutional norm

NORMATIVE LINGUISTICS Collective term for a number of linguistic schools which claim that it is the function of the linguist and grammarian to set and preserve certain standards in a language. → prescriptive linguistics.

NOTATION The process or result of representing speech by graphic symbols. Several types of notation can be distinguished: ALPHABETIC WRITING which records sound sequences by conventionalised signs called letters; ANALPHABETIC NOTATION which uses non-alphabetic signs specially created for the purpose; phonetic and phonemic TRANSCRIPTIONS which use a combination of both alphabetic and analphabetic notation to represent accurately and unambiguously the sound features of utterances in a particular language; grammatical notations which represent the morphological and syntactic features of an utterance by special symbols. (3.1, 7.2).

NOTIONAL GRAMMAR → Philosophical grammar.

colour, even when it is used as an adjectival in the sentence *This is a red book*. It is better, therefore, to define a noun by its → form and → function. In English, nouns usually distinguish between singular and a plural form, e.g. *table : tables*, and have a possessive form, e.g. *man's*. Words which do not have these distinctions but which function as nouns are called → nominals by some grammarians. A noun functions as the → head of a noun phrase, often preceded by modifier(s) and → determiners, e.g. *the long green grass*. A noun phrase may function as the subject or object of a sentence or may be part of a prepositional phrase. In inflected languages which have a system of → genders and → cases, the definition of a noun may be further modified by indicating that it is a word which is declined according to gender and case as well as → number. Nouns may be classified into proper nouns, e.g. *John, Mary, Greenland*, and common nouns, e.g. *spade, tree, garden, music*, etc. Common nouns may be divided into → unit nouns, e.g. *stone, chair, ball*, and → mass nouns, e.g. *sand, rice, water*. (4.1, 4.2, 8.23).

NOUN ADJUNCT A noun which modifies a following noun, traditionally defined as 'a noun used as an adjective', e.g. *a university student*, or *a weather vane*.

NOUN CLAUSE → Nominal clause.

NOUN CLUSTER → Noun phrase.

NOUN-EQUIVALENT → Nominal.

NOUN PHRASE A word or group of words with a → noun or pronoun as its head and functioning like a noun as the subject, object or complement of a sentence. In English a noun phrase may consist of a pronoun on its own, e.g. *he* or *me* in *He asked me*, or it may be a structure with many modifiers operating within rigid rules of word order: *Both the other two younger university students downstairs in the library.* . . . Alternative terms: nominal phrase, nominal sequence, nominal group, noun cluster. (4.1, 4.2, 8.23).

NOUN PHRASE INITIATOR A determiner which is capable of preceding the article in a noun phrase, e.g. such words as *all*, *both*, *half*.

NOUNAL FUNCTION The → frame into which a nominal will fit, e.g. as subject, object or complement of a sentence, object of a preposition, head word in a noun phrase, etc.

NUCLEUS → Syllable nucleus.

NUMBER (*a*) The grammatical category distinguishing between → singular, → dual, → plural, etc. In many languages verb forms show → agreement with number and person of the subject. (*b*) → numeral. (4.1, 4.2, 8.23).

NUMERAL A word denoting a number or quantity. Two examples of numerals are cardinal numbers (*one, two, three* . . .) answering the question *How many?* and ordinal numbers (*first, second, third* . . .) indicating the order in a sequence. Numerals are often represented in writing by special symbols, e.g. *1, 2, 3* . . . or *1st, 2nd, 3rd* . . . Alternative term: number. (4.1, 4.2, 8.23).

NURSERY LANGUAGE → Baby-talk (*a*).

O

OBJECT A term in traditional grammar for a word or group of words forming the 'complement' of certain verbs. Depending on the relationship with the verb, two types of object are distinguished. The DIRECT OBJECT is 'the person or thing which suffers the action of the verb in the sentence'. In inflected languages the direct object is usually marked by the accusative case, e.g. Latin *Pater amat filium* 'The father loves his son'. In languages such as English which do not show this type of case inflexion the direct object may be marked by word order, e.g. *The dog bites the man* as opposed to *The man bites the dog*. The INDIRECT OBJECT is 'the person or thing for whom or on whose behalf an action is carried out'. In inflected languages the indirect object is usually marked by the dative case. In languages which do not have this type of inflexion the indirect object may be marked by means of prepositions or word order: in English, for example, the direct object precedes the indirect object when the latter is marked by a preposition, e.g. *He gave a book to me*; if there is no preposition the indirect object precedes the direct object, e.g. *He gave me the book*. Note, however, that if both objects are pronouns either order is possible: e.g. *He gave me it* and *He gave it me* both occur. The use of the relationships 'direct object' and 'indirect object' differs from one language to another and exactly the same meaning may be expressed in one language by an indirect object and in another language by a direct object: e.g. German *Ich helfe Ihnen* 'I'll help you' has a dative pronoun (*Ihnen*), but there is no reason to consider the English *you* as anything other than a 'direct object'. The term object can be defined distributionally as that part of a sentence which becomes the → subject when a sentence is transformed into the passive, but again usage differs from one language to another: some languages only permit passive transforms when a direct object is present, others including English allow passive transformations of direct and indirect objects: e.g. *The boy caught the fish > The fish was caught by the boy*; *My father told me the story > I was told the story by my father*. (4.1, 4.2, 8.23).

OBJECT LANGUAGE A language which is the object of analysis through the medium of another language. In the object (or FIRST-ORDER) LANGUAGE words 'stand for' or 'refer to' things, while in a → meta-language (or SECOND-ORDER LANGUAGE) words are used to refer to other words.

OBJECT WRITING A primitive → writing system using concrete objects as signs, e.g. some North American Indian tribes use knots on a string for messages. (7.2).

OBJECTIVE CASE Term used to refer to → oblique case forms, particularly in languages which only have two inflexional case forms, e.g. the pronoun *me* in English *The man sees me* or French *Il me voit* 'he sees me' as opposed to the → subjective case: *I* in *I see the man* or *je* in *Je le vois* 'I see him'.

OBJECTIVE PRONOUN A form of a → pronoun which is governed by a verb or preposition, e.g. *I see him* where *him* is the object of the sentence, or *He gave me it* where *me* is the indirect object of the sentence, or *He did it for her* where *her* is governed by the preposition *for*.

OBLIGATIVE MOOD → Mood.

OBLIQUE CASE Any → case form in inflected languages other than the nominative, e.g. accusative, dative, instrumental, etc. In English, this term refers to forms other than the → common case, i.e. the possessive case of nouns and the → objective case of pronouns.

OBLIQUE QUESTION → Indirect question.

OBSERVATION The detailed study of all phenomena of → language with the view to discovering regularities, e.g. by → field-work. When the observing linguist is a participant in the linguistic activities of the speech community he investigates, his conclusions may be influenced by his own language habits, but he will attempt to check his abstractions and theories with the actual events, before any valid general scientific statements can be made. → metalanguage, linguistic analysis. (2.2 Garvin, 2.3 Samarin).

OBSTRUENT A category of consonants which includes → stops, → fricatives and → affricates, where the passage of the air stream is constricted at some point, as opposed to → resonant.

OBVIATIVE A form of the third person → pronoun referring to a person other than the subject. English has no special form for this, but in Russian for example, *его* 'his', 'its' cannot refer to the subject, whereas *свой* 'my', 'your', 'his', 'our', etc. can only refer to the subject, e.g. *Он читал свою книгу* 'He was reading his (his own) book' as opposed to *Он читал его книгу* 'He was reading his (someone else's) book'. → person.

OCCLUSION The period of time during the production of a → stop consonant in which the closure is maintained. → hold.

OCCLUSIVE → Stop.

OCEANIC LINGUISTICS The linguistic description of the languages spoken in Australia and on islands in the Pacific Ocean. → Malayo-Polynesian linguistics. → Appendix 1, p. 276. (2.2 Sebeok VIII, 8.8 Milner–Henderson, Wurm).

OESOPHAGEAL SPEECH Speech sounds produced with air from the oesophagus (→ diagram p. 159). This type of speech production is often used by patients who have undergone laryngectomy, the surgical removal of the → larynx.

OFF-GLIDE Movement of the speech organs after the production of a speech sound, either back to the neutral position or to a position anticipating the next sound. → on-glide. Alternative term: final glide.

OFFICIAL LANGUAGE → National language.

ON-GLIDE Movement of the speech organs, either from the position for a sound just produced or from a neutral position immediately prior to the production of a speech sound. → off-glide. Alternative term: initial glide.

ONOMASIOLOGY The study of the semantic relationships which can be set up between linguistic → symbols and the things they signify, e.g. grouping together the words with more than one meaning (→ polysemy) or the same meanings expressed in more than one word (→ synonymy). (5.2 Ullmann).

ONOMASTICS The study of the origin and meaning of names. A distinction is made in this field between TOPONYMY, the study of place names (including HYDRONYMY, the study of names of rivers and lakes) and ANTHROPONYMY, the study of personal names. → proper noun. Alternative term: onomatology. (10.1 Hymes).

ONOMATHESIA → Naming.

157

ONOMATOLOGY → Onomastics.

ONOMATOPOEIA The formation of words imitating natural sounds, e.g. *miaow, moo.* Only a very limited number of words in a language are based on this type of imitation, while the conventional nature of words as arbitrary symbols is a much more important feature of human language. → origin of speech, synaesthesia. (2.4 Jesperson, 10.1 Hymes). Alternative term: sound echoism.

ONOMATOPOEIC THEORY → Origin of speech.

ONOMATOPOEIC WORD A word intended to mimic a natural sound, e.g. *cock-a-doodle-do* or *splash.* Alternative terms: imitative word, echo word, mimetic word.

ONSET (*a*) The preliminary movement of the speech organs towards the → articulation of a speech sound. (*b*) The initial part of a → syllable, e.g. [m] in *man.*

ONTOGENY The study of one person's speech habits throughout his whole lifetime, as opposed to → phylogeny, the history of a whole language system. → idiolect, → developmental linguistics. (2.1 Hockett).

OPEN APPROXIMANT Term used by some linguists to refer to → frictionless continuant.

OPEN-CLASS WORD → Content word.

OPEN JUNCTURE → Transition.

OPEN LIST → Open set.

OPEN SET A paradigmatic series of an unlimited number of variants in a field or slot, e.g. a list of lexical items such as *chair, table, lamp,* etc. which could be continued indefinitely, as opposed to a → closed system such as a list of prepositions the number of which is fixed. Alternative term: open list. (9.11 Halliday *et al.*).

OPEN SYLLABLE A → syllable ending in a vowel sound, e.g. *me* or *high.* Alternative term: free syllable.

OPEN TRANSITION → Transition.

OPEN VOWEL A → vowel sound produced with the tongue in a relatively low position in the mouth. → diagram p. 253.

OPPOSITION A relationship between elements of a system by means of which the elements can be distinguished from each other. Opposition may be grammatical (e.g. singular as opposed to plural, present as opposed to past), or phonological. Phonological opposition is the result of a difference in sound which enables different → phonemes to be distinguished. Thus the sounds [t] and [d] are in opposition in English, since the difference between them enables speakers of English to differentiate between *tin* and *din* or *bad* and *bat.* → binarism, → distinctive feature, → contrast. (3.4 Trubetzkoy).

OPTATIVE MOOD → Mood.

OPTIONAL VARIANT → Free variant.

158

ORACY → Articulacy.

ORAL (*a*) Concerning speech, as opposed to 'writing', e.g. in oral → literature. (*b*) Concerning the mouth, as opposed to nose or other → cavities in the vocal tract. (*c*) A speech sound produced with the velum raised to seal off the nasal passage, so that no air can escape through the nose, e.g. all the sounds in [bɪd] *bid*. → nasal. (*d*) → nasal *versus* oral.

ORAL AIR-STREAM MECH-ANISM → Air-stream mechanism.

ORAL CAVITY → Cavity.

ORAL LITERATURE → Literature.

ORATORICAL → Key.

ORATORICAL SPEECH A ceremonial type of language used on very formal occasions. → manner of discourse.

ORDER (*a*) A group of consonant sounds, all produced at the same → point of articulation, e.g. the labial order [p], [b], [m], etc. → series. (*b*) Sequence of elements, e.g. words in a sentence (→ word order) or rules in a grammar (→ phrase structure rule).

ORDINAL NUMBER A → numeral which answers the question *In what order?* e.g. *first, second, third,* etc. as opposed to → cardinal number. In inflected languages ordinal numbers usually decline like adjectives.

ORDINARY LANGUAGE The speech used in everyday discourse. → common language.

ORGANS OF SPEECH Parts of the human body concerned with the → articulation of speech sounds, i.e. the lungs, larynx, pharynx, nasal cavity, oral cavity, lips, teeth, tongue, alveolar ridge, palate, velum, uvula. → diagram below. Alternative term: speech organs.

THE ORGANS OF SPEECH

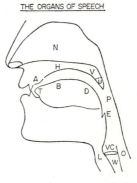

N	Nasal cavity	A	Alveolar ridge
H	Hard palate	V	Soft palate, velum
U	Uvula	T	Tip, apex
B	Blade, front	D	Dorsum, back
P	Pharynx	L	Larynx
VC	Vocal cords	W	Trachea, windpipe
O	Oesophagus, food passage	E	Epiglottis

ORIGIN OF LANGUAGE → Origin of speech.

ORIGIN OF SPEECH The questions of where and how human beings first developed → language. There is little factual evidence, since human speech is probably as old as man, and written records only go back for about 4,000 years. Attempts have been made to find out more about the origin of speech by analogies with certain forms of animal communication, with the child's acquisition of language, and with 'primitive' languages, but all these have failed to solve the problem.

Various authors have put forward hypothetical explanations: M. Müller (1823–1900) suggested a mystic connexion between sound and meaning: human speech developed from primitive man giving vocal expression to the objects he encountered (DING-DONG or NATIVISTIC THEORY). O. Jespersen (1860–1943) held that language developed from primitive inarticulate ritualistic chants (SING-SONG THEORY). L. H. Gray's (1875–1955) POOH-POOH or EXCLAMATION or INTERJECTIONAL THEORY traced language back to interjections expressing emotions. L. Noiré (1847–1889) explained the origin of speech in terms of the cries uttered during the strain of work (YO-HE-HO THEORY). R. Paget (1869–1955) claimed that language comes from the combination of certain gestures and tongue movements (TA-TA THEORY). Various explanations have been given in terms of imitation of animal cries and other sounds heard in nature (BOW-WOW, CUCKOO, ANIMAL CRY, ONOMATOPOEIC, HEY-NONNY-NONNY THEORY, etc.). → polygenesis. Alternative term: origin of language. (2.1 Gray–Wise, 2.2 Haas).

ORTHOEPY Standardised → pronunciation.

ORTHOGRAPHY Standardised → spelling.

OSCILLOGRAPH An instrument for producing a graphic representation of the variations in air pressure of sound waves, showing frequency and amplitude. → sound spectrograph.

OSCILLOSCOPE Cathode ray tube for viewing a → sound wave form.

OSTENSIVE DEFINITION → Definition.

OUTER CLOSURE → Closure.

OUTER FORM → Inner form.

OVERCORRECTION Mispronunciation of words or use of unaccepted grammatical constructions due to conscious efforts to avoid regional or → sub-standard forms of speech. Thus a Northern British English speaker in making an effort to use the Southern English [ʌ] in words like [kʌm] *come* and [bʌs] *bus* might pronounce *butcher* as [bʌtʃər] by analogy with *button* [bʌtn], or a speaker may say *between you and I* in order to avoid saying *you and me*. Alternative terms: hyper-correction, hyper-urbanism. (7.1).

OVERLAPPING DISTRIBUTION → Class cleavage.

OVERTONE (*a*) The → harmonic frequencies of a sound wave. (*b*) The → connotations in meaning of a particular word or phrase.

OXYTONE A word having the → stress on the final syllable, e.g. *under'stand*. → paroxytone.

OXYTONIC LANGUAGE A language in which most words have fixed → stress on the final syllable. (3.1, 6.1, 8.1).

P

PALAEOGRAPHY The study of ancient cursive → writing on soft surfaces. → epigraphy. (7.2).

PALATAL A consonant articulated with the tongue touching or approaching the hard → palate. If the dorsum region of the tongue acts as the articulator the sound may be called → dorsopalatal. According to the point of articulation, a sound may be called PREPALATAL, i.e. articulated at the front of the palate, MEDIO-PALATAL, i.e. articulated around the centre of the palate, or POSTPALATAL, i.e. articulated towards the rear of the palate. (3.1, 8.22).

PALATALISATION The raising of the tongue towards the hard palate, normally as a secondary feature of articulation, e.g. as in the initial sound of *dew*. In some languages the difference between non-palatalised and palatalised consonants (HARD and SOFT) is often used to distinguish words with different meanings, e.g. Russian *угол* 'corner' as opposed to *уголь* 'coal'. In IPA phonetic transcription palatalisation is normally indicated by means of an apostrophe, e.g. [ugol']. (3.1, 8.22).

PALATALISED Pronounced with some degree of → palatalisation, i.e. with the front of the tongue being raised towards the palate, e.g. in the initial sound of English *dew*. Alternative term: soft consonant.

PALATE Concave bone structure forming the roof of the mouth behind the → alveolar ridge. → diagram p. 159. Alternative term: hard palate. (3.1, 8.22).

PALATO-ALVEOLAR A consonant articulated with the front part of the tongue touching or approaching the junction of the alveolar ridge and the hard palate: e.g. [ʃ] as in *ship* or [ʒ] as in *pleasure*.

PALATOGRAM Drawing, photograph, or actual impression of the points of contact of the tongue on the palate during the → articulation of a speech sound. Alternative term: glossogram.

PALATOGRAPHY The study of → articulation by means of observing the physiological contacts between the tongue and the palate in speech, either by direct impressions taken in the mouth, by using an artificial palate, or by photography. (3.1).

PALINDROME A word or series of words or digits which read the same either forwards or backwards, e.g. *Otto*; *Anna*; *Able was I ere I saw Elba*; *18181*. → anagram.

PARADIGM (*a*) A list of all the various inflected forms of a declinable word, e.g. conjugations such as *walk*, *walks*, *walked*, etc. or declensions such as *boy*, *boy's*, *boys*, *boys'*. (*b*) Occasionally used as an alternative term for → substitution class, i.e. to refer to any set of items which are in paradigmatic relationship.

PARADIGMATIC The vertical relationship between forms which might occupy the same particular place in a structure, e.g. in

> *He walks slowly*
> *quickly*
> *as fast as he can*
> *home*

a paradigmatic relationship exists between *slowly, quickly, as fast as he can*, and *home*. Each word in a language is in paradigmatic relationship with a whole set of possible alternatives. This phenomenon is used in the idea of → substitution frames in language teaching. By contrast, the linear or horizontal relationship between words in a sentence is called → syntagmatic. (2.5 Lepschy, 4.1 Palmer, 8.23).

PARAGOGUE The addition of a sound or sounds to the end of a word for the sake of euphony or easier pronunciation. → diagram p. 75.

PARAGRAPH A unit of spoken or written discourse intermediate between the → sentence and the whole → text. In their search for narrative and conversational units beyond the single utterance, scholars associated with the linguistic school of → tagmemics have investigated how reference is made between consecutive paragraphs by varying pronouns and determiners. (2.5 Cook).

PARALANGUAGE → Paralinguistic features.

PARALINGUISTIC FEATURES Those formal patterns of speech which characterise an individual speaker of a language, e.g. voice quality such as 'falsetto', 'creak', 'staccato', 'giggle', etc. Some linguists have treated these features as lying outside the scope of linguistic communication and analysis (→ metalanguage), others have related them to features of posture and gesture (→ kinesics) or of phonology (→ prosodic features). To a certain extent these personal traits are conventionalised in different languages or in different dialects of one language. Alternative term: paralanguage. (8.22 Crystal).

PARALINGUISTICS The system and study of → paralinguistic features.

PARAMETRIC LINGUISTICS A method of analysing linguistic entities into physical variables such as voice, pitch, tongue and lip movement, etc. The co-ordination of such 'parameters' is essential in → speech production and → speech synthesis. (2.3 Heller–Macris).

PARAPHRASE The process or result of rewording an utterance from one level or variety of a language into another without altering the meaning, as opposed to → metaphrase or translation which converts the utterance into a different language. Some types of → language teaching make use of both paraphrasing and translation to develop the skills of expressing the same meaning in a number of different ways.

PARAPLASM A newly coined word replacing an older well-established form, e.g. *record player* for *gramophone*. Alternative term: paraplastic form.

PARAPLASTIC FORM → Paraplasm.

PARASITIC → Epenthetic.

PARASYNTHESIS Formation of words using → derivational affixes + a stem. → parasynthetic formation.

PARASYNTHETIC FORMATION A word consisting of a stem and one or more affixes, e.g. *denationalise* or *blue-eyed*. → derivational affix. Alternative term: parasyntheton.

PARASYNTHETON → Parasynthetic formation.

PARATAXIS The joining together of sentences or clauses by juxtaposition, without the use of conjunctions, e.g. *He dictated the letter; she wrote it*, as opposed to → hypotaxis: *He dictated the letter and she wrote it*.

PARENT LANGUAGE One of a family of related languages which is the common origin of all others. Thus, Vulgar Latin is regarded as the parent language of all Romance languages such as French, Italian and Rumanian, which are called descendant or daughter languages. → glottochronology. Alternative term: ancestor language. (6.1).

PARENTHESIS (*a*) → Punctuation. (*b*) → Parenthetical clause.

PARENTHETICAL CLAUSE A syntactic pattern inserted into a sentence, modifying a particular part of the sentence without adding to or changing its basic structure, e.g. the relative clause in *That man (who is wearing a green hat) is my uncle*. Alternative terms: inserted clause, embedded clause, constituent sentence, parenthesis.

PAROLE → Langue and parole.

PARONOMASIA → Pun.

PARONYM A word derived from the same base as another word, e.g. *childhood, childish, childlike*; or a word having the same form as a → cognate word in another language, e.g. English and German *Winter*.

PAROXYTONE A word with the → stress on the last syllable but one, e.g. *under'standing*. → oxytone.

PAROXYTONIC LANGUAGE A language in which most words have a fixed → stress on the last syllable but one. (3.1, 6.1, 8.1).

PARSING A grammatical exercise involving the description of sentences and words by giving names to the grammatical categories of various elements: e.g. subject, object, verb, number, gender, case, person, etc.

PART OF SPEECH A grammatical word class. The controversy about how many parts of speech can be recognised and what they are, goes back to the ancient Greeks. Plato distinguished only two word categories in Greek: *noun* and *verb*, but Aristotle added a third class of *indeclinables*. Later (*c.* 100 BC) Dionysius Thrax distinguished eight categories which were to become accepted for many centuries: *noun, pronoun, article, participle, verb, adverb, preposition, conjunction*. The Greek categories fitted the Latin language reasonably well with very slight modifications, and the Roman grammarians such as Priscian and Donatus adopted Thrax's categories except for the deletion of *article*, which did not occur in Latin, and the addition of *interjection*. These grammatical categories became a tradition which was further established by the

163

Modistae in the Middle Ages and which persists more or less up to the present day. It is significant that differences between the number and nature of the parts of speech recognised by grammarians through the ages depended mainly on the approach they adopted and hardly at all on the language involved. Twentieth-century linguists tried to break away from this tradition in order to define categories which would be more appropriate to the specific language in question and more consistent than the traditional categories which were based partly on 'notional' definitions and partly on 'functional' categories. The inconsistency of this approach can be seen from the following: a noun is said to be a 'naming word', a notional definition, whereas an adverb is said to be a word 'modifying a verb', a functional definition. Confusion arises in that *home* is still a 'naming word' even when it modifies a verb in a sentence such as *He goes home*. Twentieth-century grammarians realised the need for relating definitions of the parts of speech to specific languages but this did not bring about agreement between grammarians working on the same language, because different approaches to the analysis have produced different results. Some linguists have taken over the traditional terms and have redefined them, adding new terms where necessary (Sledd); others rejected completely the traditional terminology and invented new names for the categories to prevent confusion, or resorted even to numbering the categories (Fries). Probably the most 'formal definition' of part of speech is that found in → transformational grammar which assigns words to categories based on constituent structure in the deep grammar of a sentence; all words which can operate as the same constituent of a sentence are members of the same class. From the following very simple phrase structure diagram three word classes can be distinguished: (1) words which can function at A; (2) words which can function at B; and (3) words which can function at C:

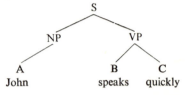

In → categorial grammar the approach is quite different in that only nouns are recognised as a separate category and all other categories are defined in accordance with the way in which they can combine with nouns to form sentences. Thus a 'verb' is a word which can combine on its own with a noun to form a sentence. It is also worthy of note that in some types of transformational grammar adjectives may be considered as a sub-category of verbs, which is in agreement with Plato's basic dichotomy *noun* and *verb*, where *verb* included what was later distinguished as *adjective*. This relationship between intransitive verbs and adjectives can be understood if *is* in *John is careless* is considered to be an 'empty' auxiliary performing the same function as the morpheme {s} in *John walks*, in other words *is careless* is a realisation of *careless* + {s} in the same way as *walks* is a realisation of *walk* + {s}. (2.1 Lyons, 4.1 Herndon, 8.23 Gleason).

PARTIAL ASSIMILATION → Assimilation.

PARTICIPIAL PHRASE A meaningful group of words containing a participle, e.g. *driving a van* in *I dislike driving a van.*

PARTICIPLE A traditional term for a non-finite form of the → verb. In Latin, participles are verbal adjectives in the sense that they can have the function of an adjective in qualifying a noun whilst at the same time having certain characteristics of a verb, distinguishing tense and voice. Most Latin verbs have three participles: active present: *amans* 'loving', active future: *amaturus* 'about to love', and passive perfect: *amatus* 'loved'. English has basically two participle forms: the present participle which usually ends in *-ing* and the past participle usually ending in *-ed* or occasionally *-en*, etc. Apart from their use in forming compound verb forms such as *I am walking* or *I have walked*, participles are used in English as adjectives, e.g. *a crying child*; *the closed door*. In addition there are a series of compound forms in English which may also be called participles, e.g. perfect active: *having walked*; perfect passive: *having been seen*; present passive: *being read*. (4.1, 8.23).

PARTICLE An invariable part of speech with grammatical meaning rather than lexical meaning, e.g. prepositions such as *on*, *at*, etc. → function word.

PARTITIVE ARTICLE A form used in some languages before → mass nouns to indicate, amongst other things, that the noun refers to only a part of a whole, e.g. French *de l'* in *de l'encre* or *some* in the English translation *some ink*. → partitive genitive.

PARTITIVE GENITIVE The use of the genitive case in some inflected languages to indicate that reference is being made only to a part of the total meaning of a word or phrase: e.g. Russian *Я куплю рыбы* 'I shall buy some fish' where *рыбы* is genitive meaning 'some fish' not 'all fish'.

PARTITIVE NUMERAL A → numeral denoting a fraction, e.g. *half, quarter, eighth.*

PASIGRAPHY A writing system using signs which are of almost universal significance, not restricted to one particular language, e.g. Arabic numbers *1, 2, 3*, etc.

PASIMOLOGY Communication by means of → gesture, e.g. the hand alphabet used by deaf-mutes.

PASSIVE The passive → voice (*b*).

PASSIVE ARTICULATOR → Articulator.

PASSIVE CAVITY → Cavity.

PASSIVE INFINITIVE An infinite form of the → verb, made up in English by *to be* plus the past participle of a transitive verb, e.g. *to be read, to be taken*, etc.

PASSIVE VOICE → Voice (*b*).

PAST ANTERIOR A compound → tense form occurring in formal written French and other Romance languages, used to express rapid accomplishment of an action. It is formed with the past historic of an auxiliary verb plus the past participle of a full verb. It can occur in the main clause of a simple sentence: e.g. *En trois heures j'eus visité la ville et ses environs* 'In three hours I had visited the town and its surroundings', or after certain conjunctions: e.g. *Aussitôt que j'eus achevé mon travail...* 'As soon as I had finished my work...' Alternative term: second past perfect.

PAST HISTORIC A past → tense form of the verb, used in formal written French and other Romance languages to refer to a completed action, e.g. in *Louis XIV régna soixante-douze ans* 'Louis XIV reigned for seventy-two years'.

PAST PARTICIPLE A → participle, in English usually ending in *-ed* or occasionally *-en*, etc. used with auxiliaries to form compound perfect tenses, e.g. *I have walked*, or as an adjectival, e.g. *a used car*.

PAST PERFECT → Pluperfect tense.

PAST TENSE A → tense form of a verb referring to an action which took place prior to the time of the utterance. The distinction past : non-past is the basic distinction of the English tense system. → aspect, → mood. Alternative term: simple past.

PATOIS A regional variant of a language. → dialect.

PATRONYMIC A name given to a person based on his father's first name, e.g. *Johnson*. Some cultures, e.g. Russian, use a system of three names: first name, patronymic, surname, e.g. Александр Сергеевич Пушкин *Alexander Sergeyevitch Pushkin.* → matronymic, → teknonymic.

PATTERN In → linguistic analysis and → language teaching, the systematic arrangement of elements according to the regularities found in the language. The term pattern may refer to the overall system of a language, e.g. sound pattern or phonology, or to the way individual units can be grouped together and within units of the next higher level, e.g. morphemes within words. (4.1, 8.23, 9.11).

PATTERN DRILL The application of the 'slot-and-filler' or → substitution frame technique to language teaching in order to practice a particular linguistic structure. The so-called parallel drill requires the student to imitate a structure, the mutation drill involves a change in the given structure, both on the basis of → analogy. Alternative terms: structure drill, substitution drill. (9.11).

PAUCAL A category of → number denoting the concept 'a few'.

PAUSE A short break in speech, often occurring before items of high → information content or low probability. → transition. (3.1, 8.22).

PEAK OF PROMINENCE → Peak of sonority.

PEAK OF SONORITY That portion of a → syllable which stands out due to highest → pitch or strongest → stress, e.g. [a] in [pai] *pie* or the consonant [s] in [psːt] *psst!* Alternative terms: crest of sonority, peak of prominence, syllabic peak.

PEAK SATELLITE That part of a vowel cluster which does

not carry the → peak of sonority, e.g. [i] in *day* [dei].

PEDAGOGICAL GRAMMAR
A grammatical description of a language specifically designed as an aid to teaching that language to native or foreign learners. It emphasises functional aspects of grammar rather than theoretical categories or, in foreign language teaching, contrastive features between the → source and target languages. (9.11).

PEDAGOGICAL LINGUISTICS
A branch of → applied linguistics which is concerned with improving the efficiency of → language teaching by providing comprehensive descriptions of the underlying processes and by using adequate teaching methods. Such pedagogical activities are relevant both in the teaching of the mother tongue and in foreign language instruction, particularly in terms of the specification of the variety of language to be learnt (e.g. → register, dialect), of the skills involved (e.g. → reading, speaking, etc.) and the selection and grading of the material to be presented (e.g. 'basic' → vocabulary, testing, etc.). (9.1).

PEDIGREE THEORY
The theory that a parent language splits up into descendant languages with a resultant geneological relationship like a → family tree. (6.1).

PEJORATION
→ Deterioration.

PEJORATIVE
Term used for a word or morphemic element with an unfavourable connotation, e.g. the suffix *-ish* in the words *childish, womanish*.

PERCEPTION
The act of hearing and interpreting speech sounds so as to be able to understand the meaning of an utterance.

PEREGRINISM
→ Alienism.

PERFECT ASPECT
→ Aspect.

PERFECT TENSE
Traditional term for the verb form occurring as *have + past participle* in English, e.g. *I have read*. This kind of time reference is now usually considered as a type of → aspect rather than → tense, since it refers more to the type and state of the action, e.g. that it is completed, than to its location in time. Alternative terms: simple perfect, present perfect, first perfect.

PERFECTIVE ASPECT
→ Aspect.

PERFORMANCE
→ Competence and performance.

PERIOD
(*a*) The time interval between crests of → sound waves or between any other corresponding points on the wave form. (*b*) → Punctuation.

PERIPHERAL AREA
→ Area.

PERIPHERAL LANGUAGE
The language used by a speech community sharing features of phonology, grammar and/or vocabulary with a neighbouring speech community, not because of historical relationship, but because of cultural or other contacts. (6.1, 7.1, 8.1).

PERIPHERAL VOWELS
Vowel sounds produced with the highest part of the tongue farthest removed from the centre of the mouth in any direction. The eight → cardinal vowels are peripheral vowels.

PERMANSIVE ASPECT → Aspect.

PERSON A deictic category relating participants one to another in a linguistic situation. In any such situation there are necessarily two basic participants: a speaker and an addressee, although under certain circumstances they may be identical. Most languages, including English, distinguish three 'persons': FIRST PERSON, used by a speaker to refer to himself, e.g. *I*, *we*; SECOND PERSON, to refer to the addressee, e.g. *you*; THIRD PERSON, to refer to people or things other than the speaker or addressee, e.g. *he*, *she*, *it*, *they*. Some languages make further distinctions, e.g. Tagolog distinguishes an EXCLUSIVE PERSONAL PRONOUN meaning 'we, i.e. I and somebody else other than the addressee' from an INCLUSIVE PERSONAL PRONOUN meaning 'we, i.e. I and the addressee'. In some languages, e.g. Eskimo and Cree, a distinction is made in the third person between PROXIMATE, the nearer or the more important, and OBVIATIVE, the more distant or the less important. English has something comparable to this in the use of *this* and *that* and *the former* and *the latter*. In many languages 'person' is marked by inflexions on pronouns or verbs or both and is thus a grammatical category, but in languages which have no such inflexions, e.g. Japanese, it may be considered a lexical category. (4.1, 4.2, 8.23).

PERSONAL ENDING The ending of a → verb form to agree with number and person, e.g. *she sings, they sing*, French *elle chante, ils chantent*.

PERSONAL INFINITIVE A form of the → infinitive which shows inflexional distinctions of person and number, e.g. Portuguese *Julgamos estares cansada* 'We think you're tired' where *estares* shows agreement for second person singular.

PERSONAL PRONOUN A → pronoun referring to one of the categories of person such as *I*, *he*, *she*, *it*, *we*, *they*, etc. as well as their inflected (→ objective and → possessive) forms *we*, *him*, *her*, *us*, *them*; *my*, *mine*, *your*, *yours*, *his*, etc. (4.1, 8.23).

PERSONAL VERB A verb used in all three persons, as opposed to an → impersonal verb which is used in the third person only.

PETROGLYPH. → Petrogram.

PETROGRAM An ancient inscription on stone. Alternative term: petroglyph. (7.2).

PETROGRAPHY → Writing on hard surfaces such as stone.

PHANTOM WORD → Ghost form.

PHARYNGEAL A speech sound articulated in the → pharynx, e.g. [ħ] as in Arabic *Ahmed*.

PHARYNGEAL AIR-STREAM MECHANISM → Air-stream mechanism.

PHARYNGEAL CAVITY → Pharynx.

PHARYNGEALISATION The articulation of a speech sound accompanied by a constriction in the → pharynx.

PHARYNX The chamber between the root of the tongue and the back wall of the throat extending from the nasal cavity to the larynx. → diagram p. 159. Alternative term: pharyngeal cavity. (3.1, 8.22).

PHASE Two → sound waves are in phase if at a particular point in time the air pressure is registered at the norm for both waves and at that point both waves show variation in the same direction. If one wave moves to its trough as the other moves to its crest, they are out of phase. (3.3 Joos).

PHASE OF ARTICULATION One of three stages in the production of a speech sound: → on-glide, → hold, → off-glide.

PHATIC COMMUNION Term coined by B. Malinowski (1887–1942) to refer to the exchange of sterotyped phrases, e.g. *How do you do?* or *Nice day!* or *mhm*. Such utterances do not have → meaning in the sense of conveying information, but serve to establish social contact between speakers or to avoid embarrassing silence. (5.1 Ogden–Richards).

PHILOLOGY (*a*) Older term for → comparative and → historical linguistics, particularly used to refer to historical linguistic research based on the study of literature and written documents. The work of the philologists of the 19th century laid the foundations for modern linguistic studies. (*b*) Philology is sometimes used in a wider sense to include the study of literature and civilisation. (6.1).

PHILOSOPHICAL GRAMMAR The study of → grammar not in consideration of the usage of a particular language, but from the point of view of the features all languages have in common (→ universal). → philosophy of language. Alternative term: notional grammar. (4.2 Jespersen, 10.3).

PHILOSOPHICAL LINGUISTICS → Philosophy of language.

PHILOSOPHICAL SEMANTICS Collective term for several approaches to the philosophical study of → meaning in language. Philosophers have often related questions of semantic meaning to the nature of naming objects (are words linked to the things to which they refer or are they just conventionalised labels?) or to the truth and validity of statements, some have demonstrated that philosophy and culture are in fact dependent on the structure of language. Linguistic → semantics, on the other hand, studies the mutual relations between the words or groups of words themselves. → semiotics, → general semantics. Alternative terms: rhematics, rhematology. (5.2 Morris, 10.3 Carnap).

PHILOSOPHY OF LANGUAGE A collective term given to a variety of efforts to explore the general nature and status of language as a human activity and the theoretical and conceptual foundations of linguistic science. Special research topics

169

under this heading include → meaning and culture, → logic in language, the study of language → universals, the concept of → language itself, and the various models, approaches and methods in linguistics. LINGUISTIC PHILOSOPHY refers to a number of approaches to language by philosophers, while the linguists' treatment of these problems is usually called PHILOSOPHICAL LINGUISTICS. → philosophical grammar, → philosophical semantics. (10.3).

PHONAESTHEME → Synaesthesia.

PHONAESTHETIC SERIES → Synaesthesia.

PHONATION (*a*) → Speech production. (*b*) → Voicing.

PHONE In → phonology the smallest possible segment of sound abstracted from the continuum of speech. → phoneme, → allophone.

PHONEMATIC UNIT In → prosodic analysis the segmental element left when all the prosodies have been abstracted.

PHONEMATICS → Phonemics.

PHONEME The smallest unit of → phonology. The concept of the phoneme arose out of the awareness that the precise phonetic realisation of a particular sound is not so important as its function within the sound system of a particular language. The phonetic realisation of a phoneme may vary: its phonetic variants are called → allophones. Each language has its own arrangement of phonemes and allophones,

i.e. its own phonemic structure, and two sounds which may be variants of a single phoneme in one language may represent different phonemes in another. The English word *room* for example may be pronounced [rum] or [ruːm], in which case [u] and [uː] are allophones of the phoneme /u/, but in German [u] and [uː] are not interchangeable in the same environment without affecting the meaning: [rum] *Rum* 'rum', but [ruːm] *Ruhm* 'fame'. In German, therefore, [u] and [uː] are realisations of separate phonemes. The precise definition of the term phoneme has been the subject of much discussion among linguists and there are two major points of view. The first is the 'classification' theory developed by D. Jones which considers the phoneme to be a group or family of related sounds, e.g. /p/ in English consisting of [pʰ], [p], etc., or /u/ consisting of [uː], [u], etc. The second or 'distinctive feature' theory developed by N. S. Trubetzkoy and the → Prague School considers a phoneme to be a bundle of distinctive features, e.g. /p/ in English is considered to be made up of bilabial + stop + voiceless (aspiration is therefore not distinctive and thus the allophones [pʰ], [p] above are allowed for). The → distinctive feature theory has gained impetus from the work of R. Jakobson and M. Halle in acoustic phonetics. Whatever the many theoretical differences in the two approaches mentioned, the practical result can be seen to be the same: the analysis of the continuum of speech into significant segments, hence the alternative term SEGMENTAL PHONEME or LINEAR PHONEME. A phonemic analysis of this type is useful for reducing a language to writing by means of a phonemic

170

alphabet (phonetic transcription) which uses one symbol per phoneme, ignoring allophones. Some features of the spoken language, however, such as pitch, stress, intonation, etc. cannot be satisfactorily reduced into segments; to accommodate these the original phoneme theory was adapted to include such features under the heading of → supra-segmental phonemes. → prosodic analysis, → opposition, → minimal pair. (3.1–3.4, 8.22).

PHONEME-GRAPHEME CORRESPONDENCE In writing systems, the correspondence between the graphic elements (such as letters, syllabic or character signs) and the phonological/grammatical units (such as phonemes, syllables or words) which they represent. In most scripts the FIT between graphic signs and the units for which they stand is imperfect, which is the main reason for difficulties in → spelling. (7.2 Wardhaugh).

PHONEMIC The difference between a pair of words is said to be phonemic or phonologically → distinctive if they differ only in one → phoneme, e.g. /b/ and /p/ in *bin*:*pin*.

PHONEMIC ANALYSIS The analysis of an utterance into → segmental and → suprasegmental features. → phoneme, → phonological analysis.

PHONEMIC CONTRAST A difference between sounds which is sufficient on its own to permit words to be differentiated. Thus the phonemes /p/ and /b/ in English show a contrast, since it is primarily the difference between them which enables speakers to distinguish the words *pin* and *bin*. → opposition.

PHONEMIC LOAN A borrowed word which retains the sounds and combinations of sound of its original language, even though these sounds are not part of the phonemic system of the borrowing language, e.g. the combination [ts] in initial position in *tsetse*, a loan word from Bantu.

PHONEMIC NOTATION→ Phonemic transcription.

PHONEMIC PRINCIPLE The theory that the continuum of speech can be analysed into a series of segmental and/or suprasegmental units of sound called → phonemes.

PHONEMIC SOUND CHANGE A type of → sound change affecting the distribution of → allophones to → phonemes and thus affecting the whole phonemic structure of the language. At one stage in the history of the English language [n] and [ŋ] were allophones of the phoneme /n/, [ŋ] occurred before /k/ or /g/ and [n] before all other sounds. The allophone [ŋ] developed into a separate phoneme /ŋ/ which now contrasts medially and finally but not initially with /n/ as in [siŋə] *singer* as opposed to [sinə] *sinner*, or [siŋ] *sing* as opposed to [sin] *sin*. Alternative terms: phonological change, sound change by phonemes, functional change. (6.1).

PHONEMIC STRESS A stress pattern is phonemic if a change of stress would result in a change of meaning or a change of word class, e.g. *pérmit* (noun) as opposed to *permìt* (verb).

PHONEMIC STRUCTURE An inventory of all the → phonemes

and the relationship existing between them together with a phonetic description of the → allophones is called the phonemic structure or SOUND SYSTEM of a language. Each language has a unique phonemic structure: languages differ in the number of phonemes, the arrangement of allophones into phonemes, the phonetic description of allophones, the relationship existing between phonemes, etc. (3.1, 8.22).

PHONEMIC TRANSCRIPTION
A broad → transcription which uses one symbol per → phoneme, with no information about → allophones. Phonemic transcription is usually written between slants, e.g. /haus/, to distinguish it from phonetic transcription which is usually written between square brackets, e.g. [haus], [hæ·ɐs], [aus], [u·s], etc. All alphabetic writing is, to a certain extent, phonemic, but some languages such as English and Danish show great inconsistency in the graphic representations of speech sounds. Others such as Finnish and Turkish come very near to using consistently one letter per phoneme. Alternative term: phonemic notation. (3.1, 8.22).

PHONEMICIST A linguist concerned with → phonemic analysis. → phonetician.

PHONEMICS Although many European linguists use the term → phonology to refer to all aspects of the study of the sound system of a particular language, the originally American usage of the term phonemics is becoming more widespread. In this sense phonemics is a branch of phonology concerned with the synchronic analysis of the sound system of a given language,

particularly with reference to reducing language to writing, as opposed to historical or diachronic phonology. Alternative term: phonematics. (3.1–3.4, 8.22).

PHONESTHEME → Synaesthesia.

PHONETIC ALPHABET An alphabet, such as the → International Phonetic Alphabet, used in → phonetic transcription. → pp. 262–263.

PHONETIC (COMPLEMENT) In some logographic systems of → writing, that component part of an elementary → character sign which gives an indication of the pronunciation of the word represented. Most Chinese written signs are composed of two elements, the radical and the phonetic. The phonetic suggests the pronunciation by association with a character for a → homonym. Alternative term: phonetic indicator. (7.2).

PHONETIC CONTEXT The environment of a speech sound in terms of its neighbouring speech sounds and prosodic features.

PHONETIC EMPATHY The behaviour of a listener when he goes through the movements of sound production as part of his act of perception. This feature plays an important part in speech perception and indicates that the process of listening to speech sounds is different from the process of listening to other sounds. (3.1 Abercrombie).

PHONETIC INDICATOR → Phonetic (complement).

PHONETIC LAW A statement in historical and comparative linguistics which seeks to explain a series of regular changes in the sound system of a language from one stage of its development to another or a series of correspondences between different languages. Examples of such laws are → Grimm's Law, → Grassman's Law, → Verner's Law. Alternative term: sound law.

PHONETIC NOTATION → Phonetic transcription.

PHONETIC REPRESENTATION → Phonology.

PHONETIC SCRIPT → Phonetic transcription.

PHONETIC SIGN A graphic sign used in → phonetic transcription. → chart, p. 262.

PHONETIC SOUND CHANGE A → sound change which does not affect the phonemic structure of a language, i.e. does not affect the relation of one phoneme to another or change the status of a sound from allophone to phoneme. Alternative terms: sound change by allophones, allophonic change. (6.1).

PHONETIC SPELLING A → spelling system which attempts to follow closely and consistently the actual sounds of speech. In popular speech the term phonetic spelling is used to refer to what would more accurately be called → phonemic transcription.

PHONETIC SYMBOL A graphic sign used in → phonetic transcription. → chart p. 262.

PHONETIC TRANSCRIPTION A system of graphic signs and → diacritic marks to represent the sounds of speech on paper. Phonetic transcriptions may be devised for widely differing purposes, e.g. teaching pronunciation of a language or studying the phonology of a language, and it is not surprising, therefore, that there are several types. The term BROAD TRANSCRIPTION is used by some linguists as an alternative to the term PHONEMIC TRANSCRIPTION, i.e. a transcription which uses one symbol per → phoneme. The term NARROW TRANSCRIPTION or COMPARATIVE TRANSCRIPTION is used to denote a transcription which uses more than one symbol per phoneme and which sets out to show → non-distinctive features of an utterance by means of special letters and/or diacritics. A broad transcription of the English word *tenth*, for example, would probably be /tenθ/ whereas a narrow transcription such as [tʰɛn̪θ] would indicate the aspiration of the initial consonant by means of the superscript h, the phonetic realisation of the phoneme /e/ by using the symbol [ɛ], the dental articulation of the usually alveolar [n] by use of the symbol [n̪]. There is no such thing as a standard phonetic transcription, nor a standard PHONETIC ALPHABET; there are several types of phonetic alphabets in common use today, but perhaps the most common is the alphabet of the International Phonetics Association, the → International Phonetic Alphabet (IPA). → analphabetic notation. Alternative terms: phonetic script, phonetic notation. → table, pp. 262–263.

PHONETIC VARIANT → Allophone.

PHONETICIAN A person engaged in the study of → phonetics. → phonemicist, phonologist.

PHONETICS The study of speech processes, including the anatomy, neurology and pathology of speech, the articulation, classification and perception of speech sounds. Phonetics is a pure science and need not be studied in relation to a particular language, but it has many practical applications, e.g. in → phonetic transcription, → language teaching, → speech therapy. Some phoneticians consider phonetics to be outside the central core of → linguistics proper, but most would include it under the heading 'linguistic sciences'. The linguistic aspects of phonetics, i.e. the study of the sound systems of particular languages, is part of → phonology. The study of phonetics can be divided into three main branches, ARTICULATORY PHONETICS, the study of the movement of the speech organs in the articulation of speech, ACOUSTIC PHONETICS, the study of the physical properties of speech sounds such as frequency and amplitude in their transmission, and AUDITORY PHONETICS, the study of hearing and the perception of speech sounds. LABORATORY PHONETICS, EXPERIMENTAL PHONETICS or INSTRUMENTAL PHONETICS are general terms for phonetic studies which involve the use of mechanical or electronic apparatus. (3.1–3.3, 8.22).

PHONIC Relating to or characteristic of sound.

PHONIC SUBSTANCE As opposed to the visual or graphic material of written language, phonic substance refers to the auditory aspects or sound features of spoken language, as studied by articulatory, acoustic and auditory → phonetics.

PHONICS A method of teaching → reading by training the learner to associate a particular sound with a particular symbol. (7.2).

PHONOGRAM (*a*) A graphic sign used in writing to represent sound elements of speech, e.g. the → letter in alphabetic scripts, the → phonetic component of a character in logographic writing systems, or the symbol used in → phonetic transcription. (*b*) A series of graphic signs representing similar sounds in different words, e.g. *igh* in *mighty*, *higher*, *bright*. (3.1, 7.2).

PHONOGRAPHY A → writing system based on the representation of individual sounds by graphic signs, as opposed to → logography which represents whole words by single characters. (7.2).

PHONOLOGICAL ANALYSIS The analysis of the sound system of a language or dialect. It may be a synchronic study, considering only contemporary forms of the language, or a diachronic study taking historical → phonology into account. (3.1–3.4, 6.1, 8.22).

PHONOLOGICAL CHANGE → Phonemic sound change.

PHONOLOGICAL COMPONENT → Component (*b*).

PHONOLOGICAL ITEM An element of the sound system of a language, e.g. the phonemes /r/, /ʌ/ and /n/ as in *run*.

PHONOLOGIST A linguist specialising in the study of → phonology. → phonemicist, → phonetician.

PHONOLOGY The study of speech sounds of a given language and their function within the sound system of that language. In contemporary usage the term covers not only the field of phonemics but also the study of sound changes in the history of a given language, i.e. diachronic phonology. Modern science of speech sounds really began with the concept of the 'phoneme' as developed by Trubetzkoy and others of the → Prague School in the 1930s. The first significant modification came in 1952 with the distinctive feature theory, which goes further in rejecting many of the notions of 'traditional' phonology. 'Classical' phonology was concerned with the analysis of the continuum of speech into distinctive segments, whereas the aim of GENERATIVE PHONOLOGY is to establish a series of universal rules for relating the output of the syntactic component of a generative grammar to its phonetic realisation. In the application of the generative rules two levels of representation are recognised: a SYSTEMATIC PHONETIC REPRESENTATION and a PHONOLOGICAL REPRESENTATION. An earlier term for the latter was SYSTEMATIC PHONEMIC but this was later rejected because of the meaning of phonemic in structural theories. Generative grammar rejects the notion of a phonemic level and the concept 'phoneme'. On the phonetic level the phones are bundles of distinctive features and phonological rules relate these phones directly to the 'lexical' level. (3.1–3.4, 8.22 Chomsky–Halle, Kurath).

PHONOMETRICS The analysis and description of the spoken language by phonological (linguistic) and phonetic (instrumental) as well as statistical means. (3.2 Malmberg).

PHONO-MORPHOLOGY → Morpho-phonology.

PHONOSTYLISTICS That branch of → stylistics which investigates the expressive function of sounds, e.g. the use of → onomatopoeia in poetry.

PHONOTACTICS The system and study of the characteristic arrangement of → phonemes in sequence. Each language has its own system of phonotactic rules, e.g. /ts/ does not usually occur in word-initial position in English, but it does in German. (3.2 Malmberg).

PHRASAL COMPOUND A → compound word made up of two or more words which can have entirely different independent meanings when used alone, e.g. *homework* made up of *home* and *work*.

PHRASAL VERB → Verb phrase (*a*).

PHRASE (*a*) In traditional grammar a phrase is a group of words forming a syntactic unit which is not a complete sentence, i.e. it does not have a subject or predicate. According to their function in the sentence the following types of phrases may be distinguished: adjectival phrase, e.g. *nice and easy*, adverbial phrase, e.g. *until yesterday*, nominal or noun phrase, e.g. *that funny man on the corner*, prepositional phrase, e.g. *along the street*, verbal or verb phrase, e.g. *haven't got*, infinitive phrase, e.g. *in order to see*, participial phrase, e.g. *on leaving the room*. (*b*) In → systemic grammar a phrase or group is one of five grammatical units recognised for English. It is of higher rank than word and hence consists of one or more words, but of lower rank than clause, which means that a clause consists of one or more phrases. Alternative term: syntactic group. (4.1, 4.2, 8.23).

PHRASE MARKER, P-MARKER

In a → phrase structure grammar a diagrammatic representation, usually in the form of labelled brackets or a so-called tree diagram, of the derivation of a sentence. A P-marker shows the structural rules. Taking the following rules as a very simple example:

$$S \rightarrow NP + VP; \quad VP \rightarrow V + NP;$$
$$NP \rightarrow Det + Nom$$

(where S = sentence, VP = verb phrase, NP = nominal phrase, Det = determiner, Nom = nominal) the following derivation:

1. S
2. NP + VP
3. NP + V + NP
4. Det + Nom + V + Det + Nom

can be represented by a P-marker as follows:

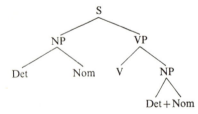

This could represent a sentence such as:

Det + Nom +   V   + Det + Nom
The   cat   catches   the   mouse

P-markers are produced by → phrase structure rules. Transformation rules operate upon the P-markers to produce new sentences, e.g. a passive sentence. The new P-marker resulting from the application of transformation rules is called a DERIVED P-MARKER. (4.1, 4.2, 8.23).

PHRASE STRUCTURE The arrangement of syntactic elements to form larger units, e.g. noun phrase + verb phrase, to make a sentence.

PHRASE STRUCTURE GRAMMAR A system of rewriting rules which will generate sentences and assign a constituent structure to them. The best known of such systems is the one devised by Chomsky, which produces sentences by means of concatenating strings and which forms the basic part of the syntactic component of a → transformational generative grammar. Alternative term: constituent structure grammar.

PHRASE STRUCTURE RULE A series of syntactic → rewrite instructions in a → generative grammar. Phrase structure rules generate strings and assign a structure to the string. Each rule is in the form of an expansion rule with only one symbol to the left of the arrow, e.g. S → NP + VP, which means that a sentence has the structure noun phrase + verb phrase:

$$VP \rightarrow \left\{ \begin{matrix} Vt + NP \\ Vi \end{matrix} \right\}$$

This means that the verb phrase consists of a transitive verb + noun phrase, or an intransitive verb standing alone. NP → det + Nom means that a noun phrase consists of determiner + nominal. These rules applied one by one in the following order:

1. S → NP + VP
2. NP → $\begin{Bmatrix} Vt + NP \\ Vi \end{Bmatrix}$
3. NP → Det + Nom

could produce a series of strings such as:

1. NP + VP
2. NP + Vt + NP
3. Det + Nom + Vt + Det + Nom

which (with words added from a lexicon and appropriate morpho-phonological rules applied) could be a sentence such as

The + boy + kicks + the + ball.

The above 'generation' could be represented diagrammatically as:

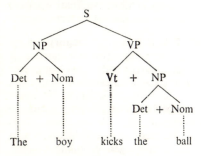

When all the phrase structure rules have been applied the result is a terminal string (as string 3 above) each element of which is called a formative. (4.1 Fowler, 8.23 Langendoen).

PHYLOGENY The study of the historical development of a language through several of its stages, as opposed to → ontogeny, the development of a single speaker's → idiolect. (2.1 Hockett).

PHYSICAL PHONETICS → Acoustic phonetics.

PHYSIOLOGICAL PHONETICS → Articulatory phonetics.

PICTOGRAM A graphic sign which represents a stretch of speech by an image, e.g. a traffic sign. → ideogram. Alternative term: pictograph. (7.2).

PICTOGRAPH → Pictogram.

PICTOGRAPHY A → writing system using → pictograms.

PIDGIN A mixture of elements from different natural languages in regions of intensive language → contact, usually restricted to certain groups, e.g. traders and seamen in some parts of South-East Asia. → lingua franca, → creole. Alternative term: contact vernacular. (8.8 Hall, 9.2 Hymes).

PITCH In acoustics, pitch is measured in cycles per second, i.e. the number of times a vibrating body vibrates in one second. The → vocal cords vibrating rapidly produce a high-pitched sound, and conversely a slow vibration produces a low-pitched sound. The phonetician is concerned with the way differences in pitch are perceived by the ear and brain as an auditory category. Not all the changes in pitch made by a human voice during an utterance are → distinctive, however, and in phonology relative pitch levels which are distinctive can be abstracted as suprasegmental phonemes. In one type of analysis of English, four pitch levels are abstracted: (1) low, (2) mid, (3) high, (4) extra high, which act as structural signals in the → intonation pattern to distinguish such utterances as [2]*What* [4]*are you* [2]*doing*[1]? and [2]*What are you* [3]*doing*[1]? (3.1, 8.22).

PITCH ACCENT Prominence of a part of an utterance created by its difference in → pitch (higher or lower) from its immediate surroundings. In a pitch-accent language a change in pitch can be part of the structure of a word and can distinguish one word from another, e.g. Swedish /bitən/ with a falling tone ('acute accent') means 'bit, piece', whereas /bitən/ with a falling-rising tone ('grave accent') means 'bitten' (past participle). Alternative term: chromatic accent. → tone language.

PLACE OF ARTICULATION → Point of articulation.

PLAIN → Flat *versus* plain.

PLANE One of the two sides of the linguistic sign, → expression (i.e. phonic and graphic forms) and → content (i.e. semantic meaning).

PLANNED LANGUAGE CHANGE → Language planning.

PLENE WRITING → Defective writing.

PLEONASM → Tautology.

PLEREME Name given by some linguists to the unit of meaning or content in → componential analysis, e.g. *cub*, *pup*, *calf*, *child* have in common the feature or component 'the young of a species'. Alternative term: semantic component. Hjelmslev used the term in → glossematics to refer to the smallest unit of expression which has content, as opposed to → ceneme which has no content. This usage is comparable to that of Hockett who, in terms of linguistics, equates plereme with → morpheme and ceneme with →

phoneme. (2.1 Hockett, 2.5 Hjelmslev).

PLOSION The movement of air outwards upon release of a → stop. Alternative term: explosion.

PLOSIVE A → stop released with an egressive pulmonic air stream, e.g. [p] in *pin*, [t] in *tin* or [k] in *kill*.

PLUPERFECT TENSE Traditional term for the verb form occurring as *had + past participle* in English, e.g. *I had read*. This kind of time reference is now usually considered as a type of → aspect rather than → tense, since it refers more to the type and state of the action, e.g. that it was completed, than to its location in time. Alternative terms: past perfect, second perfect.

PLURAL Category of → number referring to more than one (or more than two in the case of languages where a → dual exists). In languages where the plural is formed by means of special lexical markers, similar to numerals, e.g. in Japanese, it is considered a lexical category, but in many languages, including English, it is formed by inflexions on nouns and verbs and is purely a grammatical category, e.g. *The cats sleep* as opposed to the singular form *The cat sleeps*. Grammatical plurality, however, does not always coincide with 'natural' or 'referential' forms of verbs, e.g. *The United States has agreed to . . ., No news is good news*. Other nouns have plural forms and take plural verbs even when they refer to a 'naturally singular' object, e.g. *The scissors are here, My trousers are too long*. Note also the use of plural forms referring to uncountable quantities, e.g. *oats, ashes, soap-suds*. → unit noun, mass noun. (4.1, 8.23).

PLURALISER → Unit noun.

PLURATIVE An affix or adjunct denoting plural, e.g. *-s* in *boys*. → singulative.

PLURILINGUALISM → Multilingualism.

PLURISEGMENTAL FEATURE → Suprasegmental feature.

PLUS JUNCTURE → Transition.

POETIC LICENCE Deviations from the accepted norm for a given language as a stylistic device in literary prose or poetry. There may be a semantic deviation involved, such as 'widening' of meaning or the use of a → figure of speech, or there may be grammatical deviations producing new constructions. (7.3).

POETICS The linguistic study of poetry in → literature. (7.3).

POETRY Within the field of → stylistics, literary scholars and linguists are now exploring the application of linguistic knowledge to the analysis of various literary genres. Apart from → metre, → verse, and → rhyme, poetry is characterised by certain 'deviations' from the phonological, grammatical and lexical rules in the general language which are due primarily to the intended fusion of 'meaning' and 'form' into a meaningful whole, and various linguistic explanations have been proposed of these phenomena. → Poetic licence. (7.3 Freeman, 8.24 Leech).

POINT OF ARTICULATION A part of the → vocal tract which cannot move, but with which an →

articulator comes into contact during → articulation. In the articulation of the English [t], [d], [n], for example, the alveolar ridge is the point of articulation. Alternative terms: place of articulation, position of articulation.

POLITE FORM A grammatical form which denotes a relationship of respect between speakers, e.g. German *Sie* and French *vous* when talking to superiors and strangers, as opposed to the → familiar forms of *du* and *tu*. Some languages such as Japanese or Korean make extensive use of such forms, differentiating degrees of relationship. → honorific form. (4.1, 10.1).

POLYGENESIS THEORY The theory that the languages of the world developed from various sources and not from a single parent language. → monogenesis theory, → origin of speech. (2.1 Hockett).

POLYGLOT. → Multilingual.

POLYLINGUAL → Multilingual.

POLYLOGUE → Monologue.

POLYPHONY Spelling in which several different sounds are represented by the same written signs, e.g. [ʌ], [ou], [ɔː] by *o* in *son*, *sole* and *sore*. (7.2).

POLYSEMIA → Polysemy.

POLYSEMY Term used when a word or phrase has two or more meanings, e.g. *head* 'part of human body', 'top of matchstick', 'foam on glass of beer', 'person in charge', etc., as opposed to → monosemy, i.e. a word with only one meaning. Alternative term: polysemia. (5.1).

POLYSYLLABLE A word consisting of more than one → syllable. Alternative term: multisyllable.

POLYSYNDETON The linking of several clauses to form a sentence. Alternative term: syndesis. → asyndeton, syndeton.

POLYSYNTHETIC LANGUAGE → Incorporating language.

POLYSYSTEMIC → Monosystemic *versus* polysystemic.

POLYSYSTEMIC PHONOLOGY → Prosodic analysis.

POLYTONIC LANGUAGE → Tone language.

POOH-POOH THEORY → Origin of speech.

POPULAR ETYMOLOGY → Folk etymology.

POPULAR LANGUAGE → Common language.

POPULAR WORD A word used in common everyday conversation, e.g. *letter* as opposed to a → learned word such as *epistle*.

PORT ROYAL GRAMMAR → Cartesian linguistics.

PORTMANTEAU MORPH A single morph which stands for two morphemes. The best known example is French *au* /o/ 'to the' which represent *à + le*. (2.1 Hockett).

PORTMANTEAU WORD → Blend.

POSITION OF ARTICULATION → Point of articulation.

POSITIONAL VARIANT → Conditioned variant.

POSITIVE DEGREE → Degree.

POSSESSIVE ADJECTIVE Alternative term for the → first possessive form of personal pronouns when functioning as determiners: *my, your, his, her, its, our, their.*

POSSESSIVE CASE Name sometimes given to an inflexional form of English nouns and pronouns which indicates possession: e.g. *father's* and *yours* in *My father's car is right behind yours.* → genitive.

POSSESSIVE COMPOUND A compound word one part of which indicates a quality possessed by the other, e.g. *madman* or *greenfly*.

POSSESSIVE PRONOUN Alternative term for the → second possessive form of personal pronouns, e.g. *mine* and *yours* in *This is mine, and that is yours.*

POST-ALVEOLAR → Alveolar.

POST-ARTICLE → Postdeterminer.

POST-DENTAL → Dental.

POST-DETERMINER A word which can occur between the article and the noun it modifies, e.g. the two numerals in the noun phrase *the first four men*. Alternative term: post-article. (4.1, 4.2, 8.23).

POST-PALATAL → Palatal.

POST-POSITION A particle placed after the noun it governs, e.g. *homeward* as opposed to a → pre-position which is placed before the noun it governs, e.g. *towards home*.

POST-TONIC SYLLABLE The → syllable occurring immediately after the main → stress, e.g. *-ing* in *under'standing*.

POST-VELAR → Velar.

POST-VOCALIC Occurring immediately after a → vowel.

POWER (OF GRAMMARS) A measure of the ability of the grammar to account for all possible forms of a language by appropriate generalised rules. (2.1 Chomsky).

PRAGMATIC TRANSLATION → Translation.

PRAGMATICS → Semiotics.

PRAGUE SCHOOL A group of linguists associated with the Linguistic Circle of Prague in the late 1920s. Influenced by the ideas of Swiss and Russian linguists, these scholars stressed the need for a FUNCTIONAL approach to linguistic analysis, regarding language as a system of mutually related units. At the level of → phonology, great progress was made by defining the phoneme in opposition to other phonemes in terms of → distinctive features, e.g. /d/ as 'alveolar' + 'stop' + 'voice'. Phonological units are realised differently in different positions (→ neutralisation), and in connected speech the grammatical function of sound units is important, e.g. as → boundary signals. The Praguists also stressed the extra-linguistic features of language, taking into account the social background of the speaker, the subject matter that is communicated, the differences between the written and the spoken mode and many others. → Synchronic studies of the contemporary forms of language had priority over → diachronic ones, and in historical-comparative works the emphasis shifted from genetic affiliations to geographical and dialect affinities (e.g. language alliances in the Balkan area). After World War II the Prague Linguistic Circle was revived, and research concentrated on English and → Slavonic linguistics. (2.5, Fried, Vachek).

PRE-ARTICLE → Pre-determiner.

PREBASE → Prefix.

PRE-CO-ORDINATOR The first of two → correlative conjunctions, e.g. *either* as the first part of *either/or* in *He was either ignorant or a liar*.

PREDETERMINER A word or group of words which can occur in front of an article or other → determiner in a noun phrase, e.g. *some of* in *some of the men*. Alternative term: pre-article. (4.1, 4.2, 8.23).

PREDICATE A verb or verb phrase, with or without a complement, functioning as one of the two fundamental constituents of a sentence, the other constituent being the subject. In *The black cat caught the mouse, the black cat* is the → subject and *caught the mouse* is the predicate. In traditional grammar the dichotomy of noun/verb goes back to the Greeks (→ part of speech) and the notion of subject/predicate is linked with it. The terms subject and predicate suggest the traditional philosophical approach that in a sentence something is spoken about (subject) and something is said about it (predicate). In a more modern approach to this dichotomy the categories → topic and comment cut right across the traditional categories of subject and predicate. → verb phrase. (4.1, 8.23).

PREDICATE ADJECTIVAL → Predicative adjective.

PREDICATE ADJECTIVE → Predicative adjective.

PREDICATE COMPLE-MENT → Predicate nominative.

PREDICATE NOMINATIVE The use of a noun phrase as the complement of a verb, e.g. *quite a job* in *It's quite a job!* Alternative terms: predicate noun, predicate complement, subject complement.

PREDICATE NOUN → Predicate nominative.

PREDICATE PHRASE A constituent of a sentence which contains the verb and any complement or adjunct, in contrast to the subject noun phrase. In *John drinks milk every day*, *John* is the subject and *drinks milk every day* is the predicate phrase. In the → phrase structure rules of transformational-generative grammar it is more usual to refer to this part of the sentence as → verb phrase (VP).

PREDICATION The relationship between subject and → predicate in a sentence.

PREDICATIVE ADJECTIVE An adjective or equivalent word used to form the complement in the predicate. In *The green carpet is old*, *old* is a predicative adjective whereas *green* is an → attribute. Alternative terms: adjective predicate, predicate adjective, predicate adjectival.

PREDICATIVE ATTRIBUTE An adjective or equivalent word used as an attribute in the predicate of a sentence, e.g. *green* in *It is a green carpet*.

PREDICATIVE CONSTRUC-TION → Exocentric construction.

PREFIX An → affix which is added to the front of a root or stem, e.g. *un-* in *unlikely*. Alternative term: prebase.

PREFIXING LANGUAGE A type of language in which grammatical relationships are expressed by the addition of prefixes to a base or root word, e.g. Coptic or Bantu. (6.1, 8.1).

PRELITERACY The stage in the history of a language before the development of a → writing system.

PREPALATAL → Palatal.

PREPOSITION A → part of speech, usually indeclinable in form, used together with a noun phrase to show the relationship between that phrase and other words in the sentence, e.g. *with* in *She went with me*. A preposition together with the noun phrase which follows it (i.e.

which it governs) is called a PRE-POSITIONAL PHRASE or PREPOSITIONAL GROUP, e.g. *along the street*, *with me*, etc. A preposition, as its name suggests, usually precedes the noun it governs (as opposed to a → post-position), but the term DEFERRED PREPOSITION is used by some grammarians to refer to a preposition which occurs elsewhere, e.g. at the end of a sentence or clause: *Do not use a preposition to end a sentence with.* (4.1, 4.2, 8.23).

PREPOSITIONAL A → case form in some inflected languages, indicating dependence on certain prepositions, e.g. Russian *На столе* 'on the table'. → locative.

PREPOSITIONAL CONJUNC-TION → Conjunction.

PREPOSITIONAL GROUP → Preposition.

PREPOSITIONAL OBJECT The object of a → preposition which is closely attached to a verb and may be transformed into the subject in passive constructions, e.g. *him* in *You can rely on him* > *he* in *He can be relied on.*

PREPOSITIONAL PHRASE → Preposition.

PRESCRIPTIVE GRAMMAR → Prescriptive linguistics (*a*).

PRESCRIPTIVE LINGUISTICS (*a*) An attitude to language studies which seeks to establish rules for correct usage. Ancient Greek and Indian grammarians tried to fix such norms modelled on the most famous works of literary merit, a tradition which has been repeated by many

classical grammars down to the present day. The teaching of such norms rests on the assumption that an absolute standard can be established which can be derived from a certain logico-philosophical framework or from a language considered superior. Most modern linguistics is → descriptive in nature, i.e. it records actual usage. → Alternative terms: prescriptive grammar, prescriptivism. (*b*) In → institutional linguistics the term prescriptive refers to → language planning which aims at the creation of a national → standard language in a linguistically and culturally diverse country. (2.5, 10.1).

PRESCRIPTIVISM → Prescriptive linguistics (*a*).

PRESENT FUTURE → Future tense.

PRESENT PARTICIPLE A non-finite form of the → verb in English ending in *-ing*, used for forming compound tenses, e.g. *I was reading*, or as nominals, e.g. *a meeting of great minds*, or adjectivals, e.g. *the crying baby*. → participle.

PRESENT PERFECT → Perfect tense.

PRESENT TENSE A → tense form of a verb referring to an action which is contemporaneous with the utterance. What is traditionally called 'present tense' in English grammar is best described as a 'non-past' tense since it can do more than express action in the present, e.g. *Men walk*, *Birds fly*, etc. → aspect, → mood.

PRESSURE STOP → Stop.

PRESTIGE DIALECT A social or regional variant of a language which enjoys a certain prestige usually by being accepted as the standard form of a language, e.g. Parisian French. (7.1).

PRETERITE A common term in traditional grammar to refer to a simple past → tense form of a verb.

PRETERITE PRESENT A verb of which the modern → present tense derives from an older preterite form, e.g. *ought* < Old English *ahte* (preterite of *āgan*) and *must* < *moste* preterite of *mōt* (1st sing. pres.).

PRETONIC SYLLABLE The → syllable immediately preceding the main → stress, e.g. *-der* in *under'-standing*.

PREVELAR → Velar.

PREVOCALIC Occurring immediately before a → vowel.

PRIMARY ACCENT → Stress.

PRIMARY ARTICULATION → Articulation.

PRIMARY COMPOUND A compound word consisting of two simple bases, e.g. *homework*. Alternative terms: base compound, fused compound, solid compound.

PRIMARY DERIVATIVE A word consisting of two bound morphemes. → word formation.

PRIMARY LANGUAGE → Native language.

PRIMARY STRESS → Stress.

PRIMARY UNIT A basic linguistic element, e.g. the word and the sentence in grammar or the phoneme in phonology, as opposed to → secondary units such as the phrase or the syllable.

PRIMARY VOWEL → Cardinal vowel.

PRIMARY WORD A word consisting of one morpheme. → word formation.

PRINCIPAL The word or phrase which is modified by an → apposition, e.g. *My brother Julian* in which the appositive *Julian* refers back to the principal *my brother*.

PRINCIPAL CLAUSE → Main clause.

PRINCIPAL PARTS Those forms of a → verb which are necessary for deducing the whole → conjugation according to regular patterns, e.g. Latin: first person singular *fero* 'I carry', infinitive *ferre*, perfect tense *tuli*, supine *latum*, or German: infinitive *singen* 'to sing', past tense *sang*, past participle *gesungen*.

PRINCIPAL VERB → Full verb.

PRIVATIVE AFFIX An affix which denotes negation or lack, e.g. *un-* in *unlikely*, *in-* in *infinitive* or *-less* in *hopeless*.

PRIVILEGE OF OCCURRENCE The syntactic position a word may occupy in a sentence. For example, forms such as *runs*, *walks*, *drives, travels, flies, sails,* etc. all share the same privilege of occurrence in that they can all be fitted into the frame *he — home.* → substitution frame. (2.1 Hockett).

PROCEDURE A set of techniques in → linguistic analysis which ensures that only the relevant details are accounted for in the grammatical description. So-called DISCOVERY PROCEDURES are applied to a particular corpus of text with the aim of establishing the basic categories, → units and relationships that are needed to fully describe its grammatical structure. So-called DECISION PROCEDURES are designed to make explicit the combination of units into grammatical sentences. So-called EVALUATION PROCEDURES help in selecting the most appropriate grammar from a number of possible alternative approaches. → pseudo-procedure, → method. (2.1 Chomsky).

PROCESS → Item-and-process.

PROCLITIC A word which has only weak → stress and which in pronunciation forms a unit with the stressed word following it, e.g. *his* in *Give him his own* [izoún] *back.* → clitics.

PRODUCTIVE AFFIX An → affix which is in regular use in a language to coin new derived words, e.g. *-ness* in *loudness, sameness, muchness.* → unproductive.

PROGRAMMED INSTRUC-TION A method of teaching based on the principles of → behaviourism which claims that human behaviour (including verbal learning) is largely explainable in terms of stimulus and

response acts. Teaching should follow a carefully organised plan where (i) the aim of the course or terminal behaviour is properly defined, (ii) the material is presented in a series of graded steps or units called 'frames', and (iii) the student has the opportunity of checking his progress at each stage of the course. According to the type of programme being used the student may be obliged to follow a single route through the course (linear programme) or he may be able to choose several routes according to his previous performance (branching programme). Attempts have been made to apply the principles of programmed instruction to language teaching by the use of tape recorders, language laboratories, film loops and other audio-visual aids. Alternative term: auto-instruction. (9.14, 10.2).

PROGRAMMING The writing of a 'programme' for language teaching (→ programmed instruction) or automatic processing of linguistic data (→ computational linguistics).

PROGRESSIVE ASPECT → Aspect.

PROGRESSIVE ASSIMILA-TION → Assimilation.

PROGRESSIVE DISSIMILA-TION → Dissimilation.

PROHIBITIVE A sentence expressing a prohibition. It may take the form of a negative → imperative, e.g. *Do not touch!*, but can also be expressed in other ways, e.g. *No smoking,* or *It is forbidden to speak to the driver.*

PROJECTION RULES In a → transformational-generative grammar a set of rules which assign a semantic interpretation to syntactic structures. (2.1 Lyons).

PROLEPSIS Anticipation in the main clause of the subject of a following subordinate clause, e.g. *leaves* in *Do you hear the leaves, how they rustle?*

PROMINENCE The relative degree to which a sound stands out from its environment. → stress.

PRONOMINAL A name given by some grammarians to a structure which functions as a pronoun, e.g. *the one* in *That's not the one I wanted.*

PRONOMINAL ADJECTIVE → Determinative pronoun.

PRONOMINAL QUESTION A question introduced by an → interrogative pronoun, e.g. *What did you want to see?*

PRONOMINALISATION The process or result of using a → pronoun instead of some other part of speech or syntactic structure.

PRONOUN In traditional grammar a part of speech used instead of a noun or noun phrase, e.g. the pronoun *he* can replace *the angry farmer* in *The angry farmer chased the boys out of his field*, or *it* can replace *the cup of tea* in *The cup of tea is on the table*. These pronouns are called personal pronouns; other classes of pronouns include → demonstrative, → indefinite, → possessive, → reflexive, → relative pronouns. In inflected languages, pronouns usually vary in form according to number, gender and case as do nouns. In English, personal pronouns have a subjective case form and objective case form and two possessive case forms, e.g.

SUBJECTIVE	OBJECTIVE
I	*me*
we	*us*
1st POSSESSIVE	2nd POSSESSIVE
my	*mine*
our	*ours* etc.

(4.2, 8.23).

PRONUNCIATION The way an individual speaker or group of speakers within a speech community articulate speech sounds. Phonetics is concerned with the general properties of speech sounds, phonology with the part they play in a particular language, dialectology with the classification of regional and social varieties, and ORTHOEPY with the study of standardised pronunciation. (3.1, 7.1, 8.22).

PROP WORD A word such as a → pronoun which serves to replace another word for the purpose of → back-reference, e.g. *this* and *one* in *I don't want this, have you got another one?*

PROPAROXYTONE A word with the → stress on the third syllable from the end, e.g. *dis'similar*. → oxytone, paroxytone.

PROPER ADJECTIVE An → adjective formed from a → proper noun, *English* from *England*, *Victorian* from *Victoria*.

PROPER COMPOUND A → compound word which only has inflexion in the final part of the compound, e.g. *toothbrush*. → improper compound.

PROPER NAME → Proper noun.

PROPER NOUN The name of an individual person, place or object, as opposed to a → common noun which refers to any one of all things denoted by the noun. Thus, *John, Eiffel Tower, The Tyrol, London*, are proper nouns, whereas *boy*, *building, city*, are common nouns. In English, proper nouns are usually written with an initial capital letter. Alternative term: proper name.

PROSCRIPTIVE GRAMMAR An attitude to language usage which attempts to lay down rules as to which 'wrong' or 'slipshod' forms are to be avoided in speech and writing. → prescriptive linguistics (*a*).

PROSE (*a*) Written language which is not → verse. (*b*) In conventional language teaching, an exercise involving → translation into the foreign language being taught.

PROSIOPESIS → Aphesis.

PROSODEME A distinctive → prosodic feature, e.g. stress, intonation, juncture, often represented in conventional writing by punctuation. → prosodic sign.

PROSODIC ANALYSIS A method of phonological analysis based on a theory originally put forward by J. R. Firth (1890–1960) and developed by other linguists since then. Some of the weaknesses of phonemic analysis based entirely on the division of the continuum of speech into segments, i.e. → phonemes, had been recognised and partially overcome by the development of the concept of → suprasegmental phoneme, but Firth insisted on the separation of the requirements of transcription from the requirements of understanding the structure of a phonological system. Prosodic analysis establishes two types of unit: PHONEMATIC UNIT and PROSODY both of which refer to a phonetic feature or group of phonetic features of an utterance. Phonematic units are segments which are ordered serially, such as consonants and vowels. Prosodies refer to phonetic features which either extend over the whole or major part of a structure, e.g. intonation patterns, or are limited in position in such a way as to delimit or demarcate it, e.g. stress or juncture. At first sight phonematic units and prosodies seem to be equivalent to segmental and suprasegmental phonemes of the traditional phonemic analysis, but in a prosodic analysis, features which would be assigned to segmental phonemes in a phonemic analysis are sometimes assigned to prosodies, e.g. such features as palatalisation, nasalisation or lip rounding. With its emphasis on the relevance of structures such as syllable, word, sentence, prosodic analysis attempts to link phonology and grammar. In a prosodic analysis different phonological systems can be set up for different structures or different places in structures (e.g. features which can occur at the beginning of a syllable may not be the same as the features which can occur at the end of a syllable in a given language), and so prosodic analysis is also called POLYSYSTEMIC PHONOLOGY or MULTIDIMENSIONAL PHONOLOGY, as opposed to the essentially mono-systemic nature of phonemic analysis, where a phonological system is set up for the language as a whole without reference to grammatical or lexical structure. Alternative term: prosodic phonology. (3.4 Palmer, 8.22 Crystal).

PROSODIC FEATURE A feature of speech not restricted to one segment of speech, e.g. → stress, → intonation, → transition. Alternative terms: secondary phoneme, secondary feature, suprasegmental feature.

PROSODIC MARK → Prosodic sign.

PROSODIC PHONOLOGY → Prosodic analysis.

PROSODIC SIGN A graphic sign used to represent prosodic features in writing, e.g. → duration, → tone, → stress, → pitch, → transition. In normal orthography such features are usually, though in-adequately, represented by → punctuation or italics. → suprasegmental grapheme. Alternative terms: prosodic mark.

PROSODY (*a*) A phono-logical feature which extends over more than one segment in the continuum of speech, abstracted in prosodic analysis, as opposed to → phonematic unit. (*b*) The system and study of → verse structure.

PROSTHESIS → Prothesis.

PROSTHETIC → Prothetic.

PROTASIS → Conditional clause.

PROTENSITY FEATURES → Distinctive feature.

PROTHESIS, PROSTHESIS The addition of a vowel or consonant at the beginning of a word to make pronunciation easier, e.g. the Latin word *schola* 'school' > Spanish *escuela* and French *école*. → table p. 75.

PROTHETIC, PROSTHETIC A vowel or consonant added at the beginning of a word to make pro-nunciation easier. → prothesis.

PROTO- In the cronology of the different stages of the historical development of a language or language family, 'proto-' refers to those forms which are either attested or hypothetically assumed to be the earliest, e.g. the reconstructed Proto-Indo-European *dekm* is the common root of Sanskrit *dáśa*, Latin *decem*, German *zehn*, English *ten*, etc. (6.1).

PROVINCIALISM A feature of pronunciation, grammar or vocab-ulary which is restricted to a particu-lar → regional dialect.

PROXIMATE → Person.

PSEUDO-PROCEDURE A method of → linguistic analysis which is alleged to follow certain scientific principles, but which does in fact violate them, either because the investigator's original assump-tions were inconsistent or because they prove to be too difficult to be carried out in practice. Thus in → phonemic analysis and → field-work it is often claimed that findings are based on reactions of the native speaker to statements containing → minimal pairs, when in fact it is practically impossible to test all such substitution processes objectively.

PSEUDO-SYNONYM → Near-synonym.

PSYCHOLINGUISTICS Within the general framework of interdisciplinary studies concerned with human behaviour and language (→ psychological linguistics), psycholinguistics refers to the efforts of both linguists and psychologists to explain whether certain hypotheses about language acquisition and language competence as proposed by contemporary linguistic theories (→ transformational-generative grammar) have a real basis in terms of perception, memory, intelligence, motivation, etc. This sometimes involves the observation of actual linguistic behaviour in laboratory conditions (e.g. word association studies) or the close monitoring of communicative situations (e.g. description of hesitation forms, recall and sentence complexity). (10.2).

PSYCHOLOGICAL LINGUIS-TICS Collective term for a number of different approaches to language from the point of view of psychology. Against the background of several traditions such as German National and Gestalt psychology, French psychosomatics and American behaviourism, current work is aimed at obtaining factual evidence, by observation and experiment, of how we acquire language (and how we manipulate it to learn other skills), how we behave in perceiving and producing speech, whether memory and intelligence contribute to our linguistic performance, how language interrelates with thinking processes,

etc. → developmental linguistics, → clinical linguistics, → psycholinguistics. (10.2).

PSYCHOLOGICAL PHON-ETICS → Auditory phonetics.

PSYCHOLOGICAL SUBJECT → Subject.

PULMONIC AIR-STREAM MECHANISM → Air-stream mechanism.

PULMONIC CAVITY → Cavity.

PULMONIC CLOSURE → Closure.

PUN A play on the multiple meaning or similar sounds of words, e.g. *Is life worth living? That depends upon the liver.* Alternative term: paronomasia, annomination.

PUNCTUAL ASPECT → Aspect.

PUNCTUATION A collection of auxiliary graphic signs used in addition to the signs of a → writing system to denote features of speech such as special emphasis, pauses, astonishment, etc.: e.g. *"No!" he said, "can't you ...?"*. In scripts based on the Latin alphabet, punctuation marks usually include the following:

full-stop or period	.
comma	,
semi-colon	;
colon	:
quotation marks or inverted commas	"..."
	or '...'

exclamation mark   !
question mark or
   interrogation point   ?
dash   —
hyphen   -
parentheses   ( )
brackets   [ ]

These punctuation marks and other → diacritic marks may also be used in → analphabetic notations and → phonetic transcriptions. (3.1, 7.2).

PURE VOWEL → Monophthong.

PURISM An attitude towards language which disapproves of deviations from certain grammatical rules, of neologisms and borrowings from other languages. Often purists make a vain attempt to preserve the status quo of a particular language. (2.1 Hall, 7.1).

Q

QUALIFIER A word or group of words which limits or extends the meaning of another word. → modifier (*a*).

QUALIFYING CONJUNCTION → Subordinating conjunction.

QUALITATIVE ABLAUT → Vowel gradation.

QUALITY The characteristic timbre of a speech sound depending on the shape of the → resonance chambers in the vocal tract, which in turn depends on the position of the lips, tongue and velum. The difference in quality enables different sounds, e.g. [i], [e], [o], [u] to be distinguished from one another. (3.1).

QUANTIFIABLE NOUN → Mass noun.

QUANTIFIER A word indicating quantity, used to modify another word or group of words, e.g. numerals like *two*, *twenty*, etc., or words like *much, several, few*, etc.

QUANTITATIVE ABLAUT → Vowel gradation.

QUANTITATIVE LINGUISTICS → Mathematical linguistics.

QUANTITY → Duration of a speech sound as a phonological feature. Quantity is a distinctive feature in some languages, e.g. in German *Ruhm* [ʀuːm] 'fame' as opposed to *Rum* [ʀum] 'rum'. Quantity often combines with → quality as a distinguishing feature, e.g. in English the tense vowel [i] as in *bead* is *usually* long, whereas the lax vowel [ɪ] as in *bit* is *usually* short. (3.1, 8.22).

QUESTION An utterance which requests an answer. A distinction must be made between the semantic term question and the formal or grammatical term interrogative since not all questions are in the interrogative form, e.g. *He is coming?* is a question but it is not interrogative. The relationship existing between question and interrogative also exists between → command (semantic term) and → imperative (grammatical term) and between statement (semantic term) and indicative (grammatical term). → mood. (4.1, 4.2, 8.23).

QUESTION MARK → Punctuation.

QUESTION WORD → Interrogative word.

QUESTIONNAIRE In → dialectology and other types of linguistic → field-work, a series of carefully worded questions designed to obtain information about the language used by an → informant.

QUOTATION MARK → Punctuation.

R

RADIATION The → extension of the semantic meaning of a word in more than one direction, e.g. *head* 'part of human body', 'top of matchstick', 'person in charge', etc. Alternative term: irradiation.

RADICAL (*a*) → root (*b*). (*b*) In some logographic systems of writing, that component part of an elementary character sign which indicates the semantic meaning of the word represented. Almost nine-tenths of Chinese written signs are composed of two elements of which the first component, the radical, assigns the word to a semantic class, the second giving guidance as to pronunciation. Conventional Chinese dictionaries list the vocabulary by 214 radicals which may be grouped by the number and shapes of the required strokes. →

phonetic. Alternative term: determinative. (7.2).

RADICAL LANGUAGE A language without → inflexions, in which all words are radicals or roots. → isolating language. (6.1, 8.1).

RANK In → systemic grammar the relationship between one item and another on a hierarchical scale, e.g. word can be considered a higher rank than morpheme, group higher than word, clause higher than group and sentence higher than clause. → grammatical unit.

RANK-BOUND A → translation is said to be rank-bound if there is a consistent 1:1 relationship between the source language and the target language texts at the word, group, clause or sentence level. Word-for-word translation is rank-bound at the word level, literal translation is usually rank-bound at the group level, whereas free translation is usually not rank-bound at all. (9.3 Catford).

RANK SCALE In → systemic grammar the hierarchical order of linguistic units on a particular level of analysis, e.g. distinctive feature, phoneme, syllable, foot in phonology, or morpheme, word, group, clause, sentence in grammar. → rank-shift.

RANK-SHIFT The process or result of a grammatical unit being moved down the hierarchical scale of rank from sentence and clause to phrase, word and morpheme. Thus the clause *where he works* might form a part of a unit lower down the scale than itself, e.g. in *The factory where he works is old*, in which it forms part of the noun phrase. (9.11 Halliday *et al.*).

191

RATIONALISTS → Renaissance linguistics.

READING The skill of recognising and understanding written language in the form of sequences of graphic signs and its transformation into meaningful speech, either as silent comprehension or by reading aloud. There is a long tradition of several approaches to the teaching of reading, e.g. the 'analytic' method of drilling → phoneme–grapheme correspondences (PHONICS), or the 'synthetic' method of training the learner to associate the shapes of whole words with the ideas and actions they stand for (LOOK-AND-SAY). → listening, speaking, writing. (7.2 Wardhaugh, 9.11 Schlesinger, 9.12 Gunderson, 9.3 Lee).

REAL DEFINITION → Definition.

REALISM → Naturalism.

REALISATION The actual expression of a phonological, grammatical or semantic feature or unit, e.g. a 'phoneme' by a speech sound, 'modality' by auxiliary verbs, 'gender' by articles or inflexions, 'subject' by a noun phrase, 'lexeme' by a series of phonemes, etc. Alternative terms: actualisation, exponence, manifestation, representation.

RECEIVED PRONUNCIATION Pronunciation of → standard British English based on the speech of educated speakers of Southern British English. It is regarded as a useful norm and is the type of pronunciation often recommended as a model for foreign learners. (8.22 Gimson).

RECESSIVE STRESS Strong → stress on the initial syllable, e.g. '*temporary*.

RECIPROCAL ASSIMILATION → Assimilation.

RECIPROCAL PRONOUN A → pronoun expressing mutual relationship, e.g. *each other*.

RECIPROCAL VERB A type of verb involving a mutual action, e.g. *see* and *meet* in *We shall see each other next week* and *We'll meet tomorrow*.

RECOMPOSITION The process or result of using a borrowed element as an → affix to form new words, e.g. *tele* in *telecast, teleview, teleprinter*. (2.1 Martinet).

RECONSTRUCTION A method of finding the common → ancestor of a group of genealogically related languages by comparing their shared features (→ comparative method) or by determining the changes a language has undergone over several stages of its historical development (→ internal reconstruction). (6.1).

RECTION → Government.

RECURSIVENESS In → transformational-generative grammar a property of grammar which allows an infinite number of sentences to be generated by introducing the initial symbol S as an optional element in an expansion rule, thus permitting the preceding rules to be applied an infinite number of times. The following simplified example will generate an infinite number of sentences:

1. S → NP + VP
2. VP → V + NP
3. NP → Det + Nom + (S)

since (S) can be embedded in NP to account for sentences like *The man* (*who kicked the ball*) *scored the goal* (*that won the game*) where the clauses in brackets can be embedded by rule 3 above. (4.1, 8.23).

REDUCTION (*a*) An alternative term for → contraction or → abbreviation. (*b*) The process by which the meaning of a word or phrase becomes narrowed by a restriction of the contexts in which it can occur, e.g. *deer* 'animal' > 'forest ruminant'. → extension (*a*). Alternative terms: specialisation of meaning, restriction, narrowing of meaning. (5.1).

REDUNDANCY The amount of information which is communicated over and above the required minimum. Language may be said to utilise redundancy, since much more information is given in normal circumstances than is really necessary to guarantee comprehension. Such devices include repetition of lexical items, e.g. *It was terrible, dreadful, awful*, or of grammatical features, e.g. 'singular' or 'plural' agreement in the sentences *The boy goes out* and *The boys go out*. Work in → information theory has shown that redundancy correlates with frequency of occurrence, e.g. common and superfluous items such as 'clichés' give less information than infrequent unusual ones, and helps to counteract → noise: the more interference in a message, the more redundancy has to be built in. (10.5).

REDUPLICATION The repetition of some part of a form.

In Indo-European languages the repetition of part of the root of the verb was a method of tense formation, e.g. *l-* in Greek *leipo* 'I leave', perfect: *le -loip -a.*

REFERENCE (*a*) The relationship between a → referent (e.g. a concrete entity or an abstract concept) and the → symbol which is used to identify it (e.g. a verbal sound sequence or a graphic sign sequence). In semantics, this relationship between physical object and linguistic name is used to explain the → meaning of those lexical items which 'stand for' an object or idea. (5.1, 5.2).

(*b*) In writing systems, that part of the language structure which is represented by the grapheme. Thus in some alphabetic scripts the letters represent phonemes (phonemic reference), in logographic scripts the characters represent words (morphemic reference). (7.2).

(*c*) → Anaphora or back-reference.

REFERENCE THEORY OF MEANING → Semantics.

REFEREND → Referent.

REFERENT, REFEREND The physical entity or abstract concept to which we give a name by a verbal or written symbol. Thus the object which may be defined as 'luminous body which shines in the sky at night' is referred to in English by the articulated sound sequence [stɑː] or the graphic representation *star*. → reference (*a*).

REFERENTIAL MEANING → Meaning.

REFLEX A linguistic form which is derived from an older form

193

of the same language, e.g. Modern English *foot* is a reflex of Old English *fōt*. → etymon. (5.1, 6.1).

REFLEXIVE PRONOUN

A personal pronoun which refers back to the subject, e.g. *myself* in *I wash myself in hot water*, or *yourself* in *You can see for yourself*. Alternative term: intensive pronoun.

REFLEXIVE VERB

A → verb used usually with a → reflexive pronoun, e.g. *He helped himself* or French *Il se lève* 'he gets up'. In English some verbs have reflexive connotations without a reflexive pronoun, e.g. *he shaved*.

REGIONAL DIALECT → Dialect.

REGISTER

(*a*) Voice quality brought about by a specific type of phonation (→ speech production). If a small volume of air is allowed to pass through the vocal cords during production of voiced sounds, the resultant voice quality is called TIGHT PHONATION, whereas a large volume of air passing through the vocal cords produces BREATHY PHONATION or BREATHY VOICE. If part of the glottis is made to vibrate slowly whilst the rest vibrates normally, the result is a CREAKY VOICE, CREAK or LARGYNGEALISED VOICING. There are many other different registers, but, as the impressionistic labels given to the examples above indicate, they are not easy to define in objective terms. Some languages, however, make use of contrasts in register. Gujerati, for example, contrasts tight and breathy phonation and some African and Caucasian languages make use of creaks in a distinctive manner. In other languages register

differences are brought about by such features as emotional state or attitude of the speaker to the listener and constitute what may loosely be called 'tone of voice'. A tone of voice like the creak described above is typical of some speakers of Received Pronunciation of English when the voice falls below a certain pitch. (3.1 Abercrombie).

(*b*) A → variety in language used for a specific purpose, as opposed to a social or regional → dialect (which varies by speakers). Registers may be more narrowly defined by reference to subject matter (FIELD OF DISCOURSE, e.g. the jargons of fishing, gambling, etc.), to medium (MODE OF DISCOURSE, e.g. printed material, written letter, message on tape, etc.), or to level of formality (MANNER OF DISCOURSE, e.g. formal, casual, intimate, etc.). → terminology, → special language. (6.1 Ellis, 7.1–7.3, 8.24).

REGRESSIVE ASSIMILATION → Assimilation.

REGRESSIVE DISSIMILATION → Dissimilation.

REGULAR VERB

A verb which is conjugated according to the → paradigm for its class in a given language.

REGULARITY

The phenomenon of a linguistic form conforming to the normal grammatical rule, e.g. the English noun *dogs* is regular within the → paradigm of nouns forming the plural by adding *-s*. → irregularity.

REGULARITY OF SOUND CHANGE

The assumption by the

→ Neogrammarian school of linguists that phonetic laws are without exception. (6.1).

REGULATION → Speech production.

RELATED LANGUAGE → Cognate language.

RELATIVE ADVERB An → adverb which acts as a conjunction in introducing a subordinate clause. It also refers back to an antecedent, e.g. *where* in *This is the place where we met* or *when* in *At the time when I knew him, he worked hard.*

RELATIVE CLAUSE A → subordinate clause introduced by a relative pronoun or adverb, e.g. *who is sitting near the window* in *The man who is sitting near the window is my uncle* or *where he was born* in *This is the place where he was born.*

RELATIVE PRONOUN A → pronoun such as *who, whom, whose, which, that,* which refers back to a previous word in the sentence, e.g. *that* in the sentence *The house that Jack built* refers to *the house.*

RELATIVITY The view proposed by the American anthropological linguist B. L. Whorf (1897–1941), and previously by the German ethnologist W. von Humboldt (1767–1835), that a speaker's language determines his view of the world (or 'Weltanschauung') through the grammatical categories and semantic classifications that are possible in the linguistic system that he has inherited together with his native culture. It has also been alleged that → translation is severely hampered between languages with limited cultural overlap. These beliefs are in opposition to the tenets of → universal grammar which stresses the linguistic features common to all languages. Alternative terms: determinism, Whorfian hypothesis, Humboldtism. (2.4 Humboldt, Sapir, 10.1 Whorf).

RELATOR-AXIS CLAUSE A term used in → tagmemics to refer to what are traditionally known as 'subordinate clauses' introduced by means of a subordinating conjunction, e.g. *when I first spoke to him, where you came from..., which I have at home...,* etc. The conjunction is referred to as the relator and the rest of the clause as the axis.

RELATOR-AXIS PHRASE Term used in → tagmemics to refer to a phrase of the type referred to traditionally as prepositional phrase, where the preposition is the relator and the word 'governed' by the preposition is the axis.

RELEASE Movement of the speech organs from the position for the articulation of one speech sound either to the position for the → articulation of another speech sound or to a state of rest in such a way that a closure in the vocal tract is opened or a stricture removed. The type of release accompanying a stop consonant, for example, may have an important influence on the nature of sound perceived. The bilabial stop which is the phonetic realisation of the English phoneme /p/ may have several types of release, e.g. as an aspirated stop, i.e. with an audible puff of breath as at the beginning of the word *pin*; as a non-aspirated stop as in the word *spin*; as an unreleased stop as in the word *apt* where the closure is only released with the [t]. The term NASAL RELEASE (→ nasal plosion) is used to refer to the type of [p] which can be heard in the phrase *cup and saucer* when pronounced [kʌpmsɔːsə] where the stop is released by the velum being lowered and by the air being allowed to escape through the nose. The term LATERAL RELEASE (→ lateral plosion) is used to refer to a sound which is released by allowing the air to escape around the sides of the tongue, e.g. in the word *cattle* the alveolar stop is released laterally with the [l]. (3.1, 8.22).

RELEVANT → Distinctive.

RELIC AREA → Area.

REMOTE AREA → Area.

RENAISSANCE LINGUISTICS The period of linguistic scholarship following → Mediaeval linguistics and characterised by the widening of horizons beyond Greek and Latin (which continued to be taught, but with a view to rediscovering 'classical' standards) to the 'vernacular' Indo-European languages from Spanish to Polish. An improved knowledge of Hebrew and Arabic and the discovery of other non-Indo-European languages in America and Asia contributed new concepts and categories, and the study of the diachronic relationship between the Romance languages and their common ancestor Latin brought new insights into the processes of language → change. The invention of printing influenced orthographic conventions, and work on → spelling reforms renewed interest in → phonetics. 15th- and 16th-century HUMANISTS such as Erasmus and W. Lily did much to reassess the linguistic

description of Latin, and the grammarian P. Ramée described Greek, Latin and French as systems in their own right. The end of this period is marked by the controversies between the data-oriented, 'pragmatic' EMPIRICISTS, e.g. English work on stenography, cryptography and phonetics, and the theory-oriented, 'prescriptive' RATIONALISTS, e.g. Descartes and other Port Royal grammarians. The latter school was also responsible for the foundation of Academies (to guard literary and linguistic standards) and the creation of artificial 'universal' languages (to store knowledge and ease communication). (2.5 Robins).

REPERTORY The total stock of symbols of a code, e.g. the signs of a writing system such as the letters of the Latin alphabet.

REPETITIVE COMPOUND A compound word which consists of two or more similar elements, e.g. *bye-bye* or *Humpty-Dumpty*. → reduplication.

REPLACIVE MORPH A → morph which replaces another in the internal modification of a word to indicate a grammatical feature, e.g. in English *foot* /fut/ becomes plural *feet* /fiːt/ and /iː/ can be considered as a replacive morph, taking the place of /u/ and indicating plurality.

REPORTED QUESTION → Indirect question.

REPORTED SPEECH → Indirect speech.

REPRESENTATION (*a*) → Representational function. (*b*) The realisation of one or more linguistic units at one → level by a unit at the next 'lower' level. Thus the semantic and syntactic elements 'go' and 'past tense' are said to be represented at the morphological level as {went} which in turn can have either a phonological or graphic representation. → realisation.

REPRESENTATIONAL FUNCTION The use of language for the purpose of portraying a situation. → function (*a*).

RESONANCE Vibrations in sympathy with the movement of air pressures caused by another vibration. → resonator. (3.1, 8.22).

RESONANCE CHAMBER A cavity which acts as a → resonator, e.g. the nasal, pharyngeal and oral cavities in the → vocal tract.

RESONANCE CURVE → Spectrum.

RESONANT A speech sound which can be lengthened indefinitely, e.g. → vowels, → nasal or → lateral consonants, as opposed to → obstruents.

RESONATOR A body which vibrates in sympathy with another body, strengthening certain frequencies, e.g. a volume of air in one of the cavities of the → vocal tract resonating with the vibrations of the vocal cords in the larynx.

RESPONSE In behaviourist psychology and language teaching, the reaction of the speaker or learner to a situation or verbal → stimulus, which may involve the active or 'overt' production of speech or writing, e.g. an answer to a question,

or a passive or 'covert' response, e.g. comprehension of a scene described in a dialogue. (9.11, 10.2).

RESTRICTED CODE Term coined by the sociologist B. Bernstein to describe the speech of socially and educationally underprivileged sections of a speech community, who use largely ritualistic and predictable elements in their speech, as opposed to the socially and educationally privileged who may use a more ELABORATED CODE. (10.1).

RESTRICTED LANGUAGE → Special language.

RESTRICTION → Reduction (*b*).

RESTRICTIVE A structure within a sentence which specifies an antecedent structure, e.g. the relative clause in *The boy who was sitting by the window caught a cold.* Such modifying clauses, essential for the meaning of the sentence, are not usually set off from the rest of the sentence by intonation or commas. → non-restrictive.

RETAINED OBJECT An → object retained in a passive sentence. A sentence containing a direct and an indirect object usually has two passive forms in English, one of the objects being retained in each case: *He gave me a book* > *I was given a book,* or *A book was given to me.*

RETRACTED → Velarised.

RETROFLEX A speech sound articulated with the tip of the tongue curled upwards and backwards towards the hard palate, e.g. [r] in English red. → retroflexion.

Alternative terms: cacuminal, cerebral, inverted.

RETROFLEXION The → articulation of a speech sound accompanied by the curling of the tip of the tongue towards the hard palate. Some kinds of American English are characterised by a marked retroflexion, particularly in words spelled with *r*, e.g. *bird*. The retroflexion of certain *t* and *d* consonants is very marked in Hindi and other Indian languages. (3.1, 8.22).

RETROGRESSIVE ASSIMILATION → Assimilation.

RETROGRESSIVE DISSIMILATION → Dissimilation.

REVIVAL FORM → Archaism.

REWRITE RULE A rule indicating expansion of a term by replacing the term by further elements. Rewrite rules are typical, for example, of → phrase structure rules in transformational-generative grammar. The rule S → NP + VP can be expressed as 'rewrite S (i.e. sentence) by NP (noun phrase) followed by VP (verb phrase)'.

RHEMATICS → Philosophical semantics.

RHEMATOLOGY → Philosophical semantics.

RHEME → Theme and rheme.

RHETORIC The system and study of the stylistic devices of formal speech, e.g. → figures of speech, the organisation of an address to an audience, etc. (7.3).

RHETORICAL FIGURE → Figure of speech.

RHOTACISM The occurrence of [r] in place of some other speech sound.

RHYME The process or result of forming a similar sound sequence in two corresponding units. The sequence repeated usually stretches from the vocalic nucleus of the stressed syllable to the end of the word, as in 'rhyme proper' at the end of succeeding verse lines, e.g. *Mary, Mary, quite contrary.* → alliteration. (3.1, 7.3).

RHYTHM The pattern of stressed and unstressed → syllables in speech. The use a language makes of → stress has a great influence on the rhythm of the language. English, for example is a stress-timed language, i.e. the stressed syllables are approximately equidistant in time: it takes about the same amount of time to say *Jǎck and Jíll* as it does to say *Jáck ǎnd hǐs sǐster Jíll*. French, on the other hand, is syllable-timed, i.e. every syllable takes up approximately the same amount of time. Rhythm plays an important part in verse structure. → foot, → tempo. (3.1, 7.3, 8.22).

RISING DIPHTHONG → Diphthong.

RISING-FALLING An → intonation pattern where the voice rises first and then falls to a low level, e.g. on *well* in the expression of surprise *Well, of all things!*

RISING JUNCTURE → Juncture.

ROLLED (CONSONANT) → Trill.

ROMAN ALPHABET → Table p. 265.

ROMANCE LINGUISTICS Collective term for the linguistic description of Romance languages such as Latin (the → ancestor language), French, Spanish, Italian, Portuguese and Rumanian. These languages and their grammatical and lexicographical analysis played a major role in → Mediaeval, → Renaissance and → diachronic linguistics. → Appendix 1, p. 268. (2.5 Hall, 8.3, 8.6, 8.7 Posner).

ROMANISATION The → transliteration of the graphic signs of non-Latin writing systems, e.g. Chinese, Cyrillic, Arabic, into the letters of the Latin alphabet. (7.2).

ROOT (*a*) The rear part of the tongue at the front of the pharynx. → diagram p. 159. (*b*) A morpheme within a word which carries the main lexical information, e.g. *come*, as opposed to grammatical → affixes such as derivational and inflexional endings, e.g. in *coming*, *comes*, *comely*. → stem. Alternative term: base (*a*), radical. (4.1).

ROOT-CREATION A type of → word formation in which a new word is coined by onomatopoeia or invention, e.g. *ding-dong*, *fizz*, *blob*, *see-saw*, *galumphing*, etc. (4.2, 5.1).

ROOT-INFLECTED LANGUAGE A type of → inflected language such as Arabic in which the vowel distribution in word roots changes to show inflexion. (6.1, 8.1).

ROOT-ISOLATING LANGUAGE A type of → isolating language such as Chinese which shows grammatical relationships by invariable root words and word order. (6.1, 8.1).

ROUNDED Articulated with lip rounding. → labialisation.

ROUNDED versus NON-ROUNDED Cavity features in recent theories of → distinctive feature phonology. Rounded sounds are produced with a rounded lip orifice, non-rounded sounds without such lip rounding.

ROUNDING → Labialisation.

RULE A generalised statement of a regularity. In traditional grammar rules tend to be notional and prescriptive, e.g. 'The third person singular of an English verb is formed by adding -s'. In modern linguistics rules tend to be more formal and more clearly deduced from observable data, e.g. 'The plural of an English noun ending in the consonant [s] is formed by adding the plural morpheme [ız]'. In transformational-generative grammar rules are divided into → phrase structure or rewrite rules and → transformation rules. Rewrite rules assign a structure to a particular unit, e.g. A → B+C showing that A has the structure B+C, whereas transformation rules change one structure into another, e.g. A+B+C ⇒ X+Y+Z showing that the structure A+B+C becomes X+Y+Z.

RUNE A graphic sign or letter of the runic alphabet. → table p. 265.

RUNIC ALPHABET → Table p. 265.

S

SANDHI A → m u t a t i o n, contraction or ellipsis in connected speech, e.g. French *j'ai* or English *don't*. A special form of Sandhi can be observed in initial → mutation in Welsh. (3.1, 4.1, 6.1).

SATEM LANGUAGES Indo-European languages largely of the Eastern groups in which the Proto-Indo-European → velar stop *[k] changed to a voiceless alveolar fricative [s] as exemplified in Avestan *satem* 'hundred'. Satem languages include the sub-families Balto-Slavonic, Albanian, Armenian and Indo-Iranian. The distinction between satem and → centum languages was originally made by 19th-century philologists who believed there had been a direct dichotomy within the Indo-European speech community. → Historical linguistics favours the explanation that there was a sound shifting of the velar to the spirant in certain areas, rather than a direct splitting up of the speech community. (6.1).

SAUSSUREAN LINGUISTICS Collective term for a number of insights by the Swiss linguist F. de Saussure (1857–1913) who may be regarded as the founder of modern → structural linguistics. Among the basic distinctions he made are those of → diachronic and synchronic linguistics, → langue and parole, → paradigmatic and syntagmatic ('associative') relations, and the two sides of the linguistic sign ('significant' and 'signifié'). These ideas were further developed by linguists of the → Prague School and → glossematics. Alternative term: Geneva School. (2.4 Saussure, 2.5 Godel, Lepschy).

SAYING Collective lay term for → idiom and proverb.

SCALE-AND-CATEGORY GRAMMAR An earlier term for → systemic grammar.

SCHOLASTICISM The linguistic philosophy of the Schoolmen. → Mediaeval linguistics.

SCHWA → Shwa.

SCIENTIFIC GRAMMAR The linguistic description of the → grammar of a language, as opposed to a pedagogical grammar used for language teaching.

SCRIPT A set of graphic signs of an alphabetic, syllabic or logo-graphic → writing system. More specifically script refers to hand-writing in which the graphic signs within words are run together, rather than print in which the graphemes are separated by spaces, (7.2).

SECOND ARTICULATION All human languages can be subjected to a double articulation. The first articulation is the splitting up of the continuum of speech into units such as words. The second articulation is the splitting up of words into speech sounds. The word *book*, for example, may be isolated from an utterance such as *The book is on the table near the door* and it may be further divided into a sequence of phonemes /b/, /u/ and /k/. → first articulation,

→ double articulation (*b*). (2.1 Martinet).

SECOND FUTURE → Future perfect tense.

SECOND INFINITIVE The infinitive used with the particle *to*, e.g. in *I want to go.* → first infinitive. Alternative term: marked infinitive.

SECOND LANGUAGE → Foreign language.

SECOND-ORDER LANGUAGE → Metalanguage (*a*).

SECOND PAST PERFECT → Past anterior.

SECOND PERFECT → Pluperfect tense.

SECOND PERSON → Person.

SECOND POSSESSIVE The form of the → personal pronoun which can function as a nominal, e.g. *mine, yours, his, hers, its, ours, theirs*, as opposed to the → first possessive which usually functions as a determiner, e.g. *my, your, his, her, its, our, their*.

SECOND SOUND SHIFT A series of regular sound changes which first took place in the southern part of the German speaking area before the earliest written records, and gradually spread northwards, distinguishing High German (Southern) dialects from Low German (Northern) dialects. The sound shift affected mainly the stop consonants [p t k b d g]. Under certain conditions [p > pf > f]; [t > ts > s]; [k > kx > x]; [b > p]; [d > t]; [g > ɣ]. The results of some of these changes can still be observed by comparing English words descended from Old English (a West-Germanic language which was not affected by the second sound shift) and modern standard German (High German), descended from Germanic dialects which were influenced by the second sound shift: *pound*:*Pfund*; *ten*:*zehn* [tseːn]; *water*: *Wasser*; *book*:*Buch* [buːx]; *sleep*: *schlafen*; *out*:*aus*; *day*:*Tag*; *deep*: *tief*, etc. Alternative term: High German sound shift. (6.1).

SECONDARY ARTICULA-TION → Articulation.

SECONDARY DERIVATIVE A word consisting of one stem plus a derivational affix. → word formation.

SECONDARY FEATURE A feature of → articulation of speech sounds such as lip rounding, aspiration, nasalisation, retroflexion, etc. which may be phonologically less important in speech production than the basic features of phonation, point of articulation, manner of articulation. → prosodic feature. (3.1, 8.22).

SECONDARY LANGUAGE → Foreign language.

SECONDARY PHONEME → Prosodic feature.

SECONDARY STRESS → Stress.

SECONDARY UNIT A linguistic element which is set up as a derivative of a → primary unit. In traditional grammar, the word and the sentence are regarded as primary units, while the phrase and the clause are secondary units.

SECONDARY WORD A word consisting of one stem plus an affix. → word formation.

SEGMENT A linguistic unit abstracted from a continuum of speech or text, e.g. → phone or → phoneme as the smallest unit of sound, or → morph or → morpheme as the smallest unit of grammar. Features of the continuum of speech which extend over more than one segment, e.g. intonation or lip rounding, are given the name → suprasegmental, plurisegmental or → prosody. Alternative term: isolate. (3.1, 4.1).

SEGMENTAL ANALYSIS A method of → linguistic analysis in which utterances are analysed into units, e.g. → phonemes or → morphemes, which in turn may be used to construct larger units, e.g. words or sentences. → prosodic analysis. (3.1, 4.1).

SEGMENTAL PHONEME → Phoneme.

SEGMENTAL PHONOLOGY The system and study of the speech sounds in a language as separate → phonemes, in contrast to a componential approach which further subdivides speech sounds into → distinctive features, or a → prosodic analysis which recognises prosodies which extend over several segments.

SEGMENTATION The analysis of a continuum into units, e.g. speech into → phonemes, or a text into → graphemes.

SEGMENTATOR A device used in phonetic research which can play back a taped recording of the continuum of speech in small segments with pauses between them. (3.1, 8.22).

SELECTION RESTRICTION Most linguistic units (phonemes, words) are limited in the way they can combine with other units in particular environments. Thus noun and verb must agree in number: *The boy likes fishing* but *The boys like fishing*. On the semantic level, there must be compatibility between related elements: *The boy likes fishing* but not *The boy pleases fishing*. Special rules can be set up in a → generative grammar to make the selection of non-grammatical or non-sensical features impossible. → tactics.

SEMANTEME A unit of linguistic meaning understood as a 'segmental' rather than componential item. → sememe.

SEMANTIC ANALYSIS A branch of → linguistic analysis which investigates the → meaning of vocabulary items by explaining what sense relations hold between them. Different types of semantic analysis have been proposed, according to whether a referential, conceptual, contextual or other theory of meaning is taken as a basic framework. → semantics.

SEMANTIC CHANGE A shift in the → meaning of a word. The meaning may be widened or narrowed (→ extension, → reduction), changed in the positive or negative direction (→ amelioration, → deterioration), or transferred by → metaphor. Alternative terms: semantic shift, shift of meaning, vocabulary change. (5.1, 6.1).

SEMANTIC COMPONENT
(*a*) In → componential analysis, one of several features which together can be said to make up the semantic meaning of a word or utterance. Thus *raining* could be analysed into the component features 'precipitation', 'liquid' (not 'solid' as *hail*), 'average' (not 'light' as *drizzling* or 'heavy' as *pouring*), etc. → distinguisher. Alternative terms: semantic feature, semantic property, semantic marker. (*b*) In → transformational-generative grammar, that part or level of the model which interprets the structures specified in the base component.

SEMANTIC DIFFERENTIAL
A device developed by psychologists to measure experimentally the sense an individual speaker gives to a word. Thus the subject hears the word *father* and records his response to this stimulus by choosing one of two bipolar adjectives, e.g. *happy/sad*, *hard/soft*, *slow/fast*, etc. (5.2 Osgood et al.).

SEMANTIC DISTINGUISHER
→ Distinguisher.

SEMANTIC FEATURE →
Semantic component (*a*.)

SEMANTIC FIELD
A group of lexical items which are associated in meaning by occurring together in similar contexts, e.g. 'pieces of furniture' in such phrases as *I sit on a chair/settee/stool*, or *Move that bed/table/chair back!* Comparative investigations of such 'fields' as colour terms have been used for evidence that languages differ in the way they view and structure the 'external world' by means of the sense relations between vocabulary items. → value. Alternative terms: lexical field, domain. (5.1, 5.2).

SEMANTIC FIELD THEORY
The view proposed by J. Trier and other linguists that sections of the vocabulary of a language can be analysed as structured → semantic fields. (5.1 Ullmann).

SEMANTIC INFORMATION
→ Information theory.

SEMANTIC MARKER →
Marker.

SEMANTIC MEANING →
Meaning.

SEMANTIC PAIR
A pair of lexical items related in meaning, e.g. → synonyms such as *help/assist*, → converse terms such as *buy/sell*, → antonyms such as *black/white*, etc. (5.1, 5.2).

SEMANTIC PROPERTY
→ Semantic component (*a*).

SEMANTIC RANGE
The number of different contexts in which a word can occur. Thus in English *blue* has a wide range of occurrence, e.g. *The sky is blue, a blue joke, he's got the blues*, etc. (5.1).

SEMANTIC SHIFT →
Semantic change.

SEMANTIC STRUCTURE That level of language on which → meaning relations between vocabulary items may be established. Every language may be said to have its own semantic structure which linguists try to analyse, in addition to its phonological and grammatical structures. (5.1).

SEMANTIC TRIANGLE The view proposed by C. K. Ogden and I. A. Richards that linguistic meaning can be explained in terms of the triadic relationship between (1) the thing or concept to which reference is made, (2) the symbol or name used to refer to it, and (3) the mental image or sense it has for a speaker or hearer.

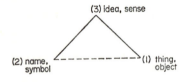

→ semantics. Alternative term: triadic theory of meaning. (5.1).

SEMANTIC VALUE The ability of a linguistic element to distinguish → lexical meaning. Thus the phonemes /p/ and /t/ distinguish the words *pin* and *tin* and have semantic value. (3.4, 5.1).

SEMANTICS The system and study of → meaning in language. Many different theories of meaning have been put forward by different authors and schools, first in the realm of philosophy (→ philosophical semantics) and more recently within the scope of → linguistics. The Greeks had introduced the controversy between the view of the 'realists' (NATURALISM) that words are linked to essential features of the things to which they refer and the view of the 'nominalists' (NOMINALISM) who insisted on the conventional nature of words as names. While philosophical approaches to meaning have often been concerned with the origin of verbal symbols and their validity in terms of truth and logical consistency, LINGUISTIC SEMANTICS has studied meaning more in terms of the connexions between speech acts and the physical and intellectual environment of the speaker. Some linguists have stressed the intimate links between the internal structure of a particular language and the way its speakers depend on it to classify the world around them (Humboldtism, Whorfian hypothesis). Others have asked whether it is possible at all to account for the relationships between utterances and the infinite number of situations in which they are made. On these grounds, many linguists, particularly those associated with one period of American distributionalism, have attempted to exclude semantic considerations from their formal analysis. On the other hand it is virtually impossible to explain linguistic phenomena without any reference to the communicative context in which they occur, and most contemporary linguists therefore emphasise that semantics must be regarded as an important branch or → level of linguistic analysis. Among the major theories in linguistic semantics have been (*a*) the CONCEPTUAL THEORY (or CONCEPTUALISM) in which meaning is defined as the 'mental image' the speaker has of the thing he is talking about, (*b*) the REFERENCE or CORRES-PONDENCE THEORY which assumes a direct relationship between a linguistic → symbol and the thing it denotes (→ semantic triangle), (*c*) the CONTEXTUAL THEORY which attempts to explain the meaning of words by the habitual 'collocations' it normally enters with other words in specific situations, (*d*) the FIELD THEORY which interprets the meaning relationships between the members of restricted → semantic fields, (*e*) COMPONENTIAL ANALYSIS which shows how sets of terms are made up of universal semantic features, (*f*) COMBINATORIAL SEMANTICS or SEMOTACTICS which looks at both the lexical meaning of individual items and their syntactic arrangement, (*g*) GENERATIVE SEMANTICS which studies underlying logical relations. Alternative terms: glossology (obsolete), sematology (obsolete), semasiology (obsolete), semology. (5.1, 5.2, 8.24, 10.3).

SEMASIOLOGY → Semantics.

SEMATOLOGY → Semantics.

SEME Unit of content or meaning, as opposed to such units as phone, morph or graph which are units of form. → semene.

SEMEME A minimum unit of → meaning. Different approaches in semantic analysis have defined the sememe in different ways, as a 'segmental' unit (the meaning of a → morpheme), or a compound of 'distinctive features' (→ componential analysis). (5.1, 5.2).

SEMEMIC STRATUM → Stratificational grammar.

SEMI-COLON → Punctuation.

SEMI-CONSONANT → Semi-vowel.

SEMIOLOGY → Semiotics.

SEMIOTIC SYSTEM A system of → signs (*b*), such as a natural language.

SEMIOTICS The systematic study of linguistic and non-linguistic → signs. Many disciplines have contributed to the elaboration of a general framework within which the philosophical, psychological, social and linguistic aspects of signs as 'symbols of communication' can be analysed. The logico-philosophical approach to language signs has been summarised by C. W. Morris and R. Carnap, who defined the field of semiotics as consisting of three main branches: PRAGMATICS, the study of how signs and symbols are used by man for communicating in a particular language, SEMANTICS (with a 'theoretical' or abstract and a 'descriptive' or empirical component), the study of the relationships between the 'symbol' and its 'referent', and SYNTACTICS, the study of symbols in relation to each other. Since F. de Saussure, → linguistics and some of its branches, notably linguistic → semantics, have been shown to be capable of solving many semiotic problems, and involved in applying semiotic procedures to practical problems, e.g. the study of → stylistics. Alternative terms: significs, semiology. (5.2 Carnap, Morris, 10.3).

SEMI-VOWEL A speech sound which can have certain features of both a vowel and a consonant. Such sounds have open approximation of the articulators and very little friction noise, but they do not normally occur as the nucleus or peak of a syllable: e.g. the phonemes /j/, /r/, /w/ in *yellow*, *red* and *well*. Alternative terms: semi-consonant, glide.

SEMOLOGY   → Semantics.

SEMOTACTICS   The system and study of the characteristic arrangement of → sememes in sequence. → semantics.

SENSE   The semantic → meaning that a word or phrase has for a speaker (writer) or hearer (reader), e.g. the different connotations of *teenager* in a report on juvenile delinquency or in a popular magazine for young people. (5.1).

SENSE RELATIONS   The semantic relationships that may be set up between individual or groups of lexical items, e.g. → synonymy, → antonymy, → complementarity.

SENTENCE   In traditional grammar a sentence is defined as the expression of a 'complete thought' with at least a → subject and a → predicate (although in some sentences the subject is said to be 'understood', e.g. imperatives such as *stand up* where *you* is said to be the subject 'understood'). In linguistics such notional definitions are inadequate since they do not take account of the empirical facts of grammatical structure. A typical structural definition of a sentence includes reference to the fact that it is the largest unit on which linguistic

analysis can be carried out, i.e. it is a grammatical form which can be analysed into constituents but which is not a constituent of any larger form. In → systemic grammar a sentence is similarly the highest grammatical unit in the hierarchy of → rank scale and it is made up of one or more clauses. In → transformational-generative grammar, too, the sentence is the highest linguistic unit and can be defined as any syntactic structure which can be generated by the phrase structure and transformation rules of an adequate grammar. The tagmemic approach, however, emphasises the need to establish categories larger than a sentence, and would thus define sentence as being intermediate between clause and paragraph. As in the case of the definition of word, some linguists would consider that the term sentence can only be used in reference to *langue* (language as a system), not to *parole* (speech), maintaining that speech does not consist of sentences but of utterances 'derived' from sentences. → Diagram p. 244. (4.1, 4.2, 8.23).

SENTENCE ADVERBIAL   → Sentence modifier.

SENTENCE COMPOUND   → Compound sentence.

SENTENCE CONNECTOR   A word, usually a → conjunctive adverb, which links two or more sentences. Unlike conjunctions, sentence connectors do not always occur at the beginning of the sentence which they introduce, e.g. *therefore* in *Our leading man fell ill; we therefore had to cancel the play.* Alternative term: connective.

SENTENCE FRAGMENT → Minor sentence.

SENTENCE MODIFIER An adjunct word, phrase or clause modifying a whole sentence rather than a particular word in the sentence, e.g. the adverb in *Fortunately, I caught the train*, or the participial phrase in *Without waiting for permission, I went in*. Alternative term: sentence adverbial.

SENTENCE PARTS Syntactic categories forming constituents of a sentence, e.g. → subject, → predicate, → object, → complement, etc.

SENTENCE PATTERN Traditional grammar distinguished four types of sentences which were given the notional labels 'statement', 'question', 'exclamation', 'command'. These distinctions were based on the syntactic-grammatical patterns of Latin and Greek, but are by no means universal. Sentence patterns need to be distinguished formally for a given language by means of an analysis of their constituents and the order in which they occur. The structure of English, for example, does not always coincide with the traditional analysis, as an examination of the concepts → question and → command will show. Many linguists find it convenient to differentiate between notional terms such as these and grammatical or syntactic terms such as 'interrogative', 'imperative' because not all questions have an interrogative construction, e.g. *He is coming?* and not all commands have an imperative construction, e.g. *No smoking*. Languages differ greatly in the syntactic patterns they

use, and an understanding of the basic sentence patterns of a given language is important in language teaching. The term favourite sentence is sometimes used to describe a pattern which is the most typical for a statement in a given language, e.g. in English, Subject + Predicate: *John is running*, and the term minor sentence for other patterns, e.g. *Is John running? Run, is something John can't do!* Alternative terms: syntactic pattern, speech act. → Clause pattern. (4.1, 8.23).

SENTENCE STRESS → Stress.

SENTENCE WORD A single word functioning as a sentence, e.g. *yes* in *Are you coming?—Yes*.

SEPARABLE An → affix which can be separated from the stem to which it is attached. In particular, certain verbal prefixes in German which are separated from the verb and occur usually at the end of the clause or sentence whenever the verb is used in a finite form, e.g. *Er geht zum Feind über* 'he defects to the enemy', as opposed to the → inseparable verb form *Er übergeht den Fehler* 'he ignores the mistake'. Alternative term: separable prefix.

SEPARABLE PREFIX → Separable.

SEQUENCE In linguistic analysis the relationship between linguistic items in succession, as opposed to their arrangement at several structural levels, e.g. the linear arrangement of phonemes in a word.

SEQUENCE OF TENSES The conditioning of the → tense to be used in a subordinate clause by the tense in the main clause, e.g. the past tense forms in *He asked me whether I wanted to come with him.* Languages differ in respect of their conventions concerning sequence of tenses.

SEQUENCING → Grading.

SERIES A group of consonant sounds, all sharing a common feature, which are produced at a number of points along the vocal tract, e.g. the voiced series [b], [v], [ð], [d], [z], [ʒ], [g], etc. → order (*a*). (2.1 Martinet).

SHARP versus NON-SHARP One of the basic oppositions in → distinctive feature phonology based on the analysis of a → spectrogram. The term 'sharp' indicates relatively high intensity of the upper frequency components of the → spectrum, and 'non-sharp' the lack of these features. In articulatory terms sharp indicates sounds produced with wide pharyngeal cavity and palatalisation. All soft or → palatalised consonants have the feature sharp, whereas all hard or non-palatised consonants have the feature non-sharp.

SHIFT OF MEANING → Semantic change.

SHORTENING A type of → word formation consisting of a shortening of one or more words, e.g. *flu* from *influenza*, *pop* from *popular*. → contraction, abbreviation.

SHWA, SCHWA A name, taken from Hebrew, given to the vowel usually represented in phonetic transcription by [ə]. → neutral vowel.

SIBILANT A → fricative produced by forcing the air stream through a groove-shaped opening between the tongue and the roof of the mouth, e.g. [s] in *sin*; [z] in *zoo*; [ʃ] in *shop*; [ʒ] in *pleasure*. Alternative terms: groove fricative, groove spirant, whistling consonant. (3.1, 8.22).

SIGN (*a*) A conventionalised visible mark on a surface used as a basic graphic unit of a → writing system to represent or record ideas and words (logogram, character), syllables (syllabogram), or speech sounds (phonogram, letter). → grapheme. Alternative term: iconic sign. (7.2). (*b*) The spoken or written word as used by speakers or hearers to refer to an object or idea, as a combination of meaning conveyed (→ signified, → content) and the phonic or graphic manifestation of it (→ signifier, → expression). Alternative terms: linguistic sign, symbol, symbolic sign. (5.1).

SIGNARY A collection of the graphic signs of a → writing system, e.g. syllabary or alphabet. (7.2).

SIGNIFIANT → Signifier.

SIGNIFICANCE (*a*) Grammatical → meaning. (*b*) → Signification.

SIGNIFICANS → Signifier.

SIGNIFICANT (*a*) Producing a difference in meaning, e.g. voice is the distinguishing feature between the initial sounds of the words *bin* and *pin*. → distinctive. (*b*) The spoken or written → signifier which is used to refer to or express a concept.

SIGNIFICATION In → semantics, the relationship between an abstract concept or concrete thing on the one hand and the linguistic symbol which is used to refer to it on the other. The concept or thing and its meaning are said to be the → signified and the verbal or graphic representation of it is said to be the → signifier. → appellation. Alternative term: significance. (5.1).

SIGNIFICATUM → Signified.

SIGNIFICS → Semiotics.

SIGNIFIÉ → Signified.

SIGNIFIED A concrete object or abstract idea which is referred to by means of an appropriate → signifier, e.g. a sequence of verbal sounds or graphic signs. Thus the word *star* (the signifier) may be used to convey the idea of a 'luminous heavenly body' (the signified or → referent). Alternative terms: signifié, significatum. (5.1).

SIGNIFIER The sequence of sounds or graphic signs by which a speaker refers to a physical entity or abstract concept of which he has a mental image. Thus the word *star* (the signifier) may be used to convey the idea of a 'luminous heavenly body' (the → signified or referent). Alternative term: significans, signifiant, signifiant. (5.1).

SILENT STRESS When a stressed syllable is omitted in colloquial or rapid speech the → stress may be retained on a period of silence, often accompanied by a nod or other gesture, e.g. *thank you* when pronounced *'kyou* [⌐kjʊ].

SIMILE A → figure of speech in which a comparison is made between persons or things usually by means of the word *like* or *as*, e.g. "*She sat like patience on a monument, smiling at grief*" (Shakespeare, *Twelfth Night*, Act II, Sc. 4) or *He drove as if possessed by the devil.* → metaphor.

SIMILITUDE The pronunciation of one segment being influenced by the pronunciation of an adjacent segment, e.g. [k] in *kill* is articulated at the front of the velum anticipating the front vowel [ɪ] whereas [k] in *call* is articulated at the back of the velum anticipating the back vowel [ɔː].

SIMPLE PAST → Past tense.

SIMPLE PERFECT → Perfect tense.

SIMPLE PREDICATE A → predicate consisting solely of a verb phrase, i.e. a single verb or auxiliary plus a full verb, e.g. *Birds fly* or *It is raining.* → compound predicate.

SIMPLE SENTENCE A syntactic pattern consisting of one → main clause without any subordinate or co-ordinate clauses.

SIMPLE STEM A word consisting of one morpheme. → word formation.

SIMPLE STOP → Stop.

SIMPLE TENSE A verb consisting of a single form without an auxiliary, e.g. the English past tense such as *he went*, as opposed to the compound future tense such as *he will go*.

SIMPLE VOWEL → Monophthong.

SIMPLE WAVE FORM → Sound wave.

SIMULTANEOUS INTERPRETING → Interpreting.

SINGLE-BAR JUNCTURE → Juncture.

SING-SONG THEORY → Origin of speech.

SINGULAR Grammatical category of → number, referring to not more than one.

SINGULATIVE An affix or adjunct denoting singular, e.g. *flake* added to *snow* to give *snowflake*. → plurative.

SINO-TIBETIAN LINGUISTICS Collective term for the linguistic description of the Chinese and Tibeto-Burman languages such as Mandarin Chinese, Wu, Cantonese, Siamese, etc. → Appendix 1, p. 271. (8.8 Kratochvíl, Shafer).

SINUSOIDAL WAVE FORM → Sound wave.

SISTER LANGUAGE → Family of languages.

SITUATION → Context (*b*).

SITUATIONAL MEANING → Meaning.

SKILL → Linguistic skill.

SLACK VOWEL → Lax vowel.

SLANG A variety of speech characterised by newly coined and rapidly changing vocabulary, used by the young or by social and professional groups for 'in-group' communication and thus tending to prevent understanding by the rest of the speech community. (7.1, 8.24).

SLAVIC LINGUISTICS → Slavonic linguistics.

SLAVONIC LINGUISTICS The linguistic description of Russian, Polish, Serbocroat and other Slavonic languages. → Appendix 1, p. 269. Alternative term: Slavic linguistics. (8.5, 8.7 de Bray).

SLENDER VOWEL → Front vowel.

SLIT FRICATIVE A → fricative produced through slit-shaped aperture, e.g. [θ] in *think*.

SLOPES → Syllable.

SLOT A defined environment into which a linguistic item will fit. It might be said, for example, that a word which fits into the following slot functions as a noun: *The ----- is good.* In → tagmemics the term slot refers to the grammatical function of a tagmeme and here the reference is not so much to linear sequence but to such grammatical functions as subject, object, predicate, etc. In the sentence *John lives here* the subject slot is filled by the tagmeme *John.* → substitution frame.

SLUR The blurred → transition from one speech sound to another.

SOCIAL DIALECT → Dialect.

SOCIOLECT   A social → dialect.

SOCIOLINGUISTICS Collective term for the applications of research techniques and findings from linguistics and various social sciences to the study of language in society. Linguistic and social problems are closely related, so much so that linguistics itself has sometimes been regarded as a 'social' science. Every speaker of a language is also part of a community, and his → idiolect or social → dialect will be largely determined by his environment which in turn will become apparent in his speech. In school and through other means such as mass media and travel, a speaker may acquire the → standard language as a 'second' or 'auxiliary' language. Some languages possess a 'high' and a 'low' standard (→ diglossia). In multilingual speech communities such as the U.S.A. or India conflicting loyalties may develop in certain groups (→ bilingualism). → anthropological linguistics, restricted code. (7.1, 9.2, 10.1).

SOCIOLOGICAL LINGUISTICS (*a*) Those linguistic studies of language which claim that language cannot be separated from the social context of man, in particular the views of a number of French linguists (A. Meillet, C. Bally) who related linguistic analysis to the different stylistic modes of expression of individuals and groups. Similar ideas may be found in certain branches of German ethnolinguistics and American anthropological linguistics (→ relativity), in Italian → Neo-linguistics and → British linguistics. (2.4 Humboldt, Sapir, 2.5 Hall, Langendoen). (*b*) → Sociolinguistics.

SOFT   → Palatalisation.

SOFT CONSONANT   → Palatalised.

SOFT PALATE   → Velum.

SOFT SIGN The Cyrillic character ь which indicates → palatalisation of the preceding consonant, e.g. in Russian *уголь* 'coal'.

SOFTENING   → Palatalisation.

SOLECISM A violation of the accepted convention, i.e. the rules of pronunciation, grammar and lexis of a particular language.

SOLID COMPOUND   → Primary compound.

SOLILOQUY   → Monologue.

SONAGRAPH Commercial name for a widely-used → sound spectrograph.

SONANT (*a*) In phonetics, a → voiced sound, as opposed to a voiceless sound. (*b*) In phonology, a syllabic consonant or → semivowel.

SONOGRAM   → Spectrogram.

SONORANT A term sometimes used to describe → nasal and → liquid sounds, which may form a whole syllable on their own, e.g. [n̩] in *button*.

SONORANT versus NON-SONORANT (OBSTRUENT) Major class features in recent theories of → distinctive feature phonology. Sonorants are produced with the vocal tract in a position where

211

spontaneous voicing is possible, e.g. vowels, glides, nasals, consonants, liquids. Sounds formed with greater constriction in the vocal tract, e.g. stops, fricatives, affricates are non-sonorants.

SONORITY A resonant quality of a sound such as 'loudness' or 'length' which makes it more prominent than another. Vowels are more sonorous than consonants, and → continuants more sonorous than → stops. (3.1, 8.22).

SONORITY FEATURES → Distinctive feature.

SOUND The impression received by the brain as a result of the vibration of the ear drum in reaction to changes in air pressure. → phonetics.

SOUND CHANGE A change in the sound system of a language from one stage in its historical development to another. If a sound change modifies the number or distribution of phonemes it is called a → phonemic sound change (or SOUND CHANGE BY PHONEMES, PHONOLOGICAL CHANGE, FUNCTIONAL CHANGE). If a sound change affects only the distribution of allophones with a phoneme it is called a → phonetic sound change (or ALLOPHONIC CHANGE, SOUND CHANGE BY ALLOPHONES). Sound changes may be caused by a variety of factors such as → assimilation, → dissimilation, and may affect parts or whole of the sound system. There are basically two ways in which a sound system can be affected: (i) by means of a → merger (or convergence) when two phonemes develop into one; (ii) by means of a → split when a single phoneme develops into two.

A sound change is said to be a CONDITIONED SOUND CHANGE (or CONDITIONAL, COMBINATIVE, COMBINATORY, DEPENDENT) when the change is restricted to certain phonetic environments, e.g. Middle English [u] became [ʌ] except after labial consonants: blod > *blood* [blʌd] whereas [u] remained in *put* [put]; but UNCONDITIONED (or UNCONDITIONAL, INDEPENDENT, ISOLATIVE, AUTONOMOUS, SPONTANEOUS, SPORADIC) when it is in no way dependent on its environment but occurs in all positions in which the sound in question occurs, e.g. Proto-Indo-European [o] and [a] merged into Proto-Germanic [ɑ]: PIE **osdos* > Gothic *asts* 'branch'. (6.1 Lockwood).

SOUND CHANGE BY ALLOPHONES →Phonetic sound change.

SOUND CHANGE BY PHONEMES → Phonemic sound change.

SOUND ECHOISM → Onomatopoeia.

SOUND LAW → Phonetic law.

SOUND SHIFT A series of regular changes in the sound system of a language or group of languages from one stage of development to another. If the sound shift involves only vowels it may be called a vowel shift (→ Great English vowel shift). If the change affects only consonants it may be called a consonant shift (→ first sound shift, → second sound shift). Sound shifts are often named after the men who first formulated them, e.g. the first and second sound shifts are often referred to as → Grimm's Law. Other such laws are → Verner's Law, → Darmesteter's Law and → Grassman's

Law. Alternative term: phonetic law. (6.1).

SOUND SOURCE The origin of sound. It may refer to the → vocal tract, or to an electronic device used to reproduce sound such as → tape recorder, record player, loudspeaker. (3.1, 8.22, 9.14, 10.5).

SOUND SPECTROGRAPH The basic instrument for the acoustic study of speech. The sound spectrograph stores 2.4 seconds of recorded speech. The recording is then played back several times at high speed each time through a differing set of filters. The recording paper on a revolving drum records time, intensity and frequency. The horizontal axis represents time, the vertical axis represents frequency, and the intensity or amplitude is shown by the blackness of the marks on the paper. The recorded output of the sound spectrograph is called a → spectrogram. (3.3).

SOUND SYMBOLISM Collective term for → onomatopoeia and → synaesthesia.

SOUND SYSTEM An account of the phonemes and allophones of a language and the relationships between them. → phonemic structure.

SOUND WAVE Disturbances in the air caused by the vibration of a body in the air. Vibrating bodies such as a tuning fork or the → vocal cords send out 'ripples' in all directions like the ripples made by a pebble thrown into water. The ripples are variations in air pressure to which the ear is sensitive. Graphic representations of these changes in air pressure produce wave forms:

regular symmetric variations produce a SIMPLE WAVE FORM, the most regular of which is a SINUSOIDAL WAVE FORM, corresponding to the path followed by a point on a wheel moving forward at a regular speed: a COMPLEX WAVE FORM is the result of a combination of two or more simple wave forms. → amplitude. (3.1, 8.22).

SOURCE In a communication channel, that part from which messages are sent, i.e. the speaker or writer, as opposed to the → addressee.

SOURCE FEATURES → Distinctive feature.

SOURCE LANGUAGE The language from which an original text is translated or from which a loan word is borrowed. In foreign language teaching, the native language from which the instruction of the foreign language starts. → target language.

SPEAKING One of the basic linguistic skills; the act of producing speech as a means of communication, sometimes used as an alternative term to parole (→ langue and parole) and performance (→ competence and performance). → listening, → reading, → writing. (9.11).

SPECIAL LANGUAGE Collective term for the → varieties in language used for particular purposes. Linguists have found it difficult to draw the line between the 'common core' or 'general' language which is known to most of its speakers, and the 'special purpose' languages used by experts in various professional and technical fields

213

from commerce to nuclear physics. Several fields of applied linguistics such as → translation, → lexicography and → language teaching have been concerned with practical aspects, particularly the use of → terminology and certain grammatical constructions, and statistical techniques such as word frequency counts have been used to differentiate special languages from each other and from the language at large (→ computational linguistics). The term RESTRICTED LANGUAGE or 'little' language refers to 'codes' such as that used between aeroplane pilots and airport control towers, or between doctors and chemists. FORMULAIC LANGUAGES are symbolic systems used in scientific reasoning such as mathematical proofs. → register (*b*).

SPECIALISATION OF MEANING → Reduction (*b*).

SPECIALISED MEANING
The use of a word in a restricted sense, e.g. *doctor* for 'medical practitioner' rather than for 'holder of a doctorate' or *undertaker* to refer to 'funeral undertaker' rather than 'entrepreneur'. Alternative term: narrowed meaning.

SPECTRAL ANALYSIS In
phonetic investigations, a technique for observing and measuring features of speech sounds by means of a → sound spectrograph. (3.3).

SPECTROGRAM A graphic
representation of sound which gives information about changes in → duration, → frequency and → intensity of sound waves along a time axis. A spectrogram is produced automatically by a → sound spectrograph. Alternative term: sonogram. (3.3).

SPECTROGRAPH → Sound spectrograph.

SPECTRUM A graph showing
the relative amplitudes of the frequency components of a sound wave. A repetitive wave form has a limited number of components and these can be represented graphically as lines of differing lengths corresponding to the relative amplitudes of the different frequencies, giving a spectrum analogous to an optical spectrum. A spectrum showing a limited number of such components is a LINE SPECTRUM. The curve joining

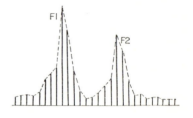

Spectrum of the vowel [eː] (Swedish). On the *x* axis the frequencies. On the *y* axis the amplitude. Spectogram obtained by the so-called Siemens Tonfrequenzspektrometer; *on top* its envelope. F_1 about 350 c/s, F_2 at 2000 c/s.
(Malmberg: *Structural Linguistics and Human Communication*, p. 40, Springer-Verlag, Berlin)

individual lines is called the ENVELOPE or RESONANCE CURVE or CONTINUOUS SPECTRUM. A continuous spectrum is a more accurate representation of any real sound because effects of damping, i.e. successive repetition of a wave having reduced amplitude, prevent wave forms being exactly identical and there is some amplitude at every frequency, represented by the curve consisting of an infinite number of points. The greater the degree of damping the greater the spread of the resonance curve.

A spectrum is also referred to as DPF 2 distribution of power among the frequencies. Since power is proportional to amplitude squared, such a graph does show its distribution.

SPECULATIVE GRAMMAR
→ Mediaeval linguistics.

SPEECH The process or result of producing a continuum of meaningful sounds in a language; spoken language as opposed to language of → gesture or → writing. Sometimes used as collective term for both → (langue and) parole or → (competence and) performance. → elocution.

SPEECH ACT (*a*) The production of speech sounds in an organised way so as to produce meaningful utterances. → speech event. (*b*) Alternative term for → function (expressive, appellative, etc.). (*c*) Alternative term for → sentence pattern (declarative, interrogative, etc.).

SPEECH COMMUNITY A group of people, usually in the same area, speaking the same variant of a → language, or the same standard language. (7.1, 9.2, 10.1).

SPEECH DEFECT A peculiarity in a person's language which is due to psycho-physiological disturbances or injuries. Such defects cause the afflicted individual to be so much at variance with other speakers that communication becomes difficult. → speech pathology, → speech therapy, → aphasia. Alternative

terms: speech disorder, speech impediment. (9.5).

SPEECH DISORDER → Speech defect.

SPEECH EDUCATION → Elocution.

SPEECH IMPEDIMENT → Speech defect.

SPEECH EVENT Collective term for the linguistic and extra-linguistic components of a self-contained act of speech. The various contributory factors may be analysed with the help of a → communication model which specifies information about the personalities involved (speaker, hearer), the form in which the message is transmitted (linguistic, → paralinguistic and → kinesic features) and the topic and context of the message. → function (*a*). Alternative term: speech act. (10.1 Hymes).

SPEECH IMPROVEMENT → Elocution.

SPEECH ISLAND A small speech community surrounded by speakers of another, more dominant language, e.g. German communities in the United States, such as Pennsylvania Dutch. (7.1, 8.1).

SPEECH ORGANS → Organs of speech.

SPEECH PATHOLOGY The study of defects and disturbances which may impede the communication effectiveness of a speaker. Speech pathology aims at finding the causes of such disorders, e.g.

damaged speech organs, neuro-muscular and sensory defects (including loss of hearing) or psychological upsets, while → speech therapy aims at curing them by adequate treatment. In both fields a thorough knowledge of the acoustic and articulatory processes (→ phonetics) as well as the psychological, anatomical and linguistic bases is required. → clinical linguistics. (9.5).

SPEECH PERCEPTION The recognition and understanding of speech sounds, syllables, words, etc. by a human listener. → speech recognition.

SPEECH PRODUCTION Collective term for the activities in the → vocal tract which convert muscular energy into acoustic energy. The muscular movement involved in setting the air in motion is called INITIATION by some linguists and → air-stream mechanism by others. REGULATION is the term used to describe the valve-like movements in the vocal tract which regulate the flow of air, generating or modifying sound waves. It is convenient to distinguish two types of regulation: (i) PHONATION activity which generates sound waves, e.g. vibration of the vocal cords in the larynx, (ii) ARTICULATION activity which modifies sound waves, e.g. closures or strictures in the pharynx, mouth and nose. → speech synthesis. (3.1 Abercrombie, Malmberg, 8.22).

SPEECH RECOGNITION The unambiguous identification of linguistic elements such as syllables or words. This concept is particularly important in efforts to imitate and mechanise human speech by

mechanical or electronic equipment. → speech synthesis, speech perception.

SPEECH SOUND A unit of sound as produced by the → organs of speech and observed by the phonetician (→ phone) and/or phonologist (→ phoneme). (3.1, 8.22).

SPEECH STRETCHER A device used in phonetic research to slow down recorded speech without changing the pitch or distorting it in any other way.

SPEECH SYNTHESIS The production of sounds of human speech by artificial means, e.g. for communicating computer output directly. The equipment may involve an artificial larynx or vibration source and an electronic → vocal tract which can change the quality of the sound produced in a way similar to the resonance chambers of the human organs of speech. Alternative term: artificial speech. (3.3, 9.5, 10.5).

SPEECH THERAPY Treatment for the elimination and/or alleviation of speech and language disorders. The treatment is carried out by speech therapists in collaboration with doctors, psychologists and occasionally linguists. → speech pathology, → clinical linguistics. Alternative term: logop(a)edics. (9.5).

SPELLING The representation of the sounds of human speech by means of standardised → writing rules. Only few languages such as Finnish and Turkish have a fairly close correspondence or fit between graphic signs and speech sounds, i.e. between spelling and pronunciation. In many languages, including English, one phoneme may be represented by different letters, as /ou/ in *foe*, *mow* and *so*, or different phonemes by the same letter(s), as /ɔ/ in *cough*, /au/ in *plough*, /ou/ in *though*. Often, written letters are not pronounced, e.g. *k* as in *knee*. The imperfections of spelling and the failure of the writing system to indicate features of intonation have led to numerous → spelling reforms. (7.2 Peters).

SPELLING PRONUNCIATION
The pronunciation of a word based upon its spelling, e.g. when *ate* is pronounced [eit] instead of [ɛt].

SPELLING REFORM A measure to improve the → spelling system by making it more representative of the sounds of speech. This includes proposals by individuals like G. B. Shaw (who left funds for the development of Shavian) and R. E. Zachrisson (Anglic) as well as official decrees by governments or academies. (8.22 Wijk).

SPIRANT → Fricative.

SPLIT The result of a single phoneme in an older form of the language becoming two phonemes at a later stage. Thus in Old English the phoneme /n/ had two allophones, [n], [ŋ], the latter only occurring before /k/ or /g/. /n/ and /ŋ/ are now separate phonemes in modern English contrasting medially and finally, e.g. /siŋər/*singer*:/sinər/*sinner*; /sin/ *sin*:/siŋ/ *sing*. → sound change.

SPLIT CLAUSE A → clause with two or more compound elements joined by conjunctions. Thus

in *He had neither attended classes nor done any homework when he took the examination*, the compound predicate *had attended classes* (*nor*) *done any homework* is composed of the verb phrases of two subordinate clauses with the common subject *he*.

SPLIT INFINITIVE A construction in which an adverbial or other adjunct is embedded between the two parts of a second infinitive, e.g. in *She was told to regularly attend classes*. In English this construction is considered by some as 'incorrect'.

SPOKEN LANGUAGE One of the modes of linguistic communication. As distinct from → written language, it is characterised by repetition, hesitation forms, pauses, variations in articulation, lapses, as well as differences in vocabulary and grammar. The primary importance of spoken language in the analysis, description and teaching of languages has been stressed frequently. → speech. → conversation. (3.1, 7.1, 9.11, 9.5).

SPONDE → Foot (*a*).

SPONTANEOUS SOUND CHANGE → Sound change.

SPOONERISM The accidental or deliberate interchanging of two initial sounds or syllables. Spooner, a warden of New College, Oxford, after whom the phenomenon is named, is once purported to have said *"Is the Bean dizzy?"* for *"Is the Dean busy?"*.

SPORADIC SOUND CHANGE → Sound change.

SPREAD VOWEL A vowel sound produced with the lips spread, e.g. [e] as in *bed*, as opposed to a rounded vowel, e.g. [u] as in *boo*. Alternative term: unrounded vowel.

STAGING → Grading.

STAMMER A speech impediment, usually due to psycho-physiological disturbances and more frequent in male than female speakers, in which consonant sounds and syllables are spasmodically repeated, particularly at the beginning of words. Alternative term: stutter. (9.5).

STANDARD DIALECT → Standard language.

STANDARD LANGUAGE The socially favoured → variety of a language, often based on the speech of the educated population in and around the cultural and/or political centre of the speech community. Such standard → dialects are imitated and used as auxiliary language by speakers of other regional and social dialects for the purpose of formal discourse and writing as well as for teaching the language to foreigners. However, each language variety (dialect, style) may be considered to have its own standard, and literary, colloquial, provincial and similar standards have been distinguished. Deviations from the respective established standards are called → non-standard or → sub-standard. → received pronunciation. Alternative terms: standard dialect, standard speech. (2.3 Quirk–Svartvik, 7.1, 8.24).

STANDARD SPEECH → Standard language.

STANDARDISATION The official acceptance by at least some groups within a speech community of certain general patterns of pronunciation, grammar, orthography and vocabulary. Standardised pronunciation is gaining ground with modern media of communication such as radio and television, and the need for national and even international co-ordination of → terminology is important in the fields of science and technology. (10.1 Tauli).

STARRED FORM → Asterisk form.

STATE OF LANGUAGE A → temporal dialect.

STATEMENT An utterance expressing an assertion or an hypothesis as opposed to a question or a command. A distinction must be made between the semantic term 'statement' and the formal or grammatical term 'indicative', since not all statements are in the indicative, e.g. *If I were you I should sit still* is a statement, but it is not in the indicative. The relationship existing between statement and indicative also exists between → command (semantic term) and → imperative (grammatical term) and between → question (semantic term) and → interrogative (grammatical term). (4.1, 4.2, 8.23).

STATIC LINGUISTICS → Synchronic linguistics.

STATISTICAL LINGUISTICS Collective term for a number of attempts to apply statistical procedures to the handling of language data, e.g. word → frequency counts and the study of an author's style. → mathematical linguistics. (10.4).

STATUS The extent to which social rank and power is expressed in language, e.g. by the use of special forms of → address or syntactic constructions. Different styles of discourse are marked in dictionaries by → usage labels. Status correlates inversely with → intimacy. (10.1 Fishman).

STATUS LABEL   → Usage label.

STEM   That which is left of a word when all inflexional → affixes have been removed. Thus the word *kindness* is a stem consisting of the root or → base *kind* and the derivational suffix *-ness*, to which can be added the inflexional suffix *-es* to form the plural. If the derivational prefix *un-* is added, a new stem *unkindness* is formed. The stem of a word is the form usually listed in dictionaries. (4.1, 4.2, 5.1, 8.23).

STEM COMPOUND   A word consisting of two stems. → word formation.

STEM-INFLECTED LANGU-AGE   A type of → inflected language such as Sanskrit, Greek or Latin where suffixes expressing different functions can be added to an unchanged base, e.g. Latin *bon-us*, *bon-a*, *bon-um*, etc. 'good'. (6.1, 8.1).

STEM-ISOLATING LANGU-AGE   → Isolating language.

STEMMA   A → phrase marker used in certain types of → dependency grammar.

STIMULUS   In behaviourist psychology and language teaching, the situation or verbal act which precedes a → response by a speaker or learner. The stimulus may be in the form of a problem or a statement or question, and in programmed instruction is usually followed up by a 'reinforced' stimulus to correct or confirm the student's response. (9.11, 10.2).

STOP   A speech sound which is the result of a complete → closure in the vocal tract. In the production of a stop consonant the velum seals off the nasal cavity so that no air can escape through the nose, and in addition the air stream is blocked at some other point(s) in the vocal tract. If the closure occurs at only one other point, say the lips, the sound is called a SIMPLE STOP, e.g. [pʰ] in *pin*. If the closure occurs at more than one other point, say at the lips and the glottis, the sound is called a COMPLEX STOP, e.g. [pʔ] often heard in French *pain* 'bread'. Stops may be classified according to the direction of air flow after release into INGRESSIVE STOP (alternative term: SUCTION STOP), i.e. with the airflow moving into the vocal tract towards the lungs, and EGRESSIVE STOP (alternative term: PRESSURE STOP), i.e. with the air stream moving out of the vocal tract away from the lungs. Another classification can be made according to the point of articulation into labial [p], [b]; alveolar [t], [d]; velar [k], [g]; glottal [ʔ], etc. A further classification distinguishes VOICED STOP [b] [d] [g], etc. in the production of which the vocal cords are allowed to vibrate, from VOICELESS STOP [p] [t] [k], etc. in the production of which the vocal cords are not allowed to vibrate. Some terms used to describe stops give information about the airstream mechanism used on their release, e.g. PLOSIVE or EXPLOSIVE refers to an egressive pulmonic air stream; IMPLOSIVE to a glottalic ingressive air stream; EJECTIVE to a glottalic egressive air stream; and

CLICK to a velaric ingressive air stream. Alternative terms: occlusive, mute (obsolete). (3.1, 8.22).

STRATIFICATION In → linguistic analysis, the setting up of a series of interrelated hierarchical → levels of language structure. Several alternative theories have been put forward, suggesting components of sound (phonology), grammar (morphology, syntax), and vocabulary (lexis), and within these further subdivisions into → ranks such as distinctive feature, phoneme, syllable, etc. or morpheme, word, phrase, etc. The most explicit formulation of this principle can be found in → stratificational grammar.

STRATIFICATIONAL GRAMMAR An approach to → linguistic analysis based on the work of the American linguist S. M. Lamb. Starting from the premise that there are two main components in language, meaning and sound, these are taken as two 'ends' (the HYPERSEMEMIC and the HYPOPHONEMIC system) between which several levels or strata can be established, each composed of units. Thus *better* can be analysed on the following strata: (1) the SEMEMIC STRATUM with SEMEMES (e.g. 'good' and 'comparative'), (2) the LEXEMIC STRATUM with LEXEMES (e.g. *good* and *-er*), (3) the MORPHEMIC STRATUM with MORPHEMES (e.g. /gud/ or /bet/ and /r/), and (4) the PHONEMIC STRATUM with PHONEMES (e.g. /b/ + /e/ + /t/ and /ə/). The units on neighbouring strata are hierarchically linked by the relation of → realisation, e.g. the lexeme *good* is represented by the morpheme {gud} which in turn is represented by the phonemic units /g/ + /u/ + /d/. Apart from the vertical stratification there are also several types of horizontal or tactic patterns (→ tactics) to account for the way units are strung together in speech. (4.2 Lamb).

STRATUM In → stratificational grammar, one of several → levels of analysis at which linguistic units may be said to realise themselves. Thus the word *raining* may be analysed at the sememic stratum as consisting of the sememes (or semantic components) 'liquid' + 'precipitation', on the lexemic stratum as the lexeme *rain* and a gerundial affix, on the morphemic stratum as two morphemes {rain} + {ing}, and on the phonemic stratum as the phonemes /r/ + /e/ + /i/ + /n/ + /i/ + /ŋ/.

STRESS Greater force exerted in the articulation of one part of an utterance compared with another, thus accentuating a certain part of the utterance, giving it more prominence. A stressed syllable is associated with what is called a reinforced → chest pulse, i.e. a chest pulse produced with extra energy. In phonology, two types of stress are distinguished: SENTENCE STRESS where extra prominence is given to a word in a sentence for the sake of emphasis: e.g. *I saw it (you didn't see it, I saw it)*, and WORD STRESS where the stress pattern is part of the phonological structure of a word, e.g. *permit* (verb) as opposed to *permit* (noun). Some languages have FIXED stress (or BOUND ACCENT or FIXED ACCENT) where the stress always occurs in the same place in relation to the word boundary, e.g. Hungarian, Czech, whereas other languages, e.g. English and Russian, have FREE STRESS (or MOVABLE STRESS) where the position of the stress can vary from word to word. Different degrees of stress can be abstracted as suprasegmental phonemes or prosodies. One type of analysis of English establishes four such degrees: (1) PRIMARY STRESS (PRIMARY ACCENT or HEAVY STRESS) /´/ the strongest, (2) SECONDARY STRESS /ˆ/ weaker than primary but stronger than tertiary, (3) TERTIARY STRESS /ˋ/ weaker than secondary, (4) WEAK STRESS or MINIMAL STRESS /ˇ/ the weakest degree of stress. The phrase *élev̌atòr ôpeřatòr* is often quoted as containing all four degrees of stress. Alternative term: accent. (3.1, 8.22).

STRESS ACCENT → Expiratory accent.

STRESS GROUP A group of syllables containing one primary → stress.

STRESS MARK A diacritic mark placed at the beginning of a syllable to indicate that the syllable carries the main stress, e.g. ʹ*syllable* or *diaʹcritic*.

STRESS-TIMED LANGUAGE → Tempo.

STRESSED PULSE → Chest pulse.

STRICTURE The relation of an active → articulator to a passive articulator, influencing to what degree the flow of air is restricted at a particular point in the vocal tract.

STRIDENT versus MELLOW One of the basic oppositions in → distinctive feature phonology based on the analysis of a spectrogram. 'Strident' indicates high intensity with predominance of high frequencies, resulting in a weakening of the lower formants. In articulatory terms this opposition is the equivalent of 'rough-ended' versus 'smooth-edged', i.e. complex obstruction at the point of articulation *versus* less complex obstruction. English phonemes /ʒ/, /z/ have the feature strident, whereas /θ/, /ð/ are 'mellow'. → Stops are mellow whereas → fricatives, or affricates, e.g. German /p͡f/ in *Pferd* 'horse', are strident.

STRING A concatenation of elements in linear sequence. In generative grammar a terminal string is the end product of a series of rewrite rules.

STRING ANALYSIS A method of grammatical analysis which considers a sentence to consist of an elementary unit with or without adjuncts. The adjuncts may occur to the left or right of the elementary unit or any of its constituent parts. Thus a string analysis of the sentence *Today we heard three shots in the park* would be as follows: *We heard shots* is the elementary sentence; *today* is an adjunct to the left of the elementary sentence; *in the park* is an adjunct to the right of the elementary sentence; *three* is an adjunct to the left of the word *shots*. The main point of contrast between this type of analysis and → immediate constituent analysis is that language is seen here as a purely linear string, whereas immediate constituents form part of a unit of a higher level. (2.3 Harris).

STRING CONSTITUENT ANALYSIS → Tagmemics.

STRONG DECLENSION A term used to denote a certain declensional paradigm of nouns and adjectives in Germanic languages. The strong declension of adjectives in Old High German was used originally to denote 'indefinite article' as opposed to the → weak declension to denote 'definite article'. This difference can still be seen in German, e.g. weak: Old High German *der guoto man* > Modern German *der gute Mann*; strong: Old High German *ein guotêr man* > Modern German *ein guter Mann*. Alternative term: indefinite declension.

STRONG VERB A verb which changes its root vowel to change the → tense, instead of adding an inflexional ending. This feature is particularly characteristic of Germanic languages: English *sing/sang/sung*; German: *trinken/trank/getrunken*. It is, however, no longer a productive feature: most new verbs introduced into these languages are regular or → weak, i.e. they add an ending for the past tense rather than change the root.

STRUCTURAL DESCRIPTION The representation of the constituent relations of an utterance in semantic, syntactic and phonological terms. → structure.

STRUCTURAL LINGUISTICS In the widest sense, any linguistic study of a language which considers it as an independent system of sound features, grammar and vocabulary in its own right. In the narrowest sense, the term 'structural linguistics' has been used to refer to the approach of groups of European linguists such as those of the → Prague School who claimed that no

element of language can be analysed in isolation from other elements of the same language. Some linguists have equated 'structural' with → descriptive linguistics, some with → synchronic linguistics, others have seen it in opposition to → atomistic linguistics. Alternative term: structuralist(ic) linguistics, structuralism. (2.5 Lepschy).

STRUCTURAL MEANING → Meaning.

STRUCTURAL SEMANTICS Collective term for several approaches to the linguistic study of → semantics which are less concerned with 'conceptual' and 'reference' aspects of → meaning than with the 'sense relations' that may be established between words or groups of words. Linguists interested in the interchangeability or incompatibility of lexical items have used several different concepts and techniques, e.g. → semantic field and → componential analysis. (5.1, 5.2).

STRUCTURAL WORD → Function word.

STRUCTURALISM → Structural linguistics.

STRUCTURALIST(IC) LINGUISTICS → Structural linguistics.

STRUCTURE The organisation of the language as a whole and of individual linguistic elements into meaningful patterns. Thus the sentence *He may go* may be regarded as structure at various → levels: syntactically it consists of a noun phrase (here: pronoun) functioning as the 'subject' and a verb phrase (here:

auxiliary + main verb) functioning as the 'predicate'; morphologically it is characterised by distinct free 'morphemes' and the lack of inflexional endings (as compared to such forms as *his*, *him* or *goes*, *going*); the phonological structure is made up of three 'syllables' consisting of the 'phonemes' /hi/, /mei/, /gou/, accompanied by a declarative 'intonation pattern', and concluded by a 'terminal juncture'; on the level of vocabulary, the lexical items *he* (as distinct from *she* or *we*), *may* (as distinct from *can* or *should*) and *go* (as distinct from *stay* or *walk*) may be established. → paradigmatic, syntagmatic, functional relationships. (2.1, 4.2, 8.23).

STRUCTURE DRILL → Pattern drill.

STUTTER → Stammer.

STYLE The personal use an individual makes in speech or writing of the language at his disposal. The choices a speaker or writer makes from among the phonological, grammatical and lexical resources of his language have been the subject of many different approaches in → stylistics, and many definitions of style have been proposed. Traditional stylistic analysis (particularly by literary scholars) has emphasised style as the deliberate use of written language for a particular effect. Language use which 'deviates' from the literary → standard and the conventions set up by writers is in this sense described as 'bad style'. Contemporary linguists take a wider view of style, recognising the less conscious personality traits in the language of an individual speaker ('idiolect') in relation to

time, place, social environment and subject matter (→ variety in language such as 'dialect', 'manner of discourse' and 'register'). Sometimes the notion of style is extended to cover the characterisation of groups of writers and their literary output, and statistical techniques may be used to compare 'texts' or 'genres' (→ computational linguistics). (6.1 Ellis, 7.3 Crystal–Davy, 8.24 Leech).

STYLISTICS The application of linguistic knowledge to the study of → style. Traditionally stylistic analysis has been mainly concerned with the analysis of literary style or the language variety characteristic of a writer, and various criteria have been set up to deal with individual or group styles in relation to biographical, psychological, social and other details reflecting the personality of its creator. More recently, emphasis has shifted to the linguistic description of the utterance itself in terms of its components and characteristic 'deviations' from the → standard language (LINGUOSTYLISTICS), and also to a widening of the notion of style within the framework of variety studies (→ register (*b*), → manner of discourse). The study of the expressive function of sounds is called PHONOSTYLISTICS, the application of computer techniques and quantitative models is labelled STYLOSTATISTICS. (7.3, 8.24, 9.4).

STYLOSTATISTICS The use of → mathematical linguistics in analysing the → style of an author.

SUBCATEGORISATION The specification, usually by a set of → rules, of what kind of items may represent a class or category in a particular environment, e.g. when a transitive verb (but not an intransitive verb) must occur together with a noun-object.

SUB-CLAUSE → Subordinate clause.

SUBJECT A nominal phrase which may function as one of two main constituents of a sentence, the other being the → predicate. In active sentences the subject usually states the 'actor', e.g. *the black cat* in *The black cat caught the mouse*; in a passive sentence it usually states the 'goal' or 'sufferer' of the action, e.g. *the mouse* in *The mouse was caught by the cat*. In inflected languages the noun or pronoun which functions as the subject is normally in the nominative case. In English, word order may play a part in distinguishing subject and object: compare *The boy hit the ball* and *The ball hit the boy*. A distinction is sometimes made between GRAMMATICAL SUBJECT, which is expressed in the surface structure of the sentence, e.g. *the mouse* in *The mouse was caught by the cat*, the LOGICAL SUBJECT, which may not be expressed but can be postulated to be 'understood' or present only in deep structure, e.g *the cat* in *The mouse was caught (by the cat)*, and the PSYCHOLOGICAL SUBJECT which is the topic of discourse, e.g. *that book* in *That book I haven't read yet*. → topic and comment, → theme and rheme. (4.1, 4.2, 8.23).

SUBJECT COMPLEMENT → Predicate nominative.

SUBJECTIVE CASE Alternative term for → nominative case, used particularly in systems where only two case forms are distinguished, e.g. English → pronouns.

SUBJECTIVE PRONOUN → Pronoun.

SUBJUNCTIVE MODE → Subjunctive mood.

SUBJUNCTIVE MOOD A verb form which is used to indicate subordination, and considered less 'factual' than the 'indicative' →mood. Different languages have different uses for the subjunctive: French, for example, requires it after certain conjunctions, German uses it to indicate → indirect speech. Subjunctive forms in English only survive in a few instances such as *God save the Queen* or *Far be it from me* or *If I were you*, etc. Alternative term: subjunctive mode.

SUBORDINATE A word which modifies, qualifies or limits the → head word in an endocentric phrase, e.g. *very* and *old* in *the very old man*.

SUBORDINATE CLAUSE A → clause which is dependent on another clause for its full meaning and which is joined to a → main clause by means of a subordinating conjunction, e.g. in the sentence: *He was reading when I came into the room*, *when I came into the room* is a subordinate clause dependent on the main clause *He was reading*. Alternative terms: sub-clause, dependent clause, hypotactic clause. (4.1, 4.2, 8.23).

SUBORDINATING CONJUNCTION A → conjunction such as *because, although, if, that*, etc. used to introduce a → subordinate clause or to join a subordinate clause to a main clause. Alternative term: subordinator, subordinative conjunction, qualifying conjunction.

SUBORDINATION The relationship between a dependent and an independent grammatical structure. In the sentence: *He sat down because he was tired*, the clause *he was tired* is a → subordinate clause joined to the main clause by means of the subordinating conjunction *because*. (4.1, 4.2, 8.23).

SUBORDINATIVE CONJUNCTION → Subordinating conjunction.

SUBORDINATOR → Subordinating conjunction.

SUBPHONEMIC VARIANT → Allophone.

SUBSTANCE As opposed to linguistic → form, the medium by which language is transmitted. Thus the English sentence *The grass is green* can be realised as → graphic substance in writing or as → phonic substance in speech.

SUB-STANDARD A → manner of discourse which deviates in pronunciation, grammar and vocabulary from a common standard. As opposed to the neutral term non-standard, sub-standard dialects may carry a social stigma.

SUBSTANTIVE → Nominal.

SUBSTANTIVE UNIVERSAL → Universal.

SUBSTITUTION The process or result of replacing a linguistic item within a larger unit by another, e.g. /p/ in *pin* by /t/, or *home* in *I went home* by *out*, in order to find → distinctive elements or to explain a particular linguistic structure to the learner. Alternative term: contrastive substitution.

SUBSTITUTION CLASS A list of items which are in → paradigmatic relationship with one another and which can function in the same slot or → substitution frame.

SUBSTITUTION DRILL → Pattern drill.

SUBSTITUTION FRAME A sequence such as a phrase or sentence which contains 'slots' that can be filled by several variable items, e.g.

I		buy		house
he	can		a	cottage
they		afford		bungalow

Such structures are used in language teaching as → pattern drills. (4.1, 9.11).

SUBSTRATE (*a*) → Substratum. (*b*) The material substance or surface used for writing on, e.g. rock or paper. → constrate.

SUBSTRATUM The forms of a language which affect those of another, more dominant speech community, particularly the speech of the indigenous population in a colonial or culturally less advanced country, which may influence the superimposed language (→ adstratum) of a conquering or culturally more advanced power. Alternative term: Substrate. (2.1 Hall).

SUCTION STOP → Stop.

SUFFIX An → affix added to the end of a word. It may be → inflexional such as case endings in Latin or the plural ending *-s* in *boys*, or → derivational such as

-ness in *kindness, happiness,* etc. Alternative term: ending.

SUFFIXING LANGUAGE A type of language in which grammatical relationships are expressed by the addition of suffixes to a base or root word, e.g. Latin, Algonquian. (6.1, 8.1).

SUPERFICIAL STRUCTURE → Surface structure.

SUPERFIX Term used to describe the suprasegmental or prosodic features of a particular word or utterance, e.g. the stress pattern which distinguishes modifier + noun *green house* from the compound noun *greenhouse.*

SUPERIOR COMPARISON A comparative form of adjective or adverb indicating that the thing possesses more of a certain quality than another. In English the inflexional ending *-er* or the word *more* is used for this purpose, e.g. in *This one is more appropriate than that one.* → inferior comparison. Alternative term: upward comparison.

SUPERLATIVE DEGREE → Degree.

SUPERORDINATE → Hyponym.

SUPERSTRATUM The forms of a language which affect those of another, subjected speech community, e.g. the English language influencing the native speech of former colonial territories such as India or East Africa. There is evidence of considerable → borrowing, particularly of vocabulary items, from the superstratum language. (2.1 Hall).

SUPINE A form of verbal noun in Latin. A supine can be used only in the accusative or ablative case, e.g. *amātum* 'in order to love', *amātu* 'for *or* in loving' from *amo* 'I love'.

SUPPLETION The use of → suppletives, i.e. different lexical forms to replace part of a paradigm, e.g. the past tense of the English verb *to go* is *went* (from *to wend*), the perfective form of the Russian verb *говорить* 'to speak' is *сказать.*

SUPPLETIVE A substitute for a missing form in a paradigm, e.g. the past tense forms of the two English verbs *be* (*was, were*) and *go* (*went*), which are derived from different roots, or *had to* for the past tense of *must.* Alternative term: forlorn element. (2.1 Hockett, 4.2, 8.23).

SUPPOSITION In → semantics, particularly that associated with mediaeval philosophical grammar, an aspect of meaning which encompasses the actual situations in which an expression is used, as opposed to → signification or conceptual meaning and → appellation or term. (5.1).

SUPRADENTAL → Alveolar.

SUPRAGLOTTAL CAVITY → Cavity.

SUPRAGLOTTAL FRICTION → Friction.

SUPRASEGMENTAL FEATURE A feature which extends over more than one speech sound in an utterance, e.g. → pitch, → stress, → juncture. Alternative terms: superfix, plurisegmental feature, multisegmental feature. → prosodic feature. (3.1–3.4, 8.22).

SUPRASEGMENTAL GRA-PHEME A graphic sign used to represent suprasegmental features such as → stress, → pitch, → duration, etc. → prosodic sign.

SUPRASEGMENTAL PHONEME A distinctive feature of speech not restricted to one phonological segment, e.g. stress, pitch, intonation, the influence of which may spread over more than one → phoneme.

SURD Older term for → voiceless sound, as opposed to → sonant or voiced sound.

SURFACE GRAMMAR → Surface structure.

SURFACE STRUCTURE The relationship which exists between elements of an actually produced sentence as a result of the linear sequencing of these elements, as opposed to → deep structure which reveals grammatical relations which underlie the surface structure and which are not immediately apparent from it. Alternative terms: surface grammar, superficial structure. (4.1).

SUSTAINED JUNCTURE → Juncture.

SWITCHING The process of changing over from one language to another, e.g. in → translation, → interpreting, or in → bilingualism.

SYLLABARY A collection of writing signs which represent syllables. → syllabogram. (7.2).

SYLLABIC → Syllable nucleus.

SYLLABIC CONSONANT A consonant which carries the → peak of sonority in a syllable; nasals and laterals in the final position in such words as *apple* and *mutton* are often pronounced in this way, i.e. [æpl̩] and [mʌtn̩].

SYLLABIC PEAK → Peak of sonority.

SYLLABIC SIGN → Syllabogram.

SYLLABIC WRITING → Syllabography.

SYLLABICATION → Syllabification.

SYLLABIFICATION The division of words into → syllables, e.g. in phonological analysis or writing. Alternative term: syllabication. (3.1, 7.2, 8.22).

SYLLABLE Although the syllable is an intuitively easily recognisable unit there is no single definition which can account for all aspects of the term's usage. A syllable can be defined in various ways, but essentially from three basic points of view: (*i*) physical or motor definition, which usually characterises it as an utterance occurring during one → chest pulse, i.e. one contraction of the intercostal muscles during exhalation of air from the lungs. In this sense the syllable is the minimum utterance since at least one such chest pulse must be involved, no matter how short an utterance we make; (*ii*) in articulatory phonetics a syllable is defined as a stretch of utterance containing one → peak of sonority occurring between two structures characterised by lack of sonority; (*iii*) in structural or phonological definitions the syllable is considered as a structure consisting of a sequence of phonemes (or a single phoneme, e.g. /n/ in English /bʌtn̩/ is a single phoneme but constitutes a → syllable nucleus, together with other features such as length or stress. There is usually considerable correspondence between syllables established phonetically and syllables established phonologically, but there is not always complete agreement. For example in the case of an intervocalic consonant VCV (where V = any vowel and C = any consonant—the usual notation for describing syllabic structure) phonetically the syllable boundary would probably occur during the articulation of the C element since this is where the greatest degree of stricture and the minimum of sonority occurs. A phonological decision, however, usually assigns the C to the following syllable. This decision is based on the fact that CV, i.e. a syllable ending in a vowel, called an OPEN SYLLABLE or FREE SYLLABLE, is universal to all known languages and hence more common than any other syllable structure. Except for the structure CV above which is universal, all languages have their own rules with regard to syllable structure. Other structures VC, CVC, V, do not occur in all languages. Some languages, e.g. Fijian, permit no syllables ending in a consonant (also called BLOCKED SYLLABLES or CHECKED SYLLABLES). Arabic, for example, only permits syllables beginning with a consonant. English and German both permit a good deal of consonant clustering both at the beginning and at the end of the

syllable, but where consonant clusters are permitted the rules describing which phonemes are allowed to cluster at which point in the syllable differ for each language and constitute an important feature of the → phonemic structure of a language. A phonological syllable is usually divided into three parts, ONSET, the initial sound or sounds occurring before the NUCLEUS, the central part, coinciding with the phonetic PEAK OF SONORITY, and the CODA, the final sound or sounds occurring after the nucleus. The terms MARGINAL ELEMENTS or SLOPES are sometimes used to refer to onset and coda collectively. It follows from what was said above that not all syllables in all languages possess all three elements and the only compulsory element is the nucleus, the distribution of onset and coda depending on the phonological structure of a particular language. → tempo. (3.1, 3.4, 8.22).

SYLLABLE NUCLEUS The sound which carries the → peak of sonority in a syllable, e.g. [æ] is the nucleus of the syllable [kæt] *cat*, [s] is the nucleus of the syllable [pst]. Alternative terms: syllabic, nucleus, centre. (3.1–3.4, 8.22).

SYLLABLE SIGN → Syllabogram.

SYLLABLE-TIMED LANGUAGE → Tempo.

SYLLABLE WRITING → Syllabography.

SYLLABOGRAM A graphic sign used in some systems of writing, e.g. Mesopotamian cuneiform, West Semitic syllabary, Hindi devanagari,

Japanese kana, to represent a → syllable. Syllabic signs are believed to be derived from → logograms where words are represented by pictorial signs, and later to have developed into more sound-based → letter signs of alphabets. → Table p. 264. Alternative terms: syllabic sign, syllable sign. (7.2).

SYLLABOGRAPHY A system of writing using → syllabograms, i.e. graphic signs representing → syllables. Alternative terms: syllabic writing, syllable writing. (7.2).

SYMBOL (*a*) An invented mark or sign representing a linguistic entity (sound, sound feature, phoneme, syllable, morpheme, word) which may be conventionalised in phonetic transcription or writing systems, e.g. letters of an alphabet, Chinese characters, Egyptian hieroglyphs, etc. (*b*) → Sign (*b*).

SYMBOLIC SIGN → Sign (*b*).

SYMMETRICAL PATTERNING The principle that the sound system of a language tends to have a symmetrical pattern of contrasts. A language which has three voiceless stops /p/, /t/, /k/ in contrast to each other and which uses voicing as a distinctive feature is likely to have three voiced stops /b/, /d/, /g/ corresponding exactly to the voiceless stops. Not all languages have this feature: there are some notable exceptions, e.g. Dutch has /p/, /t/, /k/ in the voiceless stops but only /b/ and /d/ in the voiced series. (3.1–3.4).

SYNAESTHESIA The associating of a particular sound or group of sounds with a particular meaning, e.g. *fl-* in *flare, flicker, flame, flash, flick, fleeting,* etc. Such a combination of sounds is called a PHONAESTHEME or PHONESTHEME and such a series of words a PHONAESTHETIC SERIES or CONGENERIC GROUP. Alternative term: sound symbolism.

SYNCHRONIC LINGUISTICS An approach to language studies in which the forms of one or more languages are investigated at one particular stage of their development. The synchronic study of language as carried out in the first half of the 20th century was a reaction against the predominantly → diachronic approach of 19th-century comparative philology in which the emphasis was on language → change through history. Today the value of both synchronic and diachronic linguistics is generally recognised. Alternative term: static linguistics. (2.1, 2.4 Saussure, 2.5 Robins).

SYNCOPE The loss of one or more sounds or letters from the middle of a word, e.g. Latin *domina* 'lady' > Italian *donna*, or English *extraordinary* pronounced [ekstrɔːdṇrɪ]. → Table p. 75.

SYNCRETISM The loss of → inflexional endings, resulting in the merging of inflexional forms which were once distinct, e.g. Old English *stan* (nominative) and *stāne* (dative) have merged into Modern English *stone*. → deflexion. (6.1, 8.21).

SYNDESIS → Polysyndeton.

SYNDETIC CONSTRUCTION → Syndeton.

SYNDETON A construction, parts of which are linked together by means of conjunctions or joining words, e.g. in *He came and went again*. → asyndeton. Alternative term: syndetic construction.

SYNERESIS The process or result of pronouncing a → vowel cluster as a diphthong in a single syllable. → diaeresis.

SYNESIS Syntactic agreement based on the meaning of a word rather than its grammatical form, e.g. *The crew are in good spirits*, where a collective noun which is usually singular in form takes a plural verb.

SYNONYM One of two or more words with identical meaning. True or pure synonyms, i.e. words which can be substituted for each other in all contexts are rare, e.g. *buy/purchase* or *stop/occlusive* (in phonetics). → antonym, near-synonym. (5.1, 5.2).

SYNONYMY The relationship between → synonyms.

SYNTACTIC CATEGORY A class to which a unit is assigned as a result of its relationship with other words in a syntactic construction. The constituents of a sentence, e.g. subject, predicate, object, complement, etc. are syntactic categories.

SYNTACTIC CHANGE A → grammatical change which affects the way words are linked to form larger constructions, e.g. when an originally intransitive verb like *convert* or *remember* is used with a direct object.

SYNTACTIC COMPONENT Part of a → transformational-generative grammar consisting of phrase structure and transformation rules which generate and assign a syntactic structure to sentences of a given language.

SYNTACTIC COMPOUND A → compound word consisting of two or more free forms which have a relationship similar to that which they would have in a phrase, e.g. *armchair* 'a chair with arms', *flagpole* 'a pole for a flag', etc. as opposed to a → synthetic compound in which one part of the compound is a bound form and cannot occur on its own, e.g. *untie*, *recover*, etc.

SYNTACTIC CONSTRUCTION The result of putting together free forms in a way which is in agreement with the rules of syntax for a given language, e.g. *He came home by train yesterday* as opposed to **Yesterday by came train he home*. (4.1, 4.2, 8.23).

SYNTACTIC DOUBLET Two forms of the same → morpheme, choice between which is determined by environment or function in the sentence, e.g. English *a, an*.

SYNTACTIC GROUP → Phrase.

SYNTACTIC ORDER → Word order.

SYNTACTIC PATTERN → Sentence pattern.

SYNTACTICS (*a*) The system and study of the characteristic arrangement of syntactic units in sequence. → syntax. (*b*) A branch of

→ semiotics studying the relationships existing between → symbols in relation to each other.

SYNTAGM(A) (*a*) A general term for any string of units which together form a complex larger unit, e.g. any string of words which have syntagmatic relations such as *over the hill, the green trees, no smoking, birds fly,* etc. (*b*) Used by some linguists as an alternative term for → taxeme.

SYNTAGMATIC The 'horizontal' relationship between linguistic elements forming linear sequences, e.g. in the sentence *Come quickly* there is a syntagmatic relationship between the words *come* and *quickly,* and on a different level between the phonemes /k/, /ʌ/ and /m/ in the word /kʌm/. → paradigmatic.

SYNTAGMEME In → tagmemics a group of tagmemes at one level representing a tagmeme of a higher level. A string of morphemes may represent a word, a string of words a phrase, a string of phrases a clause, etc. The rank scale of → systemic grammar deals similarly with a grammatical hierarchy.

SYNTAX That branch of → grammar which is concerned with the study of the arrangement of words in sentences and of the means by which such relationships are shown, e.g. word order or inflexion. → morphology. (4.1, 4.2, 8.23).

SYNTHESIS The process or result of combining elements to form utterances, e.g. by the addition of an inflexional or derivational ending

to a word, or by mechanical production of speech. → linguistic analysis, → speech synthesis, → synthetic language. (2.1, 4.2, 9.11).

SYNTHETIC COMPOUND A → compound word at least one part of which consists of a bound form which cannot occur on its own, e.g. *telescope, return,* etc. as opposed to a → syntactic compound which consists of free forms which have relationship similar to that which they would have in a phrase, e.g. *bookshelf* 'a shelf for books', *lawnmower* 'a mower for the lawn', etc.

SYNTHETIC INDEX → Index (*b*).

SYNTHETIC LANGUAGE A type of language such as Latin, Arabic and Finnish, in which syntactical relationships are shown by → inflexion and the close merging of affixes with the base or root, as opposed to → analytic languages. → inflected language. (6.1, 8.1).

SYSTEM (*a*) A term used to describe a language as an organised whole, with each of its component parts functioning according to an overall convention of usage to enable the members of a speech community to interchange information. Most linguists agree on the view of language as a 'system of systems', i.e. the arrangement of units on hierarchically ordered and inter-related → levels. (*b*) The relationships between the members of a paradigmatic class, e.g. number (singular or plural) or gender (masculine, feminine, neuter). → systemic grammar. (2.1, 4.1).

SYSTEMATIC PHONEMIC REPRESENTATION → Phonology.

SYSTEMATIC PHONETIC REPRESENTATION → Phonology.

SYSTEMATIC PHONOLOGICAL REPRESENTATION → Phonology.

SYSTEMATIC TRANSCRIPTION A → phonetic transcription relying to a certain extent on the phonetician's knowledge of the sound system of the language being transcribed, as opposed to an → impressionistic transcription.

SYSTEMIC GRAMMAR A theory of → linguistic analysis developed by the British linguist M. A. K. Halliday from J. R. Firth's theories. A set of categories and levels is established to account for the 'formal' aspect of language. The three primary 'levels' are: FORM (organisation of substance into meaningful events, i.e. grammar and lexis), SUBSTANCE (phonic and graphic material), and CONTEXT (relations between 'form' and 'situation', i.e. semantics). The four fundamental categories are: UNIT (a pattern-carrying segment at any level, e.g. sentence, clause, tone group), STRUCTURE (the syntagmatic arrangement of patterns, e.g. the 'clause-structure' subject – predicator – complement – adjunct), CLASS (set of items operating with a given function in a higher structure, e.g. nominal group, syllable) and SYSTEM (paradigmatic arrangement of classes in 'choice' relation). In addition, three 'scales' have been set up to inter-relate the categories within the theory and

the observed speech events: the scale of RANK refers to the hierarchical arrangement of units, e.g. from sentence to morpheme or from tone group to phoneme; the scale of EXPONENCE relates the categories to the data, e.g. the class 'noun' is represented by the particular lexical item *man*; and the scale of DELICACY differentiates certain relationships in depth, e.g. subdividing 'clause' into 'concessive' and other types of clause. Some of the main principles of systemic grammar are being applied to the description of the varieties of English (→ register (*b*)) and to the teaching of English in schools. → cline. Alternative terms: scale-and-category grammar, system-structure grammar, Neo-Firthian linguistics. (2.1 Wilkinson, 8.23 Scott *et al.*, 9.11 Halliday *et al.*).

SYSTEM-STRUCTURE GRAMMAR → Systemic Grammar.

T

TABOO The avoidance of embarrassing words in certain circumstances. Taboo words are either avoided completely or substituted by → euphemisms, e.g. *powder room* for *ladies' lavatory*. Alternative term: linguistic taboo. (5.1, 10.1).

TACHYGRAPHY The use of shorthand or abbreviated writing for the sake of speed. (7.2).

TACTICS The system and study of the characteristic arrangement of linguistic units in sequence. Such tactic rules may be established at several levels of linguistic analysis: PHONOTACTICS refers to the way speech sounds combine in a particular language; MORPHOTACTICS and SYNTACTICS are concerned with the arrangement of grammatical units such as morphemes, words and phrases; LEXOTACTICS and SEMOTACTICS control the ways in which lexical items can be combined and the sense relations between them. → selection restriction. (4.2 Lamb).

TAG QUESTION A short interrogative formula placed at the end of a declarative statement, e.g. *isn't it?* or *wouldn't it?* in English, *n'est-ce pas?* in French, or *nicht wahr?* in German. Alternative term: confirmational interrogative.

TAGMA In → tagmemics the minimum unit of substance as opposed to the tagmeme which is the minimum unit of form. Tagma is to tagmeme as phone is to phoneme and morph to morpheme.

TAGMEME The basic unit of form in → tagmemics. It is the correlation of a slot and the class of items which can occur in that slot. In the sentence *The book is on the table*, *the book* fills the subject slot and the subject tagmeme is manifested by *the book*. Alternative term: grammeme (obsolete). (2.5 Cook).

TAGMEMIC ANALYSIS → Tagmemics.

TAGMEMICS A school of → linguistic analysis based on the work of K. L. Pike. Language is seen as being structured into three semi-autonomous but interlocking levels

or MODES: phonology, grammar and lexicon. Pike and his followers reject the → sentence as the basic unit of grammar, and stress instead the hierarchical ordering of grammatical units into ranks or LEVELS (morphemes, words, phrases, clauses, sentences, paragraphs, discourses). The basic unit is the TAGMEME which is both a grammatical function or SLOT and the class of items filling that slot, e.g. the word *I* denoting 'actor-as-subject' in the utterance *I don't care.* Tagmemes combine to form 'syntagmemes' or strings of collateral constituents (STRING CONSTITUENT ANALYSIS). Some of these concepts have been employed in the description of American Indian languages, mainly under the auspices of the American Summer Institute of Linguistics. (2.5 Cook).

TALKING → Language acquisition.

TAMBER → Timbre.

TAMBRE → Timbre.

TAP A speech sound produced by a single momentary contact between → articulators, as opposed to a → trill where there may be several rapid vibrations between articulators. Many phoneticians and linguists distinguish between this type of sound and a → flap.

TAPE RECORDER An electro-mechanical device for recording and reproducing sound by means of magnetic tape. As the tape passes the recording head, the iron oxide particles on the tape are magnetized into certain patterns corresponding to the impulses received from the source, e.g. microphone or other tape recorder. During playback this procedure is reversed: an electro-magnet converts the magnetic patterns into electric impulses which are amplified and reproduced as sound through a loudspeaker or earphones. Tape recorders, developed towards the end of the first half of this century, have revolutionised the study of sound, and in teaching have done for the spoken language what books did for written language. They play a very important part in modern → phonetics, → dialectology, and many fields of → applied linguistics including speech therapy and language teaching, particularly in → language laboratories. → field-work.

TARGET LANGUAGE The language into which an original text is translated or into which a loan word is borrowed. In language teaching, the foreign language being taught. → source language.

TA-TA THEORY → Origin of speech.

TAUTOLOGY The use of → redundancy in speech or writing, e.g. the use of *absolutely* and *positively* together in *I'm absolutely positively sure*. Alternative term: pleonasm.

TAUTOPHONY Two rhyming words used contiguously, e.g. *boiling oil*.

TAXEME A significant feature of syntactic relationship such as inflexion (e.g. *The boy kicks the ball* as opposed to *The boys kick the ball*), word order (e.g. *John invited Mary* as opposed to *Mary invited John*), or stress (e.g. *I saw 'him* as opposed to *'I saw him*). Alternative term: grammatical feature. (2.4 Bloomfield).

TAXONOMIC LINGUISTICS An approach to linguistic analysis and description which looks at language phenomena with the primary aim of listing and classifying them into groups, e.g. → parts of speech in grammar, types of → consonants in phonetics, or → lexical fields in semantics. Followers of → transformational-generative grammar have often criticised such taxonomic descriptions as lacking a systematic theoretical framework.

TAXONOMIC PHONEMICS Term coined by N. Chomsky to refer to phonological procedures based on segmentation and classification.

TECHNICAL TRANSLATION → Translation.

TEETH RIDGE → Alveolar ridge.

TEKNONYMIC A name given to a parent, based on the name of a child. → matronymic, patronymic.

TELESCOPED WORD → Blend.

TEMPO The rate of articulation, usually measured in terms of syllables per second. Tempo is closely related to rhythm, and different languages have different characteristics in this respect. A STRESS-TIMED LANGUAGE such as English, German or Russian has stressed syllables occurring at approximately equal time intervals, irrespective of how many unstressed syllables occur between them. This feature, called ISOCHRONISM, results in unstressed syllables increasing in tempo according to the number occurring together between stressed syllables. Compare, for example, the tempo of the following sentences in terms of speed at which one syllable follows another:

He′ met′ two′ old′ school′ friends′.
What′ could he have said′ to them if he had chanced to see′ them in the street′.

A SYLLABLE-TIMED LANGUAGE such as French, on the other hand, has the feature known as ISOSYLLABISM where each syllable takes up approximately the same amount of time in an utterance whether spoken at slow or rapid tempo. → rhythm. (3.1, 3.4).

TEMPORAL CLAUSE
An adverbial → clause referring to the time when an action takes place, e.g. *when he comes* in *I shall see him when he comes.*

TEMPORAL DIALECT
A variety or → dialect of a language which was used at a particular stage in its historical development.

TENSE
Grammatical category of the verb expressing by means of grammatical contrasts the time relationship of the action referred to in the sentence and the time of utterance. Traditional grammar distinguished three basic tenses: past, present, and future. This tripartite distinction is by no means a universal feature: some languages have no tense forms at all, in others tense interacts with the categories of → aspect and mood. The basic distinction in English is between past and non-past, e.g. *walk(s)* is non-past whereas *walked* is 'past', but either form can combine with certain con-

junctions and adverbials to express circumstances independent of 'time', e.g. *If you went to the party...*, or *He comes here every day.* What is traditionally referred to as the 'future tense' in English, formed with the auxiliaries *will* and *shall*, is as much a question of → mood as tense, and the so-called 'perfect tenses' are now usually considered as → aspects. (4.1, 4.2, 8.23).

TENSE versus LAX
One of the basic oppositions in → distinctive feature phonology based on the analysis of a → spectrogram. 'Tense' indicates longer duration of constant state of a sound and a sharply defined resonance region in the spectrum. 'Lax' indicates shorter duration of constant state and lack of sharply defined resonance. In articulatory terms tense sounds involve greater movement of the vocal tract from its neutral central position than is the case for lax sounds. Tension in the muscles affecting the tongue and the walls of the vocal tract may also play a part here. In traditional terms the 'fortis' consonants in English /p/, /t/, /k/ are tense and the 'lenis' consonants /b/, /d/, /g/ are lax. In the case of vowels, long vowels tend to be tense and short vowels lax. Some languages have an opposition between tense and lax vowels, e.g. in French *saute* 'jump' (tense) as opposed to *sotte* 'fool' (lax) or *pâte* 'paste' (tense) as opposed to *patte* 'paw' (lax).

TENSE VOWEL
Tension in the muscles of the mouth and throat can greatly affect the quality of a vowel. A tense vowel is produced with more muscular tension than a → lax vowel, e.g. [i:] as in *beat* is a

tense vowel, whereas [ɪ] in *bit* is a lax vowel. This change in tension can be felt by placing the thumb and forefinger under the lower jaw whilst pronouncing the words one after the other.

TENUES Older term for voiceless → stops, e.g. [p], [t], [k]. → mediae. (3.1, 6.1).

TERM A vocabulary item which has a special meaning in a particular subject field, e.g. *sound* or *voice* in phonetics, or *butterfly* in swimming.

TERM OF ENDEARMENT A word or words used to show an affectionate relationship between the speaker and the person or thing to which reference is made. In many languages endearment is indicated by the use of → diminutive forms, e.g. English *pussikins* and the frequent collocation *dear little*.

TERMINAL JUNCTURE Alternative term for → juncture.

TERMINAL STRESS → Stress on the last syllable of a word, e.g. in words such as *a'bout*, *a'long* or *under'stand*.

TERMINAL STRING A → string which is the result of applying all the appropriate phrase structure rules in a → transformational-generative grammar. The elements which make up a terminal string are called formatives, e.g. Det, Nom, etc. in a terminal string such as Det + Nom + Vt + det + Nom which, after words have been substituted from the lexicon, could become a sentence such as *The boy kicks the ball*. Transformation rules operate on terminal strings.

TERMINOLOGY The sum total of → terms used in a particular subject, e.g. chemistry or phonetics or swimming, and contained in special glossaries and dictionaries. The effectiveness and possibility of → standardisation of technical terminology has been the subject of serious discussion in → lexicography. (5.1, 5.2 Zgusta).

TERRITORIAL DIALECT A regional → dialect.

TERTIARY STRESS → Stress.

TESSITURA Term borrowed from musical nomenclature to refer to the range of pitch of a voice during normal speech. A high or low tessitura is a characteristic of some speech communities compared with others. (3.1 Abercrombie).

TEST BATTERY → Testing.

TESTING The setting of exercises and tasks to measure either the student's aptitude for a particular subject or his achievement in a particular subject. Tests in → language teaching should be related to the aim of the instruction, and ideally all linguistic skills taught (comprehension, speaking, reading, writing) should be represented in language examinations. A TEST BATTERY consists of a set of test items assessing a number of different skills. → error analysis. (9.14).

TEXT A sequence of words forming an actual utterance in a language. Texts may either be transcriptions or recorded material or the result of writing down a work of → literature or a piece of information (→ message). In all of these cases the text is considered by linguists as a document containing a sample of a particular variety of language, and serves as the basis for → linguistic analysis and description. Often texts are the only clue to obtaining data about extinct languages. In → language teaching, work with texts plays an important part, either for illustrating special varieties or 'styles' in the language, or for translation and comprehension exercises. (6.1, 7.1–7.3, 8.24, 9.1).

THEMATIC INFLEXION An inflexion occurring between the root of a word and any other inflexional endings, e.g. the inflexions *-er-*, *-ir-*, *-r-* in the future tense of French verbs: *je donnerai* 'I shall give', *je finirai* 'I shall finish', *je vendrai* 'I shall sell'. → athematic.

THEME A collective term for those → morphemes in a word which are not affixes and which indicate semantic rather than grammatical features, e.g. the base or root *luck* and the stem *lucky* of such words as *luckier* or *unlucky*.

THEME and RHEME Constituents of a sentence similar to those of → topic and comment. The theme is the first element in the sentence and states what is being talked about, thus giving the starting point for the information given in the remainder of the sentence. Whereas topic and comment are restricted to clause and sentence structure, theme and rheme are more concerned with information structure. (2.5 Vachek, 4.2 Sgall).

THEORETICAL LINGUISTICS → Linguistics.

THEORY OF MEANING Collective term for the study of → meaning either by linguists or by scholars in related disciplines such as philosophy. → semantics.

THESAURUS In lexicography, a list or dictionary of lexical items, usually of the more common word-classes such as nouns, grouped together by their common or related meaning. One example in English is Roget's *Thesaurus* which classifies the vocabulary according to conceptual fields. → synonym. (5.1, 5.2, 8.25).

THIRD PERSON → Person.

THIRD PERSON IMPERATIVE → Mood.

THORN The name of the runic symbol ð used in Old and Middle English manuscripts.

THOUGHT and LANGUAGE The relationships between man's intellectual and linguistic activities on the one hand and the outside world on the other has exercised the interest of linguists, psychologists and philosophers for generations. This covers such unsolved problems as how a child acquires language (→ developmental linguistics), how our conceptualisations may be determined by the language system in which we live (→ relativity), whether 'silent' speech and reading are possible without vocalisation, how language is used for argument and reasoning (→ logic in language), and how language symbols refer to concrete and abstract entities (→ meaning). (10.2).

THRESHOLD OF HEARING The lowest → amplitude which can be heard by the human ear at a certain frequency. → audible area.

THRESHOLD OF PAIN The highest → amplitude of sound at a given frequency which can be heard by the human ear without pain. → audible area.

TIGHT PHONATION → Register (*a*).

TILDE A → diacritic mark used in phonetic transcription to indicate → nasalisation, e.g. French *bon* [bõ] 'good', and in some orthographies to indicate → palatalisation, e.g. Spanish *señor*.

TIMBRE Features of → quality of a vowel sound. There is no distinct boundary line to be drawn phonetically between oral and nasal, front and back, or rounded and unrounded, etc. A predominantly oral vowel may have traces of 'nasality' and can be said to have a 'nasal timbre'; similarly with other qualities. Alternative terms: tambre, tamber, colouring, tone-colour. (3.1, 8.22).

TIME DEPTH A formula used in → glottochronology, but by no means widely accepted as being valid, to determine the length of time for which two related languages have been separated:

$$t = \frac{\log c}{2\log r},$$

where *t* stands for time depth, *c* the percentage of → cognates in the two languages, and *r* the percentage of cognates retained after 1,000 years of separation. (6.1 Lehmann).

TMESIS The division of a word into its component parts by the interpolation of another word or words, e.g. German *woher* in *Wo kommen Sie her?* 'Where do you come from?'

TOKEN → Type and token.

TONAL QUALITY → Voice quality.

TONALITY FEATURES → Distinctive feature.

TONE A significant → pitch contour in a tone language. Mandarin Chinese, for example, has four tones: (1) high level, (2) high rising, (3) falling and rising, (4) falling. In tone languages such as Chinese these features are used to distinguish between words and/or grammatical categories. → intonation. Alternative term: lexical tone. (3.4 Pike).

TONE COLOUR → Timbre.

TONE LANGUAGE A language in which → tone or pitch patterns form part of the structure of words rather than sentences. Alternative term: polytonic language. (3.4 Pike).

TONE OF VOICE The distinctive individual characteristic of a person's voice by which we recognise it as the voice of a particular individual. → voice qualifier, register (*a*).

TONEME A particular feature of → pitch which in a tone language distinguishes two otherwise identical words or forms. There are four tonemes in one variety of modern Chinese: high as in *bā* 'eight', rising as in *bá* 'to uproot', falling and rising as in *bǎ* 'to hold', and falling as in *bà* 'harrow'. (3.1–3.4).

TONETICS The system and study of pitch and → tone in speech.

TONGUE The most important articulator in the vocal tract. For reference it is divided into several parts, e.g. BLADE (including the tip or

apex) or FRONT; CENTRE or TOP; BACK
or DORSUM (including the ROOT). →
Diagram p. 159. (3.1, 8.22, 9.5).

TONIC A sound or syllable
carrying the main → stress. → atonic.

TOPIC and COMMENT In
several different models of analysing
utterances, linguists and philosophers
have claimed that most sentences
have two basic constituents, the
subject that is announced and the
statement that is made about it.
Thus in the sentence *John came to
see me* the topic is *John* and the
comment is *came to see me*. One
characteristic of the topic is that it
usually occurs before the comment.
This would make topic and comment
synonymous with the traditional
notions of → subject and predicate.
However, in the following example
the topic, *Those plants he gave me
yesterday* is not identical with the
grammatical subject *I*: *Those plants
he gave me yesterday I'll put in this
afternoon.* Some languages, e.g.
Japanese, have special particles to
mark the topic of the sentence, and
for such languages the topic/com-
ment division is a more satisfactory
analysis than the subject/predicate
division. Topic and comment refer
to clause and sentence structure,
whereas → theme and rheme (and
'given' and 'new') are more concerned with information structure
which is often expressed by distinctive intonation contours. (2.1
Hockett).

TOPONOMASIOLOGY →
Toponymy.

TOPONOMASTICS →
Toponymy.

TOPONOMATOLOGY →
Toponymy.

TOPONYMIC A place name.

TOPONYMY That branch of →
onomastics which studies place
names. Alternative terms: toponomatology, toponomastics,
toponomasiology.

TOTAL ASSIMILATION →
Assimilation.

TOTAL DISSIMILATION →
Dissimilation.

TRACHEA The passage leading
from the lungs to the larynx. →
Diagram p. 159. Alternative term:
windpipe.

TRADE LANGUAGE A
language used by people of different
native tongues as a means of
communication for commercial purposes. → pidgin, contact vernacular,
lingua franca. (8.8 Hall).

TRADITIONAL GRAMMAR
→ Grammar.

TRANSCRIPTION The
reduction of speech to a written
form. Alphabetic transcription may
be PHONETIC, i.e. attempt to represent
all sounds in as much detail as
possible, e.g. [tʰɛɳθ] indicating aspiration of the initial [t] and dental
articulation of the [n]; PHONEMIC or
SYSTEMATIC, i.e. use one symbol per
phoneme irrespective of phonetic
variants, e.g. /tenθ/, ignoring the
features indicated above; or ORTHO-
GRAPHIC, i.e. adhere to the rules of
standard spelling for a given language, e.g. *tenth*. → phonetic transcription, → notation. (3.1–3.4, 8.22).

TRANSFER (*a*) The process or result of carrying over grammatical forms from one language to another. In → language teaching, for example, the patterns of the mother tongue may interfere in the acquisition of those of the foreign language, or in → translation lexical items may be borrowed from the source language, e.g. *sputnik* from Russian. → interference.

(*b*) The process or result of converting the symbols of speech into a different medium, e.g. the graphic signs of → writing. In the transfer from written letters to the signals of a code, the symbols are twice removed from the original ones, although the communicated information remains the same.

(*c*) → Transferred meaning.

TRANSFERRED MEANING Figurative or metaphorical use of a word, e.g. when *eyes* are described as *the windows of the soul*.

home into the interrogative sentence *Does he go home?* or embedding: *The man is at the corner* with *The man is my uncle* to form *The man at the corner is my uncle*. The process of transformation is used in formulating → transformation rules in a transformational-generative grammar. (4.2, 8.23).

TRANSFORMATION RULE In → transformational-generative grammar a rule which lays down procedures for converting one grammatical pattern into another. Such a rule may change one sentence type into another, delete or add elements, change the order of elements, or substitute one element for another. Transformation rules operate on the output, i.e. the terminal string of the → phrase structure rules, e.g. the transformation rule: NP + Pas + *be* + X ⇒ Pas + *be* + NP + X (where NP = noun phrase; Pas = past tense; X = any construction) could change a declarative sentence to an interrogative sentence, as follows:

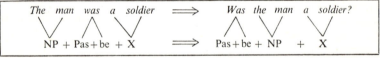

TRANSFORM A syntactic structure which is said to be derived from a basic or kernel sentence by a series of → transformations and/or deletion rules. Thus the sentence *The red book is on the table* may be regarded as a transform of the two kernel sentences *The book is on the table* and *The book is red*.

TRANSFORMATION The process or result of changing one linguistic structure or structures into another according to certain rules, e.g. the declarative sentence *He goes*

TRANSFORMATIONAL-GENERATIVE GRAMMAR A linguistic theory based on the work of the American N. Chomsky, who criticised most schools of traditional and structural linguistics as being 'taxonomic', i.e. as merely labelling and listing phonetic, grammatical and other units, and thus neglecting the underlying processes of human speech. According to Chomsky the object of linguistic analysis must be to discover what is universal and regular in man's innate ability to understand and produce new

240

'grammatical' sentences although he may never have heard them before (→ competence/performance). Grammar in this sense must account for all the sentences which may be formed in a language and judged 'correct' by the linguistic intuition of native speakers. Accepting the notion of sentence as a basic unit, relationships between items in the structure of a sentence are described in terms of abstract statements called → phrase structure rules and → transformation rules. The phrase structure rules describe the basic structures of the language concerned, whereas more complicated structures lend themselves to description as transformations of basic structures by means of transformation rules. In the earliest type of transformational-generative grammar, the rules themselves are usually referred to in terms of three 'components': firstly, the phrase structure component consisting of phrase structure rules, secondly, transformation component producing strings of → formatives; and thirdly, a morphophonemic component, a series of rules converting the string of formatives into a phonetic representation. In a later exposition of a more comprehensive theory Chomsky added a SEMANTIC COMPONENT, having come to the conclusion that meaning should have the same formal treatment as syntax. Semantics was now included as an integral part of the grammatical analysis of a language. The emphasis in transformational-generative grammar is on the elaboration of a logically consistent theory which can adequately explain and formulate explicitly the → deep structure of sentences. (2.1 Chomsky, 2.5 Chomsky, Lyons, 3.4 Harms, Postal, 4.1 Burt, Fowler, 5.2 Fill-

more–Langendoen, 6.2 King, 8.22 Chomsky–Halle, 8.23 Jacobs–Rosenbaum, etc.).

TRANSFORMATIONAL GRAMMAR A grammar which uses transformation rules in its description of a language. The most highly developed grammar of this type is the → transformational-generative grammar developed by Chomsky and his associates.

TRANSFORMED SENTENCE A sentence produced after the application of transformation rules in a → transformational-generative grammar. Alternative term: derived sentence.

TRANSITION A phonological feature relating to the way in which sounds are joined together. Two types of transition are distinguished by most linguists: (i) OPEN TRANSITION (OPEN JUNCTURE), represented in transcription by means of ⟨+⟩ and often called PLUS JUNCTURE, which occurs at a word boundary and distinguishes, e.g. /ən+eim/ *an aim* from /ə neim/ *a name*. An open transition between speech sounds within a word, e.g. in *co-operative*, is called INTERNAL OPEN JUNCTURE or INTERNAL HIATUS. (ii) CLOSE TRANSITION (CLOSE JUNCTURE), represented in transcription by writing symbols in sequence without a space, which occurs in the normal unbroken sequence of one sound to the next, e.g. /k/, /a/, /t/ > /kat/. Some linguists use the term → juncture where others use the term transition, but this use of the term *juncture* must be distinguished from its use in the sense of → terminal juncture. (3.1–3.4, 8.22).

TRANSITION AREA → Area.

TRANSITIONAL SOUND → Glide (*b*).

TRANSITIVE VERB A verb used with a direct object, e.g. in the sentence *The boy kicks the ball*, as opposed to the → intransitive verb in *The horse kicks*. Many verbs in English can be used transitively or intransitively without change of form, but in some languages the form of a verb determines its usage as either one or the other but not both, e.g. in German *beantworten* 'to answer' can only be used transitively: *Er beantwortete die Frage* 'he answered the question' whereas *antworten* 'to answer' can only be used intransitively: e.g. *Er antwortet nicht* 'he doesn't answer'. (4.1, 4.2, 8.23).

TRANSITIVITY Those grammatical features which are used systematically to express certain relationships between the participants in a communicative situation and the actions, states or circumstances in which they are involved. → transitive verb, clause pattern. (2.1 Lyons).

TRANSLATION The process or result of converting information from one language or language variety into another. In translating written or recorded material of natural languages, the aim is to reproduce as accurately as possible all grammatical and lexical features of the 'source language' original by finding equivalents in the 'target language'. At the same time all factual information contained in the original text or recording must be retained in the translation. The criterion of genuine equivalence of expression has been called 'fluency', that of corresponding content 'fidelity' or 'faithfulness'. Various types of translation have been distinguished. Depending on how closely the grammatical and other linguistic features of the two languages correspond, a translation may be WORD-FOR-WORD (or T_1 in the example below) in which the words of the source language text are rendered one by one into the target language without making any allowances for grammatical or lexical differences between them, LITERAL (or T_2) in which a few adjustments are made on the phrase level, and FREE (or IDIOMATIC or T_3) which reads like an original text.

Original: *It's pouring (with rain)*.
T_1 (German): **Es ist gießend (mit Regen)*.
T_2: **Es gießt (mit Regen)*.
T_3: *Es gießt*, or: *Es regnet in Strömen*.
Depending on the subject matter of the text, one can distinguish LITERARY TRANSLATION (of poetry, drama and other literary works), where the emphasis is on emotive connotations and stylistic features, and PRAGMATIC TRANSLATION (of technical, commercial and other material) where the emphasis is on conveying factual information. Oral translation is called → INTERPRETING, translation by computer or other mechanical means → MACHINE TRANSLATION. Through language teaching (→ grammar-translation method), bilingualism and other linguistic contact between different languages, translation may contribute to → borrowing and → change. (9.3).

TRANSLATOR A person engaged in → translation.

TRANSLITERATION The process or result of representing the graphic signs of one writing system, e.g. Chinese logographic characters, by the graphic signs of another script, e.g. letters of Latin alphabet. Internationally standardised codes for this conversion are available, e.g. for the → romanisation of Cyrillic writings. (7.2, 8.5 Shaw).

TRANSMUTATION The process or result of changing the class of a word either without changing its form, e.g. in English the word *drink* can be a noun as in *Have a drink!* or a verb as in *If you're thirsty, you must drink*, or by a change in stress or other suprasegmental feature, e.g. *cónvèrt* (noun) as opposed to *cŏnvért* (verb). Alternative terms: functional change, conversion. (4.1, 4.2, 8.23).

TREE DIAGRAM An illustration of the genealogical relationship between languages of one family (→ family tree) or the grammatical relationships between the words in a sentence (→ phrase structure rule).

TREMA → Diaeresis.

TRIADIC THEORY OF MEANING → Semantic triangle.

TRIGRAPH A combination of three written symbols to represent one speech sound, e.g. French *eau* [o] 'water'.

TRILL A speech sound produced by the air stream causing the tongue or uvula to vibrate several times, e.g. the rolled [r] in Italian or the apico-alveolar [r] or uvular [ʀ] in German. → flap. Alternative term: rolled (consonant). (3.1).

TRIPHTHONG → Diphthong.

TRISYLLABIC Having three syllables.

TROCHE → Foot (*a*).

TYPE and TOKEN Statistical terms used in various branches of linguistics to denote an actual observed item such as a speech sound or an utterance (token) and the general class into which linguistic analysis places it, e.g. → phoneme, → sentence (type). Such dichotomies as → langue and parole or 'emic' and 'etic' may also be explained in terms of type and token. (2.1 Chao, 10.4 Herdan).

TYPOLOGICAL CLASSIFICATION → Typology.

TYPOLOGY In → comparative linguistics, the → classification of languages according to features of phonology, grammar and lexis rather than historical development. Traditionally the emphasis was on showing genetic relationships, e.g. between the languages of the Indo-European 'family', but many linguists from W. von Humboldt (1768–1835) to E. Sapir (1884–1939) have stressed that each language has its own internally consistent and independent grammatical system which makes it 'different' from or 'similar' to other languages. Different types have been established, e.g. → agglutinative, → inflected, → tone languages, → synthetic languages, and a number of → indexes devised to characterise them. Most languages share more than one feature, which makes typology a matter of degree rather than absolute categories. English, for example, has elements of 'inflexion', e.g. vowel gradation in *sing–sang–sung* or plurals such as *mouse–mice*; features of 'isolation', e.g. invariable words such as *when, in, of, now*; and characteristics of 'agglutination', e.g. formation of words like *un-god-li-ness*. There is no evidence for a 'natural' development from one type to another, e.g. from → analytic to → synthetic languages. (6.1, 8.1).

U

ULTIMATE CONSTITUENTS
In → immediate constituent analysis, the smallest units which can be abstracted. In the grammatical analysis of sentences the ultimate constituents are morphemes and words, as shown on the following diagram:

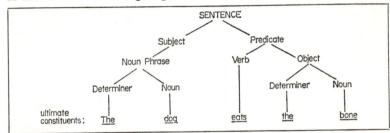

UMLAUT (*a*) A sound change which occurs as a result of a vowel in one syllable being affected by the vowel of a following syllable, e.g. OE *mūsiz > mȳs > Mod. E *mice*. Alternative term: vowel mutation. (*b*) The diaeresis ⟨ ¨ ⟩ used in German *ü*, *ö*, *ä* to indicate a fronted pronunciation which often arose from historical vowel mutation.

UNACCEPTABLE → Acceptability.

UNASPIRATED STOP A → stop consonant produced without an audible puff of breath on release, e.g. [p] in French *pain* 'bread'.

UNBOUNDED NOUN → Mass noun.

UNCHECKED → Checked *versus* unchecked.

UNCONDITIONAL SOUND CHANGE → Sound change.

UNCONDITIONED SOUND CHANGE → Sound change.

UNCOUNTABLE WORD → Mass noun.

UNDERLYING STRUCTURE → Deep structure.

UNDERSTOOD A linguistic item may be said to be 'understood' when it is not present in the surface structure of an utterance, but is considered necessary for a satisfactory explanation of the underlying grammatical structure. Thus in the imperative sentence *Come and see me tomorrow*, the pronoun *you* may be said to be the subject understood. → dummy element.

UNGRAMMATICAL An utterance is said to be ungrammatical when it does not comply with the morphological and syntactic conventions of the language. → irregularity, → grammaticality.

UNILATERAL CONSONANT → Lateral.

UNILINGUAL Involving only one language, as opposed to → bilingual and → multilingual. Alternative terms: monoglot, monolingual.

UNION LANGUAGE The deliberate creation of a → standard language and writing system to facilitate communication between dialects, e.g Union Shona for several Bantu dialects in Rhodesia and East Africa, with phonological, grammatical and lexical items from four neighbouring dialects plus a script based on the Latin alphabet. → language planning.

UNIT An element of linguistic structure. Examples of such basic units on the phonological level are → phoneme and → syllable, on the grammatical level → morpheme, → word, and → sentence, in lexis and semantics → lexeme and → sememe, in graphemics → grapheme, word, sentence and paragraph. Such a classification is arrived at by breaking up the whole language system into consecutively smaller parts. → linguistic analysis.

UNIT NOUN Term used by some grammarians to denote words, usually concrete → nouns, which may form a plural, e.g. *chair, table, dream, child*, etc. as opposed to → mass nouns which cannot be counted and which cannot form a plural without a change of meaning, e.g. *sugar, sand*, etc. Alternative terms: count noun, countable noun, pluraliser, class noun. (4.1, 4.2, 8.23).

UNIVERSAL A linguistic category common to all languages. It is now generally held that such categories as 'accusative case', 'third person', or 'future tense' are not universal. However, a number of features have been empirically shown to have universal validity. Examples of universals are the conventional character of language (words have arbitrarily agreed meanings and forms which are passed on and can be learned), the duality of transmission and reception, the presence of names and deictic elements. A distinction is sometimes made between SUBSTANTIVE UNIVERSALS, i.e. features of sound substance such as the phonological elements → phoneme and → syllable, and FORMAL UNIVERSALS which are made explicit by the linguist in the form of grammatical → rules. → relativity. (2.2 Bach–Harms, 2.3 Greenberg).

UNIVERSAL GRAMMAR The view that all languages have linguistic structures in common (→ universal). Greek and Latin grammarians had held this view which was perpetuated in the tradition of 'Latinate' grammars (→ mediaeval linguistics) and 18th-century French and English 'rationalism'. As a reaction, the discovery of non-European languages and grammatical systems (→ comparative linguistics) made linguists sceptical of whether even two languages could be described in similar categories, which more recently was underlined by the work of American anthropological linguists (→ relativity). However, interest in the universal features of all human languages is increasing again, promoted by adherents of → transformational-generative grammar. Alternative term: general grammar.

UNIVERSAL LANGUAGE A language system, especially one

245

artificially constructed, to facilitate international communication, e.g. Esperanto, Interlingua, and Novial. → artificial language (*a*).

UNIVERSAL SEMANTICS
The search for language-independent, i.e. universal, features in the → componential analysis of meaning of words.

UNIVERSALISM
Collective term for those approaches to linguistics which assume that languages are closely linked to the logical system of a supreme philosophical system, e.g. the Scholastic grammars of Latin in the 12th century or the Port Royal grammars of French in the 18th century. (2.5).

UNMARKED (MEMBER)
→ Marked (member).

UNPRODUCTIVE
A feature of a language is said to be unproductive if it is no longer used in the formation of new words or compounds, e.g. in English the affix -*th* on nouns such as *width*, *length*, *breadth*, would not be used to form new words in the same way as the suffix -*ness* would still be used, e.g. *muchness*. The same applies to the principle of → vowel gradation in the various tense forms of verbs: all new verbs in English form the past tense with an affix.

UNROUNDED
→ Unrounded vowel.

UNROUNDED VOWEL
A vowel sound produced with spread lips, e.g. [ɛ] in *bed* [bɛd], as opposed to a rounded vowel, e.g. [u] as in *boo*. Alternative term: spread vowel.

UNROUNDING
→ Delabialisation.

UNVOICED
→ Voiceless (*a*).

UPWARD COMPARISON
→ Superior comparison.

URAL-ALTAIC LINGUISTICS
Collective term for the linguistic description of Hungarian, Finnish, Estonian (FINNO-UGRIAN LINGUISTICS), Turkish, etc. → Appendix 1, p. 272. (8.8 Collinder, Meskill).

URBANISM
A feature of pronunciation, grammar or lexis which is restricted to use in cities or urban areas, as opposed to rural areas.

USAGE
The way in which the members of a speech community use their mother tongue; the sum total of all idiolects of a language. → grammar, → norm. (2.3 Quirk–Svartvik).

USAGE LABEL
A lexicographical practice of indicating different language varieties by special symbols, e.g. *archaic*, *non-standard*, *familiar*, *figurative*, *dialect*, *slang*, etc. Alternative term: Status label.

UTTERANCE
Stretch of speech between two periods of silence or potential silence, usually marked at the end by a rising or falling terminal juncture. Thus *Is John there? No, not yet*, are both separate utterances. → sentence.

UVULA
The appendage to the → velum or soft palate, hanging at the centre of the back of the mouth. → Diagram p. 159. (3.1, 8.22).

UVULAR
A speech sound the articulation of which involves the → uvula. Since it is the dorsum region of the tongue which comes

into contact with the uvula, a sound may also be called → dorso-uvular, e.g. [ʀ] French *rue* 'street'. (3.1, 8.22).

V

VALENCY → Dependency grammar.

VALUE The relative position that a linguistic → sign occupies in the semantic system of a language. Thus the French word *mouton* has a different value from the equivalent English words *mutton* and *sheep*: although it can signify the same objects, it is in opposition to a different set of terms such as 'live animals' and 'types of meat'. (2.4 Saussure).

VALUE JUDGMENT An attitude to language which cannot be confirmed by scientific → oberva-tion and analysis, e.g. statements about the use of certain 'ugly', 'incorrect' or 'debased' expressions in a variant of a language, or about the 'beauty', 'logicality' or 'primi-tiveness' of one language as com-pared with another.

VARIABLE WORD A word which can change its form by the addition of inflexional → affixes, e.g. the Latin noun *pater* 'father' which takes case endings: *patrem*, *patris*, *patrī*, *patrē*, etc. → invariable word.

VARIANT A form which may be used as an alternative, e.g. the written form *will not* or *won't* as opposed to the spoken form ['wɪl nɔt] or [woʉnt], the morphophone-mic variants of noun plural forms, e.g. [s] in *cats*, [z] in *domes*, [ɪz] in *houses* or the alternative pronuncia-tions [rum] and [ruːm] for *room*. → allophone, allograph, allomorph, allochrone, alloseme, etc. Alternative terms: alternant, alternative form.

VARIETY IN LANGUAGE No language is a uniform entity, and all languages vary according to the place, time and context in which they are used. There are many ways in which language varieties can be distinguished, but basically three criteria are important: (1) the geo-graphical and social background of the speaker and the actual situation in which the speech act takes place: → dialect, → register (*b*) or → manner of discourse; (2) the medium or 'mode' through which language is expressed: → written language, → spoken language, extralinguistic → features; (3) the subject-matter under discussion: → special language. The language of an individual speaker, which is influenced by any of these factors at a given time, is usually called → idiolect. A dialect is the regional, temporal or social variant used by a particular community. The term 'register' may refer to the varieties of language associated with different uses in particular situations, whereas 'style' refers to the speech or literary form selected by an indi-vidual for a particular occasion. There has been disagreement among linguists about a 'common core' in the language at large, but most linguists confirm that all language varieties are subject to constant → change by the mobility of their speakers. → standard language. (6.1 Ellis, 7.1, 7.2, 7.3, 8.24).

VELAR A speech sound articulated with the tongue touching or approaching the → velum. When the dorsum region of the tongue acts as the articulator, the sound may be called → dorso-velar. According to the point of articulation it may be called PRE-VELAR, articulated towards the front of the velum; MEDIO-VELAR, articulated towards the centre of the velum; the POST-VELAR, articulated towards the rear of the velum. (3.1, 8.22).

VELARIC AIR-STREAM MECHANISM → Air-stream mechanism.

VELARIC CLOSURE → Closure.

VELARISATION The → articulation of a speech sound accompanied by raising the dorsum region of the tongue towards the → velum, e.g. in English [ɫ] is velarised in a word like *call*. (3.1, 8.22).

VELARISED Articulated with the dorsum region of the tongue retracted towards the soft palate or → velum, e.g. in the pronunciation of the [ɫ] in English *table*. Alternative terms: retracted, dark.

VELIC CLOSURE → Closure.

VELUM The soft membrane forming the roof of the mouth behind the hard → palate. Alternative term: soft palate. → Diagram, p. 159.

VERB A → part of speech which may function as → predicate in a sentence. The traditional definition of verbs as 'doing words' is inadequate, since many verbs do not imply any action, e.g. in *I am cold* or *She looks happy enough*. For most European and many other languages, verbs may be defined as words which can be assigned to categories such as → number, → aspect, → person, → tense, → mood and → voice on the basis of grammatical inflexions or the use of auxiliary words, e.g. English *he talks* as opposed to *we talk* as opposed to *we will talk* as opposed to *we must talk*, etc. In English, the regular or weak verb has four inflexional forms, *walk, walks, walked, walking*, and the irregular or strong verb has five, *sing, sings, sang, sung, singing*. A distinction can be made between → transitive and → intransitive verbs, although in English there may be no formal distinction, e.g. *He drinks a pint of milk* as opposed to *He drinks (often)*. These categories, transitive and intransitive, can be further subdivided on the basis of syntactic or semantic criteria, e.g. the intransitive verbs *look, seem, is*, may be called → copulas or linking verbs. So-called compound tense forms in English make use of → auxiliary verbs. (8.23 Grady, Joos, Palmer, Svartvik, 8.4 Helbig–Schenkel, 8.5 Forsyth).

VERB–ADVERB COMBINATION A verb phrase which is made up of a verb and a movable adverbial particle, e.g. *on* in *She turned on the light* or *She turned the light on*. Note the contrast with the prepositional phrase *on the children* in *She turned on the children*.

VERB CLUSTER → Verb phrase (*a*).

VERB PHRASE (*a*) In traditional grammar a group of words having the same syntactic function as a simple verb in a sentence, e.g. *could have been seeing* in *I could have* *been seeing things*, or *rang up* in *He rang me up*. Alternative terms: phrasal verb, verb cluster, verbal group, verbal phrase. (*b*) In → transformational-generative grammar, the verb phrase is that constituent of a sentence which contains the predicate (or complement or adjunct), in contrast to the subject noun phrase. In *John drinks milk every day*, *John* is the subject and *drinks milk every day* is the verb phrase. The abbreviation VP is used in → phrase structure rules, as below. (4.1, 8.23).

S → NP + VP
John drinks milk every day.

VERBAL (*a*) A word or group of words functioning as the verb in a sentence. (*b*) Non-finite verb elements such as infinitives, gerund and participial constructions. Alternative term: verbid.

VERBAL ADJECTIVE An → adjectival which is closely related in form and/or meaning to a verb, e.g. *imaginable* 'can be imagined', or such forms as the English -*ing* forms used as adjectives, e.g. *crying* in *a crying child*.

VERBAL ASPECT → Aspect.

VERBAL CORE The → verb in a Romance language together with its subject and object pronouns which are attached in a special order, e.g. in French *J'en ai deux* 'I have two of them'.

VERBAL GROUP → Verb phrase (*a*).

VERBAL NOUN A → nominal which is closely related in form and/or meaning to a verb, e.g. *foundation*, or such forms as the

English -*ing* forms used as nouns, e.g. *crying* in *the crying of the child*.

VERBAL PHRASE → Verb phrase (*a*).

VERBAL SKILL → Linguistic skill.

VERBALISATION (*a*) The process or result of expressing a thought in words, as opposed to gesture, painting, music, etc. (*b*) The process or result of making a word or phrase into a → verb, e.g. by the addition of an appropriate derivational affix such as -*ise* in *visualise* < *visual*.

VERBID → Verbal (*b*).

VERBLESS SENTENCE → Minor sentence.

VERNACULAR (*a*) → Common language. (*b*) The indigenous language of a country, e.g. the native European languages during the Middle Ages, as opposed to Latin, the 'lingua franca'. (6.1, 7.1).

VERNER'S LAW A regular pattern of sound changes discovered by K. Verner in 1877, which explains the apparent exceptions to → Grimm's Law. If the Indo-European stops [p], [t], [k] were not initial and did not immediately follow the stress, then the voiceless spirants [f], [θ], [x] and [s] which arise in Primitive Germanic in accordance with Grimm's Law changed farther to voiced spirants [v], [ð], [ɣ], [z], e.g. Sanskrit *saptá* > Germanic *sebun*, Gothic *sebun*, English *seven*. The modern languages have occasionally levelled out such differences, but the past tense forms of some

249

modern German verbs still exhibit this change, e.g. *schneiden*—'to cut', past tense—*schnitt*. In all Germanic languages except Gothic a [z] arising from this sound change developed further into [r]. This change, called rhotacism, accounts for such differences as *was/were, lose/forlorn* in modern English. Alternative term: grammatical change. (6.1 Lockwood).

VERSE Spoken or written language with regular patterns of stressed and unstressed syllables. Certain literary forms such as poetry exploit the natural 'rhythm' in a language by assigning definite portions of speech to measures such as the → foot, a number of feet making up a metrical line. (7.3).

VIBRANT A speech sound articulated by a continuous vibration between a movable and immovable speech organ, e.g. [v] as in *vote*, where the bottom lip is the movable speech organ and the top teeth the immovable one. → resonant.

VIBRATORY FEEDBACK → Feedback (*a*).

VIRTUAL COMPOUND A → compound word which is a combination of a verb with another word, e.g. *overtake, understand*.

VISIBLE SPEECH (*a*) A system of → analphabetic notation using graphic symbols to represent the spoken word. (*b*) The observation, measurement and recording of the acoustic signals of spoken language in terms of intensity, frequency, amplitude, etc., producing → spectrograms. (3.3 Potter *et al.*).

VOCABULARY The stock of words which are at the disposal of a speaker or writer. The term vocabulary may refer to all words in the whole language, or the words and phrases used in a particular variety such as → dialect, → register, or → terminology. The number of words counted in different languages varies according to the specialised needs of its speakers and to the quality of available dictionaries. In English the 'total' vocabulary has been estimated at over 1 million words. The terms ACTIVE and PASSIVE VOCABULARY are sometimes used to distinguish the words a speaker will habitually use from those he understands, but does not use himself. The vocabulary of a language or language variety is compiled and codified by lexicographers in general or specialised → dictionaries. Linguists have found it difficult to draw a sharp line between vocabulary or lexical items (also called → content words) and those items which have only grammatical meaning (also called → function words). The lexical meaning of vocabulary items is analysed in → semantics, and the changing meaning of words through time is traced by → etymology. For certain limited purposes it has been found convenient to determine the basic (core) vocabulary of a language, i.e. those lexical items which refer to concepts and situations common and fundamental to all human activity, e.g. kinship terms, parts of the body, numerals, etc. These basic items are usually fairly stable over long periods of historical development of the language, and thus may be used for lexico-statistical comparisons between different languages; in → glottochronology, a basic list of

200 items has been suggested. In language teaching, → frequency counts have been used to compile lists of the most common vocabulary items used in a language, from which teaching items can be selected. (5.1, 5.2 Zgusta, 6.1 Lehmann, 8.25, 9.1, 9.4, 10.4).

VOCABULARY CHANGE
→ Semantic change.

VOCAL BANDS → Vocal cords.

VOCAL CHARACTERISER
→ Voice qualifier.

VOCAL CORDS The two lips or folds of tissue which vibrate in the → larynx to produce → voice. Alternative terms: vocal bands, vocal folds. → Diagram p. 159.

VOCAL FOLDS → Vocal cords.

VOCAL QUALIFIER → Voice qualifier.

VOCAL TRACT The 'speech organs' in the chest and head used for the → articulation of speech sounds by providing a source of energy (a moving stream of air), a vibrating body (vocal cords in the larynx) and a resonating chamber (oral or nasal cavities). → Diagram p. 159.

VOCALIC versus NON-VOCALIC One of the basic oppositions in → distinctive feature phonology based on the analysis of a → spectrogram. The term 'vocalic' indicates the presence of at least two clearly defined → formants, and 'non-vocalic' the lack of this feature. In articulatory terms vocalic indicates vibration of the vocal cords but no interference with the air stream above the glottis, and non-vocalic indicates interference with the air stream in the vocal tract above the glottis, with or without the vibration of the vocal cords. All vowels have the feature vocalic and all consonants except liquids (l-sounds) have the feature non-vocalic.

VOCALIC ALTERNATION
→ Vowel gradation.

VOCALISATION (*a*) The change of a → consonant into a → vowel. (*b*) → Voicing.

VOCALISED → Voiced.

VOCATIVE A → case form in inflected languages used to denote the person or personified object being directly addressed, e.g. *Brute* in the Latin *Et tu Brute!* 'You too, Brutus'. In English the term vocative may be used to refer to such nouns or noun phrases which do not have a special inflexion but which are usually set off by intonation or punctuation, e.g. *John, close the window!*

VOCOID A term used by some linguists to refer to an articulatory class of sounds more traditionally called vowels, reserving the term → vowel to refer either to the written representation, e.g. *i, a, u,* or to phonemes of a particular language. Vocoid is thus a phonetic term, and vowel a phonological term. → contoid. (3.1 Pike).

VOICE (*a*) Sound produced by vibration of the → vocal cords in the larynx. (3.1, 8.22). (*b*) A verb form or

251

particular syntactic construction indicating certain relationships between the subject and object of a verb. The ACTIVE VOICE occurs in a sentence where the grammatical subject of a verb carries out some activity or process, e.g. *The cat caught the mouse.* The PASSIVE or INACTIVE VOICE occurs in a sentence in which the grammatical subject of the verb is the goal or sufferer of the action expressed by the verb, e.g. *The mouse was caught by the cat.* In such a passive sentence the noun or noun phrase introduced by the preposition *by* is termed the agent. The term MIDDLE VOICE is used, particularly in Greek grammar, referring to a sentence expressing an action performed by the subject on himself or for his own benefit, e.g. Greek *loúomai* 'I wash myself'. The term middle voice is also used by some grammarians to refer to such constructions in English as *I am getting shaved*, etc. which could mean *I am shaving* or *I am being shaved*. (4.1, 4.2, 8.23).

VOICE QUALIFIER A → paralinguistic feature of the voice which conveys information about the state of the speaker, e.g. 'plaintive' or 'husky'. Alternative terms: tone of voice, vocal characteriser, vocal qualifier.

VOICE versus VOICELESS One of the basic oppositions in → distinctive feature phonology, based on the analysis of a → spectrogram. 'Voice' indicates the presence of periodic low-frequency vibration in the larynx; 'voiceless' the lack of this feature. In articulatory terms voice indicates vibration of the vocal cords and voiceless the lack of such vibration. In English, for example, the

→ consonants /b/, /d/, /g/, etc. have the feature voice, whereas /p/, /t/, /k/, etc. are voiceless.

VOICE QUALITY Collective term for the non-linguistic background features in the speech of an individual which allows him or her to be recognised as unique. Such sound qualities may include pitch, loudness, duration and timbre, but are not normally exploited in communication as are → prosodic and → paralinguistic features. Alternative terms: tonal quality, tone of voice, voice-set. (8.22 Crystal).

VOICE REGISTER → Register (*a*).

VOICE-SET → Voice quality.

VOICE STATE → Glottis.

VOICED Produced with vibration of the → vocal cords, e.g. [b] as in *bin*; [d] as in *din*; [v] as in *vat*; [z] as in *buzz*, as opposed to the → voiceless counterparts in *pin*, *tin*, *fat* and *bus*. Alternative term: vocalised.

VOICELESS (*a*) Produced without vibration of the → vocal cords, e.g. [s] as in *Sue*; [f] as in *fan*; [t] as in *ten*; [p] as in *pin*, as opposed to the → voiced counterparts in *zoo*, *van*, *den* and *bin*. Alternative term: unvoiced. (*b*) → Voice *vs.* voiceless.

VOICELESS VOWEL → Whispered vowel.

VOICING Vibrating the → vocal cords during the → articulation of a speech sound. In normal speech most vowels are voiced. Consonants may be voiced or unvoiced, but these are not absolute terms in phonetics, since there may be differing degrees of voicing, e.g. a voiceless consonant may become partially voiced when it occurs between vowels, e.g. /h/ in *behind*. Alternative terms: vocalisation, phonation. (3.1, 8.22).

VOLUME The intensity with which a sound is perceived, dependent on a combination of the → frequency and → amplitude of its wave. Volume is a subjective impression and cannot be measured objectively in the same way as power or amplitude can be measured, but the relative levels of volume may be indicated in decibels. Alternative term: loudness. (3.1, 8.22).

VOWEL (*a*) A speech sound produced with vibration of the → vocal cords but with no closure or stricture or close approximation in the vocal tract above the → glottis. The quality of the vowel sound, i.e. whether it is heard as [i], [e], [u], etc. is dependent upon the shape of the resonance chamber, i.e. the oral and nasal cavities, and upon which of the cavities are used. If the nasal cavity is sealed off by the velum, the result is an ORAL VOWEL, if air is allowed to pass through the nasal cavity the result is a → nasal or NASALISED VOWEL. The shape of the oral resonance chamber is affected chiefly by two factors, the position of the lips and the position of the tongue; rounded lips produce a different sound from spread lips. The following diagram indicates the approximate tongue positions of some vowels represented in → IPA. → Table pp. 262–263.

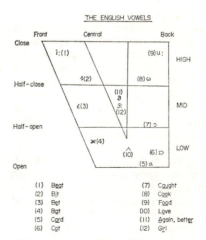

THE ENGLISH VOWELS

					(1)	Beat	(7)	Caught
(2)	Bit	(8)	Cook
(3)	Bet	(9)	Food
(4)	Bat	(10)	Love
(5)	Card	(11)	Again, better
(6)	Cot	(12)	Girl

In addition to the above a further classification can be made into TENSE and LAX according to the tension in the muscles of the vocal tract during production of the vowel, e.g. [i] in *beat* is tense, whilst [ɪ] in *bit* is lax. In phonology a vowel is defined as a sound which can occur in the nucleus of a → syllable, e.g. *cat* has the syllabic structure CVC, the sound [æ] being the nucleus. → neutral vowel, close vowel, diphthong. (*b*) A letter representing the above type of speech sound. (3.1, 8.22).

VOWEL CLUSTER A combination of more than one vowel sound such as in *Noël*, pronounced as [nouɛl].

VOWEL GRADATION A means of marking different functions of a word by varying the vowel sound in its stem, e.g. the three principal parts of many strong verbs in English (*sing/sang/sung*). Such changes may be QUALITATIVE when the articulation of the sound is modified, as in the above example, or QUANTITATIVE when the sound is omitted, shortened or lengthened, e.g. the nominative and genitive case forms of Latin *pater/patris* 'father'. → mutation. Alternative terms: ablaut, apophony, internal inflexion, internal modification, introflexion, internal change, vocalic alternation. (4.1, 6.1).

VOWEL HARMONY A feature of languages such as Turkish or Hungarian where all the vowels of a particular polysyllabic word form have a certain feature in common, e.g. Hungarian *ház* 'house', plural *házak*, *hely* 'place', plural *helyek*. (3.1, 4.1, 6.1).

VOWEL MUTATION A modification in the vowel sounds of words, brought about by neighbouring sounds and often resulting in a series of changes from one stage in the historical development of a language to the next. Thus Old English *fēt* 'feet' developed from **fōti* under the influence of the following 'front' vowel (FRONT MUTATION), and Old English *heofon* 'heaven' developed from **heƀun* under the influence of the following 'back' vowel (BACK MUTATION). → mutation. Alternative terms: umlaut, metaphony. (6.1, 8.21).

VOWEL QUADRILATERAL A diagram classifying vowel sounds according to the relative tongue positions. The diagram may also take the shape of a triangle. → Diagrams on pp. 31, 253.

VOWEL QUALITY → Quality.

VOWEL QUANTITY → Quantity.

VOWEL REDUCTION A change in the pronunciation of a vowel under special conditions, e.g. *man* as [mən] in the second (unstressed) syllable of *postman*.

VOWEL SHIFT A series of regular changes in vowels at a particular stage in the history of a language. → Great English vowel shift.

VOWEL SYSTEM An inventory of the vowel phonemes of a given language, indicating the relationship of the contrasts between them. A vowel system is often plotted on a vowel triangle or quadrilateral. → Diagram p. 253. (3.1, 3.4).

VOWEL TRIANGLE A diagram classifying vowel sounds according to the relative tongue positions. The diagram may also be in the shape of a quadrilateral. → Diagram p. 253.

VOX NIHILI → Ghost form.

VULGAR A level of language normally used by people of low social class and education and felt inappropriate in elevated discourse, e.g. 'four-letter words' which are → taboo in most general communicative situations. → manner of discourse.

WAVE FORM → Sound wave.

WAVE THEORY A model borrowed from physics and used in → historical linguistics to explain how speech forms develop from a particular dialect or language and then spread out over large areas of related languages like waves produced by throwing a stone into water. → family of languages. (6.1).

WEAK DECLENSION A term used to denote a certain declensional paradigm of nouns and adjectives in Germanic languages. The weak declension originally indicated 'definiteness' as opposed to the → strong declension which denoted 'indefiniteness'.

OH German: Modern German:

weak

    der guoto man > *der gute Mann*
                   'the good man'.

strong

    ein guotêr man > *ein guter Mann*
                   'a good man'.

Alternative term: definite declension.

WEAK FORM Form of certain common English words in unstressed position, e.g. *and* and *of* may be pronounced [ənd] and [əv].

WEAK STRESS → Stress.

WEAK VERB A → verb in a Germanic language which forms its past tense by the addition of an inflexion, e.g. *walk/walked*, as opposed to irregular or → strong verbs which change the tense forms by internal vowel gradation, e.g. *sing/sang/sung*.

WELL-FORMED A term used to describe a sentence which complies with given grammatical rules or established norms. The fulfilment of grammatical conditions does not necessarily imply that a sentence is accepted usage or even meaningful. → grammaticality, → correctness.

WERNICKE'S AREA Area in the back portion of the brain which controls the comprehension of speech, as opposed to → Broca's area which controls speech production. Alternative term: centre of Wernicke. (9.5, 10.2).

WHISPER Speech produced without voice, but with audible friction as a result of a partial closure of the → glottis.

WHISPER STATE → Glottis.

WHISPERED VOWEL A vowel sound produced without → voicing. In one sense the sound [h] in English and many other languages can be called a VOICELESS vowel, e.g. in the word *head* the vocal tract adopts its position for the vowel but allows the air to start flowing, producing the 'aspiration' before the voicing begins.

WHISTLE-SPEECH Intonation patterns of speech transmitted by whistling. This type of communication has been found among the Mazatico people of Mexico where male speakers use it to communicate over longer distances than would be possible with normal speech. Young English children often use whistle speech as a game. (3.1 Abercrombie).

WHISTLING CONSONANT
→ Sibilant.

WHORFIAN HYPOTHESIS
→ Relativity.

WIDE DIPHTHONG →
Diphthong.

WIDENED MEANING →
Meaning.

WIDENING OF MEANING
→ Extension (*a*).

WINDPIPE → Trachea.

WING BRACKETS → List
p. xvii.

WORD All native speakers of a
language seem to have an intuitive
idea of what is meant by the term
'word' in its general sense, whether
they write the language or not, but
word as a linguistic unit is more
difficult to define and has been the
subject of much discussion. In many
ways the word is a unit of *langue*
(language as a system, rather than
of *parole* or speech), and for many
writing systems a written word can
be defined as a sequence of letters
which occurs between spaces. The
most famous definition of word
which is valid for the spoken language is Bloomfield's 'minimum free
form', which means that a word is
the smallest unit which can be used
alone to constitute a sentence or
utterance, and it must consist of at
least one free morpheme. Even so
there are marginal cases, e.g. *the*, *a*
in English which can hardly stand
alone and *je* in French which can
only be used in conjunction with a
verb. The difficulties with the definition of the word have led linguists
to distinguish this concept on several
levels: the PHONOLOGICAL WORD is
bounded by pauses, the MORPHEMIC
WORD is defined in terms of its
position in the sentence, the LEXICAL
WORD is a vocabulary item with a
specific meaning. In → systematic
grammar a word is one of five
grammatical units arranged in a
hierarchy of rank scale: the unit
'word' is intermediary between 'morpheme' and 'group', i.e. a word
consists of one or more morphemes
and a group consists of one or more
words. (4.1, 4.2, 8.23).

WORD and PARADIGM
(WP) An approach to linguistic
analysis which considers the word
as the central unit of grammatical
description. Most words can be
placed in a → paradigm with their
derivational and inflexional forms
which can show both morphological
and syntactic relationships. → item-
and-arrangement. (2.2 Lyons).

WORD BOUNDARY A
phonological, prosodic, graphemic or
grammatical device to separate
words, e.g. the allophones [l] and
[ɫ] to distinguish *they lend it* from
they'll end it.

WORD CLASS A category into
which a word is placed because of
similarities in form and/or function
with other members of the class.
The → parts of speech are probably
the best known word classes. (4.1,
8.23).

WORD COUNT A → frequency
count of words.

WORD FORM The form of a
given word operating in a particular
function, e.g. the nominative form of
a noun, or the past tense form of a
verb.

WORD FORMATION Morphologically significant changes in word form are brought about by such means as the addition of an affix, e.g. *teacher/teachers,* vowel or consonant change, e.g. *sing/sang,* or change of stress, e.g. *récord/recórd.* Such changes in word form are usually divided into two main categories: inflexion and derivation. INFLEXION occurs when an → affix is added or a change is made in order to limit the grammatical functioning of a particular word form. Case endings, for example, fall into this category, since a word with a particular case form cannot be used in the same slot as a word with a different case form; plural endings and agreement of adjectives with nouns and nouns with verb forms are examples of inflexion for similar reasons. All changes which are not inflexional are derivational. DERIVATION in contrast to inflexion produces a form which has substantially the same grammatical status as the original or base form. Some derivational changes produce a word of the same class as the base form, e.g. *king/kingdom, green/greenish;* others change the word class, e.g. *modern/modernise, slow/slowly, cónvert/convért.* Inflexions can be added to a word which is a derived form, e.g. *kingdom/ kingdoms, modernise/modernises,* but note that a derivational suffix cannot be added after an inflexional suffix. Words can be classified according to the structure of their STEMS: a simple stem, PRIMARY WORD or morpheme word consists of one morpheme, e.g. *dog, cat, vegetable, blue, come, fast,* etc. A derived form, derivative or SECONDARY WORD consists of one stem plus an addition. If the addition is a derivational affix, the term SECONDARY DERIVATIVE or

DERIVED SECONDARY WORD is used, e.g. such words as *childish, catty, quickly, kingdom, actor, befriend,* etc. If the addition is another stem the term STEM COMPOUND or COMPOUND WORD is used, e.g. such words as *bookcase, armchair, backrest,* etc. PRIMARY DERIVATIVES or DERIVED PRIMARY WORDS consist of two bound morphemes, i.e. no part of the word is a stem, e.g. such words as *receive, detain, refer,* etc. (4.1, 5.1, 6.1, 8.23).

WORD-FOR-WORD TRANS-LATION → Translation.

WORD FREQUENCY → Frequency (*a*).

WORD GROUP → Phrase (*b*).

WORD LIST In linguistic fieldwork, a list of basic → vocabulary items used to check features of pronunciation, grammar and lexis with native informants. (2.3 Samarin).

WORD ORDER The placing of words in a sequence according to the conventions of a given language. This refers not only to sentence parts such as Subject + Verb + Object, but also to word order in noun phrases or verb phrases. Some languages such as Malay and to a large extent French, have the → head word occurring before the → modifier, e.g. French *une maison blanche* 'a white house'. Other languages such as Japanese and to a large extent English, have the modifier before the head word, e.g. *a tall tree* or *a low table.* Sometimes, however, English has the modifier occurring after the head word, e.g. *Postmaster General* or *the bus waiting at the corner.* In uninflected languages such as English or Chinese, word order has syntactic significance: compare *The dog bit the man* with *The man bit the dog*. A language which signals syntactic relationships by means of → inflexions is not so dependent on word order: compare Latin *Pater amat filium*; *Filium amat pater*; *Pater filium amat*, all meaning 'a father loves his son'. Alternative term: syntactic order. (4.1, 8.23).

WORD PARADIGM → Word and paradigm.

WORD SIGN → Logogram.

WORD STRESS → Stress.

WRITING The process or result of recording language in the form of conventionalised visible marks or graphic signs on a surface. Materials, tools and techniques vary in time and place (stone, paper, chisel, pen, printing, etc.), but several distinct stages or types of writing systems may be distinguished. The forerunners of written signs were pictorial devices to describe or record events in messages (pictograms). The first full writing systems consisted of → logograms representing words, e.g. Egyptian hieroglyphs or Chinese characters; a further stage was reached by abstract signs representing syllables, e.g. Mesopotamian cuneiform, West Semitic → syllabary, Japanese kana; finally, in alphabetic scripts the individual sounds of human speech are represented by phonetic signs called → letters. → graphemics, → notation, → linguistic skill, literacy. (7.2, 2.1 Trager).

WRITING SYSTEM A code of conventionalised graphic signs representing speech by reference to words (→ logography), to groups of sounds (→ syllabography) or individual phonemes (→ alphabet). (7.2).

WRITTEN LANGUAGE One of the means or modes of linguistic communication. As distinct from → spoken language, it does not usually represent all features of speech such as stress and pitch, and lacks the redundancy and lapses of spoken conversation (written dialogue and reading aloud are more akin to written than to spoken language). → literature, literary language, orthography. (7.2).

Y

YO-HE-HO THEORY → Origin of speech.

YOUNG GRAMMARIANS → Neogrammarians.

Z

ZERO A → variant morph which is characterised by lack of change. In English, for example, *sheep* can be singular or plural, but since most words add an affix to form the plural, it is convenient for the sake of regularity to consider that a zero affix has been added when *sheep* is used as a plural. (4.2, 8.23).

ZERO ANAPHORA A reference back to a previous word with the anaphoric word omitted, e.g. in

Pass me two crayons please, a red and a blue, the anaphoric word that has been left out is *one*: *a red one* and *a blue one*.

ZERO MORPH → Zero.

ZIPF'S LAW A general statement about the distribution and → frequency of words used by speakers or authors. The equation $F \times R = C$ (where F = frequency, R = rank, i.e. position on a frequency list, and C = constant) says that there is a fixed ratio between the total number of times a word is used and its position on the frequency list. The so-called LAW OF ABBREVIATION holds that the words used most frequently in a language are also the shortest ones. → economy (*a*). (10.2 Zipf).

ZOO-SEMIOTICS The study of communication between animals. (10.2 Sebeok–Ramsay).

SOME IMPORTANT CONSONANTS

Manner	Bilabial	Labio-dental	Dental	Alveolar	Post-alveolar	Retroflex	Palatal	Velar	Uvular	Pharyngeal	Glottal
Stop	p b		t̪ d̪	t d		ʈ ɖ	c ɟ	k g	q ɢ		ʔ
Nasal	m	ɱ	n̪	n		ɳ	ɲ	ŋ	N		
Fricative	ɸ β	f v	θ ð	s z	ʃ ʒ	ʂ ʐ	ç j	x ɣ	χ ʁ	ħ ʕ	h ɦ
Affricate				ts dz	tʃ dʒ						
Lateral				l		ɭ	ʎ				
Rolled				r					R		
Flapped				ɾ		ɽ			R		
Semi-vocalic	w			ɹ			j				

Consonants shown according to point and manner of articulation.
Symbols on the left of the squares indicate voiceless consonants.
Symbols on the right indicate voiced consonants.

261

THE INTERNATIONAL PHONETIC ALPHABET

Con-sonants	Bilabial	Labio-dental	Dental and Alveolar	Retroflex	Palato-alveolar	Alveolo-palatal	Palatal	Velar	Uvular	Pharyngal	Glottal
Plosive	p b		t d	ʈ ɖ			c ɟ	k g	q ɢ		ʔ
Nasal	m	ɱ	n	ɳ			ɲ	ŋ	N		
Lateral fricative			ɬ ɮ								
Lateral non-fricative			l	ɭ			ʎ				
Rolled			r						R		
Flapped			ɾ	ɽ					R		
Fricative	ɸ β	f v	θ ð | s z | ɹ	ʂ ʐ	ʃ ʒ	ɕ ʑ	ç j	x ɣ	χ ʁ	ħ ʕ	h ɦ
Frictionless continuants and semi-vowels	w ɥ	ʋ	ɹ				j (ɥ)	(w)	ʁ		

Vowels							Front Central Back				
Close	(y ʉ u)						i y i ʉ ɯ u				
Half-close	(ø o)						e ø ɤ o				
Half-open	(œ ɔ)						ə ɛ œ ʌ ɔ				
							æ ɐ				
Open	(ɒ)						a ɑ ɒ				

(Secondary articulations are shown by symbols in brackets.)

OTHER SOUNDS.—Palatalized consonants: ţ, ḑ, etc.; palatalized ʃ, ʒ: ʆ, ʓ. Velarized or pharyngalized consonants: ɫ, đ, ᵶ, etc. Ejective consonants (with simultaneous glottal stop): p', t', etc. Implosive voiced consonants: ɓ, ɗ, etc. ɼ fricative trill. σ, ʠ (labilized θ, ð, or s, z). ʇ, ʒ (labialized ʃ, ʒ). ʗ, ʖ, ʖ(clicks, Zulu c, q, x). ɺ (a sound between r and l). ŋ Japanese syllabic nasal. ɕ(combination of x and ʃ). ʍ (voiceless w). ɪ, ʏ, ᴏ (lowered varieties of i, y, u). ɜ (a variety of ə). ɵ (a vowel between ø and o).

Affricates are normally represented by groups of two consonants (ts, tʃ, dʒ, etc.), but, when necessary, ligatures are used (ʦ, ʧ, ʤ, etc.), or the marks ⌒ or ‿ (t͡s or t͡s, etc.). ⌒ ‿ also denote synchronic articulation(m͡ŋ = simultaneous m and ŋ). c, ɟ may occasionally be used in place of tʃ, dʒ, and ƻ, 2 for ts, dz. Aspirated plosives: ph, th, etc. r-coloured vowels: eɹ, aɹ, ɔɹ, etc., or eʳ, aʳ, ɔʳ, etc., or e, a, ɔ, etc.; r-coloured ə: əɹ or əʳ or ɹ or ɚ or ɝ.

LENGTH, STRESS, PITCH.— ː (full length). ˑ (half length). ' (stress, placed at beginning of the stressed syllable). ˌ (secondary stress). ‾ (high level pitch); _ (low level); ′ (high rising); ˌ (low rising); ˋ (high falling); ˌ (low falling); ^ (rise-fall); ˇ (fall-rise).

MODIFIERS.— ˜ nasality. ̥ breath (l̥ = breathed l). ̬ voice (s̬ = z). ' slight aspiration following p, t, etc. ̫ labialization (n̫ = labialized n). ̪ dental articulation (t̪ = dental t). ˙ palatilization (ż = z). ̣ specially close vowel (ẹ = a very close e). ̦ specially open vowel (ę = a rather open e). ˔ tongue raised (e˔ or ẹ = e). ꞈ tongue lowered (eꞈ or e̠ = e). + tongue advanced (u+ or u̟ = an advanced u, t̟ = t). - or ̠ tongue retracted (i- or i̠ = ɨ+, t̠ = alveolar t). ˒ lips more rounded. ˓ lips more spread. Central vowels: ï (= ɨ), ü (= ʉ), ë (= ə˔), ö (= ɵ), ë̈, ɵ̈. ̩ (e.g. n̩) syllabic consonant. ˘con-sonantal vowel. ʃˢ variety of ʃ resembling s, etc.

Reproduced by kind permission of the Association Phonétique Internationale.

SOME NON-ALPHABETIC SCRIPTS

NAME	USE	EXAMPLES	REMARKS
Chinese characters	Chinese languages. Japanese, Korean	北 京 周 报	Developed from ideographs, approx. 1500 B.C. → character
Cuneiform	Ancient Sumerian, Hittite, etc.	ᚁ ᚂ ᚃ ᚄ ᚅ	Syllabic, developed approx. 3000 B.C. → syllabogram.
Demotic → Hieroglyphics			
Hieratic → Hieroglyphics			
Hieroglyphics	Ancient Egyptian	𓂀 𓃀 𓄿 𓅓	Ideographic script, developed approx. 3500 B.C. Demotic: used for rapid writing, on clay writing, on clay Hieratic: cursive used for formal writing
Hiragana	Japanese	どういたしまして。	Syllabic script developed from Chinese characters, used for verb endings or for native Japanese words in place of characters
Kana	→ Hiragana → Katakana		
Katakana	Japanese	テ イ ー チ ン グ	Syllabic script developed from Chinese characters, used for transcribing foreign names and words

264

SOME ALPHABETIC SCRIPTS

NAME	USE	EXAMPLES	REMARKS
Arabic	Arabic	غ ع ظ ط ض ص	Developed from W. Semitic syllabary, 4th century A.D.
Armenian	Armenian	Ա ա Բ բ Գ գ Դ դ Ե ե	Developed by Mesrop, 5th century A.D.
Cyrillic	Russian, Serbian, Bulgarian, etc.	Аа Бб Вв Гг Дд Жж	Developed by Cyril and Methodius from Greek, 9th century A.D. Forerunner: Glagolitic
Devanagari	Ancient Sanskrit, Modern Indian languages	घ घा ङ ङ ज ऊ	Developed from N. Semitic syllabary. Forerunner: Brahmi script
Glagolitic	Early Slavonic		Forerunner of → Cyrillic
Gothic	Gothic, Early German, English, etc.	ʌ в г ᴆ e ʊ	Developed by Ulfilas, 4th century A.D.
Greek	Ancient Greek, Modern Greek	Αα Ββ Γγ Δδ Εε Ζζ	Developed from Phoenician, 9th century B.C.
Latin/Roman	Latin, most W. European languages, etc.	Aa, Bb, Cc, Dd, Ee, Ff, Gg, Hh, Ii, Jj, Kk, Ll, Mm, Nn, Oo, Pp, Qq, Rr, Ss, Tt, Uu, Vv, Ww, Xx, Yy, Zz	Developed from Greek via Etruscan
Runic	Early Germanic	ᚤ ⋂ ᚦ ᚠ ⟨	Developed from Greek and Latin, used for carving on wood and stone

APPENDIX 1

LIST OF LANGUAGES
OF OVER ONE MILLION SPEAKERS

Families	Number of Languages	Number of Speakers (in millions)
Indo-European	150	over 1,900
Dravidian	10	127
Sino-Tibetan	30	800
Ural-Altaic	40	90
Hamito-Semitic	20	122
African	680	150
Malayo-Polynesian	400	200
American-Indian	500	16
Other (Japanese, Mon-Khmer, Caucasian, Australian, Papuan, etc.)	over 100	over 200
TOTAL	over 2,000	over 3,600

→ Bibliography Section 8.1.

Name of Family, Language	Principal Affiliation	Predominant Location of Speech Community	Approx. No. of Speakers (in mill.)	Total
INDO-EUROPEAN				
English	W Germanic	USA, UK, Commonwealth, S Africa	320	
German	W Germanic	Germany, Austria, Switzerland	100	
Dutch-Flemish	W Germanic	Netherlands, Belgium	18	
Swedish	N Germanic	Sweden	9	
Danish	N Germanic	Denmark	5	
Yiddish	W Germanic	Jewish Communities, USA, Israel	5	
Norwegian	N Germanic	Norway	4	
Afrikaans	W Germanic	South Africa	4	
Frisian, Icelandic, Dutch Creoles, English Pidgins, Luxemburgian, etc.			1	
			——	466
Spanish	W Romance	Spain, Central and South America except Brazil	140	
Portuguese	W Romance	Portugal, Brazil	80	
French	W Romance	France, Canada	80	
Italian	E Romance	Italy	60	
Rumanian	E Romance	Rumania	25	
Provençal	W Romance	France	8	
Catalan	W Romance	Spain	5	
Sardinian, Romansch, Galician, French and Portuguese Creoles, etc.			7	
			——	405

Name of Family, Language	Principal Affiliation	Predominant Location of Speech Community	Approx. No. of Speakers (in mill.)	Total
Great Russian	E Slav(on)ic	USSR	170	
Polish	W Slav(on)ic	Poland	33	
Ukranian	E Slav(on)ic	USSR	41	
Serbo-Croat	S Slav(on)ic	Yugoslavia	15	
Czech	W Slav(on)ic	Czechoslovakia	12	
Byelo-Russian	E Slav(on)ic	USSR	10	
Bulgarian	S Slav(on)ic	Bulgaria	8	
Slovak	W Slav(on)ic	Czechoslovakia	4	
Slovenian	S Slav(on)ic	Yugoslavia	2	
Macedonian	S Slav(on)ic	Yugoslavia	2	
Sorbic, Wendish, etc.			3	
			——	300
Lithuanian	E Baltic	USSR, Lithuania	3	
Latvian/Lettish	E Baltic	USSR, Latvia	2	
			——	5
Albanian	Albanian	Albania	3	3
Armenian	Armenian	USSR, Iran, Lebanon, Turkey, Syria	4	4
Greek	Hellenic	Greece	10	10
Welsh, Breton	Celtic—Brythonic	Wales, Brittany	2	2
Irish, Scots/ Gaelic, Manx	Celtic— Goidelic	Eire, Scotland, Isle of Man	1	1

Name of Family, Language	Principal Affiliation	Predominant Location of Speech Community	Approx. No. of Speakers (in mill.)	Total
Hindi	Indic	N Central India	170	
Bengali	Indic	E India, E Pakistan	90	
Urdu	Indic	W Pakistan	80	
Bihari	Indic	NE India	40	
Marathi	Indic	W India	40	
Punjabi	Indic	N India	35	
Gujerati	Indic	W India	25	
Rajasthani	Indic	NW India	17	
Oriya	Indic	E India	16	
Nepali	Indic	N India	9	
Sinhalese	Indic	Ceylon	10	
Assamese	Indic	E India	8	
Lahnda	Indic	W Pakistan	7	
Sindhi	Indic	W Pakistan	6	
Kashmiri	Indic	Kashmir	3	
Andaman, Pahari, Bhili, Romany/Gypsy, etc.			—	556
Persian	Iranian	Iran, USSR, Afghanistan	22	
Pashto	Iranian	Afghanistan, W Pakistan	15	
Kurdish	Iranian	Iran, Turkey, Iraq	7	
Baluchi	Iranian	W Pakistan	2	
Tati, Ossetic, Tradjik, etc.			—	46
		INDO-EUROPEAN TOTAL	over 1,900	
CAUCASIAN				
Chechenian, Avaric, etc.	NE Caucasian	USSR	1	
Georgian, etc.	S Caucasian	USSR	3	
Cherkessian, Abkhaz, etc.	NW Caucasian	USSR	1	
Mingrelic, Chanic, etc.			1	
			—	6
BASQUE	Basque	S France, N Spain	1	1

Name of Family, Language	Principal Affiliation	Predominant Location of Speech Community	Approx. No. of Speakers (in mill.)	Total
DRAVIDIAN				
Telugu	Andhra	SE India	45	
Tamil	Dravidian	SE India, Ceylon	40	
Kannapese	Dravidian	SW India	20	
Malayalam	Dravidian	SW India	17	
Kurukh	Dravidian	Central E India	2	
Gondi	Dravidian	Central E India	2	
Tulu	Dravidian	SW India	1	
			——	127
SINO-TIBETAN (Tibeto-Chinese)				
Mandarin	Chinese	N & E Central China	500	
Wu	Chinese	E China (Shanghai)	50	
Cantonese	Chinese	S China	50	
Min (Fukien, Foochow, Amoy)	Chinese	S & E China	50	
Hunanese	Chinese		26	
Hakka	Chinese	S China	25	
			——	730
Thai-Siamese, Tho, etc.	Kadai/Thai	Thailand	25	
Laotian	Kadai/Thai	Laos, Thailand	5	
Shan	Kadai/Thai	Burma, Yunan	2	
			——	32
Burmese	Tibeto-Burman	Burma, Thailand	20	
Tibetan	Tibeto-Burman	Tibet, W China, Bhutan	7	
Lolo-Moso	Tibeto-Burman	SW China	3	
Bodo, Naga, Kachin	Tibeto-Burman	Assam, E India	1	
Karen, etc.	Tibeto-Burman	Burma	1	
			——	32
Miao-Yao	Miao	China	3	3
		SINO-TIBETAN TOTAL		800

Name of Family, Language	Principal Affiliation	Predominant Location of Speech Community	Approx. No. of Speakers (in mill.)	Total
JAPANESE—KOREAN				
Japanese, Ryukyu, etc.	Japanese	Japan	100	100
Korean	Korean	Korea	37	37
URAL—ALTAIC				
Turkish	W Turkic	Turkey	28	
Uzbek	W Turkic	S USSR, Afghanistan	7	
Azerbaidjani	W Turkic	S USSR	7	
Kazakh	W Turkic	S USSR, Mongolia	5	
Tatar	W Turkic	USSR	5	
Uighur	W Turkic	S USSR, Sinkiang	4	
Kirghiz	E Turkic	S USSR	2	
Turkmen	W Turkic	S USSR	2	
Altaic	E Turkic	USSR	1	
Bashkir	W Turkic	USSR	1	
Chuvash	W Turkic	USSR	1	
Yakut, etc.	E Turkic	NE USSR		
			——	64
Hungarian	Ugric	Hungary	15	15
Finnish	Finnic	Finland	5	
Estonian	Finnic	USSR, Estonia	1	
Mordvin	Finnic	USSR, Ural	1	
Karelian, Komi, Votyak, Lappish, Samoyed, etc.		USSR	1	
			——	9
Khalka, etc.	Mongolian	USSR, Mongolia	1	1
Manchu, Tungus, etc.	Manchurian	E USSR, Siberia	1	1
		URAL—ALTAIC TOTAL		90

Name of Family, Language	Principal Affiliation	Predominant Location of Speech Community	Approx. No. of Speakers (in mill.)	Total
HAMITO-SEMITIC (Afro-Asiatic)				
Arabic	SW Semitic	Middle East (Egypt and other Arab states), North Africa	80	80
Amharic, Harani, Tigre, etc.	Semitic	Ethiopia	9	9
Hebrew	W Semitic	Israel	2	2
Hausa, etc.	Chad (-Hamitic)	Nigeria, Chad, Volta	15	15
Galla	Cushitic (-Ham.)	Ethiopia, Kenya	6	
Somali, Beja, etc.	Cushitic (-Ham.)	Somalia, Ethiopia	4	
			——	10
Shilha, Kabyle, Tuareg, Rif, etc.		Algeria and neighbouring regions	6	6
HAMITO-SEMITIC TOTAL				122
AFRICAN				
(Ki) Swahili	E Bantu	Kenya, Uganda, Tanzania, Congo	15	
(Ki) Luba, etc.	Central Bantu	S Congo	4	
(Isi) Xhosa	SE Bantu	S Africa	4	
(Isi) Zulu Sotho/(Se) Suto,	SE Bantu	S Africa	4	
(Se) Chuana/ Tswana, Swazi	SE Bantu	Lesotho, Botswana	5	
(Uru-nya) Rwanda	NE Bantu	Rwanda, Tanzania, Uganda, Twanda	5	
(Iki) Rundi	NE Bantu	Twanda, Tanzania, Congo, Burundi	2	
(Ki) Kongo	Central Bantu	E Congo	2	
(Lo) Mongo, (Li) Ngala	Central Bantu	N Congo	3	
Kikuyu, (Ki) Kamba	NE Bantu	Kenya	1	
(Lu) Ganda	N Bantu	Uganda	2	
			——	55

273

Name of Family, Language	Principal Affiliation	Predominant Location of Speech Community	Approx. No. of Speakers (in mill.)	Total
Ibo	S Central Sudanese/Niger	S Nigeria	6	
Yoruba	Sudanese/Niger	W Nigeria	5	
Igbira, Bamum, etc.	Sudanese/Niger	Nigeria, Cameroon	4	
Kanuri, etc.	Nilo-Saharan	Nigeria, Chad	2	
Talodi, etc.	Sudanese	Sudan	5	
Zande, Banda, etc.	S Sudanese	Congo	4	
Bagirmi, etc.	Central Sudanese	Central African Republic	1	
			——	35
Ful(ani)	W Atlantic/ N Guinean	Senegal, Nigeria, Gambia, Guinea, Mali, Sierra Leone	6	
Wolof, Temne, etc.	W Atlantic/ W Guinean	Senegal, Guinea, Liberia	4	
Akan, etc.	Kwa/SE Guinean	Ghana	5	
Ewe	Kwa/SE Guinean	Togo, Ghana		
Fon, etc.	Kwa/SE Guinean	Dahomey, Togo, Ivory Coast	2 3	
Mossi, Senufo, etc.	Gur/Central Guinean	Upper Volta, Mali	4	
Kpelle, Mande, etc.	Mande/NW Guinean	Mali, Guinea	4	
			——	35
Hottentot, etc.	Khoisan	SW Africa		
Bushman, etc.	Khoisan	S Africa	1	

AFRICAN TOTAL   150

Name of Family, Language	Principal Affiliation	Predominant Location of Speech Community	Approx. No. of Speakers (in mill.)	Total
MALAYO-POLYNESIAN (Austronesian)				
Malay	W Indonesian	Malaysia, Republic of Indonesia	⎫ 80	
Bahasa Indonesia	W Indonesian	Malaysia, Republic of Indonesia	⎭	
Javanese	W Indonesia	Java	45	
Sundanese	W Indonesian	Java, Sunda Islands	15	
Malagasy	W Indonesian	Madagascar	5	
Batak	W Indonesian	Sumatra	4	
Madurese	W Indonesian	Java	4	
Buginese	W Indonesian	Borneo	3	
Makassarese	W Indonesian	Borneo, Celebes	3	
Gorontalo, etc.	W Indonesian	Celebes	3	
Balinese	W Indonesian	Bali	3	
Achinese	W Indonesian	Sumatra	1	
			——	170
Bisayan, etc.	N Indonesian	N Borneo, Philippines	12	
Tagalog, etc.	N Indonesian	Philippines	6	
Ilocano, etc.	N Indonesian	Philippines	3	
Formosan	N Indonesian	Taiwan, Hainan	1	
Dayak	N Indonesian	Borneo	2	
			——	24
Various	E Indonesian	Lesser Sundas, Moluccas	1	1
Nauru, etc.	Micronesian	N Pacific Islands	1	1
Fiji, Mola, etc.	Melanesian	Central Pacific Islands	1	1
Hawaiian, Maori, Tahitian, Samoan, etc.	Polynesian	E Pacific Islands	1	1

MALAYO-POLYNESIAN TOTAL   200

Name of Family, Language	Principal Affiliation	Predominant Location of Speech Community	Approx. No. of Speakers (in mill.)	Total
AMERICAN-INDIAN (Amerindian)				
Quechua, etc.	Quechua-Aymara	Peru, Ecuador, Boliva	7	
Tsimshian, etc.	Penutian	W USA	1	
Guaraní, etc.	Tupi-Guaraní	Paraguay, Brazil	1	
Carib, etc.	Arawak	Venezuela, Caribbean	1	
Hopi, Shoshone, etc.	Uto-Aztec-Tanoan	Mexico, SW USA	1	
Karok, Musko-gean, Trognoian, Dakota, etc.	Hoka-Siouan	SW, N, S USA	1	
Quiche, Yucatec	Zoque-Mayan	Mexico, Guatemala, Honduras, Yucatan	1	
Eskimo, Apache, Algonquian, Zapotec, etc.				
	AMERICAN-INDIAN TOTAL			16
OTHER LANGUAGES				
Vietnamese	Vietnamese	Vietnam	27	
Cambodian	Mon-Khmer	Cambodia	4	
Cham, Mon, etc.	Mon-Khmer	E India, Burma	1	
Santali, Mundari	Munda	E India	5	
Papuan, Australian, Palaeo-Asiatic, etc.		Oceania, Australia, E Asia		
	OTHER LANGUAGES TOTAL			40

APPENDIX 2

BIBLIOGRAPHY

Contents

0   *Bibliographies, Periodicals*
    0.1 General
    0.2 Specialised
    0.3 List of Periodicals

1   *Glossaries of Linguistic Terminology*
    1.1 General
    1.2 Specialised

2   *General Linguistics*
    2.1 General Introductions, Textbooks
    2.2 Anthologies, Readings, Surveys
    2.3 More Specialised Works
    2.4 Classics
    2.5 Linguistics as a Science, Schools, Biographies

3   *Phonetics and Phonology*
    3.1 General Introductions, Textbooks
    3.2 Anthologies, Readings, Surveys
    3.3 Specialised Works—Phonetics
    3.4 Specialised Works—Phonology

4   *Grammar*
    4.1 General Introductions, Textbooks
    4.2 More Specialised Works—Morphology and Syntax

5   *Lexicology and Semantics*
    5.1 General Introductions, Textbooks
    5.2 More Specialised Works

6   *Historical and Comparative Linguistics*
    6.1 General Introductions, Textbooks
    6.2 More Specialised Works

7   *Spoken and Written Varieties*
    7.1 Social and Regional Varieties, Dialectology
    7.2 Writing, Reading, Graphemics
    7.3 Literature, Stylistics, Rhetoric

0 Bibliographies, Periodicals

0.1 GENERAL BIBLIOGRAPHIES (→ Periodicals 0.3 below)

PERMANENT INTERNATIONAL COMMITTEE OF LINGUISTS (Ed.),
Linguistic Bibliography/Bibliographie Linguistique, Spectrum, Utrecht-Antwerp 1949 ff.

MLA, *1969 International Bibliography of Books and Articles on the Modern Languages and Literatures*
      Vol. I: General, English, Medieval and Celtic Literatures
      Vol. II: European, Asian, African, Latin American Literatures
      Vol. III: Linguistics
      Vol. IV: Pedagogy in Foreign Languages
   MLA/ACTFL New York; Banta, Menasha, Wisconsin 1970.

0.2 SPECIALISED BIBLIOGRAPHIES (→ Periodicals 0.3 below)

H. B. ALLEN, *Linguistics and English Linguistics* (Goldentree Bibliographies), Appleton-Century-Crofts, New York 1966.

R. W. BAILEY and D. M. BURTON, *English Stylistics: A Bibliography*, M.I.T. Press, Cambridge, Massachusetts 1968.

K.-R. BAUSCH, *et al.*, *The Science of Translation. An Analytical Bibliography* (1962–1969), TBL, Tübingen 1970.

B. A. BLASS, *et al.*, *A Provisional Survey of Materials for the Study of Neglected Languages*, CAL, Washington D.C. 1969.

CILT/ETIC (Ed.), *A Language Teaching Bibliography*, Cambridge University Press, London 1968, 1972.

E. I. HAUGEN, *Bilingualism in the Americas. A Bibliography and Research Guide*, American Dialect Society/Alabama University Press 1956.

R. D. HUGONIOT (Ed.), *A Bibliographical Index of the Lesser-Known Languages of India and Nepal*, SIL 1970.

H. KRENN and K. MÜLLNER, *Bibliographie zur Transformationsgrammatik*, C. Winter, Heidelberg 1968.

W. F. LEOPOLD, *Bibliography of Child Language*, Northwestern University Press, Evanston, Illinois 1952, 1970.

D. I. MULGRAVE, *et al.*, *Bibliography of Speech and Allied Areas 1950–1960*. Chilton, Philadelphia, Pennsylvania 1962.

G. D. MURPHY and H. GOFF, *A Bibliography of African Languages and Linguistics*, Catholic University of America Press, Washington D.C. 1969.

G. PRICE, *The Present Position of Minority Languages in Western Europe. A Selective Bibliography*, University of Wales Press, Cardiff 1969.

F. A. RICE, *Study Aids for Critical Languages*, CAL, Washington D.C. rev. ed. 1968.

E. STANKIEWICZ and D. S. WORTH (Eds.), *A Selected Bibliography of Slavic Linguistics*, 2 vols., Mouton, The Hague 1970.

I. TEOK, *Selected Bibliography in Linguistics and the Uncommonly Taught Languages*, CAL/ERIC, Washington D.C. 1967.

H. TONKIN, *A Research Bibliography on Esperanto and International Language Problems*, Esperanto Information Center, New York 1967.

UNESCO (*Ed.*), *Literacy Teaching. A Selected Bibliography*, UNESCO, Paris 1956.

T. W. WALTERS, *The Georgetown Bibliography of Studies Contributing to the Psycholinguistics of Language Learning*, Georgetown University Press, Washington D.C. 1965.

0.3 LIST OF PERIODICALS (with abbreviations)

ACTA LINGUISTICA HAFNIENSIA (ALH), International Journal of Structural Linguistics, Irregular, Munksgaard, Copenhagen 1953 ff.

AFRICAN LANGUAGE STUDIES (AfrLS), 1 issue per year, SOAS/Luzac, London 1960 ff.

AMERICAN SPEECH (AS), A Quarterly of Linguistic Usage, 4 issues per year, Columbia University Press, New York 1926 ff.

ANTHROPOLOGICAL LINGUISTICS (AnL), 9 issues per year, Indiana University, Bloomington, Indiana 1959 ff.

ARCHIVUM LINGUISTICUM (ArchL), A Review of Comparative Philology and General Linguistics, 2 issues per year, Scolar Press, Menston, Yorks 1949/1970 ff.

AUDIO-VISUAL LANGUAGE JOURNAL (AVLJ), Journal of Applied Linguistics and Language Teaching Technology, 3 issues per year, AVLA, Hanbury, London 1964 ff.

BABEL (Ba), International Journal Devoted to Information and Research in Translation, 4 issues per year, FIT, Avignon 1955 ff.

BEITRÄGE ZUR LINGUISTIK UND INFORMATIONSVERARBEI-TUNG (BLI), Irregular, Oldenbourg, Munich 1963 ff.

The BIBLE TRANSLATOR, 4 issues per year, United Bible Societies, London 1950 ff.

The BRITISH JOURNAL OF DISORDERS OF COMMUNICATION, 2 issues per year, College of Speech Therapists/Livingstone, Edinburgh 1966 ff.

CAHIERS DE LEXICOLOGIE (CLex), 2 issues per year, Didier-Larousse, Paris 1957 ff.

The CANADIAN JOURNAL OF LINGUISTICS (CJL), 2 issues per year, University of Toronto Press, Toronto 1955 ff.

ENGLISH LANGUAGE TEACHING (ELT), English as a Foreign or Second Language, 4 issues per year, Oxford University Press, London 1946 ff.

ENGLISH STUDIES (ES), A Journal of English Letters and Philology, 6 issues per year, Swets & Zeitlinger, Amsterdam 1920 ff.

ETC, A Review of General Semantics, 4 issues per year, ISGS, San Francisco, California 1943 ff.

FOLIA LINGUISTICA (FL), Acta Societatis Linguisticae Europaeae, 2 parts per year, Mouton, The Hague 1967 ff.

FOUNDATIONS OF LANGUAGE (FoL), International Journal of Language and Philosophy, 4 issues per year, Reidel, Dordrecht 1965 ff.

INTERNATIONAL JOURNAL OF AMERICAN LINGUISTICS (IJAL), 4 issues per year, Indiana University, Bloomington, Indiana 1917 ff.

INTERNATIONAL JOURNAL OF SLAVIC LINGUISTICS AND POETICS (IJSLP), 1 issue per year, Mouton, The Hague 1959 ff.

INTERNATIONAL REVIEW OF APPLIED LINGUISTICS IN LANGU-AGE TEACHING (IRAL), 4 issues per year, Groos, Heidelberg 1963 ff.

JOURNAL OF THE INTERNATIONAL PHONETIC ASSOCIATION, 2 issues per year, IPA/Austin, London 1886/1971 ff.

JOURNAL OF LINGUISTICS (JL), 2 issues per year, Cambridge University Press, London 1965 ff.

JOURNAL OF SPEECH AND HEARING DISORDERS (JSHD), 4 issues per year, American Speech and Hearing Association, Washington D.C. 1936 ff.

JOURNAL OF VERBAL LEARNING AND VERBAL BEHAVIOR (JVL), 6 issues per year, Academic Press, New York 1962 ff.

LANGAGES, 4 issues per year, Didier-Larousse, Paris 1966 ff.

LANGUAGE (Lg), Journal of the Linguistic Society of America, 4 issues per year, Waverley, Baltimore, Maryland 1924 ff.

LANGUAGE AND AUTOMATION, An International Reference Publication, 4 issues per year, CAL, Washington D.C. 1970 ff.

LANGUAGE AND LANGUAGE BEHAVIOR ABSTRACTS (LLBA), 4 issues per year, CRLLB/BELC, Mouton, The Hague 1967 ff.

LANGUAGE AND SOCIETY, 2 issues per year, Cambridge University Press, London 1972 ff.

LANGUAGE AND SPEECH (L & S), 4 parts per year, Draper, Teddington, Middlesex 1958 ff.

LANGUAGE AND STYLE, 4 issues per year, S. Illinois University Press, Carbondale 1968 ff.

LANGUAGE LEARNING (LL), A Journal of Applied Linguistics, 4 issues per year, University of Michigan, Ann Arbor, Michigan 1948 ff.

LANGUAGE SCIENCES, 5 issues per year, Research Center for the Language Sciences, Bloomington, Indiana 1968 ff.

LANGUAGE TEACHING ABSTRACTS (LTA), 4 issues per year, ETIC/ CILT, Cambridge University Press, London 1968 ff.

LINGUA, International Review of General Linguistics, 4 issues per year, North-Holland, Amsterdam 1948 ff.

LINGUISTIC INQUIRY, 4 issues per year, M.I.T. Press, Cambridge, Massachusetts 1970 ff.

LINGUISTIC REPORTER (LR), Newsletter of the Center for Applied Linguistics, 6 issues per year, CAL, Washington D.C. 1959 ff.

LINGUISTICS, An International Review, Irregular, Mouton, The Hague, 1963 ff.

LA LINGUISTIQUE, Revue internationale de linguistique générale, 2 issues per year, Presses Universitaires de France, Paris 1965 ff.

MECHANICAL TRANSLATION AND COMPUTATIONAL LIN-GUISTICS (MT), Irregular, University of Chicago Press 1954 ff.

MODERN LANGUAGE JOURNAL (MLJ), 8 issues per year, NFMLTA/ Banta, Menasha, Wisconsin 1917 ff.

MODERN LANGUAGES (ML), Journal of the Modern Language Association, 4 issues per year, MLA, London 1950 ff.

MONDA LINGVO PROBLEMO, 3 issues per year, Mouton, The Hague 1969 ff.

ONOMA, Bibliographical and Information Bulletin, 3 issues per year, ICO, Leuven 1950 ff.

ORBIS, Bulletin international de documentation linquistique, 2 issues per year, CIDG, Louvain 1952 ff.

PHONETICA, International Journal of Phonetics, 4 issues per year, Karger, Basel 1954 ff.

PUBLICATIONS OF THE MODERN LANGUAGE ASSOCIATION OF AMERICA (PMLA), 7 issues per year, MLA/Banta, Menasha, Wisconsin 1884 ff.

QUARTERLY JOURNAL OF SPEECH (QJSp), 4 issues per year, Speech Association of America, New York 1915 ff.

READING, A Journal for the Study and Improvement of Reading and Related Skills, 3 issues per year, Asher-Cashden, Edinburgh 1966 ff.

ROMANCE PHILOLOGY (RomPh), 4 issues per year, University of California Press, Berkeley, California 1949 ff.

SEMIOTICA, 4 issues per year, Mouton, The Hague 1969 ff.

STUDIA LINGUISTICA (SL), Revue de linguistique générale et comparée, 2 issues per year, Gleerup, Lund 1947 ff.

VOPROSY YAZYKOZNANIYA (VJa), 6 issues per year, Akademia Nauk, Moscow 1952 ff.

WORD, Journal of the International Linguistics Association, 3 issues per year, City College of New York 1945 ff.

THE YEAR'S WORK IN MODERN LANGUAGE STUDIES (YWMLS), 1 issue per year, Modern Humanities Research Association, Cambridge 1929 ff.

ZEITSCHRIFT FÜR DIALEKTOLOGIE UND LINGUISTIK (ZDL), 4 issues per year, Steiner, Wiesbaden 1934/1969 ff.

ZEITSCHRIFT FÜR PHONETIK, SPRACHWISSENSCHAFT UND KOMMUNIKATIONSFORSCHUNG (ZPhon), 4 issues per year, Akademie-Verlag, Berlin 1948 ff.

1. Glossaries of Linguistic Terminology

1.1 GENERAL GLOSSARIES

S. GERSON, *A Glossary of Grammatical Terms*, University of Queensland Press, St Lucia 1969.

A. R. MEETHAM (Ed.), *Encyclopedia of Linguistics, Information and Control*, Pergamon, Oxford 1969.

R. NASH (Ed.), *Multilingual Lexicon of Linguistics and Philology* (English, Russian, German, French), University of Miami Press, Coral Gables, Florida 1968.

M. PEI, *A Glossary of Linguistic Terminology*, Doubleday-Anchor, Garden City, New York 1966.

D. J. STEIBLE, *Concise Handbook of Linguistics*, P. Owen, London 1967.

1.2 SPECIALISED GLOSSARIES

J. H. BLAIR, *A Glossary of Language-Learning Terms*, Blackie, London 1963.

E. P. HAMP, *A Glossary of American Technical Linguistic Usage, 1925-1950*, Spectrum, Utrecht-Antwerp (reprinted with addenda) 1963.

R. PALMATIER, *Dictionary of Transformational-Generative Terminology*, Appleton-Century-Crofts, New York (forthcoming).

J. VACHEK and J. DUBSKY (Eds.), *Dictionnaire de Linguistique de l'Ecole de Prague*, Spectrum, Utrecht-Antwerp 1966.

K. S. WOOD, 'Terminology and Nomenclature' in *Handbook of Speech Pathology and Audiology* (→ 9.5 TRAVIS).

2. General Linguistics

2.1 GENERAL INTRODUCTIONS, TEXTBOOKS

G. BARRY et al. (Eds.), *Communication and Language. Networks of Thought and Action*, Macdonald Illustrated Library, London 1965.

D. L. BOLINGER, *Aspects of Language* (with *Workbook* 1970), Harcourt, New York 1968.

Y. R. CHAO, *Language and Symbolic Systems*, Cambridge University Press, London 1968.

N. CHOMSKY, *Selected Readings*, Ed. by J. P. B. Allen, P. van Buren, Oxford University Press, London 1971.

D. CRYSTAL, *What is Linguistics?* E. Arnold, London 1968.

D. CRYSTAL, *Linguistics*, Penguin Books, Harmondsworth, Middlesex 1971.

J. P. DINNEEN, *An Introduction to General Linguistics*, Holt, Rinehart & Winston, New York 1967.

P. A. GAENG, *Introduction to the Principles of Language*, Harper & Row, New York 1971.

H. A. GLEASON, Jr., *An Introduction to Descriptive Linguistics* (with *Workbook*), New York–London 1955.

G. W. GRAY and C. M. WISE, *The Bases of Speech*, Harper, New York–London 1958.

J. H. GREENBERG, *Anthropological Linguistics: An Introduction*, Random-House, New York–London 1968.

R. A. HALL, Jr., *Introductory Linguistics*, Chilton, Philadelphia–New York 1964.

R. A. HALL, Jr., *Linguistics and Your Language*, 2nd rev. ed., Doubleday-Anchor, New York 1960.

S. I. HAYAKAWA, *Language in Thought and Action*, 2nd ed., Harcourt, New York/Allen & Unwin, London 1965.

L. HJELMSLEV, *Language: An Introduction* (Translated from the Danish by F. J. Whitfield), University of Wisconsin Press, Madison 1970.

C. F. HOCKETT, *A Course in Modern Linguistics*, Macmillan, New York 1958.

R. W. LANGACKER, *Language and its Structure. Some Fundamental Linguistic Concepts*, Harcourt, New York 1968.

J. LYONS, *Introduction to Theoretical Linguistics*, Cambridge University Press, London 1968.

B. MALMBERG, *Structural Linguistics and Human Communication. An Introduction into the Mechanism of Language and the Methodology of Linguistics*, Springer, Berlin 1963.

A. MARTINET, *Elements of General Linguistics* (Translated from the French by E. Palmer), Faber, London 1966.

J. ORNSTEIN and W. W. GAGE, *The ABC's of Languages and Linguistics*, Chilton Books, Philadelphia 1964.

S. POTTER, *Language in the Modern World*, Penguin Books, Harmondsworth, Middlesex 1960.

R. H. ROBINS, *General Linguistics. An Introductory Survey*, 2nd ed., Longman, London 1971.

G. L. TRAGER, *Language and Languages*, Chandler, San Francisco 1972.

J. F. WALLWORK, *Language and Linguistics. An Introduction to the Study of Language*, Heinemann, London 1969.

A. WILKINSON, *The Foundations of Language. Talking and Reading in Young Children*, Oxford University Press, London 1971.

2.2 ANTHOLOGIES, READINGS, SURVEYS

W. L. ANDERSON and N. C. STAGEBERG (Eds.), *Introductory Readings of Language*, 2nd ed., Holt, Rinehart & Winston, New York 1966.

E. BACH and R. T. HARMS (Eds.), *Universals in Linguistic Theory*, Holt, London 1968.

C. E. BAZELL *et al.* (Eds.), *In Memory of J. R. Firth*, Longman, London 1966.

M. BIERWISCH and K. E. HEIDOLPH (Eds.), *Progress in Linguistics*, Mouton, The Hague 1970.

P. L. GARVIN (Ed.), *Method and Theory in Linguistics*, Mouton, The Hague 1970.

E. HAMP *et al.* (Eds.), *Readings in Linguistics II* (European Linguistics), Chicago University Press, Chicago–London 1966.

A. A. HILL (Ed.), *Linguistics Today*, Basic Books, New York 1969.

J. B. HOGINS and R. E. YARBER, *Language. An Introductory Reader*, Harper & Row, New York 1969.

M. JOOS (Ed.), *Readings in Linguistics I. The Development of Descriptive Linguistics in America 1925–56*, 4th ed., Chicago University Press, Chicago–London 1966.

E. H. LENNEBERG (Ed.), *New Directions in the Study of Language*, M.I.T. Press, Cambridge, Massachusetts 1964.

J. LYONS (Ed.), *New Horizons in Linguistics*, Penguin Books, Harmondsworth, Middlesex 1970.

N. MINNIS (Ed.), *Linguistics at Large. 14 Linguistic Lectures Presented by the Institute of Contemporary Arts 1969–70*, Gollancz, London 1971.

C. MOHRMANN *et al.* (Eds.), *Trends in Modern Linguistics*, Spectrum, Utrecht–Antwerp 1961.

C. MOHRMANN *et al.* (Eds.), *Trends in European and American Linguistics 1930–1960*, Spectrum, Utrecht–Antwerp 1961.

I. RAUCH and C. T. SCOTT (Eds.), *Approaches in Linguistic Methodology*, University of Wisconsin Press, Madison 1967.

T. A. SEBEOK (Gen. Ed.), *Current Trends in Linguistics*
  Vol. I   Soviet and East European Linguistics (1963)
  Vol. II   Linguistics in East Asia and S.E. Asia (1967)
  Vol. III   Theoretical Foundations (1966)
  Vol. IV   Ibero-American and Caribbean Linguistics (1968)
  Vol. V   Linguistics in South Asia (1969)
  Vol. VI   Linguistics in S.W. Asia and N. Africa (1970)
  Vol. VII   Linguistics in Sub-Saharan Africa (1971)
  Vol. VIII Linguistics in Oceania (1971)

Vol. IX   Linguistics in W. Europe (forthcoming)
Vol. X   Linguistics in N. America (forthcoming)
Vol. XI   Diachronic, Areal and Typological Linguistics (forthcoming)
Vol. XII   Linguistics and Adjacent Arts & Sciences (forthcoming)
Mouton, The Hague.

G. WILSON (Ed.), *A Linguistics Reader*, Harper & Row, New York 1967.

2.3   MORE SPECIALISED WORKS

R. L. BIRDWHISTELL, *Kinesics and Context. Essays on Body Motion Communication*, Pennsylvania University Press, Philadelphia 1970.

W. L. CHAFE, *Meaning and the Structure of Language*, University of Chicago Press, Chicago–London 1971.

J. H. GREENBERG, *Language Universals with Special Reference to Feature Hierarchies*, Mouton, The Hague 1966.

M. R. HAAS, *The Prehistory of Languages*, Mouton, The Hague 1969.

M. A. K. HALLIDAY and A. McINTOSH, *Patterns of Language*, Longman, London 1966.

Z. S. HARRIS, *Papers in Structural and Transformational Linguistics*, Reidel, Dordrecht 1970.

L. G. HELLER and J. MACRIS, *Parametric Linguistics*, Mouton, The Hague 1967.

F. W. HOUSEHOLDER, *Linguistic Speculations*, Cambridge University Press, London 1971.

J. J. KATZ and P. M. POSTAL, *An Integrated Theory of Linguistic Descriptions*, M.I.T. Press, Cambridge, Massachusetts 1964.

R. E. PITTENGER *et al.*, *The First Five Minutes. A Sample of Microscopic Interview Analysis*, P. Martineau, Ithaca, New York 1960.

R. QUIRK and J. SVARTVIK, *Investigating Linguistic Acceptability*, Mouton, The Hague 1966.

W. J. SAMARIN, *Field Linguistics. A Guide to Linguistic Field Work*, Holt, New York–London 1967.

S. K. ŠAUMJAN, *Principles of Structural Linguistics* (translated from the Russian by J. Miller), Mouton, The Hague 1971.

2.4   CLASSICS

L. BLOOMFIELD, *Language* (1st ed. 1933), 8th ed. Allen & Unwin, London 1962.

F. BOAS, *Introduction to the Handbook of American Indian Languages* (1st ed. 1911), Georgetown University Press, Washington D.C. 1963.

J. R. FIRTH, *Papers in Linguistics 1934–1951*, Oxford University Press, London 1957.

D. E. HAYDEN *et al.* (Eds.), *Classics in Linguistics*, Owen, London, 1968.

W. von HUMBOLDT, *Linguistic Variability and Intellectual Development* (1st ed. 1836), (translated from the German by G. C. Buck and F. A. Raven), Miami University Press, Coral Gables 1971.

O. JESPERSEN, *Language. Its Nature, Development and Origin* (1st ed. 1922), 10th ed. Allen & Unwin, London 1954.

285

E. SAPIR, *Language. An Introduction to the Study of Speech* (1st ed. 1922), Harvest Books, New York–London 1955.
F. de SAUSSURE, *Course in General Linguistics* (1st ed. 1915, translated from the French by W. Baskin), McGraw-Hill, New York–London 1966.
H. SWEET, *The Practical Study of Languages* (1st ed. 1899), Oxford University Press, London 1964.

2.5 LINGUISTICS AS A SCIENCE, SCHOOLS, BIOGRAPHIES

N. CHOMSKY, *Cartesian Linguistics. A Chapter in the History of Rationalist Thought*, Harper & Row, New York 1966.
W. A. COOK, *Introduction to Tagmemic Analysis*, Holt, New York–London 1971.
R. M. W. DIXON, *What IS Language? A New Approach to Linguistic Description*, Longman, London 1965.
V. FRIED (Ed.), *The Prague School of Linguistics and Language Teaching*, Oxford University Press, London 1972.
R. GODEL (Ed.), *A Geneva School Reader in Linguistics*, Indiana University Press, Bloomington, Indiana 1969.
R. A. HALL, *Idealism in Romance Linguistics*, Cornell University Press, Ithaca, New York 1963.
L. HJELMSLEV, *Prolegomena to a Theory of Language* (1st ed. 1943, translated from the Danish by F. J. Whitfield), 2nd ed. University of Wisconsin Press, Madison 1961.
C. F. HOCKETT, *The State of the Art*, Mouton, The Hague 1968.
M. IVIĆ, *Trends in Linguistics* (translated from the Serbo-Croat by M. Heppell), Mouton, The Hague 1965.
D. T. LANGENDOEN, *The London School of Linguistics. A Study of the Linguistic Theories of B. Malinowski and J. R. Firth*, M.I.T. Press, Cambridge, Massachusetts 1968.
G. C. LEPSCHY, *A Survey of Structural Linguistics*, Faber, London 1970.
J. LYONS, *Chomsky*, Fontana, London 1970.
H. PEDERSEN, *The Discovery of Language. Linguistic Science in the 19th Century* (1st ed. 1931, translated from the Danish by J. W. Spargo), Indiana University Press, Bloomington, Indiana 1962.
P. M. POSTAL, *Constituent Structure. A Study of Contemporary Models of Syntactic Descriptions*, Indiana University Press, Bloomington 1964.
R. H. ROBINS, *A Short History of Linguistics*, Longman, London 1967.
T. A. SEBEOK (Ed.), *Portraits of Linguists. A Biographical Source Book for the History of Western Linguistics 1746–1963* (2 vols.), Indiana University Press, Bloomington–London 1966.
B. SIERTSEMA, *A Study of Glossematics*, 2nd ed. Nijhoff, The Hague 1965.
J. VACHEK, *The Linguistic School of Prague*, Indiana University Press, Bloomington, Indiana 1966.
J. T. WATERMAN, *Perspectives in Linguistics. An Account of the Background of Modern Linguistics*, 2nd ed., University of Chicago Press, Chicago, Illinois 1970.

3. Phonetics and Phonology
(→ also Sections 1 and 2 above and 8.22 below)

3.1 GENERAL INTRODUCTIONS, TEXTBOOKS

D. ABERCROMBIE, *Elements of General Phonetics*, Edinburgh University Press, Edinburgh 1967.

L. F. BROSNAHAN and B. MALMBERG, *Introduction to Phonetics*, Heffer, Cambridge 1970.

C. D. BUCHANAN, *A Programmed Introduction to Linguistics: Phonetics and Phonemics*, Heath, Boston, Massachusetts 1963.

R. S. HEFFNER, *General Phonetics*, Wisconsin University Press, Madison, Wisconsin 1950, 1964.

P. LADEFOGED, *Elements of Acoustic Phonetics*, Oliver & Boyd, London/ University of Chicago Press, 1962.

B. MALMBERG, *Phonetics* (1st ed. 1960, translated from the French), Dover, New York 1963.

J. D. O'CONNOR, *Phonetics*, Penguin Books, Harmondsworth, Middlesex (forthcoming).

K. L. PIKE, *Phonetics. A Critical Analysis of Phonetic Theory and a Technic for the Practical Description of Sounds*, University of Michigan Press, Ann Arbor, Michigan–London 1944, 1962.

H. SWEET, *The Indispensable Foundation*, Ed. by E. J. A. Henderson, Oxford University Press, London 1971.

3.2 ANTHOLOGIES, READINGS, SURVEYS

D. ABERCROMBIE *et al.* (Eds.), *In Honour of Daniel Jones. Papers Contributed on the Occasion of his Eightieth Birthday 1961*, Longman, London 1964.

I. LEHISTE (Ed.), *Readings in Acoustic Phonetics*, M.I.T. Press, Cambridge, Massachusetts 1967.

B. MALMBERG (Ed.), *Manual of Phonetics*, 2nd ed., North-Holland, Amsterdam 1968.

3.3 SPECIALISED WORKS—PHONETICS

D. H. ECROYD *et al.*, *Voice and Articulation. A Handbook*, Scott-Foresman, Glenview, Illinois 1966.

R. JAKOBSON *et al.*, *Preliminaries to Speech Analysis. The Distinctive Features and Their Correlates*, 2nd ed., M.I.T. Press, Cambridge, Massachusetts 1963.

M. JOOS, *Acoustic Phonetics*, L.S.A. Language Monograph, Baltimore, Maryland 1948.

P. LADEFOGED, *Three Areas of Experimental Phonetics*, Oxford University Press, London 1967.

P. LIEBERMAN, *Intonation, Perception and Language*, M.I.T. Press, Cambridge, Massachusetts 1967.

H. MOL, *Fundamentals of Phonetics*, Vol. I: Hearing; Vol. II: Acoustical Models, Mouton, The Hague 1963–70.

R. K. POTTER *et al.*, *Visible Speech*, 2nd ed., Dover, New York 1966.

3.4 Specialised Works—Phonology

E. J. BRIÈRE, *A Psycholinguistic Study of Phonological Interference*, Mouton, The Hague 1968.

J. E. GRIMES, *Phonological Analysis I*, S.I.L., Santa Ana, California 1969.

R. T. HARMS, *Introduction to Phonological Theory*, Prentice-Hall, Englewood Cliffs, New Jersey 1968.

C. F. HOCKETT, *A Manual of Phonology*, Indiana University Press, Bloomington 1955.

I. LEHISTE, *Suprasegmentals*, M.I.T. Press, Cambridge, Massachusetts 1970.

V. B. MAKKAI, *Phonological Theory. Evolution and Current Practice*, Harper & Row, New York 1970.

F. R. PALMER (Ed.), *Prosodic Analysis*, Oxford University Press, London 1969.

K. L. PIKE, *Phonemics. A Technique for Reducing Languages to Writing*, University of Michigan Press, Ann Arbor, Michigan 1947, 1963.

K. L. PIKE, *Tone Languages*, University of Michigan Press, Ann Arbor, Michigan 1948, 1967.

P. POSTAL, *Aspects of Phonological Theory*, Harper & Row, New York 1968.

E. PULGRAM, *Syllable, Word, Nexus, Cursus*, Mouton, The Hague 1970.

N. S. TRUBETZKOY, *Principles of Phonology* (1st ed. 1939, translated from the German by C. A. M. Baltaxe), California University Press, Berkeley, California, 1969.

4. Grammar

(→ also Sections 1 and 2 above and 8.23 below)

4.1 General Introduction, Textbooks

M. K. BURT, *From Deep to Surface Structure: An Introduction to Transformational Syntax*, Harper & Row, New York, 1971.

B. ELSON and V. B. PICKETT, *Introduction to Morphology and Syntax* (with *Laboratory Manual* 1968), 4th ed., Summer Institute of Linguistics, Santa Ana, California 1965.

R. FOWLER, *An Introduction to Transformational Syntax*, Routledge, London 1971.

J. H. HERNDON, *A Survey of Modern Grammars*, Holt, New York–London 1970.

F. R. PALMER, *Grammar*, Penguin Books, Harmondsworth, Middlesex 1971.

4.2 More Specialised Works—Morphology and Syntax

O. S. AKHMANOVA and J. MIKAELAN, *The Theory of Syntax in Modern Linguistics*, Mouton, The Hague 1969.

J. M. ANDERSON, *The Grammar of Case. Towards a Localistic Theory*, Cambridge University Press, London 1971.

E. BACH, *An Introduction to Transformational Grammars*, Holt, New York–London 1964.

N. CHOMSKY, *Aspects of the Theory of Syntax*, M.I.T. Press, Cambridge, Massachusetts 1965.

S. C. DIK, *Coordination. Its Implications for the Theory of General Linguistics*, North-Holland, Amsterdam 1968.

M. GROSS and A. LENTIN, *Introduction to Formal Grammars* (translated from the French by M. Salkoff), Springer, Berlin/Allen & Unwin, London 1970.

O. JESPERSEN, *Analytic Syntax* (1st ed. 1937), Holt, New York-London 1969.

A. KOUTSOUDAS, *Writing Transformational Grammars. An Introduction*, McGraw-Hill, New York 1966.

G. LAKOFF, *Irregularities in Syntax*, Holt, New York 1970.

S. M. LAMB, *An Outline of Stratificational Grammar*, Georgetown University Press, Washington D.C. 1966.

R. E. LONGACRE, *Grammar Discovery Procedures: A Field Manual*, Mouton, The Hague 1964.

E. A. NIDA, *Morphology. The Descriptive Analysis of Words*, 2nd ed., University of Michigan Press, Ann Arbor, Michigan 1949.

P. A. M. SEUREN, *Operators and Nucleus. A Contribution to the Theory of Grammar*, Cambridge University Press, London 1969.

P. SGALL et al., *A Functional Approach to Syntax*, Elsevier, Amsterdam 1969.

5. Lexicology and Semantics
(→ also Sections 1 and 2 above and 8.24–8.25 below)

5.1 GENERAL INTRODUCTIONS, TEXTBOOKS

R. BARTHES, *Elements of Semiology* (translated from the French by A. Lavers and C. Smith), Cape, London 1967.

F. H. GEORGE, *Semantics*, English Universities Press, London 1964.

D. E. HAYDEN and E. P. ALWORTH (Eds.), *Classics in Semantics*, Philosophical Library, New York 1965.

G. N. LEECH, *Semantics*, Penguin Books, Harmondsworth, Middlesex (forthcoming).

C. K. OGDEN and I. E. RICHARDS, *The Meaning of Meaning* (1st ed. 1923), 10th ed. Routledge, London 1949.

L. B. SALOMON, *Semantics and Common Sense*, Holt, New York 1966.

S. ULLMANN, *Semantics. An Introduction to the Science of Meaning*, Blackwell, Oxford 1962.

R. A. WALDRON, *Sense and Sense Development*, Deutsch, London 1967.

5.2 MORE SPECIALISED WORKS

E. H. BENDIX, *Componential Analysis of General Vocabulary. The Semantic Structure of a Set of Verbs in English, Hindi and Japanese*, Indiana University Press, Bloomington, Indiana/Mouton, The Hague 1966.

B. BERLIN and P. KAY, *Basic Colour Terms. Their Universality and Evolution*, University of California Press, Berkeley, California 1969.

289

R. CARNAP, *Introduction to Semantics*, M.I.T. Press, Cambridge, Massachusetts 1948.

C. J. FILLMORE and D. T. LANGENDOEN (Eds.), *Studies in Linguistic Semantics*, Holt, New York 1971.

F. W. HOUSEHOLDER and S. SAPORTA (Eds.), *Problems in Lexicography. Conference at Indiana University 1960*, Indiana University Press, Bloomington, Indiana 1962.

C. MORRIS, *Signification and Significance. A Study of the Relations of Signs and Values*, M.I.T. Press, Cambridge, Massachusetts 1964.

C. E. OSGOOD *et al.*, *The Measurement of Meaning*, University of Illinois Press, Urbana, Illinois 1957.

W. Van O. QUINE, *Word and Object*, M.I.T. Press, Cambridge, Massachusetts 1960.

D. D. STEINBERG and L. A. JAKOBOVITS (Eds.), *Semantics. An Interdisciplinary Reader in Philosophy, Linguistics and Psychology*, Cambridge University Press, London 1971.

S. ULLMANN, *The Principles of Semantics* (2nd rev. ed.), Blackwell, Oxford 1960.

L. ZGUSTA *et al.* (Eds.), *Manual of Lexicography*, Mouton, The Hague 1971.

P. ZIFF, *Semantic Analysis*, Cornell University Press, Ithaca, New York 1960.

6. Historical and Comparative Linguistics

(→ also Sections 2 above and 8 below)

6.1 GENERAL INTRODUCTIONS, TEXTBOOKS

J. ELLIS, *Toward a General Comparative Linguistics*, Mouton, The Hague 1966.

W. P. LEHMANN, *Historical Linguistics: An Introduction*, Holt, New York–London 1962.

W. B. LOCKWOOD, *Indo-European Philology*, Hutchinson, London 1969.

R. LORD, *Teach Yourself Comparative Linguistics*, English Universities Press, London 1966.

P. WOLFF, *Western Languages A.D. 100–1500* (translated from the French by F. Partridge), Weidenfeld & Nicolson, London 1971.

6.2 MORE SPECIALISED WORKS

I. FODOR, *The Rate of Linguistic Change: Limits of the Application of Mathematical Methods in Linguistics*, Mouton, The Hague 1965.

H. HOENIGSWALD, *Language Change and Linguistic Reconstruction*, University of Chicago Press, Chicago, Illinois 1960.

K. M. HORNE, *Language Typology, 19th and 20th Century Views*, Georgetown University Press, Washington, D.C. 1966.

R. D. KING, *Historical Linguistics and Generative Grammar*, Prentice-Hall, Englewood Cliffs, New Jersey 1969.

W. P. LEHMANN (Ed. & Translator), *A Reader in Nineteenth-Century Historical Indo-European Linguistics*, Indiana University Press, Bloomington, Indiana 1967.

7. Spoken and Written Varieties

(→ also Section 2 above and Sections 8.24, 9.1 and 10.1 below)

7.1 SOCIAL AND REGIONAL VARIETIES, DIALECTOLOGY

P. S. DOUGHTY *et al.*, *Language in Use*, Arnold, London 1971.

S. ELLIS (Ed.), *Studies in Honour of Harold Orton on the Occasion of his 70th Birthday*, Leeds Studies in English (New Series Vol. II) 1969.

H. KURATH, *Areal Linguistics. Problems, Methods, Results*, Indiana University Press, Bloomington, Indiana (forthcoming).

R. W. SHUY *et al.*, *Field Techniques in an Urban Language Study* (Urban Language Series, 3), CAL, Washington D.C. 1968.

7.2 WRITING, READING, GRAPHEMICS

D. DIRINGER, *Writing*, Thames & Hudson, London 1962.

I. J. GELB, *A Study of Writing. The Foundations of Grammatology*, 2nd ed., University of Chicago Press, 1963.

INTERNATIONAL BUREAU OF EDUCATION (Ed.), *Literacy and Education for Adults*, Geneva 1964.

H. JENSEN, *Sign, Symbol and Script* (translated from the German by G. Unwin), 3rd ed., Allen & Unwin, London 1970.

M. L. PETERS, *Spelling: Caught or Taught*, Routledge, London 1967.

R. WARDHAUGH, *Reading. A Linguistic Perspective*, Harcourt, New York 1969.

7.3 LITERATURE, STYLISTICS, RHETORIC

D. CRYSTAL and D. DAVY, *Investigating English Style*, Longman, London 1969.

E. A. DARBYSHIRE, *The Grammar of Style*, Deutsch, London 1971.

N. E. ENKVIST *et al.*, *Linguistics and Style*, Oxford University Press, Oxford 1964.

D. C. FREEMAN, *Linguistics and Literary Style*, Holt, New York 1970.

T. A. SEBEOK (Ed.), *Style in Language*, M.I.T. Press, Cambridge, Massachusetts 1966.

K. D. UITTI, *Linguistics and Literary Theory*, Prentice-Hall, Englewood Cliffs, New Jersey 1969.

R. E. YOUNG *et al.*, *Rhetoric, Discovery and Change*, Harcourt, New York 1970.

8. The World's Languages

8.1 LINGUISTIC GEOGRAPHY (→ also Section 2 above)

S. MULLER, *The World's Living Languages*, F. Ungar, New York 1964.

D. S. PARLETT, *A Short Dictionary of Languages*, English Universities Press, London 1967.

M. A. PEI, *The World's Chief Languages*, 3rd ed., Allen & Unwin, London 1949.

8.2 DESCRIPTIONS OF ENGLISH
(→ Sections 2–7 above and 9 below)

8.21   *English—General and Historical Works*

C. L. BARBER, *Linguistic Change in Present-Day English*, Oliver & Boyd, Edinburgh–London 1964.

F. BRENGELMAN, *The English Language. An Introduction for Teachers*, Prentice-Hall, Englewood Cliffs, New Jersey 1970.

W. N. FRANCIS, *The English Language. An Introduction*, Norton & Co., New York 1965.

H. HUNGERFORD (Ed.), *English Linguistics. An Introductory Reader*, Scott, Foresman & Co., London 1968.

W. NASH, *Our Experience of Language*, Batsford, London 1971.

T. PYLES and J. ALGEO, *English. An Introduction to Language*, Harcourt, New York 1970.

R. QUIRK, *The Use of English*, 2nd ed., Longman, London 1969.

A. G. RIGG, *The English Language. A Historical Reader*, Appleton-Century-Crofts, New York 1968.

B. M. H. STRANG, *A History of English*, Methuen, London 1970.

8.22   *English—Phonetics and Phonology*

N. CHOMSKY and M. HALLE, *Sound Pattern of English*, Harper & Row, New York 1968.

D. CRYSTAL, *Prosodic Systems and Intonation in English*, Cambridge University Press, London 1969.

A. C. GIMSON, *An Introduction to the Pronunciation of English*, 2nd ed., Arnold, London 1970.

H. KURATH, *A Phonology and Prosody of Modern English*, University of Michigan Press, Ann Arbor, Michigan 1964.

J. D. O'CONNOR, *Better English Pronunciation*, Cambridge University Press, Cambridge 1967.

J. L. M. TRIM, *English Pronunciation Illustrated*, Cambridge University Press, London 1965.

A. WIJK, *Rules of Pronunciation for the English Language*, Oxford University Press, London 1966.

8.23   *English Grammar*

C. C. FRIES, *The Structure of English. An Introduction to the Construction of English Sentences*, Harcourt, New York 1952.

H. A. GLEASON, Jr., *Linguistics and English Grammar*, Holt, Rinehart & Winston, New York–London 1965.

M. GRADY, *Syntax and Semantics of the English Verb Phrase*, Mouton, The Hague 1970.

S. GREENBAUM, *Studies in English Adverbial Usage*, Longman, London 1969.

R. A. JACOBS and P. S. ROSENBAUM, *English Transformational Grammar*, Blaisdell, Waltham, Massachusetts 1968.

O. JESPERSEN, *Essentials of English Grammar* (1st ed. 1933), Allen & Unwin, London 1959.

M. JOOS, *The English Verb. Form and Meanings*, University of Wisconsin Press, Madison, Wisconsin 1964.

D. T. LANGENDOEN, *Essentials of English Grammar*, Holt, New York–London 1970.

W. H. MITTINS, *A Grammar of Modern English*, 2nd ed., Methuen, London 1967.

E. A. NIDA, *A Synopsis of English Syntax*, 2nd ed., Mouton, The Hague 1966.

F. R. PALMER, *A Linguistic Study of the English Verb*, Longman, London 1965.

D. A. REIBEL and S. A. SCHANE (Eds.), *Modern Studies in English. Readings in Transformational Grammar*, Prentice-Hall, Englewood Cliffs, New Jersey 1969.

F. S. SCOTT *et al.*, *English Grammar. A Linguistic Study of its Classes and Structure*, Heinemann, Auckland–London 1968.

B. M. H. STRANG, *Modern English Structure*, 2nd ed., Arnold, London 1968.

J. SVARTVIK, *On Voice in the English Verb*, Mouton, The Hague 1966.

S. YOTSUKURA, *The Articles in English. A Structural Analysis of Usage*, Mouton, The Hague 1970.

8.24 Varieties of English

R. D. HUDDLESTON, *The Sentence in Written English. A Syntactic Study Based on an Analysis of Scientific Texts*, Cambridge University Press, London 1971.

M. JOOS, *The Five Clocks. A Linguistic Excursion into the Five Styles of English Usage*, Harcourt, New York 1967.

C. LAIRD, *Language in America*, World Publications, New York 1970.

G. N. LEECH, *English in Advertising. A Linguistic Study of Advertising in Great Britain*, Longman, London 1966.

G. N. LEECH, *A Linguistic Guide to English Poetry*, Longman, London 1968.

R. B. Le PAGE, *English in the Caribbean*, Longman, London (forthcoming).

W. H. MITTINS *et al.*, *Attitudes to English Usage*, Oxford University Press, London 1970.

M. M. ORKIN, *Speaking Canadian English. An Informal Account of the English Language in Canada*, Routledge, London 1971.

H. ORTON and E. DIETH, *Survey of English Dialects*, A. Introduction, B. Basic Material, 4 vols. Arnold, Leeds 1962–71.

C. E. REED, *Dialects of American English*, World Publ. Co., Cleveland, Ohio 1967.

R. W. SHUY (Ed.), *Social Dialects and Language Learning. Proceedings of Conference, Bloomington 1964*, NCTE, Champaign, Illinois 1965.

J. SPENCER (Ed.), *The English Language in West Africa*, Longman, London 1971.

G. W. TURNER, *The English Language in Australia and New Zealand*, Longman, London 1966.

J. V. WILLIAMSON and V. M. BURKE (Eds.), *A Various Language. Perspectives on American Dialects*, Holt, New York 1971.

8.25 Dictionaries of English

P. DAVIES (Ed.), *The American Heritage Dictionary of the English Language*, Dell, New York 1970.

P. B. GOVE (Ed.), *Webster's Third New International Dictionary of the English Language*, 3rd ed., Merriam-Webster, Springfield, Massachusetts 1961.

E. KLEIN, *A Comprehensive Etymological Dictionary of the English Language*, 2 vols., Elsevier, Amsterdam 1966.

G. N. LEECH, *Towards a Semantic Description of English*, Longman, London 1969.

M. PEI (Ed.), *Language of the Specialists. A Communication Guide to Twenty Different Fields*, Funk & Wagnalls/Reader's Digest, New York 1966.

J. L. ROGET, *Thesaurus of English Words and Phrases*, Longman, London 1962.

M. WEST (Ed.), *A General Service List of English Words*, Longman, London 1953.

K. G. WILSON *et al.*, *Harbrace Guide to Dictionaries*, Harcourt, New York 1963.

8.3 DESCRIPTIONS OF FRENCH
(→ also Section 9.13 below)

J. C. CHEVALIER *et al.*, *Grammaire Larousse du français contemporain*, Larousse, Paris 1964.

J. DUBOIS and F. DUBOIS-CHARLIER, *Eléments de linguistique française. Syntaxe*, Larousse, Paris 1970.

A. JUILLAND *et al.*, *Frequency Dictionary of French Words*, Mouton, The Hague 1970.

G. PRICE, *The French Language, Present and Past*, Arnold, London 1971.

P. ROBERT, *Dictionnaire alphabétique et analogique de la langue française*, Presses universitaires, Paris 1956–64.

8.4 DESCRIPTIONS OF GERMAN
(→ also Section 9.13 below)

E. AGRICOLA *et al.* (Eds.), *Die deutsche Sprache*, 2 vols., Bibliographisches Institut, Leipzig 1969.

W. E. COLLINSON, *The German Language Today. Its Patterns and Historical Background*, 3rd ed., Hutchinson, London 1968.

G. HELBIG and W. SCHENKEL, *Wörterbuch zur Valenz und Distribution deutscher Verben*, Bibliographisches Institut, Leipzig 1969.

R. E. KELLER, *German Dialects*, Manchester University Press, Manchester 1961.

G. WAHRIG (Ed.), *Deutsches Wörterbuch*, 3rd ed., C. Bertelsmann, Gütersloh 1972.

8.5 Descriptions of Russian
(→ also Section 9.13 below)

J. FORSYTH, *A Grammar of Aspect. Usage and Meaning in the Russian Verb*, Cambridge University Press, London 1970.

M. HALLE, *The Sound Pattern of Russian. A Linguistic and Acoustical Investigation*, Mouton, The Hague 1959.

I. M. PULKINA, *A Short Russian Reference Grammar*, Progress Publishers, Moscow 1960.

J. T. SHAW, *The Transliteration of Modern Russian for English-Language Publications*, University of Wisconsin Press, Madison, Wisconsin 1967.

M. WHEELER (Ed.), *The Oxford Russian–English Dictionary*, Oxford University Press, London 1972.

8.6 Descriptions of Spanish
(→ also Section 9.13 below)

R. L. HADLICH, *A Transformational Grammar of Spanish*, Prentice-Hall, Englewood Cliffs, New Jersey 1971.

J. W. HARRIS, *Spanish Phonology*, M.I.T. Press, Cambridge, Massachusetts 1969.

M. MOLINER, *Diccionario del uso del Español*, 2 vols., Gredos, Madrid 1966–67.

8.7 Descriptions of other Indo-European Languages
(→ also Section 9.13 below)

R. G. A. de BRAY, *Guide to the Slavonic Languages*, Dent, London–New York 1951.

N. COSTABILE, *La struttura della lingua italiana. Grammatica generativo-trasformativa*, Patron, Bologna 1967.

E. HAUGEN and T. L. MARKEY, *The Scandinavian Languages. Fifty Years of Linguistic Research*, Mouton, The Hague (forthcoming).

A. LYALL, *A Guide to 25 Languages of Europe*, 3rd ed., Sidgwick & Jackson, London 1966.

V. MILTNER, *Theory of Hindi Syntax. Descriptive, Generative, Transformational*, Mouton, The Hague 1970.

R. POSNER, *The Romance Languages. A Linguistic Introduction*, Doubleday-Anchor, Garden City, New York 1966.

M. SALTARELLI, *A Phonology of Italian in a Generative Grammar*, Mouton, The Hague 1970.

R. A. ZISIN, *The Phonological Basis of Latin Prosody*, Mouton, The Hague 1971.

8.8 Descriptions of Other Languages

A. F. L. BEESTON, *The Arabic Language Today*, Hutchinson, London 1970.

J. J. CHEW, *A Transformational Analysis of Modern Colloquial Japanese*, Mouton, The Hague 1967.

B. COLLINDER, *An Introduction to the Uralic Languages*, University of California Press, Berkeley–Los Angeles 1965.

J. H. GREENBERG, *The Languages of Africa*, 2nd ed., Mouton, The Hague, 1966.

R. A. HALL, *Pidgin and Creole Languages*, Cornell University Press, Ithaca, New York 1966.

P. KRATOCHVÍL, *The Chinese Language Today. Features of an Emerging Standard*, Hutchinson, London 1968.

R. E. LONGACRE, *Philippine Languages. Discourse, Paragraph and Sentence Structure*, SIL, Oklahoma (forthcoming).

MATTESON (Ed.), *Comparative Studies in American Languages*, Mouton, The Hague (forthcoming).

R. H. MESKILL, *A Transformational Analysis of Turkish Syntax*, Mouton, The Hague 1970.

R. ANDREW MILLER, *The Japanese Language*, University of Chicago Press, Chicago, Illinois 1967.

G. B. MILNER and E. J. A. HENDERSON (Eds.), *Indo-Pacific Linguistic Studies* (Conference London 1965), Special issues *Lingua*, Vol. **14** (1961) and **15** (1962).

E. C. POLOMÉ, *Swahili Language Handbook*, CAL, Washington D.C. 1967.

P. S. RAY *et al.*, *Bengali Language Handbook*, CAL, Washington D.C. 1966.

R. SHAFER, *Introduction to Sino-Tibetan*, Harrassowitz, Wiesbaden 1966.

S. A. WURM, *Languages of Australia and Tasmania*, Mouton, The Hague (forthcoming).

9. Applied Linguistics

9.1 LANGUAGE LEARNING AND LANGUAGE TEACHING

9.11 *General Introductions, Textbooks*

W. A. BENNETT, *Aspects of Language and Language Teaching*, Cambridge University Press, London 1968.

J. BRITTON, *Language and Learning*, The Penguin Press, London 1970.

M. A. K. HALLIDAY *et al.*, *The Linguistic Sciences and Language Teaching*, Longman, London 1964, 1970.

R. LADO, *Language Teaching. A Scientific Approach*, McGraw Hill, New York 1964.

W. P. MACKEY, *Language Teaching Analysis*, Longman, London 1965.

W. G. MOULTON, *A Linguistic Guide to Language Learning*, 2nd ed., MLA, Washington D.C. 1970.

I. M. SCHLESINGER, *Sentence Structure and the Reading Process*, Mouton, The Hague 1968.

H. H. STERN, *Foreign Languages in Primary Education. The Teaching of Foreign or Second Languages to Younger Children*, 2nd ed., Oxford University Press, London 1967.

R. TITONE, *Teaching Foreign Languages. An Historical Sketch*, Georgetown University Press, Washington D.C. 1968.

D. A. WILKINS, *Linguistics in Language Teaching*, Arnold, London 1972.

9.12 Anthologies, Readings, Surveys

E. M. BIRKMAIER (Ed.), *Britannica Review of Foreign Language Education*, Vol. I, Encyclopedia Britannica, Chicago, Illinois 1968.

CILT (Ed.), *Languages for Special Purposes*, CILT Reports and Papers 1, London 1969.

D. V. GUNDERSON (Ed.), *Language and Reading. An Interdisciplinary Approach*, CAL, Washington D.C. 1970.

G. E. PERREN and J. L. M. TRIM (Eds.), *Applications of Linguistics. 52 Papers Selected from the 2nd International Congress of Applied Linguistics at Cambridge 1969*, Cambridge University Press, London 1971.

C. E. REED (Ed.), *The Learning of Language*, Meredith Appleton-Century-Crofts, New York 1971.

H. H. STERN (Ed.), *Languages and the Young School Child*, Oxford University Press, London 1969.

H. G. WIDDOWSON (Ed.), *Language Teaching Texts*, Oxford University Press, London 1971.

9.13 Learning and Teaching Specific Languages, Contrastive Studies
(→ also Sections 8.2–8.8 above)

F. B. AGARD and R. J. di PIETRO, *The Grammatical Structures of English and Italian*, University of Chicago Press, Chicago–London 1965.

F. B. AGARD and R. J. di PIETRO, *The Sounds of English and Italian*, University of Chicago Press, Chicago–London 1965.

J. E. ALATIS (Ed.), *Contrastive Linguistics and Its Pedagogical Implications*, Georgetown University Press, Washington D.C. 1968.

J. C. BARATZ and R. W. SHUY (Eds.), *Teaching Black Children to Read*, CAL, Washington D.C. 1969.

P. DELATTRE, *Comparing the Phonetic Features of English, French, German and Spanish*, Harrap-Gross, London–Heidelberg 1965.

R. J. di PIETRO, *Language Structures in Contrast*, Newbury House, Rowley, Massachusetts 1971.

D. M. FELDMAN and W. D. KLINE, *Spanish. Contemporary Methodology*, Blaisdell, Waltham, Massachusetts–London 1969.

P. J. T. GLENDENING, *Teach Yourself to Learn a Language*, English Universities Press, London 1965.

H. L. KUFNER, *The Grammatical Structures of English and German*, University of Chicago Press, Chicago–London 1962.

R. LADO, *Linguistics Across Cultures. Applied Linguistics for Language Teachers*, Michigan University Press, Ann Arbor, Michigan 1957.

W. R. LEE, *Spelling Irregularity and Reading Difficulty in English*, National Foundation for Educational Research in England and Wales, London 1960.

W. R. LEE (Ed.), *English Language Teaching Selections*, 2 Vols., Oxford University Press, London 1967.

A. H. MARCKWARDT, *Linguistics and the Teaching of English*, Indiana University Press, Bloomington, Indiana 1966.

W. G. MOULTON, *The Sounds of English and German*, University of Chicago Press, Chicago–London 1962.

G. NICKEL (Ed.), *Papers in Contrastive Linguistics AILA Congress 1969*, Cambridge University Press, London 1971.

R. L. POLITZER, *Teaching French. A Linguistic Orientation*, 2nd ed., Blaisdell, Waltham, Massachusetts–London 1965.

R. L. POLITZER and C. N. STEINBACH, *Teaching Spanish. A Linguistic Orientation*, Blaisdell, Waltham, Massachusetts–London 1965.

R. L. POLITZER, *Teaching German. A Linguistic Orientation*, Blaisdell, Waltham, Massachusetts–London 1968.

E. REICHMANN (Ed.), *The Teaching of German. Problems and Methods.* National Carl Schurz Association, Philadelphia/Hueber, München 1971.

R. P. STOCKWELL and J. D. BOWEN, *The Sounds of English and Spanish*, University of Chicago Press, Chicago–London 1965.

R. P. STOCKWELL et al., *The Grammatical Structures of English and Spanish*, University of Chicago Press, Chicago–London 1965.

J. and F. STODDART, *The Teaching of English to Immigrant Children*, University of London Press, London 1968.

O. THOMAS, *Transformational Grammar and the Teacher of English*, Holt, New York–London 1965.

L. G. TURKEVICH (Ed.), *Methods of Teaching Russian*, Van Nostrand, Princeton, New Jersey 1967.

A. VALDMAN, *Applied Linguistics French. A Guide for Teachers*, Heath, Boston 1965.

J. P. VINAY and J. DARBELNET, *Stylistique Comparée du Français et de l'Anglais*, Didier–Harrap, London 1960.

9.14 *Teaching and Testing Methods*

S. P. CORDER, *The Visual Element in Language Teaching*, Longman, London 1966.

A. DAVIES (Ed.), *Language Testing Symposium. A Psycholinguistic Approach*, Oxford University Press, London 1968.

B. C. GOODGER, *Modern Languages*, Morgan–Grampian, London 1967.

D. P. HARRIS, *Testing English as a Second Language*, McGraw-Hill, New York 1969.

A. S. HAYES, *Language Laboratory Facilities*, Oxford University Press, London 1968.

L. G. KELLY, *25 Centuries of Language Teaching. An Inquiry into the Science, Art and Development of Language Teaching Methodology, 500 B.C.–1969*, Newbury House, Rowley, Massachusetts 1969.

G. E. PERREN (Ed.), *Teachers of English as a Second Language. Their Training and Preparation*, Cambridge University Press, Cambridge 1968.

L. S. POWELL, *Communication and Learning*, Pitman, London 1969.

E. M. STACK, *The Language Laboratory and Modern Language Teaching*, 2nd rev. ed., Oxford University Press, New York 1966.

R. M. VALLETTE, *Modern Language Testing. A Handbook*, Harcourt, New York–London 1967.

9.2 BILINGUALISM, MULTILINGUALISM

D. HYMES (Ed.), *Pidginization and Creolization of Languages. Proceedings of the 1968 Conference at Mona, Jamaica*, Cambridge University Press, London 1971.

W. R. JONES, *Bilingualism and Intelligence*, University of Wales Press, Cardiff 1966.

L. G. KELLY (Ed.), *Description and Measurement of Bilingualism. International Seminar Moncton 1967*, Toronto University Press 1969.

J. McNAMARA, *Bilingualism and Primary Education. A Study of Irish Experience*, Edinburgh University Press, Edinburgh 1966.

V. VILDOMEC, *Multilingualism. General Linguistics and Psychology of Speech*, A. W. Sythoff, Leiden 1963.

U. WEINREICH, *Languages in Contact. Findings and Problems*, 3rd ed., Mouton, The Hague 1964.

9.3 TRANSLATION, INTERPRETING
(→ also Section 9.4 below)

R. A. BROWER (Ed.), *On Translation*, Oxford University Press, London 1966.

J. C. CATFORD, *A Linguistic Theory of Translation. An Essay in Applied Linguistics*, Oxford University Press, London 1965.

P. E. LONGLEY, *Conference Interpreting*, Pitman, London 1968.

E. A. NIDA, *Toward a Science of Translating*, Brill, Leiden 1964.

E. A. NIDA and C. R. TABER, *The Theory and Practice of Translation*, Brill, Leiden 1969.

9.4 COMPUTATIONAL LINGUISTICS

ALPAC (Eds.), *Language and Machines. Computers in Translation and Linguistics*, National Academy of Sciences/National Research Council, Washington D.C. 1966.

P. L. GARVIN and B. SPOLSKY (Eds.), *Computation in Linguistics. A Case Book*, Indiana University Press, Bloomington, Indiana 1966.

D. G. HAYS, *Introduction to Computational Linguistics*, Elsevier, New York 1967.

W. TOSH, *Syntactic Translation*, Mouton, The Hague 1965.

Y. A. WILKS, *Grammar, Meaning and the Machine Analysis of Language*, Routledge, London 1972.

R. A. WISBEY (Ed.), *The Computer in Literary and Linguistic Research*, Cambridge University Press, London 1971.

9.5 CLINICAL LINGUISTICS

A. A. BOSMAJIAN (Ed.), *Readings in Speech*, Harper & Row, New York–London 1971.

R. BRAIN, *Speech Disorders. Aphasia, Apraxia and Agnosia*, 2nd ed., Butterworth, London 1965.

299

A. V. S. de REUCK and M. O'CONNOR (Eds.), *Disorders of Language*, Churchill, London 1964.

L. E. TRAVIS (Ed.), *Handbook of Speech Pathology and Audiology*, Meredith/ Appleton-Century-Crofts, New York 1971.

9.6 DEVELOPMENTAL LINGUISTICS
(→ also Section 10.2 below)

A. BAR-ADON and W. F. LEOPOLD, *Child Language. A Book of Readings*, Prentice-Hall, Englewood Cliffs, New Jersey 1971.

Carol CHOMSKY, *The Acquisition of Syntax in Children from 5 to 10*, M.I.T. Press, Cambridge, Massachusetts 1969.

J. R. HAYES (Ed.), *Cognition and the Development of Language, Conference Pittsburgh 1968*, Wiley, New York 1970.

R. HUXLEY and E. INGRAM (Eds.), *Language Acquisition: Models and Methods*, Academic Press, New York 1971.

M. M. LEWIS, *Language and the Child*, National Foundation for Educational Research in England and Wales, Slough/London 1969.

D. McNEILL, *The Acquisition of Language. The Study of Developmental Psycholinguistics*, Harper & Row, New York 1970.

P. MENYUK, *The Acquisition and Development of Language*, Prentice-Hall, Englewood Cliffs, New Jersey 1971.

10. Linguistics and Other Fields

10.1 LANGUAGE AND SOCIAL STUDIES, ANTHROPOLOGICAL LINGUISTICS

B. BERNSTEIN, *Class, Codes and Control*, Vol. 1, Routledge, London 1972.

R. BURLING, *Man's Many Voices. Language in its Cultural Context*, Holt, New York–London 1970.

J. A. FISHMAN, *Sociolinguistics. A Brief Introduction*, Newbury House, Rowley, Massachusetts 1971.

J. A. FISHMAN (Ed.), *Readings in the Sociology of Language*, Mouton, The Hague 1968.

P. P. GIGLIOLI (Ed.), *Language and Social Context. Selected Readings*, Penguin Books, Harmondsworth, Middlesex 1972.

J. J. GUMPERZ and D. HYMES (Eds.), *Directions in Sociolinguistics*, Holt, New York 1970.

D. H. HYMES (Ed.), *Language in Culture and Society. A Reader in Linguistics and Anthropology*, Harper & Row, New York 1964.

D. LAWTON, *Social Class, Language and Education*, Routledge, London 1968.

J. B. PRIDE, *The Social Meaning of Language*, Oxford University Press, London 1970.

V. TAULI, *Introduction to a Theory of Language Planning*, Uppsala University Press, Uppsala 1968.

B. L. WHORF, *Language, Thought and Reality. Selected Writings of Benjamin Lee Whorf*, Ed. by J. B. CARROLL, M.I.T. Press, Cambridge, Massachusetts–New York 1956.

F. WILLIAMS (Ed.), *Language and Poverty. Perspectives on a Theme*, Markham, Chicago 1970.

10.2 LANGUAGE AND PSYCHOLOGY, BIOLINGUISTICS

P. ADAMS (Ed.), *Language in Thinking. Selected Readings*, Penguin Books, Harmondsworth, Middlesex 1972.

D. G. BOYLE, *Language and Thinking in Human Development*, Hutchinson, London 1971.

P. HERRIOT, *Introduction to the Psychology of Language*, Methuen, London 1970.

H. HÖRMANN, *Psycholinguistics. An Introduction to Research and Theory* (translated from the German by H. H. STERN), Springer, Berlin–New York 1971.

L. A. JAKOBOVITS and M. S. MIRON (Eds.), *Readings in the Psychology of Language*, Prentice-Hall, Englewood Cliffs, New Jersey 1967.

E. H. LENNEBERG, *Biological Foundations of Language*, Wiley, New York 1967.

J. LYONS and R. J. WALES (Eds.), *Papers in Psycholinguistics. Conference, Edinburgh 1966*, Edinburgh University Press 1967.

R. C. OLDFIELD and J. D. MARSHALL (Eds.), *Language. Selected Readings*, Penguin Books, Harmondsworth, Middlesex 1968.

T. A. SEBEOK and A. RAMSAY (Eds.), *Approaches to Animal Communication*, Mouton, The Hague 1969.

G. K. ZIPF, *The Psycho-Biology of Language. An Introduction to Dynamic Philology*, 2nd ed., M.I.T. Press, Cambridge, Massachusetts 1965.

10.3 LANGUAGE AND PHILOSOPHY

H. G. ALEXANDER, *Language and Thinking. A Philosophical Introduction*, D. van Nostrand, London 1967.

J. L. AUSTIN, *How to Do Things with Words*, Clarendon Press, Oxford 1962.

Y. BAR-HILLEL, *Aspects of Language. Essays and Lectures*, Magnes, Jerusalem 1970.

R. CARNAP, *Meaning and Necessity*, 2nd ed., University of Chicago Press, Chicago, Illinois 1956.

R. M. DIXON, *Linguistic Science and Logic*, Mouton, The Hague 1963.

J. A. FODOR and J. J. KATZ (Eds.), *The Structure of Language. Readings in the Philosophy of Language*, Prentice-Hall, Englewood Cliffs, New Jersey–London 1964.

S. HOOK (Ed.), *Language and Philosophy. A Symposium at New York University 1968*, University of London Press/New York University Press 1969.

J. J. KATZ, *The Philosophy of Language*, Harper & Row, New York–London 1966.

W. Van O. QUINE, *Word and Object*, Wiley, New York 1960.

J. F. ROSENBERG and C. TRAVIS (Eds.), *Readings in the Philosophy of Language*, Prentice-Hall, Englewood Cliffs, New Jersey 1971.

J. R. SEARLE (Ed.), *The Philosophy of Language*, Oxford University Press, London 1971.

Z. VENDLER, *Linguistics in Philosophy*, Cornell University Press, New York 1967.

10.4 LANGUAGE, MATHEMATICS, STATISTICS
(→ also Section 9.4 above and 10.5 below)

B. BRAINERD, *Introduction to the Mathematics of Language Study*, Elsevier, Amsterdam 1971.

L. DOLEŽAL and R. W. BAILEY (Eds.), *Statistics and Style*, Elsevier, New York 1969.

G. HERDAN, *Quantitative Linguistics*, Butterworth, London 1964.

C. F. HOCKETT, *Language, Mathematics and Linguistics*, Mouton, The Hague 1967.

S. MARCUS, *Algebraic Linguistics*, Academic Press, New York 1967.

10.5 LANGUAGE AND COMMUNICATION TECHNOLOGY

C. CHERRY, *On Human Communication. A Review, a Survey and a Criticism*, 2nd ed., M.I.T. Press, Cambridge, Massachusetts 1966.

D. M. MACKAY, *Information, Mechanism and Meaning*, M.I.T. Press, Cambridge, Massachusetts 1969.

A. G. SMITH (Ed.), *Communication and Culture. Readings in the Codes of Human Interaction*, Holt, New York 1966.